CISI
CHARTERED INSTITUTE FOR
SECURITIES & INVESTMENT

Investment Advice Diploma

Derivatives

Edition 7, September 2016

This learning manual relates to syllabus
version 6.0 and will cover examinations from
31 December 2016 to **30 December 2017**

APPROVED WORKBOOK

Welcome to the Chartered Institute for Securities & Investment's Derivatives study material.

This workbook has been written to prepare you for the Chartered Institute for Securities & Investment's Derivatives examination.

Published by:
Chartered Institute for Securities & Investment
© Chartered Institute for Securities & Investment 2016
20 Fenchurch Street
London
EC3M 3BY
Tel: +44 20 7645 0600
Fax: +44 20 7645 0601

Email: customersupport@cisi.org
www.cisi.org/qualifications

Author:
Bob Morrissey

Reviewers:
Rupert Clewley MCSI
Alan Green

This is an educational workbook only and the Chartered Institute for Securities & Investment accepts no responsibility for persons undertaking trading or investments in whatever form.

While every effort has been made to ensure its accuracy, no responsibility for loss occasioned to any person acting or refraining from action as a result of any material in this publication can be accepted by the publisher or authors.

All rights reserved. No part of this publication may be reproduced, stored in a retrieval system, or transmitted, in any form or by any means, electronic, mechanical, photocopying, recording or otherwise without the prior permission of the copyright owner.

Warning: any unauthorised act in relation to all or any part of the material in this publication may result in both a civil claim for damages and criminal prosecution.

A learning map, which contains the full syllabus, appears at the end of this workbook. The syllabus can also be viewed on cisi.org and is also available by contacting the Customer Support Centre on +44 20 7645 0777. Please note that the examination is based upon the syllabus. Candidates are reminded to check the Candidate Update area details (cisi.org/candidateupdate) on a regular basis for updates as a result of industry change(s) that could affect their examination.

The questions contained in this workbook are designed as an aid to revision of different areas of the syllabus and to help you consolidate your learning chapter by chapter.

Learning workbook version: 7.2 (October 2016)

Learning and Professional Development with the CISI

The Chartered Institute for Securities & Investment is the leading professional body for those who work in, or aspire to work in, the investment sector, and we are passionately committed to enhancing knowledge, skills and integrity – the three pillars of professionalism at the heart of our Chartered body.

CISI examinations are used extensively by firms to meet the requirements of government regulators. Besides the regulators in the UK, where the CISI head office is based, CISI examinations are recognised by a wide range of governments and their regulators, from Singapore to Dubai and the US. Around 50,000 examinations are taken each year, and it is compulsory for candidates to use CISI learning workbooks to prepare for CISI examinations so that they have the best chance of success. Our learning workbooks are normally revised every year by experts who themselves work in the industry and also by our Accredited Training Partners, who offer training and elearning to help prepare candidates for the examinations. Information for candidates is also posted on a special area of our website: cisi.org/candidateupdate.

This learning workbook not only provides a thorough preparation for the examination it refers to, it is also a valuable desktop reference for practitioners, and studying from it counts towards your Continuing Professional Development (CPD).

CISI examination candidates are automatically registered, without additional charge, as student members for one year (should they not be members of the CISI already), and this enables you to use a vast range of online resources, including CISI TV, free of any additional charge. The CISI has more than 40,000 members, and nearly half of them have already completed relevant qualifications and transferred to a core membership grade. You will find more information about the next steps for this at the end of this workbook.

What next?
See the back of this book for details of CISI membership.

Need more support to pass your exam?
See our section on Accredited Training Partners.

Want to leave feedback?
Please email your comments to learningresources@cisi.org

Chapter One
Introduction to Derivatives

This syllabus area will provide approximately 4 of the 80 examination questions

1.   General Introduction

Mention 'derivatives' and people tend to think of high-risk instruments that are impenetrably complex. Derivatives *can* be high-risk; after all, it was mainly trading in derivatives that brought about the collapse of Lehman Brothers and massive monetary losses at many other organisations during the recent credit crunch. However, it is not necessarily true that these instruments are inherently dangerous – they are chiefly designed to be used to reduce the risk faced by organisations and individuals (technically referred to as hedging).

In fact, many of these derivatives are not particularly complex either. To illustrate the underlying simplicity, imagine that you wanted to purchase a new sofa from a furniture showroom.

You make your choice of sofa and see that it will cost £1,000. On enquiry, you discover from the sales assistant that the sofa is currently out of stock in the warehouse. However, you can sign a contract to accept delivery of the sofa in two months' time (when the stock will be replenished) and at that stage the store will charge the £1,000 to your credit card. If you sign, you have agreed to defer delivery for two months – and you have entered into a derivative (it is **derived** from something else – here, a sofa). This is very similar to a **futures contract**. You have contracted to buy an underlying asset (the sofa) and pay a pre-agreed sum of money (£1,000) in two months' time (the **future** date). As far as the furniture store is concerned, they have contracted to sell the underlying (the sofa) in exchange for £1,000 in two months' time.

So, this is an example of a futures-type contract that we could refer to as a **sofa future**. In the jargon of the derivatives markets, you are **long** a sofa future because you have agreed to buy at a future date. The furniture store is **short** a sofa future because they have agreed to sell at a future date.

Futures are not the only type of derivative – there are also **options**. To illustrate how options differ from futures, we can use the same example of a sofa in a furniture store. This time, the sales assistant tells you the sofa you want is not in stock at present, but there is a small batch of ten sofas due for delivery in two months' time. Of these ten sofas, nine have been pre-sold. You cannot make up your mind whether to go ahead and commit to buy the tenth sofa or to try a few other stores to see if anything else catches your eye. Noticing this, the sales assistant makes you an offer. If you pay £30 now he will give you the right to **reserve** the tenth sofa. It will become yours on the payment of £1,000 in two months' time and, in the intervening period, the sales assistant cannot sell it to anyone else.

Again, this is a derivative transaction (**derived** from something else – the sofa). If you agree to it, you will be paying a non-returnable sum of money (£30) that gives you the right to buy the sofa for £1,000 in two months' time. This is a **sofa option** and, using derivatives jargon, you are **long** the option because you have the right to do something (here, the right to buy the sofa for £1,000). However, you are not obliged to buy the sofa, but if you decide not to buy then you will lose the £30 you paid over at the outset. As far as the furniture store is concerned, they are **short** the option because they have granted the right to do something (by giving you the right to buy the sofa for £1,000) in return for the receipt of an agreed sum (here £30).

2. Futures and Forwards

Learning Objective

1.1.1 Understand the core concepts and key characteristics of forwards, futures and options contracts: forward and futures contracts; contracts for differences

2.1 What is a Future?

A future is a legal agreement between two parties to make or take delivery of a **specific quantity and quality** of a **specified asset** on a **fixed future date** at a **price agreed today**.

Unlike our example of a 'sofa future' above, futures are often described as **futures contracts** because they are traded on organised exchanges, such as ICE Futures, Europe, Euronext Derivatives (Europe), the CME Group in the US, the Singapore Exchange (SGX) or the Dubai Mercantile Exchange (DME) in the United Arab Emirates (UAE).

The terms of each contract are **standardised** in a legal document called the **contract specification**. This is because it would not be financially viable for an exchange to satisfy every single trader's requirements regarding particular underlying assets precisely. The aim of the contract specification is to allow participants to take positions on general price movements in any given market. Contract specification also promotes transparency across all users of the exchange.

Futures originated in the agricultural market, where they were based on commodities, such as grain. The Chicago Board of Trade (CBOT), now part of the CME Group, trades wheat futures, where the contract is based on a set of specific grades of wheat and the **specific quantity is 5,000 bushels**, ie, each individual contract represents 5,000 bushels of wheat. The **specified asset** is obviously wheat, but of what **quality**? The contract specification goes to great lengths to detail precisely what is acceptable under the terms of each contract. For example, the CBOT's wheat future specifies that the grain must be a specific **deliverable grade**, a list of which is set out by the exchange. It also specifies what form of delivery is acceptable by listing the names of storage/warehouses to which delivery must be made.

The **price** is agreed between the buyer and the seller. In fact, it is the sole element of the futures contract that is open to negotiation. However, the exchange does specify the minimum permitted movement in price and the method of quotation. For a wheat future contract the quote is on a per bushel basis and the minimum movement is 0.25 of a cent ($0.0025) per bushel (known as the **tick size**), and, because each contract represents 5,000 bushels, the value of the minimum price movement per contract (the **tick value**) is $12.50 per contract.

The **fixed future date** is also laid down by the exchange. Although it is a set day within the month, the fixed future date is often referred to as the **contract month**. In respect of wheat futures traded on the CBOT, there are delivery months in March, May, July, September and December.

Alongside these **commodity futures** there are also **financial futures**, which are based on interest rates, bonds, currency exchange rates or stock market indices.

For all futures contracts, the **contract specification standardises the futures product** and, as long as the contracts have a common underlying asset and a common delivery date, the contract is said to be **fungible**, ie, identical to, and substitutable with, others traded on the same exchange.

For example, all March long gilt futures on ICE Futures London are fungible. A March long gilt future on ICE Futures London is **not** fungible with a June long gilt future on the same exchange, because the delivery dates are different.

The consequences of standardisation and fungibility are:

- traders know what they are trading
- traders know what their delivery obligations are (buyers know the cost of the asset they have bought, and sellers know the amount they will receive and the quality of the asset they have sold)
- contracts are easy to trade as they have set terms
- it is possible to trade large volumes (multiple contracts), and
- the concentration of activity provides liquidity and, therefore, efficiency to the market.

The fungible nature of contracts also means that a trader can remove any delivery obligations by taking an equal and opposite position. For example, a trader who has bought a future and is required to buy a specified quantity of the underlying asset can simply sell a fungible future. The result is that they have agreed to both buy and sell the same item at the same future date. The trader is described as having **closed out** his position.

2.1.1   How Do Futures Work?

Futures positions are opened by going long (buying) or short (selling).

By opening either a long or short futures position, the trader becomes exposed to changes in the futures price and the position will incur profits or losses as a result of the movement in price.

Holding the contract to expiry will oblige the trader to meet the delivery obligations. If the price of the asset rises, the futures buyer will make a profit. The trader will take delivery at the lower price and be able to sell the asset in the cash market at the higher price. Conversely, if the price is lower than the agreed price, the trader's counterparty (the futures seller) will make a profit.

2.2   Forwards

Forwards are very similar to futures contracts, as they are similarly legally binding agreements to make or take delivery of a specified quantity of a specific asset at a certain time in the future for a price that is agreed today. They may not be marked-to-market daily or, if they are, then the resulting profits are not paid out until maturity and any losses must be paid to the exchange clearing house if they are traded on-exchange. Forwards are, therefore, settled only on the delivery date.

They are usually traded off-exchange, commonly known as **over-the-counter** (OTC), but they also can be traded on-exchange. For example, the London Metal Exchange (LME) lists a number of forward contracts.

The LME trades and clears both futures and OTC contracts for certain non-ferrous metals, steel and plastics. An OTC-like steel forward would allow a construction company to lock in today the price of steel, which is a major input cost, when submitting a bid for a building project. In this case, a steel forward is similar to any other forward, in that it allows the contract's buyer to lock in today the price of steel that will be delivered at a future date.

Most forwards are OTC contracts, usually with banks and investment banks. Outright forwards are a common product traded on the foreign exchange (FX) market. Companies, institutional investors and banks use forwards to manage their FX transaction risks. If an organisation is importing or exporting goods (or investing) in a foreign currency, they can use forwards to protect against adverse currency movements. Forward contracts are also used to lock in the price of physical commodities, such as energy, metals (see the example above) and foodstuffs.

In the physical markets (where physical delivery is common), an airline might use forward prices on jet fuel to lock in one of their major costs. They would agree a price today for delivery in a future month.

Forwards are derivatives – the future price agreed for a forward is based on the spot price of the underlying asset; in the case of a currency it would be adjusted for the interest rates in the relevant currencies.

The main advantages of forwards compared with futures (which are always, by definition, exchange-traded) are:

- flexibility (in terms of details such as size and date)
- wide range of underlyings
- forwards are available from most commercial banks.

Their main potential disadvantages are counterparty risk, cost and, in some cases, liquidity. With exchange-traded futures, counterparty risk is reduced considerably by **novation** through the central clearing house (see Chapter 5, Sections 1.1 and 1.2).

Forwards can also be used for the same purposes as futures.

2.3   Contracts for Difference

Some futures contracts are based on **tangible** goods such as grain and oil. If the contract is carried through to expiry there will be an exchange of the underlying asset (also known as just 'the underlying') for the pre-agreed cash sum. These contracts are described as being **physically deliverable**.

However, many people trade in futures contracts where the underlying is **intangible** – a stock market index, for example. At the end of the contract, physical delivery of the underlying is either impossible or impractical. These contracts, where the underlying is intangible, are known as **contracts for difference** and are **cash-settled**.

Example 1

An investor buys a FTSE 100 future at an agreed price of 6550 points and at expiry the index stands at 6700 points. The investor has made a profit, not by buying or selling a tangible asset such as grain or a bond, but by receiving a set amount of cash for each point gained. The amount of money for each point is specified in the futures contract.

In the case of ICE Futures London's traded FTSE 100 futures, that amount is £10, so the seller of the future simply pays the buyer 150 points multiplied by £10, ie, £1,500.

Exercise 1

An investor has the view that economic growth will be in slowdown over the next 12 months. This slower growth will cause metals' prices to fall, due to a drop in demand. Based on this view, he sells 20 contracts of the LME's June (one-year maturity) LMEX futures at 3400.

The LMEX is a cash-settled index-based futures contract that is based on the weighted average of the price of the LME's six primary metals.

One month before its maturity the June LMEX future is trading at 3190. The contract's specification is $10 per index point and its tick size is 0.1 index point. What is the investor's profit or loss?

The answer to this exercise can be found in the Appendix at the end of the chapter.

2.4   Spread Betting

An alternative way of entering into a contract for difference is to place a bet with a spread betting firm. One of the most popular of these types of trades involves a short-term interest rate contract, such as the three-month short-sterling future.

Example 2

If an investor thinks a particular market will rise over a specified period, he could place an up bet. Say he believes the FTSE 100 index of leading UK shares is going to rise after their recent sell-off. If the FTSE 100 is currently 6300 index points, a spread betting firm may be quoting 6550/6575 for three months into the future.

Let's say the investor places an up bet at £10 a point at the quote of 6575 (the choice of pounds per point is up to the investor), and a month later the index has risen to 6600. The quote from the spread betting firm is now 6650/6675 and the investor decides to cash in his profitable position (close out). This is achieved by placing a down bet at £10 per point at 6650. The difference between the buy and sell prices is 75 index points (6550 – 6675), which multiplied by £10 gives a gain of £750.

This gain is not subject to capital gains tax.

Obviously, if an investor felt it likely that the FTSE 100 would fall, he could speculate by placing a down bet via a spread betting firm.

Learning Objective

1.1.3   Understand the purpose, risks and rewards associated with derivatives: uses of derivatives: hedging, speculation and arbitrage; counterparty, market and liquidity risk

2.5   Uses of Futures

There are three ways futures can be used:

2.5.1   Speculation

Speculators take a view on the market's direction and look to make a profit from price movements by buying or selling futures contracts. Speculative investments involve a high degree of risk and usually have short holding periods. If an investor feels the price of the underlying is going to go up, he can speculate by buying the underlying itself or, alternatively, by buying futures contracts on that underlying.

Futures are often seen to be more attractive than the underlying asset itself because they are highly **geared**. Put simply, this means that a small expenditure/initial investment gives the holder a big exposure to a market, ie, the potential for large profits or losses. However, a speculator has to allow for margin requirements (see Section 4.2) and must have sufficient liquidity to open the position.

2.5.2   Hedging

People who want to guard themselves against adverse price movements hedge using futures. A hedger seeks to protect a position, or anticipated position, in the spot market by taking an opposite position in the futures market. A perfect hedge is a risk-free position. For example, a fund manager can remove his exposure to a stock market fall that will affect the portfolio of shares he manages. He does this by taking a temporary short position in futures in an equity index. This will deliver profits to offset the impact a fall in the stock market would have. Fund managers often use these hedging strategies as temporary shields against market movements.

2.5.3   Arbitrage

An arbitrageur exploits price anomalies in two markets. He observes that the same underlying asset or financial instrument is selling at two different prices in two different markets. He undertakes a transaction whereby he buys the asset or instrument at the lower price in one market and sells it at the higher price in the other market. Arbitrage gives him a risk-free profit that will be realised when the prices in the two markets come back into line and the arbitrageur closes out the position.

2.6   Futures Profit and Loss Profiles

2.6.1   Long Futures

The outcome for a buyer or seller of a future when it reaches its expiry date is driven by the price of the underlying asset at that time. Because the market price can vary, this is known as the '**market risk**'.

A futures buyer commits to buy at a pre-agreed price (eg, £115) and will make a profit as long as the underlying asset is trading above this price at expiry. This can be represented graphically as follows:

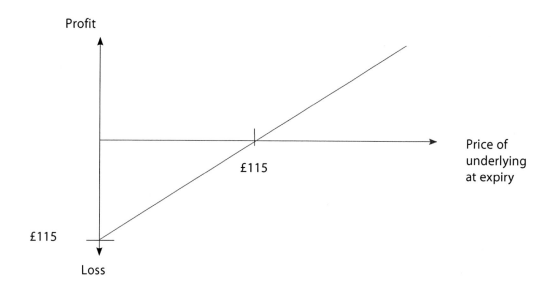

As shown, the **risk** to the buyer of a futures contract is maximised when the value of the underlying at expiry falls to zero. In that case, the buyer would pay the pre-agreed sum (£115) for an asset worth nothing, losing the £115. The **reward** to the buyer is, theoretically, unlimited – the higher the price of the underlying at expiry, the higher the profit made by the futures buyer.

2.6.2 Short Futures

Because the seller of a future is the other side of the transaction from the buyer of the future, the outcome is a mirror image of the outcome for the buyer. It is driven by the price of the underlying asset at expiry and a profit is made if the underlying asset's price falls below the pre-agreed level. A loss will be made if the underlying asset at expiry is priced above the pre-agreed futures price. This can be represented graphically as follows:

The **risk** to the seller of a futures contract is, theoretically, unlimited. As the price of the underlying asset rises above the pre-agreed level at expiry, the futures seller suffers a loss since he must pay the higher market price and sell at the lower pre-agreed price to the futures buyer. The futures seller's **reward** increases as the price of the underlying asset falls below the pre-agreed level and is limited to the futures price, where the seller can deliver the underlying asset that has cost nothing in exchange for the pre-agreed futures price.

2.7   Other Risks

In addition to the market risk, there are two other risks that arise on futures contracts.

The first is that, whenever a buyer or seller enters into a futures contract, there is a risk that the other side (the counterparty) of the contract does not or cannot honour their obligations. This is known as '**counterparty risk**'. It should be noted that in the case of futures, counterparty risk is extremely low, when compared to many OTC derivatives. This is due to the fact that futures are exchange-traded contracts; therefore, once a trade takes place, the exchange becomes the counterparty to both the buyer and the seller. This will be explained in Chapter 3.

As will be developed later in this workbook, counterparty risk exists between:

- the broker and their client, and
- the broker and the clearing house.

The second risk is **liquidity risk**. Liquidity risk arises from situations in which a party interested in trading a specific contract or asset cannot do it because no one in the market is willing to quote a reasonable price for that contract or asset at which the party is prepared to trade. Liquidity risk becomes particularly important when a market participant wishes to buy or sell a contract/asset that they currently hold, since it affects their ability to close out an open position. See Section 5 of this chapter for a full explanation of liquidity.

The third type of risk is **operational risk**, which is defined as a risk incurred by a failure in an organisation's internal activities: eg, the risk associated with a loss from a derivative trade that was caused by a problem/fault in a firm's processing of the transaction. Operational risk is broadly defined as focusing on the risks arising from the people, systems and processes through which a company operates. It can also include other classes of risk, such as fraud, legal, physical and environmental.

A widely used definition of **operational risk** is in the Basel II regulations. This states that operational risk is *'the risk of loss resulting from inadequate or failed internal processes, people and systems, or from external events'*.

Operational risk management differs from other types of risk because it is not used to generate profit. It occurs only due to a failure within a firm's/market participant's internal structure/systems.

Basically, operational risk is the prospect of any loss resulting from inadequate or failed procedures, systems or policies due to:

- employee errors
- systems failures
- fraud or other criminal activity
- any event that disrupts business processes.

3. Options

Learning Objective

1.1.1   Understand the core concepts and key characteristics of forwards, futures and options contracts: puts and calls; options on cash, equities and futures; American, European and Bermudan; common path-dependent and average pricing options

3.1   What is an Option?

An option is a contract that gives the buyer the right, but not the obligation, to sell or buy a particular asset at a particular price, on or before a specified date. The seller of the option, conversely, assumes an obligation in respect of the underlying asset upon which the option has been traded. As illustrated by the 'sofa option' in the introduction to this chapter, an option is a contract that allows an investor to buy (or sell) a product for a fixed price, on or before a future date.

Options are available on a variety of underlying assets – physical assets, like oil and sugar, and financial assets, such as individual shares and equity indices. The option may be based on a futures contract, where the underlying asset is a future; these are known as 'options on futures'.

As with futures, investors attempting to make money by investing in options are known as **speculators**, but options can also be used to hedge existing positions. As will be seen later in this workbook (see Chapter 8), options are trading and risk management tools which offer an extremely wide set of choices for investors and fund managers with differing attitudes to market direction and volatility and with differing appetites for risk.

3.2   Options Terminology

A **call option** is an option to buy an asset (the underlying) for a specified price (the strike or exercise price), on or before a specified date. Remember this by thinking that the buyer can **call** away the asset from the seller.

A **put option** is an option to sell an asset for a specified price on or before a specified date. Remember this by thinking that the buyer can **put** the asset on to someone else (the seller of the option), demanding the pre-agreed sum in exchange.

The **buyer** of an options contract is said to be **long**, or the **holder** or **owner** of the contract. The **seller** of an options contract is said to be **short**, or the **writer** of the contract.

An option's **premium** is the cost of the option to the buyer. Premiums are non-returnable and are paid by the option holder to the option writer.

The **exercise style** of an option describes how it may be exercised. A **European-style** option is an option that can be exercised on its expiry day only (remember 'E' for 'European' and 'expiry day'). An **American-style** option is an option that the holder can exercise on any day during its life (remember 'A' for 'American' and 'any day'), while a **Bermudan-style** option is one that allows its holder to exercise it at specific dates between its purchase and expiration. These dates are normally once a month over the life of the option.

There are also a number of exotic **path-dependent** types of options (ie, those whose pay-offs are based on how the underlying's asset price moves over the whole or part of the option's life). Here is a brief list of the most common types that are currently traded:

*   A **lookback option** is a path-dependent option where the option owner has the right to buy (sell) the underlying instrument at its lowest (highest) price over some preceding period.
*   A **barrier option** is a type of option whose existence and payoff depends on whether or not the underlying asset has reached a predetermined price. There are two types of barrier options: a 'knock-in' and a 'knock-out'. A knock-in option is one that is 'activated' or starts to exist once the underlying asset has reached the predetermined price, while a knock-out option is the opposite: when it is purchased, it exists, but it ceases to exist if the underlying asset reaches the predetermined price.
*   A **binary option** (also known as a digital option) pays a fixed amount, or nothing at all, depending on the price of the underlying instrument at maturity.
*   An **Asian option** (average pricing option) is an option where the payoff is not determined by the underlying price at maturity, but by the average underlying price over the entire length of or a specified part of the contract. For example, a three-month Asian call option might pay the difference between the underlying asset's average price over the call's three-month life and its price at expiration.
*   A **Bermudan option** is an option (call or put) where early exercise is restricted to certain dates during the life of the option. It derives its name from the fact that its exercise characteristics are somewhere between those of the American (exercisable at any time during the life of the option) and the European (exercisable only at the expiration of the option) styles of option. Bermudan options offer the buyer several exercise dates over the life of the option. This can be a series of dates over the contract's life that are usually spaced in regular intervals. Since Bermudan options are more flexible than European options, but less flexible regarding exercise than American-style options, their premiums are more expensive than the former but cheaper than the latter, if all other factors are the same.

3.3 Options – Risks, Rewards and Profit and Loss Profiles

Learning Objective

1.1.3 Understand the purpose, risks and rewards associated with derivatives: specific risks to buyers, writers and sellers

1.1.6 Understand options diagrams and the characteristics and implications of long and short positions

The following examples are based on American-style options on the shares of two fictional companies – ABC plc and XYZ plc.

3.3.1 Buying a Call

eg, March ABC plc 700 Call @ 30

The buyer of the option pays the premium (30p), which is the amount due per share, quoted in pence to the seller. The buyer is the holder of the option (and said to be long a call). The holder now has the right, but not the obligation, to buy one share in ABC plc for 700p.

He can do this at any point on any business day during the published trading times until the defined time on the expiry day in March. The option premium is paid up-front and is non-returnable.

As will be developed later in this workbook, the premium is paid by the buyer via his broker and then passed on to the clearing house for the account of the counterparty's broker.

What Happens at Expiry

It will depend on the price of ABC shares on the expiry day.

- If the share price prevailing in the market is below 700p, the option expires worthless and the holder will abandon the option. Would you pay 700p for the share if you could buy it for less in the market?
- If the prevailing share price is above 700p, the holder has the right to buy the shares for 700p, a lower price than in the cash market. They will, therefore, exercise the option, paying 700p for the share, and then may sell it in the market for the higher price. Even if the market price is 701p the option is worth exercising as the holder will make a profit of 1p, which can then be used to offset the up-front cost of the premium.
- The break-even price of the call is its strike plus its premium; in this case the break-even is 730p.

The potential for gain or loss can be represented diagrammatically, with profit or loss shown on the Y axis and the price of the underlying at expiry on the X axis.

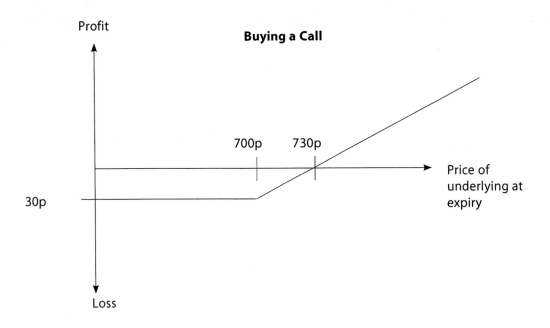

In Summary

- The maximum cost to the buyer is limited to the premium paid, which is paid regardless of the outcome at expiry.
- A net profit will be made by the buyer if the profit on exercise exceeds the premium paid.
- The break-even point is the strike price plus the premium.
- The maximum potential profit is unlimited as the long call option will become increasingly valuable to the buyer as the share price rises above the exercise price.

3.3.2   Selling a Call

eg, March ABC plc 700 Call @ 30

The seller of the option immediately receives the premium (30p) from the buyer, which is the amount due per share. The seller is now under an obligation to deliver the share should the holder of the option decide to exercise at any time up to and including expiry (as it is an American-style exercise).

What Happens at Expiry?

- If the share price prevailing in the market is below 700p, as indicated in the first example, the holder will abandon the option and the seller/writer will no longer hold any obligation. The premium has already been received and provides the seller's profit.
- If the prevailing share price is above 700p, the holder will exercise the option against the writer. The writer is obliged to deliver the share for 700p. They may not already own the share and have to acquire it in the market at a higher price and take the loss. As long as the loss is lower than the premium received, the writer will still make an overall profit.

Diagrammatically:

In Summary

- The maximum loss for the seller is potentially unlimited.
- A net loss will be made by the seller if the loss on exercise exceeds the premium already received.
- The seller's break-even point is the strike price plus the premium.
- The seller's maximum potential profit is limited to the premium received.

3.3.3 Buying a Put

eg, March XYZ plc 450 Put @ 17

Similarly to the earlier examples, the buyer of the option pays the premium (this time, say, 17p) to the seller and becomes the holder of the put option (he is now long a put). The holder now has the right to sell one share in XYZ plc for 450p, again under American-style terms.

What Happens at Expiry?

It will depend on the price of XYZ shares on the expiry day.

- If the share price is above 450p, the holder will abandon the option. The option is worthless. Would you sell the share for 450p if you could sell it for more in the market?
- If the share price is below 450p, the holder can buy the share in the cash market at the lower price, then exercise the option at the 450p strike price, thus selling the share at the higher price (450p) to make a profit. Even if the market price is 449p, the option is worth exercising as the holder will make a profit of 1p, which can then be used to offset the cost of the original premium.

Diagrammatically:

In Summary

- The maximum loss to the buyer is limited to the premium paid.
- A net profit will be made by the buyer if the profit on exercise exceeds the premium paid.
- The break-even point is the strike price less the premium.
- Maximum potential profit will arise if the share price falls to zero, and is the strike price less the premium.

3.3.4   Selling a Put

eg, March XYZ plc 450 Put @ 17

The seller of the option receives the premium (17p) from the option buyer and is the writer of the option. The writer is now under an obligation to buy XYZ plc shares for 450p each if the holder decides to exercise.

What Happens at Expiry?

As you might by now expect, it will depend on the price of XYZ shares on expiry day.

- If the share price is above 450p, the holder will abandon the option (as he can receive a higher price in the market for the share, as explained earlier). The seller keeps the premium received.
- If the share price is below 450p, the holder will exercise the option (as the holder can achieve a higher price by exercising than is possible in the market). The option writer will be obliged to buy the share for 450p and sell it on in the market at the lower price and take the loss. As long as the loss is lower than the premium received, the writer will still make an overall profit.

Diagrammatically:

In Summary

- The seller's maximum profit is limited to the premium received.
- A net loss will be made by the seller if the loss on exercise exceeds the premium received.
- The seller's break-even point is the strike price less the premium.
- Maximum potential loss will arise if the share price falls to zero, and is the strike price less the premium.

3.4   Risk and Reward Summary

The following table summarises the potential risks and rewards in each of the four option positions.

Position	Risk	Reward
Long call	Limited to premium	Unlimited
Short call	Unlimited	Limited to premium
Long put	Limited to premium	Strike price less premium (asset price would have to fall to zero)
Short put	Strike price less premium (asset price would have to fall to zero)	Limited to premium

The **counterparty risk** associated with options reflects the fact that, when an option is out-of-the-money, there is no risk that it will be exercised. Therefore, for an **option seller**, under normal circumstances, he/she does not have any counterparty risk, once they have received the premium, since after that the buyer has no obligation to the seller.

In the case of an **option buyer**, they do have counterparty risk relative to the seller, but only when the option has intrinsic value – that is, when it is at-the-money or in-the-money. This is based on the fact that the seller will have to either buy the underlying asset, in the case of a put, or sell the underlying asset, in the case of a call, at a loss, based on its current market price.

3.5   Profit and Loss Calculator

The following table provides the formulae for calculating the profit or loss made on each of the four positions at expiry.

	Expiry price < strike	Expiry price > strike
Long call	Loss = premium	Gain/(loss) = (expiry price – strike price) – premium
Short call	Profit = premium	Gain/(loss) = (strike price – expiry price) + premium
Long put	Gain/(loss) = (strike price – expiry price) – premium	Loss = premium
Short put	Gain/(loss) = (expiry price – strike price) + premium	Profit = premium

3.6   Flex Options

The **FL**exible **EX**change option concept was pioneered by the Chicago Board Options Exchange (CBOE) in 1993. Since then a number of other options and derivatives exchanges have launched similar products. They are hybrid exchange-traded products which introduce some over-the-counter (OTC) features. OTC features are negotiated between the two parties to the contract, rather than standardised in the contract specification. The concept is to provide an exchange-traded product which will offer greater flexibility by mixing the strengths of classic exchange-traded (ie, fully standardised) options with OTC (freely negotiable terms) options.

They differ from standardised exchange products by allowing users to specify certain parameters that are normally specified by the exchange within the terms of the contract. They give the ability to customise key contract terms like exercise price, exercise style and expiry date. For example, FLEX options are available on the FTSE 100 Index on ICE London and investors can specify the exercise price and expiry day of the contract.

FLEX options have the added benefit of reducing the credit risk normally associated with OTC contracts. The credit risk is substantially reduced due to the exchange's use of a central clearing house.

For an explanation of block trades, Exchange for Physicals (EFPs) and Exchange for Swaps (EFSs), see Chapter 3, Section 2.

3.7   Options on Futures

Unlike an option on a physical asset, such as gold or a share, an option on a future gives the holder the right, but not the obligation, to become the buyer or seller (depending on whether the option is a call or a put) of a specified futures contract. All major derivatives exchanges offer options based on their futures contracts. In this way they are a derivative of a derivative – an option on a future.

If an investor were to hold a call option on a December EURIBOR future (see Chapter 2, Section 4 for a definition of EURIBOR), he would become the buyer of the futures contract upon exercise at, or before, expiry depending upon the exercise style of the option. On exercise, the option seller would be assigned a short futures position.

Example 3

You sell two February calls on Euronext Paris's rapeseed oil futures contract. If at expiration the corresponding future's contract is above the call's strike price, it will be automatically exercised and you will now be short two futures at the option's strike price.

CHARTERED INSTITUTE FOR
SECURITIES & INVESTMENT

4. Gearing

Learning Objective

1.1.2 Understand the significance of gearing to exchange-traded derivatives: how margin facilitates gearing; effect on derivative positions; reward versus outlay; reward versus risk

In the derivatives market, **gearing** is the measure of the amount of cash/initial investment spent on establishing a futures or options position, compared to the actual value of the underlying position.

At its simplest, gearing is the ability for the value of a derivative to rise by 100% in a very short timescale, when the underlying security has only risen by a far smaller amount, say 10%. The principle can be illustrated by looking at gearing in the context of buying a house and taking out a mortgage.

Example 4 – Gearing Illustration

Assume a person buys a £100,000 flat by putting up £10,000 and taking out a mortgage for the remaining £90,000. If the flat increases in value by 10% to £110,000, and the individual still owes £90,000, their stake has risen to £20,000 – a 100% increase on their investment on a 10% increase in the underlying property.

Futures, options and warrants are all highly geared and the principle is the same as in the above example – a small change in the price of the underlying asset can result in a much bigger proportionate change in the value of the derivative position. This is due to the fact that the initial investment, such as the option premium, is relatively small compared to the face value of the underlying asset.

A **warrant** is a type of security that is similar to an option, in that it gives its owner the right to buy an asset at a set price. Warrants are normally attached to/or are part of a bond. Warrants can be separated from the bond and traded on their own.

4.1 Options Gearing

As the option premium is usually only a small fraction of the value of the asset, changes in the price of the underlying can produce disproportionate changes in the price of the option.

Example 5

You buy an XYZ plc 850 call for a premium of 20 when the share price is 800.

On expiry, the share price is 880. You would exercise the option and crystallise a net profit of 10, ie, (880 – 850) – 20. Your return on investment is 10 ÷ 20, ie, 50%.

However, if you had bought the share for 800 and later sold it for 880, your return on investment would have been 80 ÷ 800, ie, 10%.

Buying the call option might appear to be a more attractive reward than buying the share, but it is also more risky. If the share price only rises to, say, 808, you would lose 100% of your investment (the premium of 20), whereas holding the underlying share would have produced a profit of 8 ÷ 800, ie, 1%. The amount of gearing in an option is a direct function of the premium paid for it; **the smaller the premium, the higher the potential gearing**.

Options can also be volatile, offering high potential returns and losses (although the loss is limited to the initial investment) to investors. Time is also a factor, as options and warrants have limited lives and their value erodes as the expiry date approaches.

4.2   Futures Gearing

Gearing in a futures contract comes about through the margining system. When you buy a future, although you don't pay for the asset, you have to keep some collateral aside in case things go badly wrong. **This collateral (initial margin) is a small fraction of the contract's face value, but when you make any profits or suffer any losses it is based on the contract's full face value.** See Chapter 5, Section 2 for an in-depth explanation of the concept of initial margin.

The fact that exchanges and therefore brokers require only a small percentage of a contract's full value as an initial investment, in the form of initial margin, leads to the ability to gear futures trading positions.

Example 6

The Singapore Exchange (SGX) Japanese Government Bond (JGB) futures contract is based on a bond with a face value of JPY100 million. A broker normally requires only a percentage of the contract's full face value as initial margin – say, 20%. This means that its client will incur profits or losses on each contract based on JPY100 million, with only an initial payment of, say, JPY20 million. This is how gearing works.

Example 7

You go long a FTSE future at 6550. You will need to put aside, say, 300 points. Remember, each point is worth £10, which equals £3,000 of collateral. Later you close your position for 6610, a profit of 60 points = £600, a return of 600 ÷ 3,000, ie, 20% on your collateral. In contrast, the index has only moved 60 points, which is just 1.2%.

Exercise 2

If a call option with a premium of 10p gave the buyer the right to buy a share for 100p, what would be the gain (or loss) if at expiry the share was priced at:

a.   120p
b.   100p
c.   95p

The answer to this exercise can be found in the Appendix at the end of the chapter.

The gearing on a future is simply because the buyers or sellers of futures only pay a small proportion of the price of the underlying asset as initial margin, and potentially gain from the whole movement in the underlying asset.

5.   Liquidity

Learning Objective

1.1.4   Understand the differences between the two major measures of exchange-traded liquidity (open interest and volume)

Liquidity is a term used to describe **how easy it is to trade without incurring excessive costs**. It represents the market's ability to absorb sudden shifts in supply and demand without dramatic price distortions. Liquid markets are alternatively described as **deep**. A security is said to be **liquid** if the spread between bid and asked price is narrow and trades of a reasonable size can be done at those quotes. In the market for shares it represents the ease with which shares can be converted into cash.

In principle, derivatives markets are the same. Market prices will be established by the process of price discovery, with buyers and sellers stating their bid and offer prices. The difference between the bid and the offer is the **bid/offer spread** (or dealing spread); the tighter this spread, the more liquid the market. Furthermore, if there is a high volume of willing buyers and sellers either side of the bid/offer spread, any changes in demand will not move the price significantly. This is referred to as a **low price elasticity of demand**. A consequence of this is that it is cheaper to trade on liquid markets as a dealer has to give up less value when agreeing a trade with the other side of the market because dealing spreads are close.

One of the main goals of derivatives exchanges is to have contracts that are liquid and easily traded. Liquidity encourages trading. This gives confidence that positions can be entered into and closed out (offset) without too much difficulty or expense. This creates a virtuous circle that encourages more investors, which further adds to liquidity.

The main elements of a liquid market are:

- many buyers and sellers
- small bid/offer spreads
- low commissions, and
- large amounts can be traded without causing major price movements.

Liquidity can be quantified by assessing the **volume** traded in a given period, or by looking at the number of cumulative open positions (the 'open interest').

Volume typically quantifies the number of contracts traded on a particular day, with each contract being counted once. It is, therefore, either the total number of short positions entered into during that day or the total number of long positions entered into during that day.

Open interest looks at the total number of long positions (or short positions) that remain outstanding at the end of a particular trading day. These are contracts which remain open and must, by definition, eventually be closed out (or settled by delivery if remaining open at the date of final maturity of the defined contract), hence open interest is a good indicator of the market's willingness to take and hold a position, and of long-term commitment to the market.

The higher the figures, the greater the liquidity.

There are two other measures of liquidity.

- **Immediacy** refers to the time needed to successfully trade a certain amount of a contract or asset at a specific cost.
- **Resilience**, the final dimension of liquidity, is the speed with which prices return to former levels after a large transaction. Unlike the other measures, resilience can only be determined over a period of time.

6. Exchange-Traded versus OTC-Traded Products

Learning Objective

1.1.5   Understand the main features and differences of OTC-traded products in contrast to exchange-traded products: how an OTC-traded product is traded; standard versus bespoke OTC contracts; set maturity or expiry dates versus bespoke OTC contracts; margin requirements versus collateral; central clearing versus counterparty risk; liquidity from standard versus bespoke OTC contracts; risk profile of actively managed exchange-traded versus OTC hedging; market transparency versus confidential transactions

Derivatives can be entered into via standardised contracts provided on derivatives exchanges (such as ICE Futures Europe, the CME Group or the Osaka Exchange) or they can be negotiated and entered into away from any exchange, directly between the two counterparties. These contracts entered into away from an exchange are referred to as **over-the-counter** or **OTC** products.

The term **future** is exclusively used for exchange-traded obligations, with the equivalent OTC derivative being termed a **forward**. You probably recall that the **sofa future** encountered in the introduction was not traded on an exchange so, technically, it should have been described as a **sofa forward**. The term **option** is used for both on-exchange transactions (exchange-traded options, or traded options for short) and OTC transactions.

As seen earlier, exchange-traded derivative products, like futures, require the participants to put collateral aside in the form of margin to mitigate the risk of one of the participants not fulfilling their obligations under the contract. The margin is administered by a central counterparty (the clearing house, such as ICE Clear Europe's ICE Guardian). The use of margin is also common in many OTC transactions, but here the margin approach is agreed between the parties and is managed without any third-party involvement. The instances where third parties do participate, are those cases where an official clearing system is part of the transaction's clearing and delivery process. The requirements for margin will be explored in more detail later in the workbook (see Chapter 5, Section 2).

The following table shows the fundamental **points of comparison** between exchange-traded and OTC derivatives.

	Exchange-Traded	OTC-Traded
Contract terms	Standardised and size/quantity defined in the product specification.	Customised, specifically negotiated, totally confidential, flexible, large size possible.
Delivery	Standardised, under the exchange's product specification. Fixed dates.	Negotiable.
Liquidity	Excellent on major contracts, fast order execution. Largely an electronic environment.	Can be limited, varies dramatically on the underlying asset. Slower execution. Some markets may be made by fewer competing firms, perhaps only one.
Financial integrity	Existence of central counterparty means counterparty risk is removed. Daily mark to market.	Counterparty default possibility exists, hence credit rating is important.
Margin	Margin is normally required, in the form of initial and variation margin.	While formal margin payments are not usually required, some contracts do require the payment or pledging of collateral. It is agreed on a case-by-case basis to secure the trade; it does not have a fixed payment, such as the margin payments associated with exchange-traded derivatives (ETD) trades.
Documentation	Standard and concise.	Tends to be one-off and more complex, although certain standard documentation is provided by trade associates, eg, the International Swaps & Derivatives Association (ISDA).
Regulation	Subject to significant regulation.	OTCs have been less actively regulated historically, but since 2008 have become increasingly more regulated (EMIR in the EU, Dodd-Frank in the US).
Price quotes	Highly transparent, public dissemination.	Limited. Need to 'shop around'.
Transaction costs	Standardised, lower.	Individually priced, more expensive than exchange-traded like-for-like derivatives.

The following table highlights the **relative merits** of exchange-traded contracts compared to entering into similar contracts over-the-counter.

Feature	Exchange-Traded	OTC-Traded
Standardisation and flexibility	The exchange standardises the expiry dates and underlying for each contract. As a result, the contracts are relatively inflexible.	Contracts are tailor-made between the participants, with expiry date and underlying agreed between the participants. Highly flexible.
Fungibility	Individual contracts (with the same expiry) are totally fungible.	The contracts are customised and are not as fungible.
Trading and liquidity	Contracts are easily traded on the exchange and therefore liquid. Trading can be conducted with any member of the market, and the fungible nature means that contracts can be opened with one member and closed with another.	Contracts are not standardised and are not easily traded – so liquidity can be restricted. The tailor-made nature of contracts means that closing the contract will involve negotiating with the original counterparty. However, some products (like interest rate swaps) are regularly traded between dealers in banks.
Counterparty risk	The counterparty in exchange-traded contracts is the central counterparty (the clearing house). The counterparty risk is relatively small.	The counterparty risk will be driven by the credit standing of the counterparty to the deal. However, some OTC products (eg, swaps and repos) are able to be cleared centrally through a clearing house, reducing counterparty risk.
Regulation	There is reasonable regulation for exchange-traded products.	OTCs have been less actively regulated historically, but since 2008 have become increasingly more regulated (EMIR in the EU, Dodd-Frank in the US).
Public information	Trading activity and prices on the exchange are published on a real-time basis – trading details are revealed to the market, although the identification of the participants remains confidential.	While both EU and US regulators require public reporting of most OTC derivative trades as close to real-time as possible, US regulations apply to a more limited category of trades.
Hedging	The standardised nature of contracts means that precisely hedging a particular position may not be possible due to the restricted contract sizes and expiry dates available.	The negotiation of the terms and conditions between participants can result in precisely hedging the underlying position.
Speculation	The available speculative exposures are restricted to exchange-traded products.	The availability to speculate is restricted only by the inability to find a suitable counterparty.

As mentioned in the table above, actively hedging a portfolio using either exchange-traded or OTC derivatives carries its own particular risks. While OTC derivatives contracts allow one to structure a hedge that exactly matches the underlying exposure (in amount, specific asset characteristics and maturity), these contracts do have counterparty risks and may have limited liquidity. In contrast, exchange-traded contracts do not have counterparty risk, but, given their standardised nature, risks may arise from any slight mismatch in maturity, contract size or slightly different asset characteristics. This should be taken into account when analysing the hedge's risk profile.

7. Markets and Participants

Learning Objectives

1.1.7   Understand the main markets, and roles of key participants: FX, money markets, equity, fixed income, commodity; regulators in major markets; quote-driven versus order-driven; floor versus voice versus electronic; price-givers – central banks, banks, major market corporates; price takers – central banks, banks, corporates, asset managers, insurance companies, hedge funds, pension funds and private clients; brokers/intermediaries including Futures Commission Merchants (FCMs)

Derivatives are based on a wide range of underlying markets. The main ones are:

*   money markets/short-term interest rates
*   bonds – government and corporate
*   equities (indices)
*   foreign exchange (FX)
*   commodities – softs, agricultural, energy and metals
*   credit – credit default swaps and swaptions
*   exotics – emissions, climate control (see Chapter 2, Section 7).

As we will see in Chapter 2, the above-mentioned markets cover a wide range of products and, while they are structured differently, they do have a number of aspects in common. Most have some sort of **regulator**, whether it be the respective central bank, such as the Federal Reserve, Bank of England or European Central Bank (ECB), or a government agency, such as the Financial Conduct Authority (FCA) or Securities and Exchange Commission (SEC). In addition, all exchanges have authorities that set the minimum standards, such as trading hours, contract specification, margin requirements and delivery procedures. The following is a summary table of the **main regulatory bodies** for the main markets.

UK	Bank of England with its Prudential Regulation Authority (PRA) and Financial Policy Committee (FPC), and the Financial Conduct Authority (FCA)
EU	European Central Bank (ECB) European Banking Authority (EBA), European Securities and Markets Authority (ESMA) European Central Bank, respective country central banks and regulators such as: Autorité des Marchés Financiers (AMF) in France; Central Bank of Ireland in Ireland; Bundeszentrale für Finanzdienstleistungsaufsicht – Bundesbank and German Financial Supervisory Authority (BaFin) in Germany
US	Federal Reserve Bank (Fed) Securities and Exchange Commission (SEC) Commodity Futures Trading Commission (CFTC) Federal Deposit Insurance Corporation (FDIC)
Japan	Financial Services Authority (FSA) Securities and Exchange Surveillance Commission (SESC)
India	Reserve Bank of India (RBI) Securities and Exchange Board of India (SEBI)
China	China Securities Regulatory Commission (CSRC) China Insurance Regulatory Commission (CIRC) China Banking Regulatory Commission (CBRC)

Also, for the most part they have the same main participants, ie, the major global commercial and investment banks, fund managers (both hedge funds and pension funds), sovereign wealth funds and international corporations. Most of the wide range of funds, insurance companies and corporations are mainly price takers, which means that they principally deal off other market participants' prices or leave orders for these participants to execute for them. In addition, most will also have local entities, which in the case of smaller or newly developing markets have links with international players, for either regulatory or customer reasons.

Electronic trading is widely used in both OTC markets, such as FX, as well as many exchanges. Some organised exchanges (often referred to as exchange-traded markets) have both screen-based trading and floor brokers, although more and more have moved to screen-based only, such as ICE (effective since 2005) and Euronext (effective since 2000). Exchanges that still have floor trading include the CME Group and the LME (the only London-based exchange that still has floor trading).

Liquidity in most markets comes from both market-makers and order-driven prices from customer orders. While most participants are 'price-takers' (see below), ie, fund managers, corporate clients, non-market-making brokers – there are times when even market-makers and central banks are also price-takers.

Market-makers are market participants who quote both a buy and a sell price for a financial instrument or commodity. They are found in OTC markets, such as FX; they are known as **price-makers**. They quote both sides of a price with the aim of making a profit 'on the turn' by making the **spread** (the difference between their bid and offer prices). They also hope to increase their profits, since the positions that they hold after making a price are ones where they have not 'paid the spread' to establish them. A market that relies on market-makers for its price is known as a **price-driven** market.

A **price-taker** is the market participant who either requests the price or deals via an intermediary on another participant's price. By doing so, he **pays away the spread**. That is, they deal on someone else's price.

The **buy side** market participants are mainly institutional buyers, such as pension-funds, hedge funds and portfolio managers. Individual investors are normally excluded from the buy side because they are not considered formal participants in the securities market. This side of the market is traditionally made up of users of investment advisory and trading services of brokers, commercial and investment banks.

The part of the market or securities business that executes orders and is made up of market or price makers is known as the **sell side**. Their business is the creation, promotion, analysis and sale of securities. They include investment bankers, institutional brokers and traders and large commercial banks.

Many market participants will find themselves as both price-makers and price-takers at any given time, depending on the circumstances and their positions.

Example 8

Bank GHI might quote a two-way (bid/offer) price in spot GBP-USD to a client. If the client deals and the bank trader does not like the resulting position, he might call a few other banks for a spot GBP-USD price and deal on their price to regain the original position.

In the first case, Bank GHI is a market-maker/price-maker, while in the second case it is a price-taker (since they are dealing on another bank's price).

In contrast, most exchanges operate on an **order-driven** or **matched bargain basis**. Such a system does not have designated market-makers; instead, a deal is done when a buyer's bid meets a seller's offer. When this happens, the exchange's matching system will decide that a trade has taken place.

In summary, an **order-driven** market is one where the order flow determines prices. It displays all of the orders from both the buyers and sellers for each security, giving both the price and quantity of each security that is listed.

In a **price-** or **quote-driven** market, it is the market-makers who determine the prices and the order flow. This type of market only displays the bids and offers of the designated market-makers. The advantage of this type of market is the liquidity that the market-makers provide, since they are required to meet their quoted prices. But a major drawback is that it lacks the degree of transparency of an order-driven market.

As new products are developed, the relationship between derivatives and their underlying assets and their markets will become more inter-dependent.

7.1   Different Market Participant Roles

There is a wide range of roles and functions that different market participants fulfil to provide market liquidity. Some of these may seem to be far from the market-maker's role as price-maker but, without these other services, most markets would not exist or be as liquid or efficient as they are:

- **Prime broker** – refers to the central trade processing, reporting, financing and servicing of the account activities of clients and traders that a broker may provide. These normally include:
    - clearance and settlement of trades in global markets
    - central custodianship of assets and using consolidated positions for the extension of leverage
    - financing in multiple currencies, as required
    - stock-borrowing capabilities to support trade strategies
    - integrated web reporting of positions, activities and performance
    - hedge fund consulting services
    - facilitated communication between sales, trading and research.
- **Clearing broker** – a broker-dealer that acts as clearing agent in connection with a transaction. In addition to handling its own transactions, a clearing broker can provide clearing agent services to other broker-dealers, such as introducing brokers.
- **Introducing broker** – a broker-dealer that effects transactions with its customers through a clearing broker and does not hold customer funds or securities.
- **Executing broker** – a broker that finalises or executes an order on behalf of a client. That client could be another financial institution, a corporation, a hedge fund or a private individual.
- **Inter-dealer broker (IDB)** – an inter-dealer broker acts as an intermediary between other market participants, such as brokers and/or market-makers, who wish to buy or sell large quantities without revealing their identities. Inter-dealer brokers may also be able to deal in securities and derivatives that are not traded on exchanges.
- **Futures Commission Merchant (FCM)** – an individual or company that is registered with the Commodities Trading Commission, which solicits business from others for execution on a listed commodities exchange. FCMs can also extend credit to their customers.

Appendix

Answer to Exercise 1

The investor would have a profit of $42,000.

Index value sold	3400
Less index value at closed out	3190
	210 index points

Profit = 210 index points x $10 per index point x 20 contracts = $42,000.

Answer to Exercise 2

a. If the share were worth 120p, then the buyer of the option would exercise and buy the share for 100p – making an immediate gain of 20p (120p – 100p), but having paid 10p as a premium. This represents a profit of 10p – a 100% return on the cash outlay compared to only a 20% return on the underlying. This is the essence of gearing.

b. If the share were worth 100p, then the buyer of the option would be indifferent whether to exercise or not; the share is no cheaper under the terms of the option than it is on the market. So, the buyer of the option would 'lose' the 10p premium – 100% of the 'investment', when the underlying share did not rise or fall.

c. If the share were worth 95p, then the buyer of the option would not exercise; the share is cheaper on the market. Again, the premium has been paid up-front as required by the option contract. The buyer of the option would have paid the 10p premium – 100% of the 'investment', when the underlying share fell by just 5%.

End of Chapter Questions

1. Describe a future.
   Answer reference: Section 2.1

2. What are the main advantages of forwards compared with futures?
   Answer reference: Section 2.2

3. What is operational risk?
   Answer reference: Section 2.7

4. How does a put option differ from a call option?
   Answer reference: Section 3.2

5. With what style of option can the holder exercise on any day during its life?
   Answer reference: Section 3.2

6. What is the purpose of gearing in the derivatives market?
   Answer reference: Section 4

7. Why is one of the main goals of derivatives exchanges is to have contracts that are liquid?
   Answer reference: Section 5

8. Describe the relative merits of over-the-counter contracts, compared to entering into similar exchange-traded contracts, in relation to hedging.
   Answer reference: Section 6

9. List the seven main underlying markets that derivatives are based on.
   Answer reference: Section 7

10. What are the main activities of an IDB?
    Answer reference: Section 7.1

Chapter Two
Underlying Assets

This syllabus area will provide approximately 10 of the 80 examination questions

1. Introduction

This chapter outlines the underlying (or cash) markets and details the nature and type of derivative products that are available. These include both financial and commodity-based markets, upon which wide ranges of derivative products are traded. While commodity-based contracts are where the derivative market first developed, trading in financial derivatives has become significantly greater in recent years. The major asset classes that will be covered in this chapter are:

- money market instruments
- bonds
- foreign exchange
- short-term debt/money markets
- equities
- commodities such as softs and agriculturals; metals; energy
- other products (exotics).

2. Money Market Instruments

2.1 Short-term Rates

Learning Objective

2.1.2 Analyse the main investment characteristics and risks of interbank deposits: purpose and method of issue; minimum denomination; term; redemption; determination of interbank offer rates; LIBOR, LIBID and EURIBOR, EONIA

While the bond markets are populated by issuers (borrowers) and investors seeking to raise and invest capital over the medium- to long-term, the money markets are geared towards short-term liquidity and providing a temporary safe haven for investment funds. Money markets are normally classed as covering cash and other instruments that **mature within one year** of the point of issue.

An **interbank market** for money exists simply because banks' balances with their central bank rise and fall as cash is received and paid. A bank with a shortfall will need to borrow from a bank with a surplus – hence there is an interbank market.

ICE LIBOR (formerly known as BBA LIBOR) is a benchmark rate produced for five currencies with seven maturities quoted for each – ranging from overnight to one-year, producing 35 rates each business day.

ICE LIBOR provides an indication of the average rate at which a LIBOR contributor bank can obtain unsecured funding in the London interbank market for a given period, in a given currency. Individual ICE LIBOR rates are the end-product of a calculation based upon submissions from LIBOR contributor banks.

Calculating ICE LIBOR

Definition

- Every contributor bank is asked to base their ICE LIBOR submissions on the following question: *'At what rate could you borrow funds, were you to do so by asking for, and then accepting, interbank offers in a reasonable market size just prior to 11.00 am London time?'*
- Therefore, submissions are based upon the lowest perceived rate at which a bank could go into the London interbank money market and obtain funding in reasonable market size, for a given maturity and currency.
- 'Reasonable market size' is intentionally unquantified; it would have to be constantly monitored and, in the current conditions, would have to be changed very frequently. It would also vary between currencies and maturities, leading to a considerable amount of confusion.
- All ICE LIBOR rates are quoted as an annualised interest rate. This is a market convention. For example, if an overnight pound sterling rate from a contributor bank is given as 2.00000%, this does not indicate that a contributing bank would expect to pay 2% interest on the value of an overnight loan. Instead, it means that it would expect to pay 2% divided by 365.

Calculation

- Every ICE LIBOR rate is calculated using a trimmed arithmetic mean. Once each submission is received, they are ranked in descending order and then the highest and lowest 25% of submissions are excluded. This trimming of the top and bottom quartiles allows for the exclusion of outliers from the final calculation.
- Details are shown in the following table. The remaining contributions are then arithmetically averaged and the result is rounded to five decimal places to create an ICE LIBOR rate. This is repeated for every currency and maturity, producing 35 rates every business day.

Number of Contributors	Methodology	Number of Contributor Rates Averaged
18	Top 4 highest rates, tail 4 lowest rates	10
17	Top 4 highest rates, tail 4 lowest rates	9
16	Top 4 highest rates, tail 4 lowest rates	8
15	Top 4 highest rates, tail 4 lowest rates	7
14	Top 3 highest rates, tail 3 lowest rates	8
13	Top highest rates, tail 3 lowest rates	7
12	Top highest rates, tail 3 lowest rates	6
11	Top highest rates, tail 3 lowest rates	5

ICE Benchmark Administration (IBA) maintains a reference panel of between 11 and 18 contributor banks for each currency calculated. IBA currently fixes in the following five currencies:

- CHF (Swiss Franc)
- EUR (Euro)
- GBP (Pound Sterling)
- JPY (Japanese Yen)
- USD (US Dollar).

ICE LIBOR was previously known as BBA LIBOR until 1 February, 2014, the date on which the ICE Benchmark Administration (IBA) took over the Administration of LIBOR.

ICE LIBOR is the world's most widely-used benchmark for short-term interest rates. It serves as the primary indicator for the average rate at which banks that contribute to its determination of LIBOR may obtain short-term loans in the London interbank market.

LIBOR or ICE LIBOR's primary function is to serve as the benchmark reference rate for debt instruments, including government and corporate bonds, mortgages, student loans, credit cards; as well as derivatives such as currency and interest swaps, among many other financial products.

For example, take a Swiss franc-denominated Floating-Rate Note (or floater) that pays coupons based on LIBOR plus a margin of 35 basis points (0.35%) annually. In this case, the LIBOR rate used is the one-year LIBOR plus a 35 basis point spread. Every year, the coupon rate is reset in order to match the current Swiss franc one-year LIBOR, plus the predetermined spread.

If, for instance, the one-year LIBOR is 0.4% at the beginning of the year, the bond will pay 0.75% of its par value at the end of the year. The spread usually increases or decreases depending on the credit worthiness of the institution issuing debt.

Another prominent trait of LIBOR or ICE LIBOR is that it helps to evaluate the current state of the world's banking system as well as to set expectations for future central bank interest rates. This is based on the view that a dramatic spike in ICE LIBOR is caused by a significant rise in demand for short-term funding by the world's largest banks, which in turn could be an indication of a liquidity crisis.

In contrast, **ICE LIBID**, the London Interbank Bid Rate, is the rate at which banks are willing to accept/pay for larger or 'market-sized' deposits. There is no official bid rate fixing, so the conventional practice is for most banks to simply reduce the corresponding ICE LIBOR rate by 0.0625%–0.125% to get their LIBID rate.

LIBID is the rate at which banks take deposits from each other. Historically, it has normally been around one-eighth of a percentage point lower than the London Interbank Offered Rate (ICE LIBOR), the rate at which banks lend to each other. This bid-offer spread reflects the liquidity and depth in the money market on any given day. Responsibility for the administration of LIBOR was handed over to Intercontinental Exchange Benchmark Administration Ltd on 31 January 2014. The website address for the new administrator is theice.com/iba.jhtml.

The equivalent of the ICE LIBOR in the US is the Federal Funds rate (abbreviated to the **Fed Funds rate**), although this only refers to the overnight rate at which US banks lend money to each other.

In the short-term euro market, the Euro InterBank Offered Rate (EURIBOR) is the interbank rate that is the equivalent of sterling's LIBOR. It is the rate that one bank offers funds to other banks or borrowers within the market.

The Euro OverNight Index Average (**EONIA**) is the effective overnight reference rate for the euro. It is calculated as a weighted average of all overnight unsecured lending transactions undertaken in the interbank market, initiated within the euro area by the contributing banks. The panel of contributing banks includes euro-based banks as well as several major international non-euro banks. The European Central Bank is also involved in EONIA's calculation. Since its launch, EONIA has become a key underlying rate of numerous derivatives transactions.

2.2   Risk Implications

Learning Objective

2.1.4   Assess the risk implications of trading in money market contracts: as a depositor; as a source of funding

One of the key aspects that allows the interbank money market to operate efficiently is confidence. Banks and other investors who lend their funds in the short-term market do so with little or no guarantee that the borrower to whom they are lending is creditworthy, ie, is financially strong enough to ensure that they will return their funds back at maturity. Most banks and other participants use internal guidelines or credit limits to determine how much they are willing to lend to another market counterparty. If the market loses confidence in a borrower or in the market structure overall, that funding will simply dry up. Should this occur, those in need of short-term funding must be willing to pay a higher rate to attract funding or seek funding from their respective central bank.

For borrowers who use the money market as a key source of funding, the lack of confidence which causes funding to dry up is a major risk, as was the case with Northern Rock, the British bank in 2007 that used this market for up to 75% of its funding. Despite the fact that it was willing to pay a premium over the prevailing interbank rate, once investors and lenders lost confidence in the bank, it faced a major funding crisis. This eventually led to it being nationalised by the Bank of England (BoE).

Another example of the sensitivity of the interbank money market can be seen from the more active role the European Central Bank (ECB) has played during the euro government bond crisis. The ECB has become an active source of funding of euros to a large number of European banks.

For depositors, the main risk is counterparty risk, ie, the risk that the borrower lent to will not be able to repay the funds at maturity. Again, given the nature of these contracts, it is internal guidelines (within the lender) and credit ratings that help the lender evaluate a borrower's financial situation and their ability to repay.

2.3   Treasury Bills

Learning Objective

2.1.1   Analyse the main investment characteristics and risks of treasury bills: purpose and method of issue; minimum denomination; term; redemption

Treasury bills (T-bills) is the term given to the short-term debt that a number of governments issue. In the UK, the Debt Management Office (DMO) makes new issues on a weekly basis on behalf of the UK government to cover its liquidity needs.

They are typically issued with a maturity of 91 days (approximately three months), although some are issued with 182-day maturity (approximately six months). In the US, the Treasury Department also offers a weekly issue of new debt, with maturities of 28 days (one month) as well as three and six months like its UK counterpart. Several other governments also issue similar short-term debt, which have the same characteristics.

Since T-bills are backed by the promise of their respective government, they are often referred to as **promissory notes**. The yield they offer provides a **benchmark level of risk-free returns** available on other short-term money market instruments in their respective markets. T-bills pay **no coupon**. They are issued at a discount to their nominal value with the discount providing the return to the investor. T-bills are simply redeemed at their par value.

2.4   Certificates of Deposit

Learning Objective

2.1.3   Analyse the main investment characteristics and risks of certificates of deposit (CDs): purpose and method of issue; minimum denomination; term; redemption

A certificate of deposit (CD) is a time deposit commonly offered to consumers by banks and other financial institutions. A CD is a promissory note issued by a bank or other financial institution. It is a time deposit that restricts holders from withdrawing funds on demand. Although it is still possible to withdraw the money, this action will often incur a penalty.

The most common maturities for CDs are three and six months. They are purchased at their face, or par, value and pay a specified interest rate at maturity. CDs usually pay a yield slightly higher than that of T-bills, reflecting their slightly higher credit risk. They can be issued in any denomination.

2.5   Commercial Paper

Commercial paper is a money market instrument that is issued by large financial and non-financial institutions, as a short-term borrowing facility. The debt is unsecured, but is normally backed by unused bank-based credit lines. Maturities normally range from two to nine months and are denominated in minimums of US$500,000 or similar amounts in other currencies.

While the US domestic commercial paper market is the largest, similar markets also exist in the UK, Europe and Japan. The interest rate paid on commercial paper depends on the market conditions, as well as the issuing company's credit rating.

3. Fixed Income Securities

3.1 Government Bonds

Learning Objective

2.2.1 Analyse the main issuers of government debt, and the key investment characteristics and risks of sovereign and government fixed income securities: supranationals; sovereign governments; public authorities: local government/municipalities; index-linked; short, medium, long, undated and dual-dated; floating rate; zero coupon

A **bond** is a debt security, in which the authorised issuer owes the holders a debt and is obliged to pay interest (the coupon) at predetermined dates and repay the principal at a later date, termed **maturity**.

A bond is simply a **loan**, but in the form of a security, although the terminology used is rather different. The **issuer** is equivalent to the **borrower**, the **bond-holder** to the **lender**, and the coupon to the **interest**. Bonds enable the issuer to finance long-term investments with external funds.

A **government bond** is a bond issued by a national government which is most often denominated in the country's own currency. Governments issue bonds to finance their expenditure. They are used to finance the 'shortfall' between their revenues and the spending that has been approved as part of their budget. Bonds fund or finance the national debt (the cumulative difference between government spending and income). The annual difference is formally known as the Public Sector Net Cash Requirement (PSNCR), and often referred to as the Public Sector Borrowing Requirement (PSBR).

Bonds issued by governments in a foreign currency are called sovereign bonds.

UK government bonds are known as **gilts**, which is shorthand for gilt-edged securities. Gilts are issued by the Debt Management Office (DMO) on behalf of the government.

Most other governments also issue bonds. In the US, the Treasury is responsible for issuing **T-bonds**, while in Germany the Bundesbank issues **Bunds**. The following is a list of some of the overseas government bonds and their main features:

Country	Name	Coupon Frequency	Maturity	Trade Settled
US	Treasury bonds (T-bonds)	semi-annual	over 10 years	T+1
France	Obligations Assimilable du Trésor (OATs)	annual	up to 30 years	T+2
Germany	Bund	annual	over 10 years	T+2
Japan	Japan Government Bond (JGB)	semi-annual	long (10 years, most common), super long (20 years)	T+2
UK	Gilts	semi-annual	up to 50 years	T+1
Italy	Buoni del Tesoro Poliennali (BTPs)	semi-annual	from three to 30 years	T+2 (primary market)/T+3 (secondary market)

Like most bonds, each particular of the above specifies a nominal amount (eg, £100), a coupon (which is an interest rate, eg, 1.9% per annum) and a maturity (or redemption) date (eg, 2025). The coupon for the majority of government bonds is paid in half-yearly intervals, so the 1.9% on the £100 nominal amount would be paid in two instalments each year of £0.95, six months apart. This will take place throughout the life of the instrument; the final interest payment will be paid together with the redemption amount (the nominal) at maturity.

Government bonds are classified in a variety of ways, such as by the time remaining until they reach maturity and the government repays the debt:

* **Short** – less than seven years remaining.
* **Medium** – seven to 15 years remaining.
* **Long** – greater than 15 years remaining.

Some bonds with no fixed maturity date are known as **undated** or **perpetual bonds**.

In countries with high inflation, some are **index-linked**, where both the coupons and the principal amounts are linked to increases in the Retail Prices Index (RPI) or Consumer Prices Index (CPI).

Secondary market transactions in gilts are usually settled on the next business day (T+1).

In addition to national governments, there is a wide variety of bond issuers. In many countries, regional, state and city governments also use the bond market to finance their budgets. International organisations, such as the World Bank, also issue bonds, to finance their projects.

3.1.1 Strippable Bonds

Certain government bonds have been designated as **strippable** by their issuer. Strippable means that the individual coupons and the principal amount can be separately traded. STRIP stands for Separate Trading of Registered Interest and Principal.

By enabling investors to purchase an individual coupon, or principal cash flow, the strippable bonds can produce financial instruments that more precisely meet the investor's needs. For example, an investor might want to guarantee the receipt of £500,000 in 15 years to cover the repayment of a mortgage, and buying an individual strip could precisely meet this need.

3.1.2 Zero Coupon Bonds

Zero coupon bonds are bonds which do not pay periodic interest payments, or so-called **coupons**. Zero coupon bonds are purchased at a discount from their value at maturity. The holder of a zero coupon bond is entitled to receive a single payment, usually of a specified sum of money at a specified time in the future.

Some zero coupon bonds are inflation-indexed, so the amount of money that will be paid to the bondholder is calculated to have a set amount of purchasing power rather than a set amount of money, but the majority of zero coupon bonds pay a set amount of money known as the **face value** of the bond.

In contrast, an investor who has a regular bond receives income from coupon payments, which are usually made semi-annually. The investor also receives the principal or face value of the investment when the bond matures.

3.1.3 Yield Curves

The yield on a bond is the rate of interest it provides based on the current market price. It is usually expressed as a percentage. A yield curve is a graph that shows the relationship between yields and maturities for a set of similar securities or deposits.

In most government bond markets there is a range of bonds available with various periods until maturity. By plotting the yields of these bonds on a graph, with yields on the vertical or Y axis and time remaining on the horizontal or X axis, a pattern emerges. The line of best fit across these points is the **yield curve**. It shows the yields available to investors in bonds over different time horizons.

The Normal Yield Curve

Typically, the shape of the yield curve is upward-sloping to the right, as shown here:

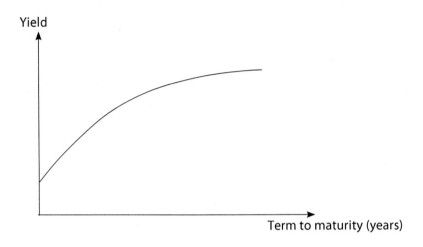

This is known as the **normal yield curve**, and its shape captures the fact that investors have a **liquidity preference** – they prefer more liquidity to less. As a result of this, they are willing to accept a lower yield on more liquid, short-dated bonds, and demand a higher yield on less liquid, longer-dated bonds. Investors are rewarded for lending their money for long periods by receiving a higher yield on instruments with longer maturities. Given the same coupon rate, the price of a short-dated gilt will be higher than that of a longer-dated bond, resulting in a higher yield for the longer-dated bond than for the equivalent shorter-dated bond. In other words, a **normal yield curve** represents investors' requirements to be paid a higher yield for longer maturities as compensation for the increased price risk associated with longer-dated securities.

The Inverted Yield Curve

Occasionally, the yield curve may not exhibit its normal upward slope. Instead, it might be downward-sloping – known as the **inverted yield curve**.

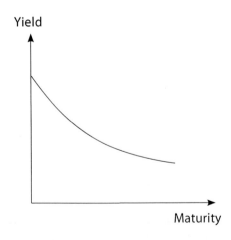

In an inverted yield curve, yields available on short-term bonds exceed those available on long-term bonds. This occurs when there is an expectation of a significant reduction in interest rates at some stage in the future. There is an inverse relationship between interest rates and bond prices. The consequence of this is, when investing in longer-term gilts that will be outstanding when the interest rates fall, the investor is willing to accept a lower yield. For shorter-term bonds that will not be outstanding when the interest rate falls, the investor is demanding a higher yield.

The existence of an inverted yield curve does not remove any liquidity preference; rather, the impact of the anticipated interest rate fall outweighs the effect of the liquidity preference.

Horizontal Yield Curve

If short-term rates are the same as long-term ones, the curve is said to be **flat** or **horizontal**. This might happen if the government temporarily raises short-term rates while the market does not reflect this in higher long-term yields.

3.2   Other Bond Issuers

Learning Objective

2.2.2   Analyse the main issuers of corporate debt, and the key investment characteristics and risks of secured and unsecured corporate fixed income securities: corporates; financial institutions and special purpose vehicles; unsecured and secured debt; fixed and floating charges; asset-backed securities; mortgage-backed securities

A **corporate bond** is a bond issued by a corporation, as the name suggests. The term is usually applied to longer-term debt instruments, generally with a maturity date falling at least 12 months later. Corporate bonds can be issued in any currency.

Corporate bonds are often listed on major exchanges (such bonds being described as **listed** bonds) and electronic communications networks (ECNs) like MarketAxess, and the coupon (ie, interest payment) is usually taxable. However, despite being listed on exchanges, the vast majority of trading volume in corporate bonds in most developed markets takes place in decentralised, dealer-based, over-the-counter markets.

Compared to government bonds, corporate bonds generally pay a higher yield than the respective government bond. This is related to the higher risk of default (although this risk depends, of course, upon the particular corporations, the current market conditions and the credit rating of the company, which plays an important role). The reason corporate and most other bonds pay a higher yield than their respective government bond is the market's view that a government has the best credit and has the lowest risk of default in its own currency's/domestic debt market. This is why government bonds are the **benchmark yield** in most markets.

As is the case for all markets, the entity's credit rating is a major factor in determining the coupon or yield an investor demands to buy and hold a bond. The major credit rating agencies – Moody's, Fitch and Standard & Poor's – give each government and all other issuers a rating. A good example of how this works is the significant rise in yields/fall in the prices of Greek, Portuguese, Irish, Spanish and Italian government bonds in 2011/12. They reflect investors' increased concern that these governments will not be able to fully repay their existing debt.

The higher the credit rating, the lower the yield required by investors to hold a specific bond/security.

Government bonds	Investment grade corp bonds	Junk bonds
←		→
Lowest yields		Higher yields

The highest ratings are what the market considers 'investment grade'; this allows securities to pay a lower yield, since investors see these securities as having a lower risk of default.

3.2.1 Secured and Unsecured and Other Types of Debt

Corporate and other bond issues can be divided into two main types. The first is **secured debt**, which is a bond where the borrower pledges some asset (eg, a factory, office building or other property) as collateral for the debt. The bond is thus secured against the collateral – in the event that the borrower defaults, the creditor takes possession of the asset used as collateral and may sell it to regain some or all of the amount originally lent to the borrower.

From the creditor's perspective, this is a category of debt in which a lender has been granted a portion of the bundle of rights to specified property. If the sale of the collateral does not raise enough money to pay off the debt, the creditor can often obtain a deficiency judgement against the borrower for the remaining amount. The opposite of secured debt/loan is **unsecured debt**, which is not connected to any specific piece of property and instead the creditor may only satisfy the debt against the borrower rather than the borrower's collateral and the borrower.

There are two purposes for a bond or other loan to be secured. First, by extending the loan through securing the debt, the creditor is relieved of some degree of the financial risks involved because it allows the creditor to take the collateral in the event that the debt is not properly repaid. In exchange, this permits the second purpose: that the debtor may receive more favourable terms than those that are available for unsecured debt, or he may be extended credit under circumstances when credit under terms of unsecured debt would not be extended at all. The creditor may offer a loan with attractive interest rates and repayment periods for the secured debt.

An **asset-backed security (ABS)** is a security whose value and income payments are derived from, and collateralised (or 'secured') by, a specified pool of underlying assets. The pool is typically a group of small and illiquid assets that are difficult to sell individually. The pooling of the assets into financial instruments allows them to be sold to individual investors, a process called **securitisation**, and allows the risk of investing in the underlying assets to be diversified, since each security will represent a fraction of the total value of the diverse pool of underlying assets. The pools of underlying assets can include common payments from credit cards, auto loans and mortgage loans, to esoteric cash flows from aircraft leases, royalty payments and movie revenues.

A convertible bond is one issued by a company that, unlike a regular bond, gives the bondholder the option to exchange it for shares of the issuing company. This gives the bondholder both a fixed-income investment with regular coupon payments as well as the potential to profit from an increase in the company's share price.

The additional value of this conversion option means that the bond's coupon will be lower than that of an equivalent bond without a conversion option.

A convertible bond, like other bonds, has a fixed maturity and pays a regular coupon rate. A convertible bond also has information about the conversion option, such as how many shares will be received for the bond if it is converted.

Typically a separate entity, called a **special purpose vehicle**, is created to handle the securitisation of the asset-backed securities. The special purpose vehicle, which creates and sells the securities, uses the proceeds of the sale to pay back the bank that created, or supplied, the underlying assets. The special purpose vehicle is responsible for bundling the underlying assets into a specified pool that will fit the risk preferences and other needs of investors who might want to buy the securities, for managing credit risk – often by transferring it to another company after paying a premium – and for distributing payments from the securities.

As long as the credit risk of the underlying assets is transferred to another institution, the originating bank removes the value of the underlying assets from its balance sheet and receives cash in return as the asset-backed securities are sold, a transaction which can improve its credit rating and reduce the amount of capital that it needs.

In this case, the credit rating of the asset-backed securities would be based only on the assets and liabilities of the special purpose vehicle. A higher credit rating could allow the special purpose vehicle and, by extension, the originating institution to pay a lower interest rate (that is, charge a higher price) on the asset-backed securities than if the originating institution borrowed funds or issued bonds.

A **mortgage-backed security (MBS)** is a specific type of asset-backed security or debt instrument that represents a claim on the cash flows from mortgage loans through the same process of securitisation. In this case, all of the underlying assets that are pooled as part of the securitisation to create the security are mortgages. These can be based on exclusively residential or commercial mortgages or a combination of both.

3.2.2   Fixed and Floating Charges

All of the above-mentioned types of bonds/debt can be issued with a **fixed charge or rate**. This means that the interest rate that the borrower/issuer pays over the life of the bond/debt is a fixed rate, which is set at the time of issue. Therefore, the cost of borrowing does not change for the debtor.

The other type of debt is one that has a **floating rate or charge**. This type of debt has a rate that is linked to a specific index or reference rate, usually adjusted by a predetermined margin. For this type of debt, the cost of borrowing varies over the life of the debt.

3.3   What Affects Bond Prices

Learning Objective

2.2.3   Analyse the relationship between interest rates and bond pricing: accrued interest, clean and dirty prices; interest rates, government bond prices and the risk-free rate; inflation, nominal and real interest rates; flat, normal and inverted yield curves; government and corporate bond yields; yield spread: government benchmark versus LIBOR-based spread; investment grade and non-investment grade bonds

2.2.4   Analyse the main determinants of bond prices and bond valuation: yield to maturity; role of rating agencies; credit rating and impact of changes; economic outlook, interest rates, inflation and the impact of changes; trading volume and liquidity of domestic and international securities markets

In this section we will discuss various factors which can affect a bond's price, which in effect are **a measure of its riskiness**; these include liquidity, interest rates, real rates of return, issuing institutions, its credit ratings, and methods of credit enhancement.

Bonds are, generally, 'negotiable' or 'marketable' securities – that is, they can be bought and sold. When considering buying bonds one needs to consider the factors that will influence prices in the bond markets. As with any market, this is driven by **supply and demand**. The following factors affect the supply of, and demand for, bonds in the market:

- Current market interest rates.
- Changes in the credit rating of the issuer.
- A change in the economic environment – for example, in the UK, the public sector net cash requirement has a large effect on the gilt and domestic bond market. The recent budget deficit problems of Greece has forced the prices of their government bonds to fall; this drop in prices was also caused by the downgrading of their credit ratings and increasing concern that the Greek government will not be able to meet its debt repayment requirements.
- The coupon and redemption date of the bond.

While bond prices are less volatile than many other asset classes, their bond prices do change. The following are the main factors that influence bond prices.

3.3.1   Liquidity

As with other investments, bonds can carry liquidity risk – the risk that the bond is hard to sell quickly, or can only be sold quickly at a price which does not reflect a fair market value.

Liquidity risk is not a problem for large issues, or issues where there is a guaranteed market such as UK gilts and other government bonds. However, it can be a much greater problem for smaller issues and those where the issuer's credit rating is less stable.

3.3.2 Interest Rates

Interest rate risk is the risk that market rates rise. A by-product of the interest rate rise is to equalise the bond yield with market interest rates. The consequence of this for holders of fixed interest securities is that:

- the bond's coupon becomes comparatively less attractive than it was before, relative to rates in the market
- consequently the bond's price falls, as demand for it dries up and/or investors sell in order to use their cash up to lock into higher rates elsewhere.

Thus the bondholders suffer a double hit: they are locked into a bond paying rates which are below market rates, and the price of their holding has also fallen, in line with the rise in market interest rates.

3.3.3 Real Returns

The returns on bonds can be eroded by inflation; indeed, if inflation reaches very high levels the real return on the bond could be negative, which will cause bond prices to fall. The exceptions to this are index-linked bonds, which provide protection against inflation risk, in that both income and capital are adjusted for changes in the RPI (Retail Prices Index).

3.3.4 Issuer Risk and Credit Rating

Issuer risk is the risk that the issuer of the bond gets into financial difficulties and cannot keep up the interest payments, or defaults on the bond. One way to measure this risk is done by the credit rating agencies. Therefore, the higher or better the credit rating of a bond, the lower its yield and higher its price.

A number of issues may affect a bond's safety, in terms of the likelihood of its being repaid. Generally speaking, bonds issued by governments might be regarded as the most secure – although it is not unheard of for governments to default on their debts. In any event, it can be hard for investors to assess the creditworthiness of either a government or a company.

In order to help them do so, a number of specialist agencies provide **credit ratings** using standardised scales, to bond issues. Among the most well known are:

- Moody's
- Standard & Poor's, and
- Fitch Ratings.

If a bond issuer wishes to be rated (and many do, because some investors will simply not buy debt which does not have an independent credit rating attached to it) then they will invite the rating agencies to inspect its financial status and operations. The agencies then assign a rating to the issuer, and often different ratings to individual debt issues from the same issuer, depending on the seniority or otherwise of the specific issue.

The rating agencies consider the following main areas:

- the issuer's current financial strength
- the financial and commercial management of the organisation
- the economic and political background in the environment in which the organisation operates
- competition in the industry in which the organisation operates.

An issuer's rating can change from time to time, with its own fortunes and those of the environment in which it operates. Ratings generally use a series of letters and numbers, which are available for investors to refer to so they can understand what they are seeing.

For example, at Standard & Poor's the most secure credit rating is AAA (or triple A), with AA being somewhat less secure, and A and A– being progressively less secure yet. The permutations are too numerous to set out here, but you should be aware that (for example):

- AAA-rated debt is more secure than AA-rated debt
- A-rated debt is more secure than B-rated debt
- B-rated debt is more secure than C-rated debt, and so on.

Bonds that have a credit rating of BBB– or above are referred to as **investment grade**. Any bond that has a credit rating of BB+ or below is commonly referred to as speculative grade (also sometimes as non-investment grade or a **junk bond**).

3.3.5 Yield Spreads

As mentioned above, a bond's credit rating is a measure of its risk. Investors use both the economic fundamentals and credit ratings to determine their demand and the risk of an issuer and its bonds.

The yield spread is a way of comparing any two financial products. In bond markets the yield spread or 'credit spread' is the difference between the quoted rates of return on two different bonds that have the same or very similar maturities. It reflects the market's view and is based on the market's/investor's perception of the different credit quality (or credit risk) between the two bond issuers. It is calculated by subtracting the yield of one bond from the other. In simple terms, the yield spread is an indication of the risk premium for investing in one issuer's/government's bond over another issuer's/government's bond. Therefore, the wider the yield spread between two bonds, the greater the risk premium associated with the bond that has the higher market yield.

When the yield spread widens between two bonds which have different quality or credit ratings, it implies that the market is factoring in more risk of default on lower-grade bonds, ie, the bonds that have the higher yield.

An excellent example of this is what has been happening in the EU euro government bond market since 2011. Since most investors view Germany, with its high credit rating and strong economy, as the 'safest' of the euro government borrowers, it is usually the benchmark from which all other euro government bond yields are compared. For example, as investors lost confidence in the Greek government's ability to repay its debt, the yield spread on Greek government bonds over German government bonds (Bunds) of the same maturity increased. In July 2015 the yield spread between ten-year Greek government bonds and ten-year Bunds widened from 29bp, before the current debt crisis began, to 1,654bp at their widest.

This represents the increased risk premium demanded by investors to buy or hold Greek government debt causing ten-year yields to rise to 16.54%, while Bunds of the same maturity were trading at 0.74%. Investor confidence has been slowly returning, since the spread between 10-year Bunds and Greek bonds has narrowed to just under 800bp in June 2016. Similar widening of spreads was also seen with Spanish, Portuguese, Cypriot and Italian government bonds in the past few years, but these too have narrowed, based on the fall in interest rates overall and an increased confidence by investors in these governments' ability to cut their budget deficit and increase economic growth.

One of the main reasons why the yield spread widened was growing concern by investors that the Greek government would follow the Irish and Portuguese governments and renegotiate its debt and that bond-holders would be forced to take a significant loss. This, in fact, turned out to be the case. Note that, when analysing the yield spread between government bonds, the bonds must have the same or very similar maturities and the same currency.

The key point to remember, therefore, is: the yield spread between government bonds or any other bond or financial instrument is a measure of the 'relative' risk premium demanded by investors to hold that bond/instrument.

4. Foreign Exchange Instruments

Learning Objective

2.3.1 Understand the role, structure and main characteristics of the foreign exchange market: market structure; quotes, spreads and exchange rate information; market participants and access to markets; margin and transaction costs; volume, volatility and liquidity; settlement dates and systems; risk mitigation: rollovers and stop losses

The **foreign exchange market** (**Forex**, **FX**, or **currency market**) is a worldwide decentralised OTC financial market for the trading of currencies. It has worldwide financial centres that provide access to trading between a wide range of different types of buyers and sellers around the clock, with the exception of weekends. The foreign exchange market determines the relative values of all free-floating currencies. The foreign exchange market is unique because of its:

- huge trading volume, leading to high liquidity
- geographical dispersion
- continuous operation: 24 hours a day except weekends, ie, trading from 20:15 GMT on Sunday until 22:00 GMT Friday
- variety of factors that affect exchange rates.

The **spot FX market** involves the exchange of one currency for another at an agreed rate, with spot settlement very soon after the date of transaction. For most currency transactions in the wholesale spot market this is T+2. For all FX trades, settlement requires that both domestic markets must be open. Therefore, in order for a EUR/JPY trade to settle, its value date must be when the banks in both the EU and Japan are open.

The FX market is used by a wide range of participants from companies and investors who need to exchange one currency for another as part of a trade or investment transaction to the market-makers and speculators who look to profit from providing liquidity and betting on one currency against another.

Many commercial and investment banks provide spot FX quotes, in their role as market-makers. This provides the FX market with liquidity, as they quote to other market participants and to their clients.

Remember that, in foreign exchange, one currency is quoted in terms of another currency. Therefore, in the quote GBP/USD = 1.3510/15, sterling (GBP) is the base currency – the first currency quoted by FX market convention is the base or action currency – while the dollar is being quoted in terms of sterling.

- 1.3510 is the **bid** for GBP – this means that the quoting bank will buy sterling and sell dollars at this rate, since it is cheaper: £1,000,000 costs $1,351,000.
- 1.3515 is the **offer** for GBP – here the quoting bank will sell sterling and buy dollars. At this rate sterling is more expensive: £1,000,000 costs $1,351,500.

Note that in most cases the amounts traded are also based on set amounts of the base currency. Since settlement in the spot FX market is usually T+2, margin does not come into play; on the settlement date the seller of one currency delivers the full amount to the buyer's account and receives the full amount of the currency that he has purchased. The only settlement risk is due to the time difference that exists between deliveries. For example the seller of yen versus US dollars has paid the yen to their counterparty's account in Tokyo, when US banks are closed and must wait several hours before the receipt of the US dollars can be confirmed.

Example 1

An American company has to pay an invoice issued by its German supplier. The German company has charged its American customer €15 million that needs to be paid in two days. In order to pay this, the American company calls one of its banks and gets the following quote:

EUR/USD = 1.1005/10

The American company agrees to the rate and buys €15 million at 1.1010 and will pay its bank $16,515,000 (€15 million x 1.1010) in two days. At the same time its bank will arrange the euro payment to its German supplier's account.

Example 2

But what could the same American company do if it gets an invoice in yen from a Japanese supplier, that is not due for two months?

In such situations, the American firm might consider entering into a forward contract. A forward contract is simply a deal between two participants to agree now the rate at which a certain amount of foreign currency will be exchanged at some pre-agreed date in the future. These forward FX contract rates are quoted over-the-counter by banks. The quotation is based on applying a margin to the spot quotes to arrive at a forward rate. For example:

USD/JPY	Bid	Offer
Spot	102.60	102.65
2mth forward points	0.65	0.60
2mth outright rate	101.95	102.05

In the second example above, the margin applied to the spot rate is a discount. The discount indicates that the base currency (the dollar, in the above example) is becoming cheaper relative to the yen. As a result, the forward points are deducted from the spot rate, so that in the forward deal the dollar will buy fewer yen (the bid column), and the yen will buy more dollars (the offer column).

Remember that, since FX spot rates are quoted in terms of one currency versus another, when the base currency is at a discount, the traded currency must be at a premium. Therefore in this example, the US dollar is at a discount in the forward market, making the yen at a premium.

When quoting forward points it is the market convention that when the forward points decrease, and the bid decrease is greater than the offer decrease as in the example above – 65/60 – then they would be subtracted from the spot rate. When the forward points quote increases, the base currency is more expensive in the forward market and the points would then be added to the spot rate. This is described as a **premium for forward delivery**. The banks will calculate the necessary premium or discount considering the relevant short-term interest rates of the two currencies.

The key advantage of forward contracts is certainty. The US firm could use the forward contract to lock into a rate of 102.05 today, rather than worry that the yen might strengthen over the next two months.

As well as commercial users, the forward market is used extensively by speculators, for example, hedge funds and the proprietary trading desks at investment banks. Since forward rates are based on the interest rate differential between the two currencies, the FX forward market is used to speculate on expected changes in the difference between these two interest rates. Speculators on the movements in spot rate mainly take spot or forward outright positions.

One final use of foreign currency forwards is in portfolio management. Suppose a UK asset manager has US investments expected to yield dividends and gains of 7% in the coming year. This could be reduced or even eliminated by foreign currency rate movements, assuming that the UK manager reports in GBP. Forward rates can be used to hedge this translation risk.

4.1 What Determines Spot FX Rates

Learning Objective

2.3.2 Understand the determinants of spot foreign exchange prices: currency demand – transactional and speculative; economic variables; cross-border trading of financial assets; interest rates; free and pegged rates

There are two main types of exchange rates. The first, known as **floating** or **free exchange rates**, are the most common in the major economies. The spot value of this type of spot exchange rate is determined by the market, which in turn is influenced by the factors described below.

The other and less common is known as a **fixed exchange rate**, sometimes called a pegged exchange rate. This is a type of exchange rate regime wherein a currency's value is linked to the value of another single currency or to a basket of other currencies, or to another asset, such as gold. A fixed exchange rate is usually used to stabilise the value of a currency against the currency it is pegged to. This makes trade and investments between the two countries easier and more predictable, and is especially useful for small economies where external trade forms a large part of their GDP.

It is understood from many models that a range of macro-economic factors affects the exchange rates but in the end currency prices are a result of dual forces of **demand** and **supply**. The world's currency markets can be viewed as a huge melting pot: in a large and ever-changing mix of current events, supply and demand factors are constantly shifting, and the price of one currency in relation to another shifts accordingly. No other market constantly looks at what is going on in the world at any given time as foreign exchange. Supply and demand for any given currency, and thus its value, are not influenced by any single element, but rather by several.

These elements generally fall into three categories: economic factors, political conditions and market psychology.

4.1.1 Economic Factors

These include: (a) **economic policy**, disseminated by government agencies and central banks, and (b) **economic conditions**, generally revealed through economic reports and other economic indicators.

- **Economic policy** – comprises government fiscal policy (budget deficit/surplus) and monetary policy (the means by which a government or its central bank influences the supply and 'cost' of funding, which is reflected by the level of interest rates).
- **Government budget deficits or surpluses** – the market usually reacts negatively to widening government budget deficits, and positively to narrowing budget deficits. The impact is reflected in the value of a country's currency. An example of this is the pressure that the euro was under when the Greek crisis started in 2010.

- **Balance of trade** – the trade flow between countries illustrates the demand for goods and services, which in turn indicates demand for a country's currency to conduct trade. Trade surpluses and deficits reflect the competitiveness of a nation's economy. For example, trade deficits may have a negative impact on a nation's currency – the reason the US dollar has steadily been weakening against the Chinese currency.
- **Inflation** – typically a currency will lose value if there is a high level of inflation in the country or if inflation levels are perceived to be rising. This is because inflation erodes purchasing power, thus demand, for that particular currency. However, a currency may sometimes strengthen when inflation rises because of expectations that the central bank will raise short-term interest rates to combat rising inflation.
- **Economic growth** – key statistics such as gross domestic product (GDP), employment, retail sales and capacity utilisation detail the levels of a country's economic growth and health. Generally, the more bullish the reports, the more robust a country's economy and the better its currency will perform.
- **Productivity** – increasing productivity in an economy should positively influence the value of its currency.

4.1.2   Political Conditions

Internal, regional and international political conditions and events can have a significant effect on currency markets. All exchange rates are influenced by political instability such as a change in the governing party. Political instability can have a negative impact on a nation's economy. For example, the sudden collapse of a government or a snap election can negatively affect the value of the currency. A prime example of this is the significant fall in sterling's value after the vote to leave the EU in June 2016, where it lost over 12% of its value in the two weeks following the vote.

Similarly, in a country experiencing financial difficulties, the rise of a political faction that is perceived to be fiscally responsible can have the opposite effect. Also, events in one country in a region may spur positive/negative interest in a neighbouring country and, in the process, affect its currency.

4.1.3   Market Psychology

Market psychology and trader perceptions influence the foreign exchange market in a variety of ways:

- **Flights to quality** – unsettling international events can lead to a 'flight to quality', with investors seeking a safe haven. There will be a greater demand, thus a higher price, for currencies perceived as stronger over their relatively weaker counterparts. Reserve currencies such as the US dollar and Swiss franc, as well as gold, have been traditional safe havens during times of political or economic uncertainty.
- **Buy the rumour, sell the fact** – this market truism can apply to many currency situations. It is the tendency for the exchange rate to reflect the impact of a particular action before it occurs and, when the anticipated event comes to pass, to react in exactly the opposite direction. This may also be referred to as a market being oversold or overbought. To buy the rumour or sell the fact can also be an example of the cognitive bias known as anchoring, when investors focus too much on the relevance of outside events to currency prices.

- **Economic figures** – while statistics can certainly reflect economic policy, some reports and numbers take on a talisman-like effect: the number itself becomes important to market psychology and may have an immediate impact on short-term market moves. What to watch can change over time. In recent years, for example, money supply, employment, trade balance figures and inflation numbers have all taken turns in the spotlight.
- **Long-term trends** – currency markets often move in visible long-term trends. Although currencies do not have an annual growing season like physical commodities, business cycles do make themselves felt. Cycle analysis looks at longer-term price trends that may arise from economic or political trends.
- **Technical trading considerations** – as in other markets, the accumulated price movements in a currency pair such as EUR/USD can form apparent patterns that traders may attempt to use. Many traders study price charts in order to identify such patterns.

4.2　Forward FX Rates and Interest Rate Parity

Learning Objective

2.3.3　Calculate forward foreign exchange rates: relationship between spot and forward market; forward points, premiums and discounts; interest rate parity (IRP) and interest rate differential (IRD); factors determining forward rates; quotation

We have seen that the forward rates of exchange are linked to the spot rate by applying a discount or premium. The factor that links spot rates is the relative interest rates between the two currencies.

The link between spot and forward rates is based on the principle of **arbitrage**. Put simply, if the forward rate quoted were not in line with relative interest rates, there would be an opportunity to make a guaranteed profit by borrowing funds and entering into a forward foreign exchange contract. This is the theory of interest rate parity (IRP). This is best illustrated by looking at an example.

Example 3

The spot FX rate for GBP/EUR is 1.2065, while 12-month sterling interest rates are 0.9% compared to 0.5% for the euro.

Suppose the one-year forward FX rate for GBP/EUR is 1.2020. An arbitrageur could borrow €12.065 million at 0.5% and convert the euros into sterling in the spot market. This would give him £10 million to invest at 0.9% for one year. At the same time, the arbitrageur could enter into a one-year forward contract to sell the principal and interest from the deposit of £10.009 million at 1.4070. The net result would be:

Borrowing €12.065 million at 0.5% produces interest of €60,325, resulting in a repayment of €12,125,325.

The deposit of £10 million at 0.9% produces interest of £90,000 at maturity resulting in a total of £10,090,000.

The one-year forward FX contract of selling £10,090,000 at 1.2020 produces €12,128,180.

The net result is an arbitrage profit of €2,855. The €2,128,180 that is received from converting the sterling deposit back into euros, less the €12,125,325 that is the required repayment for the euro borrowing.

In order to avoid such arbitrage opportunities existing, the one-year forward rate must be based on the interest rate differential between the euro and sterling. In other words, the one-year GBP/EUR forward rate should be 1.2017. The arbitrage-free one-year GBP/EUR forward rate is based on the current interest rate differential, therefore from the information listed above it is equal to €12,128,180/£10,090,000 or 1.2017.

The link between relative interest rates and the forward foreign exchange rate can be summarised as follows:

Higher interest rate currency	=	**Discount in the forward foreign exchange market**
Lower interest rate currency	=	**Premium in the forward foreign exchange market**

When calculating forward foreign exchange rates for periods of less than one year, we have to take into account the different **day count conventions** of the different currencies' money markets. For example, both the euro and dollar use an Actual/360 day count, while sterling uses Actual/365.

The following shows how to calculate a forward foreign exchange rate using the two currencies' interest rates.

$$\textbf{Forward rate = Spot rate x } [1 + (n \times r_1)] / [1 + (n \times r_2)]$$

where:

r_1 = relevant interest rate for the traded or international currency.
r_2 = relevant interest rate for the base or domestic currency.
n = period in question.

Example 4 ───

Given the following spot FX, spot and money market rates, what should be the theoretical six-month forward FX rate?

$$\text{Spot EUR/USD rate} = 1.0950$$

$$\text{USD 6-month LIBOR } (r_1) = 0.45\%$$

$$\text{Euro 6-month rate } (r_2) = 0.57\%$$

$$\text{6mth EUR/USD Forward Rate} = 1.0950 \times \frac{[1 + ((182/360) \times 0.0045)]}{[1 + ((182/360) \times 0.0057)]} = 1.0943$$

	Description	Sample Data
FX_spot	Spot price of underlying currency (domestic per 1 unit of foreign)	1.0950
rate_traded (r_1)	Traded currency's interest rate (for term of forward)	0.0045
rate_base (r_2)	Base currency's interest rate (for term of forward)	0.0057
d_s	Trade date	1 Sept 15
d_del	Forward delivery date	1 March 16
acc_dom	Accrual method for domestic rate	actual/360
acc_for	Accrual method for foreign rate	actual/360

Result

The six-month forward EUR/USD rate is 1.0943.

The FX rate adjustment or 'fair basis', which is based on the interest rate differential, is $0.0001, ie, 1 pip (a pip is the smallest change that a given exchange rate can make).

The euro is at a slight discount versus the US dollar, since its interest rate is higher than the dollar's.

4.2.1 Premiums and Discounts

As previously discussed, the forward rates are closely related to the spot rates and interest rates of the two countries. A result of the interest rate parity (IRP) theory is that, for the country with the higher interest rate, its currency is weaker in the forward market than in the spot market. As shown in the previous example, the euro's interest rate was slightly higher than the US interest rate, and the resulting theoretical forward rate is 1.0943 EUR/USD, compared with the spot rate of 1.0950.

The terms 'premium' and 'discount' refer to whether the forward rates are higher or lower than the spot rates. A premium means the forward price is higher than the spot price and a discount means lower. In this case the forward rate is then at a discount of seven points.

In order to apply forward points to a spot rate to come up with an outright quote for the forward price, one needs to know whether the forward points are premiums or discounts. For **premiums**, bid forward points are added to bid spot prices and ask forward points are added to ask spot prices. For **discounts**, bid forward points are subtracted from ask spot prices, and ask forward points are subtracted from bid spot prices.

If all this seems confusing, just remember the rule that the bid-ask spreads of the forward price should always be greater than the spot price, and that the sum of the bid-ask spreads of the spot price and forward points should equal the spread of the forward price. The bigger spread in the forward market can be viewed as compensation for the increased risk the market-maker takes in the forward market relative to the spot market.

4.3 Non-Deliverable Forwards (NDFs)

Learning Objective

2.3.4   Understand the nature, characteristics, markets and uses of currency forward contracts including: non-deliverable forwards; commercial and speculative uses; hedging uses in portfolio managements; effect of time on open positions

A non-deliverable forward (NDF) is a cash-settled, short-term forward contract on a thinly traded or non-convertible foreign currency, where the profit or loss at the time of the settlement date is calculated by taking the difference between the agreed-upon exchange rate and the spot rate at the time of settlement, for an agreed-upon notional amount of funds.

All NDFs have a fixing date and a settlement date. The fixing date is the date at which the difference between the prevailing market exchange rate and the agreed upon exchange rate is calculated. The settlement date is the date by which the payment of the difference is due to the party receiving payment.

NDFs are commonly quoted for time periods of one month up to one year, and are normally quoted and settled in USD (although EUR and GBP are also fairly common). They have become a popular instrument for corporations seeking to hedge exposure to foreign currencies that are not internationally traded.

As is the case with spot FX, forward FX contracts are used for a wide range of reasons. Since their prices are mainly based on the change in the relative difference between the two currencies' interest rates, those taking a speculative position are mainly betting on interest rate and not exchange rate movements. The latter, as we discussed earlier, is done using the spot FX market.

Other uses of forward FX contracts are for hedging, for commercial contracts such as future trade-related payments, or future receipts from foreign operations to fund managers, who use these contracts to hedge the FX risk associated with holding foreign assets within their fund. Unlike options, time does not affect the price of these contracts.

5. Equities

Learning Objective

2.4.1 Analyse the key investment characteristics and risks of the main types and classes of equity: ordinary, bearer, preference and registered shares; voting rights, voting and non-voting shares; cumulative, participating, redeemable and convertible preference shares; ranking for dividends; ranking in liquidation; tax treatment of capital gains and dividend income

Companies raise their initial capital – the money to carry on their activities – in two ways; through **share capital** and through **loan stock**.

One important contrast to keep in mind is that people who hold loan stock are creditors of the company. The company owes them a debt, which they have to repay – but they have no ownership interest in the company.

On the other hand, the people who own shares in a company are its owners. An individual may only have a few shares out of many thousands (or even millions) issued by the company – nevertheless, that individual still owns a small part of the company and has the rights that go with that ownership.

This means that shareholders bear a fair amount of risk compared to investors in bonds issued by companies. Bond-holders expect to receive a certain sum in interest – no more, no less, no matter how well the company is doing. (The exception, as you should remember, is where the bond pays a variable rate of interest – but even then the interest is determined by a set formula.) In addition, the bond-holder normally expects to receive a set amount of capital back on maturity; there is generally no additional profit or gain if the company is doing very well. The only real risk is that of the company running into difficulties that are so serious that it cannot repay its creditors – thankfully, not a very regular occurrence, though it can happen.

Shareholders, however, generally have a much greater exposure to the financial fortunes of the company they have invested in. If the company does well, they may receive a rising income stream, and the value of their shares can also increase substantially (giving them capital growth); but if a company does badly it may, as we shall see, pay falling dividends – or no dividend at all. Its share price may also fall, potentially becoming worthless if the company gets into real trouble.

We will examine this concept in more depth as we progress through the chapter; for now, it is enough to remember that shares are generally characterised by relative insecurity of both income and capital over the short term (some types more so than others), but they offer a much higher probability of producing real growth over time than, for example, cash and bonds.

There are different types of share in a company, with different rights and investment risks attached to them; these risks are the main factors that determine the equity's valuation.

5.1 Ordinary Shares

As we have said, when investors buy a share in a company, they become a part-owner of that company. Under company law this brings an entitlement to certain rights. Some of these rights relate to the financial aspects of owning shares, and some relate to the communications between the company and the shareholder, including the actions they can take to make their views known on the company's performance and actions.

Ordinary shares, also known as common stock or common shares in other markets, are the most common form of share in the global equity markets. Often referred to as **equity**, ordinary shares are usually issued in **registered** form. Registered form is where the ownership is recorded in a register, often maintained by a registrar on behalf of the company.

This contrasts with **bearer** shares, where the issuer does not maintain a register and simple possession of the certificate is sufficient evidence of ownership. These are shares whose owners are not listed or registered; dividends are paid by clipping a coupon from the share certificate and submitting it to the paying agent. For bearer shares, the physical possession of the share certificate is the sole evidence of ownership. Bearer shares are negotiable (traded) without endorsement and are transferred on delivery.

5.1.1 Shareholders' Rights

A shareholder acquires a collection of rights and entitlements, and companies may issue different classes of share capital offering different rights. These rights are established when issuing the shares and are set out in the company's Articles of Association.

An ordinary shareholder's principal rights will be:

- **dividends** – discretionary cash distributions paid out of profits earned by the company
- **capital repayment** – if and when the business is legally wound up, although as an ordinary shareholder they are the last category to be repaid and only when all other creditors have been repaid in full
- **voting rights** – the extent to which the shareholder can influence the conduct of the business, eg, appointment/removal of directors, the level of dividend payments and approval of a takeover bid;
- to receive advance notices of all **meetings** of the company and to attend, speak and vote at such meetings
- to be given the opportunity to **subscribe for a rights issue** on a pro-rata basis (if this were not so it would be easy for new shares to be issued to certain shareholders only, thus giving them effective control of the company). These are called **pre-emption rights**
- to **sell** their shares or **transfer** them without restriction. The London Stock Exchange (LSE), for example, insists on free transferability for listed company shares, although the Articles of Association of some unlisted companies may restrict the transfer of shares.

5.1.2 Voting and Non-Voting Shares

Normally, shares are voting shares, which confer the right to vote on company resolutions at annual and extraordinary general meetings. Non-voting shares do not confer such formal voting rights but do provide their holders with the same rights to receive dividends and capital return. They are sometimes called **A shares** or **participation certificates**. These non-voting shares exist to raise equity financing without diluting voting control from the remaining ordinary shareholders.

5.1.3 Partly Paid Shares

This occurs in an issue of shares where only a portion of the purchase price or capital sum due has been paid to the issuing company. The balance is usually payable in one or more instalments at predetermined future dates. The firm's directors normally have discretion as to when to require the payment of additional tranches.

5.2 Preference Shares

All companies that are quoted on the LSE must have ordinary shares, but they need not have preference shares. Preference shares are a separate class of shares that usually receive preference over ordinary shares as far as dividends and capital repayment are concerned. Their rights are:

*   **dividends** – if any profits are available to pay dividends, they must firstly be used to pay preference dividends, since preference shares have a fixed dividend payment. In addition, any past unpaid preference dividends will take priority over ordinary share dividends. Any profits remaining belong, in full, to the ordinary shareholders. Preference shareholders, therefore, receive priority but are only entitled to a fixed rate of dividend, whereas ordinary shareholders own whatever is left – the equity.
*   **capital repayment** – if the business fails and the company goes into liquidation, preference shareholders are entitled to the repayment of their capital prior to ordinary shareholders but the amount repayable is restricted to the nominal value of the preference shares. Therefore, preference shareholders rank just behind other creditors (including debt holders) in a company's liquidation. Ordinary shareholders receive whatever is left after the claims of all creditors and preference shareholders have been met. Ordinary shareholders, therefore, own all of the reserves of the company.
*   **voting rights** – in the vast majority of cases, preference shares do not carry voting rights except when the company has failed to pay its preference dividend, ie, when the preference dividend is in arrears.

5.2.1 Types of Preference Share Capital

In addition to the general characteristics of preference share capital described above, a variety of refinements may be built into the terms of issue.

Cumulative or Non-Cumulative

A company may make insufficient profits to cover the payment of its preference dividend in a particular period. If the preference shares are **cumulative**, the company must pay in later years not only the current year's preference dividend but also the accumulated **arrears of preference** dividend from previous periods. This arrears of preference dividend must be paid before any ordinary dividend.

Participating

Preference shares usually are **non-participating**, in the sense that the fixed rate of dividend is the limit of their entitlement to participate in profits, and their nominal value is the limit of their entitlement to capital repayment. If the shares are **participating** preference shares, the holders are also entitled to participate in surplus profits available for dividend after the fixed preference dividend has been paid. If they are **fully participating**, they are also entitled to a share in capital repayment in excess of nominal value.

Redeemable

Companies may issue redeemable preference shares. The terms of issue enable the company to repay the shareholders at a predetermined price (often more than nominal value, ie, at a premium) on a future specified date or dates.

Convertible Preference Shares

Convertible preference shares offer the shareholder the usual preferential rights to dividend and capital repayment, plus the option to convert their holding into ordinary shares on predetermined future dates at specified prices.

In the past, convertible preference shares were popular in company restructurings; if the company had been in financial difficulties a lender might accept convertible preference shares in exchange for providing a loan. In the short term there were elements of reassurance in receiving a 'preferential' dividend with the option of converting into equity if the company recovered and became highly profitable.

5.3   Warrants

Learning Objective

2.4.3   Analyse the key investment characteristics and differences between equity warrants and equity options: purpose and issuers; benefits to an investor or speculator; time to expiry; where traded; strike prices; effect of exercise; settlement; gearing against the underlying; effect of corporate actions on equity warrants

An **equity warrant** gives its holder the right to buy a company's shares over the life of the warrant at a fixed exercise price, which is usually at a premium over its current price at the time the warrant is issued. It is often issued by the company on which the warrant is based or another private party. Warrants are commonly attached to a **corporate bond** but, unlike convertible bonds, the bond itself continues to exist if the warrant is exercised. They can also be attached to preferred stock, to attract investors. The attachment of a warrant is seen as an inducement and usually allows the issuer to pay a lower coupon.

Equity warrants are very similar to **equity options** in that both represent the right to buy a set amount of a company's shares over a predefined time frame at a set price. They differ in that, while equity options are traded on a public exchange and the seller is usually not the issuing company, most warrants are traded privately and, as stated above, the issuing company itself is the most common issuer.

Note that warrants are traded on some financial markets such as Deutsche Börse and the Hong Kong Stock Exchange. But it should be noted that these exchanges do not trade equity options.

The lower coupon that is paid on a corporate bond with an equity warrant attached represents the premium the investor pays for the warrant (the equivalent of an option's premium). It allows the investor/speculator to take a view on the company's shares, and to profit if their price rises over the life of the warrant. Until the warrant is exercised, its holder is not entitled to receive any dividend that the company might pay.

Since the company issues equity warrants, it will include provisions to adjust the warrant's exercise price, or its number of shares in the case of share splits or bonus issues. Provisions for takeovers and mergers are more issue-specific.

Warrant certificates have stated particulars regarding the investment tool they represent. All warrants have a specified **expiry date**: the last day the rights of a warrant can be executed. Warrants are classified by their exercise style: an American warrant, for instance, can be exercised any time before or on the stated expiry date, and a European warrant, on the other hand, can be carried out only on the day of expiration.

The **underlying** instrument the warrant represents is also stated on warrant certificates. A warrant typically corresponds to a specific number of shares, but it can also represent a commodity, index or currency.

The **exercise or strike price** is the amount that must be paid in order to either buy the call warrant or sell the put warrant. The payment of the strike price results in a transfer of the specified amount of the underlying instrument.

The **conversion ratio** is the number of warrants needed in order to buy (or sell) one investment unit. Therefore, if the conversion ratio to buy an individual share is 3:1, this means that the holder needs three warrants in order to purchase one share. Usually, if the conversion ratio is high, the price of the share will be low, and vice versa. In the case of equity warrants, with any **corporate actions** such as rights issues, share splits, share buybacks and takeovers and mergers, the conversion ratio and strike price may be adjusted to reflect such activity. The reason for this is to ensure that listed products investors are not disadvantaged or do not gain undue benefit by equity adjustments.

Since warrants are usually part of another financial instrument and are exclusively traded on an OTC basis, the **settlement** process is very similar to that of any other OTC option (see Chapter 4).

5.4 Valuation Techniques

Learning Objective

2.4.2   Analyse how the following factors influence equity markets and equity valuation: trading volume and liquidity of domestic and international securities markets; relationship between cash and derivatives markets, and the effects of timed events; market consensus and analyst opinion; changes to key pricing determinants such as credit ratings, economic outlook and significant events

Calculating a share's/stock's value is not an exact science. There is a wide range of models that everyone from individual investors to large fund managers uses when evaluating a share's price. Most are based on forecasts of the company's cash flow, future earnings and/or dividend payments.

Here are a few of the most widely used equity valuation methods. These three measures are used by both credit rating agencies and market analysts, who produce regular evaluations and opinions on how well the company is performing and, therefore, forecasts of future movements on its share price.

Any significant change in any of key pricing determinants, or unexpected news, such as a potential hostile takeover of a company, will have a significant impact on that company's share price and market valuation. It will most likely cause a shift in opinion by analysts and the credit agencies.

5.4.1   Earnings Per Share

Not all of a company's profits are distributed to its shareholders through dividend payments – many are retained for reinvestment into the business. It is important that this happens, if a company is to grow and remain competitive, and if its share price is to remain strong over the long term.

Investors who are not reliant on their dividend stream to live on may therefore be more interested in a company's overall earnings, instead of just the element it distributes by way of dividend.

Earnings per share = Company's profits/Number of outstanding common shares

Steady growth in a company's earnings should, in theory, ensure that its ordinary shareholders can continue to receive stable and rising dividends in future. So the **earnings yield** calculation can be a good indicator of one company's comparative strength of earnings against that of another.

The formula is as follows:

$$\text{Earnings yield (\%)} = \frac{\text{Earnings per share (gross)} \times 100}{\text{Market price of share}}$$

5.4.2   Price/Earnings Ratio

The price/earnings ratio (or **P/E ratio**) of a company is simply the current market price of its shares, divided by the annual earnings per share (EPS):

$$\text{P/E ratio} = \frac{\text{Current market price of share}}{\text{EPS}}$$

Some of the main reasons why the P/E ratio is a useful tool for investors in equities are:

*   **Relevance** – that is, it may be more relevant to analyse a share's performance on the basis of its earnings than its dividend record.
*   **Comparisons** – P/E ratios can be useful for comparing the shares in different companies, particularly those in similar industries.
*   **Risk** – a company's P/E ratio can show how risky the market believes an investment in the company to be: a low P/E ratio, relative to those of similar companies, may indicate a high perceived level of risk (or poor prospects for profit growth); whereas a high P/E ratio may indicate a relatively low perception of risk, or an expectation of good profits growth.

A company with a P/E ratio which is lower than the average for its sector or industry could, however, have the potential for an upward correction in its price – provided the market expects its profits to improve in the future (ie, you could regard its shares as cheap).

Alternatively, a low P/E ratio could indicate that the company is in difficulties and that prospects for its recovery are seen as uncertain.

5.4.3   Net Asset Value Per Share

The net asset value (NAV) of a company is, in essence, everything it owns less everything it owes – thus:

Net asset value = assets – liabilities

We can calculate the net asset value per share of a company by calculating the total net asset value of the company and dividing this by the number of shares in issue:

$$\text{NAV per share} = \frac{\text{assets – liabilities}}{\text{shares in issue}}$$

The importance of the NAV per share of a company depends on the type of business it is in. For those companies whose resources are mainly made up of people skills (for example, architects' practices, advertising agencies or law firms), most of the value of the business may be tied up in the skills and knowledge their employees possess, and the relationships and ideas they have. There is relatively little in the way of physical or financial assets. For other companies, however, with most of their resources committed to plant, property and equipment, it may be more valuable. In this case, an investor who buys a share at 100p may be interested to know that the NAV of the company is 130p, because if the company goes into liquidation there is, in effect, a 30p buffer supporting that share price.

5.5   Major Stock Exchanges

The following is a list of the ten largest stock exchanges by the total value of shares traded as of 31 October 2015 (USD trillions):

NYSE Euronext (US & Europe)	$18.33
NASDAQ OMX (US & North Europe)	$6.72
London Stock Exchange	$6.10
Tokyo Stock Exchange Group	$4.45
Shanghai Stock Exchange	$3.92
Hong Kong Stock Exchange	$2.93
Euronext	$3.14
Shenzhen Stock Exchange	$2.65
Toronto Stock Exchange (TMX)	$1.64
Deutsche Börse	$1.56

Source: World Federation of Exchanges (industry association)

Note that the NYSE sold off part of the old Euronext, keeping the old London LIFFE operation. The London Stock Exchange (LSE) is one of the world's leading equity exchanges and an international provider of services that facilitate the raising of finance and the trading of shares and debt securities. It is home to some of the world's most successful companies, giving them access to one of the deepest pools of capital in the world. The LSE offers both primary market activity, where issuers raise finance for the first time, and secondary market activity, where investors can use the exchange facilities to sell their shares to others.

The LSE also provides a number of information products and services. Its Regulatory News Service (RNS) enables companies to meet their regulatory requirements easily when making announcements and financial communications.

The LSE also provides market data via its InfolectTM service, which provides information ranging from real-time data on individual share price movements to company announcements.

5.5.1 Emerging Markets

Equity trading has become truly global, as more countries have opened their markets to international investors. The following is a list of some of the largest emerging stock markets and the total value of shares traded on them in 2014:

Bovespa – São Paulo Stock Exchange	$1,320bn
Bombay Stock Exchange – Mumbai	$1,700bn
National Stock of India – Mumbai	$1,650bn
Moscow Exchange	$277bn

Source: World Federation of Exchanges (industry association)

Two instruments that have helped the movement of investment capital from investors in developed economies to emerging markets are **American Depositary Receipts (ADRs)** and **Global Depositary Receipts (GDRs)**.

An ADR represents ownership of shares in a foreign company (usually one whose main listing is an emerging equity market) that are traded on a US market. The shares of many non-US companies trade on US exchanges through the use of ADRs. ADRs enable US investors to buy shares in foreign companies without undertaking cross-border transactions. ADRs are priced in US dollars, pay dividends in US dollars and can be traded like the shares of US-based companies.

Each ADR is issued by a US depository bank and can represent a fraction of a share, a single share, or multiple shares of the foreign companies. An owner of an ADR has the right to obtain the foreign stock it represents, but US investors usually find it more convenient simply to own the ADR. The price of any ADR is close to the price that the foreign share is trading at in its home market, once there has been an adjustment to take into account the ratio of ADRs to the foreign shares.

GDRs are the global version of ADRs. While they are structured in the same way, they trade on non-US exchanges, such as the LSE.

6.   Commodities

A commodity is a raw, or primary, product – for example, commodities include agricultural products (such as livestock, grain and fruit), energy products (such as oil and gas) and metals (such as copper and aluminium). Commodity derivatives are based on commodities, as distinct from financial derivatives based on financial instruments or financial data.

The commodity derivatives markets provide market participants with similar instruments to those available in the financial markets (eg, futures and options), and many commodity products pre-date the financial derivatives market, which only commenced in the 1970s and 1980s. The Chicago Board of Trade (CBoT), which was established in 1848, lays claim to being the oldest futures exchange in the world. Although it is where the modern form of the futures market originates, the trading of commodities contracts has been going on for many centuries within Europe and Japan: the London Metal Exchange, founded in 1877, can in fact trace its roots back to 1571 and the opening of the Royal Exchange.

The concepts covered in Chapter 1 apply equally to both financial and commodity derivatives markets. However, further factors may need to be taken into account when dealing in the commodity derivatives markets; for example, agricultural markets are heavily affected by the growing cycle of the crop and by the weather.

Some of the main global commodity derivatives markets, with examples of some of their contracts, are:

- **CME Group** – Chicago Board of Trade for agricultural and soft commodities, gold, metals and ethanol, and the Chicago Mercantile Exchange for energy – products including gas oil, crude oil and natural gas.
- **Euronext Derivatives** – soft commodities, eg, butter, fertilizer, wood pellets; and agricultural commodities, eg, wheat, corn, rapeseed.
- **Dubai Mercantile Exchange (DME)** – crude oil.
- **Intercontinental Exchange (ICE)** – crude oil, refined energy products, natural gas, and soft commodities, such as cotton, cocoa and wood.
- **LME (London Metal Exchange)** – base metals, steel billet, minor metals (cobalt and molybdenum).
- **Tokyo Commodities Exchange (TOCOM)** – base metals, oil and rubber.
- **Shanghai Metal Exchange (SHME)** – base metals.
- **Multi Commodity Exchange (MCX) Mumbai** – soft and agricultural commodities, gold, ferrous and base metals, and energy.
- **New York Mercantile Exchange (NYMEX)** – metals and energy contracts.
- **European Climate Exchange (ECX)** – environmental contracts.

6.1   Softs and Agriculturals

Learning Objective

2.5.1   Understand the main softs and agriculturals and the influences on supply: coffee, cocoa, white sugar, soya bean, wheat, rapeseed oil, grains, livestock; change in demand; change in production; holding cost

Softs is a label for a particular set of commodities that includes cocoa, sugar and coffee. **Agricultural** commodities include the grains such as wheat and soya beans, as well as livestock and seed oils.

The price influences on soft commodities (ie, coffee, sugar and cocoa) and agricultural products (ie, wheat, soya beans, etc) can be summarised as simply supply and demand.

Supply is the amount of the particular commodity that is being provided to the market. Obviously, this will be driven *inter alia* by such factors as the amount of land that is given over to producing a crop, weather conditions over the growing season and the impact of any other factors such as disease or insect activity, the application of better technology and the availability of transport and warehouse facilities. For example, the extremely hot and dry weather that parts of Russia and Central Asia experienced in 2010 had a significant effect by reducing the supply of wheat on global markets, which sparked higher prices.

Furthermore, the greater the number and diversity of sources for a particular soft or agricultural commodity, the more stable the supply. For example, if cocoa is grown in multiple locations, harmful weather in any one location will have less impact.

Both softs and agricultural commodities are also capital-intensive produce, have considerable lead times and in many cases are politically controlled, through subsidies, taxes or trade restrictions. All of these factors are important and have considerable influence on their cost of production, their export potential and their prices.

Demand will be driven by whether nations have a deficit of the particular commodity, rather than a surplus. Additionally, the wealth of the population, economic and industrial growth, consumer tastes and habits, tax incentives, etc, will be important factors. The increased wealth and changing tastes of a number of consumers in Asia has also been a key factor to increased demand for certain agricultural products and increased prices.

Example 5

Euronext Derivatives trades a variety of commodity products, including wheat, white sugar and cocoa futures. The essential details that are relevant to the examination are contained in the table below.

Product	Contract Size (tonnes)	Tick Size (per tonne)	Tick Value (per contract)
Corn	50	€0.25	€12.50
Rapeseed	50	€0.25	€12.50
Milling Wheat	50	€0.25	€12.50

The commodity products trade on Euronext Derivative's Universal Trading Platform (UTP).

There are options available on the futures. The options are American-style (see Chapter 1, Section 3.2).

The option premiums are not paid up front, but are paid futures style. These soft commodity futures are all physically delivered and use LCH SA as central counterparty.

For those futures contracts that reach delivery, the **exchange delivery settlement price (EDSP)** is broadly the price at which the future traded at the end of the trading period on the last trading day. The sellers choose where to deliver, based on the exchange's specified delivery points (eg, for Euronext Paris' corn futures, delivery is made to a listed European port; for Euronext's corn futures, a listed international port; and for futures, an approved grain store). The delivered commodities are matched to buyers by LCH SA.

For options on the futures, the options expire in the month before the delivery month, eg, March corn options that enable the buyer to enter into a March cocoa future expire on the last business day of February.

Similar to financial assets, commodities also have their own version of a **carrying cost**. But, in the case of commodities, it is referred to as its holding cost. This refers to the costs associated with keeping any commodity inventory, which may include warehousing, spoilage, obsolescence, interest and taxes. For soft and agricultural commodities, spoilage is a key concern, since many of the commodities in the category may have a limited product life. When calculating the profits and losses from a commodities trade, holding costs must be taken into account.

6.2 Base and Precious Metals

Learning Objective

2.6.1 Understand the main base and precious metals and the influences on supply: copper, nickel, aluminium, zinc, tin, lead, gold and silver; change in demand; change in production; marginal costs of mining; changes in industry; political or strategic; holding cost

There are numerous metals produced worldwide and, subsequently, refined for use in a large variety of products and processes. Derivatives products have been introduced on some of the major metals. Trading is concentrated on two exchanges: the London Metal Exchange (LME) and the COMEX division of NYMEX in New York. However, these two exchanges do not compete on all metals, with only copper and aluminium trading on both exchanges.

As with soft commodities, metal prices are influenced by supply and demand. Factors influencing **supply** include the availability of raw materials and the costs of extraction and production. A producer will measure the cost of extraction against a metal's price: when the marginal cost of mining rises above a metal's current price, production will stop. This follows the basic economic principle that marginal cost must be less than the price in order to contribute to the other costs incurred, and potentially provide a profit. Such costs may be affected by political stability and environmental legislation. **Demand** comes from underlying users of the commodity, for example, the growing demand for metals in rapidly industrialising economies, including China and India. It also originates from investors such as hedge funds, who might buy metal futures in anticipation of excess demand or incorporate commodities into specific funds. Producers use the market for hedging their production. Traditionally, the price of precious metals such as gold will rise in times of crisis – gold is seen as a safe haven.

All metal commodities, like softs, have **holding or warehousing costs** associated with taking delivery and holding the commodity. As with all other costs of carry types of cost, the longer one holds the asset (commodity), the higher the holding cost. Finally, metals used in packaging, for example, are influenced by the cost of **alternatives** such as glass and plastic, and by consumer/government concerns about sustainable resources and recycling.

The major metals can be subdivided into base metals and precious metals. The major metals and their uses are summarised in the following table:

Metal	Major Uses
Base	
Copper	Electrics, electronics, building
Aluminium	Aerospace, packaging, kitchen equipment, windows, car manufacture, buildings, canning
Zinc	Galvanising, production of brass
Nickel	Production of stainless steel and other alloys
Lead	Batteries, petrol additive, buildings

Tin	Packaging, power
Precious	
Gold	Jewellery, dentistry, computers, electronics, investments
Silver	Jewellery, ornaments, photography, dentistry, electronics

6.3   Energy Products

Learning Objective

2.7.1   Understand the main energy products and the influences on price: crude oil, natural gas and emissions; change in demand; change in production; marginal costs of production; delivery costs; political or strategic; Organisation of Petroleum Exporting Countries (OPEC)

The energy market includes the market for refined oil products and natural gas products. Like the market for any other product, the price influences can be summarised as supply factors and demand factors.

Supply is finite, and countries with surplus oil and gas reserves are able to export to those countries with insufficient oil and gas to meet their requirements. Prices could be raised by producers restricting supply, for example, by the activities of the major oil producers in the Organisation of Petroleum Exporting Countries (OPEC).

Demand for oil and gas is ultimately driven by levels of consumption, which in turn is driven by energy needs (for example, from manufacturing industry and transport). Intercontinental Exchange (ICE) is Europe's largest energy exchange, listing a wide range of crude and refined oil and natural gas contracts.

Prices can react sharply to political crises, particularly in major oil-producing regions of the world such as the Middle East. Furthermore, since the level of demand is directly determined by the consuming economies' growth, economic forecasts and economic data also have an impact on energy prices.

Prices also react quickly to changes in supply resulting from bad weather and accidents, such as oil spills from offshore sources. The BP Gulf of Mexico oil spill of 2010 might have a longer-term effect on prices, if environmental concerns delay or block any future licences for offshore drilling in a number of regions.

Oil includes both crude oil and various fractions produced as a result of the refining process, eg, naphtha, butanes, kerosene, petrol and heating/gas oil.

Crude oil is defined by three primary factors:

*   Field of origin, for example, Brent, West Texas, Dubai.
*   Density, ie, low-density or 'light', high-density or 'heavy'.
*   Sulphur content, ie, low-sulphur (known as 'sweet') or high-sulphur (known as 'sour').

For emissions, see Section 7.

7. Other Products

Learning Objective

2.8.1 Understand the purpose and investment characteristics of futures contracts on weather, emissions, hybrids and property

Recent developments have seen the expansion of derivatives trading into a wide range of **exotic contracts**. These include weather, emissions and property, to name a select few.

A **weather** derivative is a contract that obligates the buyer to purchase the value of the underlying weather index – measured in **heating degree days (HDD)** or **cooling degree days (CDD)** – at a future date. The settlement price of the underlying weather index is equal to the value of the relevant month's HDD/CDD multiplied by $20. Weather futures can enable businesses to protect themselves against losses caused by unexpected shifts in weather conditions.

As expected, one of the main influences on price is the short- and long-term weather forecast. Contract prices are also subject to shock when unexpected weather events happen, such as hurricanes and snowstorms. This is an aspect that they have in common with many agricultural contracts.

Growing environmental concerns have prompted several exchanges to start trading several different types of **emissions** contracts. Exchanges in Europe, Asia and North America have listed several types of futures contracts for carbon dioxide, sulphur dioxide, methane and nitrogen dioxide emissions. These contracts set a price for a set amount of emissions allotment, with the goal of getting emissions to a predetermined level, such as those set by the Kyoto Accord. Those entities that are heavy polluters buy these to offset what they produce. As regulations get stricter and pollution targets are reduced, prices are expected to rise.

Freight derivatives, which include forward freight agreements (FFAs), container freight swap agreements and options, are financial contracts that are based on the future levels of freight rates, for dry bulk carriers, tankers and container ships. These instruments are settled against various freight rate indices, which are published by the Baltic Exchange (for dry and most wet contracts) and Platt's (Asian wet contracts).

FFAs are often traded over-the-counter, through broker members of the Forward Freight Agreement Brokers' Association (FFABA), but recently screen-based trading has become more popular. Trades can be given up for clearing by the broker to one of the clearing houses that support such trades. Currently, there are four clearing houses for freight: NOS Clearing, ICE Guardian, NYMEX and the Singapore Stock Exchange.

Freight derivatives are primarily used by ship-owners and -operators, oil companies, trading companies and grain houses as tools for managing freight rate risk. Recently, with commodities now standing at the forefront of international economics, the large financial trading houses, including banks and hedge funds, have entered the market.

Hybrid derivatives basically combine two different types of derivatives in one contract. They do this by incorporating two or more types of risks into a single derivative. One of the most widely used examples is a swaption = swap + option.

Hybrids very often combine features and risks from different markets. For example, a hybrid derivative could be a contract that gives its owner the right to the sell a bill paying LIBOR + 200bps for an individual share at specified prices when a specific share index reaches certain point. The option involves two markets: the money market and the equity market.

Any multi-asset derivative whose components don't belong to the same asset class can be considered to be a hybrid derivative. In general, financial derivatives can be divided into basic derivatives and hybrid derivatives, where the latter result from combining a host contract with an embedded derivative:

Hybrid derivative = host contract + embedded derivative

Hybrid derivatives allow investors, speculators, and hedgers to take a view on combinations of asset classes in a single contract. For example, a fund manager with multi-asset exposures can use hybrid derivatives as a hedging tool.

Example 6

Hybrid derivative = A GBP 1.56 put vs. the USD that depends on the price of gold reaching USD 1,200 per ounce.

A **property derivative** is a financial derivative whose value is based on the value of an underlying real estate asset. Since real estate prices are sometimes subject to market inefficiencies and are hard to price accurately, property derivatives are often based on a real estate property **index**. In turn, the real estate property index attempts to reflect price movements in the aggregate real estate market to provide a more accurate representation of underlying real estate asset's performance.

Trading or taking positions in property derivatives is also known as **synthetic real estate**.

Property derivatives usually take the form of a total return swap, forward contract or futures, or can adopt a funded format where the property derivative is included as part of a bond or note structure. Under the total return swap or forward contract, the parties will usually take contrary positions on the price movements of a property index.

End of Chapter Questions

1. What time spans are the money markets typically geared towards?
   Answer reference: Section 2.1

2. Every contributor bank is asked to base their ICE LIBOR submissions on what?
   Answer reference: Section 2.1

3. What is EONIA?
   Answer reference: Section 2.1

4. At what length of maturity are T-bills typically issued?
   Answer reference: Section 2.3

5. Describe commercial paper.
   Answer reference: Section 2.5

6. Name the four main reasons why the foreign exchange market is unique.
   Answer reference: Section 4

7. What are bearer shares?
   Answer reference: Section 5.1

8. Why is the price/earnings ratio a useful tool for investors in equities?
   Answer reference: Section 5.4.2

9. When did commodities derivatives markets originate?
   Answer reference: Section 6

10. How does a weather derivative operate?
    Answer reference: Section 7

Chapter Three
Exchange-Traded Futures and Options

This syllabus area will provide approximately 13 of the 80 examination questions

1. Derivatives Exchanges

1.1 Introduction to Derivatives Exchanges

Learning Objective

3.1.1 Understand the structures, physical and electronic trading processes, clearing mechanisms and main products of the major derivatives exchanges: CME Group including CME, CBOT and NYMEX; Intercontinental Exchange (ICE) including ICE Futures Europe, US and Canada; Euronext including NYSE Liffe and Liffe US; Turquoise Derivatives Europe; NASDAQ Options Market and NASDAQ OMX Group; London Metal Exchange (LME); Eurex; Tokyo Stock Exchange (TSE); Shanghai Stock Exchange (SSE); China Financial Futures Exchange (CFFEX); Singapore Exchange (SGX); National Stock Exchange of India (NSE); Dubai Gold and Commodities Exchange (DGCX)

A derivatives exchange is an exchange which provides a marketplace where one can buy and sell futures, options and other contracts of specific quantities of a commodity or financial instrument at a specified price with delivery set at a specified time in the future.

In providing the marketplace, the exchange will have established a trading mechanism or platform, ie, trading can take place using the traditional pits or floor trading, or electronically via computer screens using a trading platform. Some exchanges, for some contracts, do use both.

UK	
Euronext Derivatives	Euronext group's global derivatives market. Electronic trading via the Universal Trading Platform (UTP). Trades futures and options on currencies, equities, ETFs, indices and commodities. Some of its main contracts are Long Gilt, EURIBOR, EUR/USD, as well as universal stock futures and track options. It uses Exchange Data Publisher to provide clear market prices and data to its clients. All trades are cleared via LCH.Clearnet. Even though Euronext London is a cash based market, it is still an important part of the Euronext Group and its links to their European derivatives market, is one that candidates should be aware of.
LME – London Metal Exchange	Both open outcry physical trading, and electronic via LME Select and inter-office on the telephone. Trades futures and options on: aluminium, copper, nickel, tin, zinc, lead and steel, plus aluminium alloy, and its own metal-based index.
ICE Futures Europe	All trading is done electronically. Trades futures and options on a wide range of energy products, such as: Brent Crude, West Texas Intermediate (WTI), gas oil, electricity, coal and natural gas. It also trades a range of interest rates, such as LIBOR, bond and equity index and single stock futures. Trades are cleared via ICE Clear Europe.

LSE Derivatives	All trading is done electronically. Trades standardised and flexible futures and options of the shares and indices on the FTSE 100, FTSE Super Liquid (largest 35 shares) and the Norwegian OBX index. It also has contracts linked to the most liquid Russian shares and indices. Trades which are processed are cleared and guaranteed by CCP Clearing with LCH.Clearnet.

Euronext is Europe's largest exchange spanning Amsterdam, Brussels, Lisbon and Paris, referred to respectively as the Amsterdam, Brussels, Lisbon and Paris markets. These are linked to Euronext's London market via Universal Trading Platform (UTP), which in effect creates one pan-European securities market.

Bclear, which is accessible via ICE London or Amsterdam, combines the flexibility of OTC markets with the benefits of exchange-traded and cleared contracts. B-Clear offers options on a wide range of individual companies' shares, UK and European index futures and options, universal stock futures and variance futures on the AEX, CAC 40 and FTSE 100 indices. B-Clear can also be used by member firms to process OTC derivatives business, to help reduce their operational risk and manage the contract's counterparty risk. In addition to its clearing of OTC derivatives, BClear also clears a range of commodity and interest rate and bond contracts.

NASDAQ OMX Group is a US-based company that owns and operates the NASDAQ stock market and eight European stock exchanges in Armenia, the Nordic and Baltic regions. Given the wide range of exchanges, the group has several different trading systems to fit each market and product traded; these include the Genium INET trading platform, CONDICO – which is used for commodities trading and clearing – and CLICK XT. The group trades a wide variety of futures and options on a range of underlying assets that include shares, indices, interest rates and commodities. The group's two main clearing systems include Genium INET Clearing and SECUR.

NASDAQ Options Market (NOM) is one of NASDAQ OMX Group's two electronic options markets. All trading is run on NASDAQ's INET technology. The NOM is a US-based options markets, that trades a wide range of NASDAQ and PHLX options. NOM uses the same clearing systems as its parent.

US	
CBoT – Chicago Board of Trade – part of the CME Group	Both 'open outcry' physical trading and electronic via EOS Trader and CME Direct. Trades futures on a wide range of agricultural products, gold, silver, interest rates (US notes, bonds, swaps), the Dow indices, and has a joint trading agreement with SGX to trade several of its contracts. All trades processed under the JADE agreement, by the Front End Clearing System (FEC) and Front End Clearing Plus (FEC+), which are based on CME Direct.
Chicago Board Options Exchange (CBoE)	The Chicago Board Options Exchange (CBOE) is the largest US options exchange, established by the CBOT in 1973. It was the first exchange to list standardised, exchange-traded stock options and its contracts are cleared by the Options Clearing Corporation (OCC).
CME – Chicago Mercantile Exchange – part of the CME Group	Both 'open outcry' physical trading, and CME Globex electronic trading platform. Trades futures on a wide range of commodities, short-term interest rates, FX, US economic data, equity indices, weather and real estate. All trades processed via CME Direct.

NYMEX – New York Mercantile Exchange – part of the CME Group	Both 'open outcry' physical trading, and via CME Globex and NYMEX ClearPort, for OTC transactions; also after-hours trading on CME Global electronic trading platform for futures only. Trades futures and options on a wide range of metals, energy products and options on spreads between different grades of oil such as the Brent/WTI spread. All trades are processed via the exchange's clearing house.
OneChicago	The OneChicago Match Engine is accessible from either CBOEdirect or CME Globex systems. An electronically traded market via both CBOEdirect and Globex systems. Trades single stock futures (known as security futures), as well as futures on narrowly defined share indices and exchange-traded funds. Trades are processed through either CME Clearing or OCC depending on membership.
PHLX – Philadelphia Stock Exchange	Combination of floor trading and PHLX XL, the exchange's electronic trading platform. Trades stock, index, equity sector and currency options. Both offer standardised and FLEX options. All trades are processed via the exchange's clearing house.

Europe	
Eurex	An electronically traded market, the world's largest derivatives exchange. Trades a wide range of futures and options on: short-term interest rates, equities, index and single stock futures, volatility index, credit derivatives and exchange-traded funds. Also FLEX options. All trades processed via Eurex Clearing AG.
Euronext exchanges (Amsterdam, Brussels, Lisbon and Paris)	Electronic trading via the Universal Trading Platform (UTP). Trades futures and options on currencies, swaps, equities and commodities. All four exchanges use Clearnet SA to process their trades.
MEFF – Spanish Exchange for Financial Futures and Options	All trading is done via the MEFF Derivative Trading Platform. Trades futures and options on interest rates, bonds, the IBEX-35 index and leading Spanish shares. Trades are processed directly from the MEFF Derivatives Trading Platform by the exchange's clearing house.

Asia	
Singapore Exchange Ltd (SGX)	All trading is done electronically via the SGX QUEST system. Trades futures and options on interest rates, bonds and regional equity indices. Main contracts include JGB, Eurodollar and Euroyen, Nikkei 225 contracts. All trades are processed and cleared via SGX-DC (SGX Derivatives Clearing).
Osaka Securities Exchange (OSE)	A physical and electronic market. Trades futures and options on the Nikkei 225 index, as well as individual Japanese shares. Trades processed via the exchange's clearing house.
Tokyo Stock Exchange (TSE)	An electronic market that trades futures and options on several TOPIX and TSE indices, as well as individual shares and government bonds. Trading is done via the Tdex+ system.

Korea Exchange (KRX) Futures Market Division	The KSE, KOSDAQ and KOFEX markets have been consolidated and now all derivative products are traded on the Futures Market Division of KRX. On KOFEX all orders are processed via the exchange's automatic trading system. KOFEX trades futures and options of several Korean and US indices as well as gold and CD interest rate futures. All trades are processed via the KRX's clearing house.

Emerging Markets	
Brazilian Mercantile & Futures Exchange (BM&F)	Some agricultural contracts are traded physically; all other contracts are traded electronically via NSC screen trading system. Trades futures on a range of agricultural products. Futures and options on gold, coffee, corn, soybeans, USD, the Bovespa share index and a range of domestic interest rates. Trades are cleared through the three BM&F clearing houses for the respective contract product.
Dubai Mercantile Exchange (DME)	A fully electronic exchange. Trades an Oman crude oil future and two spread futures, Brent/Oman crude and WTI/Oman crude. Trades are cleared through the NYMEX clearing house.
Dubai Gold & Commodities Exchange (DGCX)	Trading is done electronically using DGCX electronic trading system. Trades of a wide range of commodity and currency futures, as well as options on gold and Indian rupee futures. All trades are cleared through the Dubai Commodities Clearing Corporation (DCCC).
National Commodities & Derivatives Exchange Ltd (India) (NYDEX)	Trading is done on the exchange's Automated Trading System. Trades futures on agro products, precious, base and ferrous metals, energy products and polymers. Trades are processed via the exchange's clearing house, with physical delivery through its Depository Clearing System, while margin payments and cash settlement are via an approved clearing bank.
South African Futures Exchange (Safex) – part of the JSE – Johannesburg Stock Exchange	Trading is done electronically using the JSE's TALX system, also accessed via the SETS trading system. Trades a wide range of futures contracts on agricultural products, gold, interest rates, FX, the JSE index and Single Stock futures.
Shanghai Futures Exchange (SHFE)	Trading takes place on its trading floor and via its electronic trading system. Trades futures contracts on a number of metals (aluminium, copper, zinc), rubber and fuel oil. Trades are processed via the exchange's clearing system, with physical delivery using any of its approved warehouses.
China Financial Futures Exchange (CFFEX)	All trading is done electronically, using the CFFEX's system, which is also linked to the exchange's clearing house. CSI 200 index futures are currently the only contract traded.
Bombay Stock Exchange (India) (BSE)	A fully screen-based exchange, using the exchange's DTSS system, as well as internet-based trading. Trades a range of individual equity, equity index and currency-based derivatives. Uses its internal system for clearing and delivery.
Multi Commodity Exchange (India) (MCX)	A fully electronic exchange. Trades futures in a wide range of commodities, including bullion, energy, ferrous and non-ferrous metals, oil seeds, and spices. Trades are cleared and delivered via the exchange's Demat@MCX system.

National Stock Exchange of India (NSE)	Trading is done electronically using the exchange's system, NEAT. Trades a wide range of equity, currency and interest rate derivatives. Uses its internal system for clearing and delivery.
Shanghai Stock Exchange (SSE)	Trading is done electronically using the SSE's trading system. The SSE trades a wide range of B-shares and share indices. All trades are cleared through the China Securities Central Clearing & Registration Corporation (CSCCRC).

1.2 Membership Structure and Trading Rights

Learning Objective

3.1.2 Understand the membership structures (brokers, dealers and broker-dealers, general clearing, individual clearing and non-clearing) and their principal rights: executing trades for third parties; executing trades for their own account; executing trades for other members; capacity as broker; capacity as dealer; capacities of clearing members

Access to most exchange markets is via **membership**. Firms may join in a number of different membership categories.

- **Brokers** – may only trade for third parties (including clients and other members).
- **Dealers** – may trade for their own account. They can also trade for other members provided that they are authorised by the appropriate regulatory body.
- **Broker-dealers** – are entitled to trade both for third parties and their own account.

The forms of membership also depend on whether the firm wishes to clear business traded on the market, and for whom the contracts will be cleared.

All exchanges have a **clearing house**, which serves as the central counterparty to all trades executed on the exchange between clearing members. Remember that one of the key attractions of exchange-traded contracts is that there is no counterparty risk: the clearing house guarantees the delivery of all contracts.

As we have seen earlier, exchanges have different types of membership that determine the types of trading services a firm can execute, and the same is true of clearing services. Clearing members can be **general clearing members (GCMs)**, which enables them to clear their own principal trades, on behalf of their clients and on behalf of other non-clearing members. Alternatively, they can be **individual clearing members (ICMs)**, only able to clear their own principal trades and on behalf of their clients. Also, **non-clearing members** may be party to a maximum of two clearing agreements, one in respect of commodity contracts and one in respect of other exchange contracts. Most clearing houses require that their general clearing members have a higher level of financial resources than they require from individual clearing members.

Each and every contract (transaction) traded on the exchange will be supported by a clearing member in whose name the transaction is registered.

2. Trading Platforms

Learning Objective

3.2.1 Understand the essential details of the trading mechanisms: open outcry, telephone and electronic platforms; quote- versus order-driven; order matching; order types accepted by the markets; recognised trading strategies; record keeping

3.2.2 Understand the significance, implications and uses of wholesale trading facilities

3.3.2 Understand the trading mechanisms used for: block trades; exchange for physicals (EFPs) and exchange for swaps (EFSs); FLEX products

---

Pit trading or open outcry (called ring trading at the LME) is the original trading method. It is a **quote- or price-driven system**, where traders quote the prices for which they are willing to buy or sell specific contracts. The LME is one of the few European exchanges that operate both ring trading during its most liquid times and LMEselect, an electronic platform, for extended trading. The LME has four five-minute ring trading sessions per day for each of its major metal contracts. These take place over different times of the main trading day and are limited to the specific contract during its allotted time.

The other markets that also use this pit trading and are found in the US are the Chicago Board of Trade and the CME. But even on these exchanges, screen-based trading is becoming increasingly more popular.

A key aspect of the LME's ring trading is its **ring dealing** membership category. Each ring dealing member is allowed to trade during each ring dealing session, in addition to the 24-hour inter-office trading that takes place on the LME. Note that seats on open outcry markets are normally more valuable given the limited number of seats due to capacity limitations. This results in waiting lists for seats and an open market for seat sales and leases.

Telephone trading is exclusively limited to trades and orders between clients and their executing brokers. This is most often the case when a client calls their broker, who has a direct line to the trader, who quotes a price. If the client deals on it, the trader will trade on the market price. Electronic trading systems have replaced telephone trading in most of the main exchanges.

Most exchange trading is purely electronic via an **electronic system**, which is an anonymous, **order-driven** system, where traders are unaware of their actual counterparty, both pre-trade and post-trade. To access the system, an order is submitted into the central order book by, or via, an exchange member.

While on the LME trading takes place both on the ring trading or its LMEselect system, ICE trading takes place on ICE Clear. Examples of other electronic trading systems are CME Globex and CME Direct, which is used for several of the agricultural contracts trading on the CME Group. Many exchanges in developing markets such as the Shanghai Futures Exchange and the NCDEX also use electronic trading systems.

Once the order has been received, the system stores the order on the central order book. Orders are matched on the basis of price, and then time priority. After the trades have been executed, trade details are fed to a trade registration system, such as ICE Clear, as used by ICE London market.

In the case of ICE London, trades that have been registered using ICE Clear are passed automatically to ICE Clear Europe. The trade then **novates** and ICE Clear Europe becomes the central counterparty to the buying and selling clearing members. (Novation is covered in more detail in Chapter 5, Clearing.)

As with all electronic trading systems, ICE Clear accepts a variety of order types:

- **Normal limit orders** – to be executed at the stated price or better.
- **Market orders** – to be executed at the best price immediately available.
- **Market on open orders** – these may be submitted prior to the opening of the day's trading with the intention of being executed at the opening price for the day.

Some order types can be given certain periods of validity, such as **good 'til cancelled (GTC)**. Additionally, they can be given certain quantity requirements, such as **immediate and cancel** (do as much as possible now and cancel any remaining), **complete volume** (do the whole order or none at all) or **minimum volume** (only do the order if a certain minimum can be achieved).

Where permitted by the exchange rules, **cross trades** (where a match has been established by negotiation prior to entry in the system) are allowed as long as they are entered into the system as separate buy and sell orders.

The **strategies** that are recognised by most exchanges are many and varied. Amongst the acceptable strategies are all those covered in the syllabus, ie, spreads, straddles, strangles and synthetics (more detail on derivatives strategies can be found in Chapter 8, Trading, Hedging and Investment Strategies).

Additionally, most exchanges recognise two types of **wholesale trades**: block trades and basis trades. A block trade is a large transaction made between an exchange member and a wholesale client. The exchange specifies the size of the transaction that is required before it becomes a block trade. Block trades are allowed to be negotiated away from the central order book as long as they are reported into the exchange once they are agreed.

The block trade facility allows members and their wholesale clients (those with sufficient knowledge, expertise and understanding) to transact business as bilaterally agreed transactions without delay and with certainty of price and execution. The block trade facility complements the central markets, which continue to be the primary method for trading.

Each exchange determines which products can be block-traded. The transaction sizes required to be classified as a block trade vary. For example, ICE London has set for short sterling and gilt futures the minimum of 500 contracts, while for FTSE futures it is 750 contracts. Block trades must be reported within five minutes and are denoted by the letter 'K'. The HKEx defines a minimum number of contracts in a block trade for its stock index futures and options as 100 contracts, while for individual stock options it is 500 contracts. Once reported, these trades are denoted by 'INT' on the HKEx in the ticker window to differentiate them.

A **basis trade** is the simultaneous exchange of a financial asset or instrument (eg, a government bond or a basket of shares), together with an appropriate offsetting number of futures contracts, in a privately negotiated transaction between two parties. Similarly to block trades, the exchange allows the futures part of the basis trade to be executed outside the central order book. As with block trades, basis trades are reported into the exchange once they are agreed.

FLEX facility, such as the one offered by ICE for FTSE 100 index options, gives any exchange member the freedom to customise the trades with respect to the strike/exercise price and expiration date. The FLEX facility is one that combines the flexibility of the OTC market with the clearing and other advantages of exchange trading. The FLEX concept was originally introduced by the Chicago Board Options Exchange (CBOE). Some FLEX facilities offered by exchanges are another way to increase trading volumes based on advances in risk management and systems. See also Chapter 1, Section 3.6.

On most exchanges, **wholesale trading facilities** enable participants to enter off-order-book trades into the exchange's system. With these facilities the participants can benefit from the flexibility of customised trading and the advantages of standardised clearing and settlement. Most facilities are pure OTC trade entry facilities, with bilateral agreement of price and quantities.

Two aspects of wholesale trading facilities are:

- **Exchange for Physical (EFP)** – an off-market transaction that involves the swapping (or exchanging) of an OTC position for a futures position. In order that an EFP transaction can take place, the OTC side and futures components must be substantially similar in terms of either value and or quantity.
- **Exchange for Swaps (EPS)** – similar to EFP, in that it involves the swapping (or exchanging) of an OTC swap with a series of futures contracts. The OTC interest rate swap must have a price correlation so that the futures are a suitable instrument for hedging the cash market transaction.

EFP transactions have a number of benefits for market participants, which explains their existence. These are:

- Counterparty credit exposure can be reduced when an existing OTC position is reversed and replaced with a futures position. In so doing, an EFP allows counterparties to release 'credit', clearing their credit limits for further OTC trading.
- Reduced balance sheet and margin requirements – by netting OTC positions against offsetting futures positions, margin and credit limit requirements can be reduced.
- 24-hour trading – EFP transactions can normally be negotiated around the clock but must be registered during exchange business days between explicit time brackets.

3.   Exchange-Traded Derivatives Contracts

Learning Objective

3.3.1   Analyse the range, key features and investment characteristics of the main types of exchange-traded derivatives on: equities; indices; interest rates and credit; foreign exchange; commodities; contracts for differences; exchange-traded funds

As mentioned earlier, exchange-traded derivatives are based on a wide range of underlying markets. The main ones are:

- money markets/short-term interest rates and credit rates
- bonds – government and corporate
- equities (indexes)
- foreign exchange (FX)
- commodities – softs, agricultural, energy and metals
- contracts for difference
- exchange-traded funds.

The exchange-traded contracts based on these underlying assets are mainly in the form of futures and options contracts. As mentioned in Chapter 1, the key features of these contracts are standardised, which makes them easily traded. Therefore, their uses/investment characteristics range from being used as a method for hedging/reducing one's risk to speculation (taking on new risk, for profit) to arbitrage, when different markets provide a risk-free price, due to their prices being misaligned.

4.   Clearing Mechanisms

Learning Objective

3.4.1   Understand the matching and clearing process: trade capture and order-matching processes; delivery and settlement; physical versus cash settlement; establishment of settlement price; options into futures; initiation of delivery; purpose of mutual offset and where it exists

3.4.2   Understand how the physical delivery methods for commodities operate and where they differ from other derivatives: warehouses, warrants and good delivery; large position reporting; price discovery – official and closing price

Every exchange uses a clearing house, which clears all trades and supervises the processing and delivery of all trades executed on that exchange. The process by which the clearing house becomes counterparty to all trades is **novation**.

Each contract, as part of its specification, has details of its settlement procedure. While most contracts are closed out before maturity, each has a settlement/delivery process the clearing house supervises to ensure that both sellers and the buyers receive proper payment or delivery of the underlying asset.

The **physical settlement** approach is part of the mechanism which ensures that price convergence of futures to cash market prices will occur.

Cash settlement, which is another final settlement mechanism, is straightforward, since it requires the net cash payment of the difference between the value at the final position's closing price and the value based on the previous day's closing price. This is due to the fact that all contracts are marked-to-market at the end of each trading day and the clearing house either receives or pays that day's variation margin.

The details of physical delivery are set out as part of the contract's details. The specifications of each contract clearly define the details of what is an acceptable asset that can be delivered. Since exchange-traded contracts have standard amounts, they also have specific standards of what can be delivered. This is particularly the case for commodity contracts, where each exchange has specific quality requirements.

It is the seller who initiates the delivery process. Once advised, the clearing house will assign a buyer at random and advise them that delivery will take place. For most financial futures the delivery process is straightforward, since, with the exception of long-dated government bond contracts, most have a single underlying asset that can be delivered. For government bond contracts, such as gilts or T-bonds, the exchange will have a list of bonds that are eligible for delivery and each bond will have a price factor, from which the final invoice payment is based.

For options, it is the buyer who initiates delivery by exercising the option. In the case of **options on futures**, upon exercise the exchange will automatically replace the exercised option position with the corresponding future at the option's strike price.

With commodities, the delivery process is a little more involved, since, depending on the contract, there might be a choice of acceptable grades of the commodity that can be delivered. Also, the exchange will have a list of authorised warehouses or agents where the seller can deposit/deliver the commodity. In some cases, such as with the LME, the exchange will have a network of **authorised warehouses** that can issue warrants (as warehouse receipts), which are recorded and held within their LMEsword delivery system (LMEsword was launched in 1999 as SWORD, and it is a secure transfer system for LME warrants which can be held in a central depository; it acts as a central database, holding details of ownership, and is subject to stringent security controls). This assures the buyer that the metal he has purchased is of the correct deliverable quantity and grade and that he will have ownership upon payment.

4.1 Mutual Offset

CME Group and the Singapore Exchange (SGX) allow common settlement or offset for five of the contracts that are traded on both exchanges. These contracts are the Euroyen TIBOR, Eurodollars, the yen and the US-dollar-denominated Nikkei 225 and E-micro CNX Nifty (Nifty 50) futures.

4.2   Calculating the Profit/Loss

Learning Objective

3.4.3   Calculate the profit/loss on delivery/expiry of futures and options

The syllabus requires that candidates are able to calculate the profit (or loss) on the delivery of equity index futures and options. This is best achieved by studying the following examples and then attempting the exercises.

Example 1 – The FTSE 100 Index Future

An investor sells five FTSE 100 futures at 6720 and holds them to delivery. The EDSP, which is the official price at the expiry of the contract, is 5957.

The contract size for the ICE Futures, London FTSE 100 future is the index x £10 per point, the tick size is 0.50 index points and tick value is £5 per tick.

The profit/loss is calculated by taking the number of ticks moved x tick value x number of contracts.

The investor's position has moved into profit by 763 index points (she has agreed to sell at 6720 something that costs 5957).

Since each index point represents two ticks, that is a movement of 763 x 2 = 1526 ticks.

The investor's total profit = 1526 x £5 x 5 contracts = £38,150.

While £38,150 is the investor's total profit of this position, the final payment will be based on the difference between the previous day's closing price and the contract's official price at expiry, 5957. This is due to the exchange's daily margin payments.

Example 2 – SHFE Natural Rubber Future

A manufacturer buys ten SHFE July Natural Rubber futures at CNY (yuan) 19,650. One month ahead of its maturity, the position is closed out at CNY 20,250.

The contract specification is as follows: contract size is five tons, quotation is in yuan per ton and the tick size is five yuan.

The profit/loss is calculated by obtaining the difference between the opening and close-out prices and then multiplying this by the contract's size and then by the number of contracts.

The manufacturer's position moved in his favour by CNY 600 (the futures were bought at CNY 19,650 and sold at CNY 20,250.

On each contract a profit of CNY 3,000 (CNY 600 x 5 tons, the contract size) has been made.

The total profit for the position = CNY 30,000 (CNY 3,000 per contract x 10 contracts).

Exercise 1

An investor buys six FTSE 100 contracts on ICE at 6550. At expiry the exchange delivery settlement price (EDSP) is 6425. What is the investor's gain or loss?

The answer can be found in the Appendix at the end of this chapter.

Example 3 – FTSE 100 Index Option

An investor buys three FTSE call options with a strike of 6500 for a premium of 12. At expiry, the cash index stands at 6510.

The investor's options are worth exercising because the value of the underlying (the cash index) exceeds the strike price at expiry. The gain on exercise will be ten index points (6510 – 6500), but the investor has incurred a premium cost of 12 index points. So, the overall position is a loss of two index points per contract.

The investor's overall loss is 2 index points x £10 x 3 contracts = £60.

Exercise 2

An investor buys seven FTSE put options with a strike of 6500 for a premium of 15. At expiry, the cash index stands at 6475. What is the gain or loss to the investor?

The answer can be found in the Appendix at the end of this chapter.

Exercise 3

A fund manager sells 20 LMEX (London Metal Exchange Index) put options with a strike of 4180 and receives a premium of 18. At expiry the index stands at 4,170. What is the fund manager's profit or loss?

The answer can be found in the Appendix at the end of this chapter.

5. Futures Pricing

Learning Objective

3.5.1 Understand the mechanisms for futures pricing and the relationship with the underlying cash prices, together with the significance of contributing factors: contango and backwardation; price convergence at maturity; the concept of fair value according to IAS

5.1 Futures Pricing Relationships

We already know that a future is a derivative. It is derived from the underlying asset, and the price of the future will be derived from the price of the underlying asset in the cash market, plus the net cost of holding the position over the term of the contract, such as any financing associated with owning the underlying asset as well as any storage costs.

However, it is normal to find that the cash price is different from the price for various deliveries in the future. Why? Well, it is tempting to think that the futures price is the market's perception of what the price of the underlying asset will be at the time of delivery, but this is not the case.

The price of the future is NOT the market's perception of what the price of the asset will be at the time of delivery.

Although prices in both markets are set by the interaction of buyers and sellers, there is a mathematical relationship that binds them together. It is important to understand the nature of this relationship. The following comments will be based on this simple illustration:

Example 4

Cash price (January)	=	400
March futures price	=	417
June futures price	=	433

Why should anyone want to pay 417 in March for an asset that is only worth 400 today?

The price relationship between the cash asset and the same asset in the future is based on an arbitrage principle.

5.2 Cost of Carry

Learning Objective

3.5.2 Understand the purpose, features and implications of the cost of carry including: interest rates and asset yields; storage costs, insurance and interest costs

It is January and an investor who wants a particular asset in March has two choices:

- go long the March future and lock in the buying price for the asset at 417, or
- buy the asset today for 400 and store it until it is needed in March.

However, by buying the asset today, the investor is forgoing the interest which could be earned on the funds until March. Furthermore, there might be costs associated with storing the asset until it is needed (in the case of a commodity). The result is that anyone wanting delivery of the asset in March will be willing to pay the higher price because they are earning interest on their funds, in the meantime, and not incurring any storage costs.

Similarly, the person holding the asset will require a higher price for future delivery to compensate for the costs involved. These are referred to as **cost of carry**.

The main components of costs of carry are:

- finance costs (interest) over the period
- storage costs, and
- insurance.

As mentioned above, 'cost of carry' can be significant for all commodity futures. Therefore, this will cause a major difference between the current cash and futures price. As would be the case with the three-month LME lead futures contract, given the contract's size of 25 tonnes, the combination of storage and insurance costs for this amount of lead, in addition to any financing costs (which also apply to financial futures), is a major factor in determining that contract's fair value.

As will be seen in Section 5.3.1 below, there may also be **benefits of carry**, such as dividend yields when equity derivatives are considered.

5.3 Fair Value (Arbitrage-Free Value)

Learning Objective

3.5.3 Calculate the fair value of a future from relevant cash market prices, yields and interest rates

Knowing what the cash price of an asset is, and how much it will cost to carry the asset up to the moment of delivery, it is possible to calculate a futures price that will be fair to both the buyer and seller of the contract. This is known as the **fair value of the future**.

If the differential between the cash price and futures price were less than the cost of carry, the investor would be better off buying the future rather than buying the asset and holding it.

If the differential were greater than the cost of carry, an investor would be better off buying the asset and holding it.

It is only when the differential exactly reflects the cost of carry that the buyer is indifferent as to whether to buy in the cash market or the futures market.

Therefore:

Fair value of the future = cash price + cost of carry

5.3.1 Calculating the Fair Value

To calculate the fair value of a particular future, simply take the cash price, calculate the interest for the period and calculate the other costs involved. The total of the cash price plus the interest plus the other costs equals the fair value.

Example 5

The cash price of a commodity is £1,250, interest rates are 6% pa, storage costs are 1% pa.

The fair value of a future with 90 days to delivery would be:

Cash price	£1,250.00
Finance	£1,250 x 0.06 x (90/365) = £18.49
Storage	£1,250 x 0.01 x (90/365) = £3.08
Fair value	£1,271.57

Note, this is the method that should be used in the exam.

Exercise 4

If the cash price of a particular asset is £750, the prevailing rate of short-term interest is 3% pa and the estimated storage costs (including insurance) for the asset are 0.5% pa, what is the fair value of a futures contract with 45 days to expiry?

The answer can be found in the Appendix at the end of this chapter.

5.3.2 Calculating the Fair Value for Equity Index Futures

In calculating the fair value of an equity index future, only the net finance costs need to be considered, as the other costs are negligible.

Net finance costs = interest – present value of dividends

This is because, by holding the underlying, the investor forgoes the interest on the funds invested in the shares, but receives dividends from those shares.

The pricing of all stock futures takes this into account, such as the Cathay Pacific futures traded on the Hong Kong exchange, whose pricing will be based on the net difference between the net of the cost of financing to buy the shares less the share's current dividend.

Example 6

The S&P 500 index is currently 2080, one-year US interest rates are 0.55% and the index's dividend yield is 2.25% pa.

The fair value of a future with 182 days to delivery would be:

Cash index   = 2080
Interest rate   = 0.55%
Index dividend yield = 2.25%
Fair value = cash price x interest rate (1 + (0.0055 x (182/360))) – dividend points (see below)

Dividend yield conversion:

S&P 500 dividend yield   = 2.25%
Conversion to dividend points   = 2080 x (0.0225 x (182/360)) = 23.66 points
Fair value of the future   = 2085.78 – 23.66 = 2062.12

Exercise 5

The FTSE 100 cash index is 6500, interest rates are 0.5% pa and the dividend yield on the index is 2.5% pa. What is the fair value of a FTSE 100 future with 91 days to run?

The answer is in the appendix at the end of this chapter.

5.3.3   IAS Definition of Fair Value

The International Accounting Standards (IAS) Board defines the fair value of a future or any other derivative instrument as the amount or price at which the future/instrument can be exchanged/traded between two market participants at a given time, as an arm's length market transaction.

In other words, the IAS's definition of a future's fair value is its current market price. For market participants the IAS requires at least a daily mark-to-market valuation of all futures positions.

5.4 Contango and Backwardation

In markets where there is a **net cost of carry** in holding the asset to delivery, **futures prices are higher than cash prices**, ie, the market is said to be in **contango** – a contango market.

This is the **normal situation for equity markets** – interest rates are higher than dividend yields, therefore there is a net cost of carry.

In markets where there is a **net benefit** in holding the asset to delivery, **futures prices are lower than cash prices**, and the market is said to be in **backwardation** – a backwardation market.

Backwardation is most common in both the bond and short-term interest rate (STIR) markets when long-term interest rates are higher than short-term rates. Backwardation can also occur within commodities markets when there is a very steep premium for material available for immediate delivery, indicating a perception of a current shortage in the underlying commodity.

Example 7

The cash price of a bond is £110.50. Interest rates available on 30-day deposits are 0.25% pa and the bond yields 1.6% pa.

The fair value of a one-month future would be:

Cash price	=	£110.500
Finance costs £110.50 x (0.0025 – 0.016) x (1/12)	=	(0.124)
Fair value		£110.376

ie, the futures price is lower than the cash price.

Exercise 6

The approximate cash price of the notional long gilt is £104.30. Interest rates available on two-month deposits are 0.25% pa and the bond yields 1.5% pa. What is the fair value of the long gilt future with two months to expiry?

The answer is in the Appendix at the end of this chapter.

5.5 Convergence

The cost of carry determines the differential between cash and futures prices and is the cost associated with holding the asset from now until expiry. It follows that, as the point of expiry approaches, the costs of carry diminish and the differential must narrow. At expiry, the cost of carry is zero, so the cash and futures prices must converge over the life of the future until they meet at expiry.

5.6   Basis

Learning Objective

3.5.4   Analyse the effect of basis: behaviour at expiry; causes of basis strengthening or weakening; response to strengthening of basis; response to basis risk

Basis is a measure of the **difference between cash and futures prices.**

Basis = cash price – futures price

This is also sometimes referred to as **crude basis.**

The term 'basis' can also be used to describe the difference between two futures prices (eg, March futures price versus June futures price).

In contango markets, the futures price is greater than the cash price, so the basis will be a negative number. **Basis is negative in contango markets.**

In backwardation markets, the futures price is less than the cash price, so the basis will be a positive number. **Basis is positive in backwardation markets.**

Because of convergence, in both types of market the basis must narrow to zero as the contract moves towards expiry.

In a perfect market, the basis should reflect the cost of carry and the future would always trade at its fair value. However, as markets are not perfect, the actual difference between two prices will be influenced by short-term supply-and-demand pressures. It is unlikely that the future will be trading exactly at its fair value at any moment in time.

Basis can change as a result of:

* changes in supply and demand
* changes to the cost of carry, eg, interest rates, insurance costs, dividend yields
* changes in time remaining to expiry (convergence).

As we will see, movements in basis can adversely impact hedging strategies, and correctly anticipating the changes in basis can provide trading opportunities.

5.6.1 Changes in Basis – Terminology

Strengthening of Basis

When basis moves in a positive direction it is said to be 'strengthening'. This is the expected situation in a **contango** market – as the future moves towards expiry, and the cash and futures price converge, the basis becomes less negative. The strengthening basis narrows the gap in prices in a contango market, as price differentials become less significant. This is shown in the following illustration:

	March futures price	June futures price	Basis
Today	417	433	−16
Tomorrow	410	420	−10

In contrast, a strengthening of basis in a **backwardation** market results in a widening gap between the two prices. This is because basis is already a positive number and any movement in a positive direction will increase the difference between the two prices. This is shown in the following illustration:

	March futures price	June futures price	Basis
Today	110.15	110.02	+0.13
Tomorrow	111.00	110.75	+0.25

Weakening of Basis

When basis moves in a negative direction, it is said to be 'weakening'. A weakening of basis in a **contango** market widens the gap in prices, with the negative price differential increasing. This is shown in the following illustration:

	March futures price	June futures price	Basis
Today	417	433	−16
Tomorrow	410	429	−19

A weakening of basis in a **backwardation** market narrows the gap between prices because the positive basis moves in a negative direction to become less positive. This is shown in the following illustration:

	March futures price	June futures price	Basis
Today	110.15	110.02	+0.13
Tomorrow	111.00	110.92	+0.08

In summary, due to the **convergence** of futures and cash prices as a contract nears maturity, the following is expected:

- In **contango** markets (eg, equity index), the basis **strengthens** towards expiry.
- In **backwardation** markets (eg, STIR and bond futures), the basis **weakens** towards expiry.

5.6.2 Changes in Basis – The Trades

Whenever the basis is expected to **strengthen** (irrespective of whether the market is in contango or backwardation), a trader should **buy the spread**. This involves buying the near-dated instrument and simultaneously selling the far-dated instrument, eg, buy March future and sell June future. This is shown in the following example:

Example 8

Assume that a trader is anticipating a strengthening of basis between the March and June FTSE 100 futures. At present, March is trading at 6480 and June is trading at 6450 – a basis of plus 30. The trader buys the spread by buying 500 March FTSE 100 futures and simultaneously selling 500 June FTSE 100 futures. Two days later, the basis has strengthened with the March FTSE 100 still trading at 6480 and the June contract trading at 6445. The trader closes out his positions.

The outcome:

March FTSE 100 contracts	bought 500 at	6480
	sold 500 at	6480
	result = no gain/loss	
June FTSE 100 contracts	sold 500 at	6450
	bought 500 at	6445
	result = gain of 5 index points	

Overall gain 5 points x £10 per point x 500 contracts = £25,000.

Whenever the basis is expected to **weaken** (irrespective of whether the market is in contango or backwardation), a trader should **sell the spread**. This involves selling the near-dated instrument and simultaneously buying the far-dated instrument, eg, sell March future and buy June future. Selling the spread is illustrated in the following example:

Example 9

Currently the March futures price is 417 and the June futures price is 433.

A trader expects a weakening of basis over the next week. The trader sells the spread today. The following week the March future is still trading at 417, whilst the June future is trading at 439. The price difference has widened, so the trader's anticipated weakening of basis was correct.

The outcome is as follows:

March futures	sold at	417
a week later	purchased at	417
	no gain/loss	0
June futures	bought at	433
a week later	sold at	439
	gain	6

Overall gain = 6 = the amount of the change in basis.

5.6.3   Summary of Basis Changes and Trades

Market	Gap	Basis	Action
Contango	Narrowing	Strengthening	Buy the spread
Contango	Widening	Weakening	Sell the spread
Backwardation	Narrowing	Weakening	Sell the spread
Backwardation	Widening	Strengthening	Buy the spread

5.6.4   Basis Risk

Basis risk is defined as the risk that a futures price will move differently from that of its underlying asset.

As we have seen in the previous sections, there are a number of reasons why a futures price differs from that of its underlying asset. But there is a relationship between the two, which means that a futures price should broadly follow the price movements of its underlying asset. Additionally, the difference between the two should become less as the future approaches its expiration – convergence.

However, other factors can occasionally influence the futures price and have a lesser effect, if any, on the cash market, or vice versa. When this happens, the basis will change. However, this basis risk is significantly less than the risk associated with price changes of the underlying asset.

The only foolproof method of eliminating basis risk would be to hold a futures contract to its expiration. At expiry, the futures price and the cash price will converge.

5.7 Arbitrage Trades

Learning Objective

3.5.5 Apply appropriate strategies for cash/futures arbitrage trades: identifying opportunities and risks of arbitrage; arbitrage calculations; arbitrage channel and effect of transaction costs; cash and carry; reverse cash and carry; hedging basis risk

The term 'arbitrage' refers to a trader's attempt to profit by exploiting price differentials between identical, or similar, financial instruments that are trading on different markets, or in different forms. The examples considered above, of buying or selling the spread, could be described as arbitrage trades because they attempt to exploit pricing differentials between futures on the same underlying asset, with different maturities.

However, there is also the potential to arbitrage mispricings between the underlying (cash) instrument and the futures available on that instrument. Such arbitrage opportunities exist when the future is not trading at its fair value.

The following two subsections (5.7.1 and 5.7.2) consider firstly how to arbitrage when a future is above its fair value and, secondly, how to arbitrage when a future is trading below its fair value.

5.7.1 Cash and Carry Arbitrage

If the future is currently trading **above its fair value** it means that it is expensive relative to the price of the underlying asset.

The appropriate arbitrage trade is to buy the relatively cheap underlying asset and simultaneously sell a future. This is known as a **cash and carry** trade because the underlying cash asset is carried to satisfy the sale of the future. This is illustrated in the following example:

Example 10

Current cash price	Fair value for future	Current futures price
1450	1485	1497

The trader buys the underlying for 1450. She incurs a further 35 in cost of carry over the period, giving an effective buying price of 1485. However, by selling the future, the trader is guaranteed a selling price of 1497, thus locking in a profit of 12.

The trader can either hold the position to expiry and realise the profit of 12, or wait for an opportunity to close out before expiry if the basis changes earlier.

5.7.2 Reverse Cash and Carry Arbitrage

If the future is currently trading **below its fair value** it means that it is cheap relative to the price of the underlying asset.

The appropriate arbitrage trade to exploit this mispricing is to sell the relatively expensive underlying cash asset and to buy the relatively cheap future. This is known as a 'reverse cash and carry' trade. A reverse cash and carry trade is illustrated in the following example:

Example 11

Current cash price	Fair value for future	Current futures price
1450	1485	1477

The trader sells the underlying for 1450, releases funds which can be placed on interest and saves storage costs, etc, over the period. This gives an effective selling price of 1485. However, by buying the future, the trader is guaranteed a buying price of 1477, thus locking in a profit of 8.

The trader can either hold the position to expiry and realise the profit of 8, or wait for an opportunity to close out before expiry if the basis changes earlier.

5.7.3 The Arbitrage Channel

In the examples above, the fact that trading incurs expenses by way of commissions and fees, as well as bid and offer spreads, has not been considered. The effect of these **trading costs** is to make arbitrage unprofitable if they outweigh the arbitrage profits achievable.

Therefore, the futures price can move away from its fair value without there being any arbitrage activity, as long as the movement is less than the trading costs that would be incurred. This creates what is referred to as an **arbitrage channel** – the range of prices within which there will be no possibility to arbitrage owing to transaction costs outweighing any potential benefits.

If, however, the futures price moves beyond the limits of the channel, arbitrage becomes profitable. The arbitrage activity forces the futures price back into the channel and ensures that the futures price does not move too far away from fair value. This explains the strong correlation between cash and futures prices.

5.8 Hedging and Basis Risk

An unhedged position is at risk from changes in the price of the asset held.

Futures can be used to offset this risk, with the underlying cash position being mirrored by an opposite position in the futures market.

Although the cash and futures prices are strongly correlated, there is, as we have seen, some flexibility in that relationship. Basis changes will affect the performance of the hedge.

The future might not have been trading at its fair value at the time the hedge was undertaken. This will, in time, be rectified by market pressure or convergence, and will therefore lead to some profits/losses on the hedge.

Basis might have changed from the time the hedge was placed to the time it was offset, thus resulting in profits/losses on the hedge.

The hedge might over- or under-perform due to changes in basis. However, the risk of significant underperformance is small because arbitrage will keep the futures price close to its fair value.

6. Options Pricing

Learning Objective

3.6.1 Calculate the intrinsic and time value of an option and understand the factors determining option premiums and pricing including: influences on intrinsic value and time value; volatility; time to expiry; strike or exercise price; underlying asset price; interest rates; dividends/coupons

Unlike a futures contract, where both parties enter into an obligation to deliver the asset (for the seller) or agreed sum (for the buyer), an options contract allows one of the counterparties a choice – the holder has the right to exercise the option, but not the obligation. The writer is obliged to meet the delivery obligations if the option is exercised. Clearly, the writer requires compensation to take on the risk and the holder is willing to pay for the flexibility that the option allows. This payment takes the form of a premium.

6.1 The Premium

The premium is the price of the option – the price paid. The level of the premium is determined by buyers and sellers trading in the market and is the cost of the option. Option buyers must pay the agreed premium to the option sellers. It is non-returnable.

There are a number of factors that determine the level of the premium. Changes in these factors will result in a change in the option's premium. The two most obvious factors are the strike (or exercise) price and the time to run until the option expires. These are illustrated in the following example:

Example 12

ABC plc shares are currently trading at 550, and the following call options are available, conferring the right to buy at the various strike prices:

Strike price	Premium for March expiry	Premium for April expiry
500 call	70	85
525 call	49	61
550 call	37	46
575 call	25	39
600 call	19	28

The various strikes and expiries have different premiums reflecting the risks involved in holding/selling those options. The longer-dated expiries are more expensive than the near months, and the lower strike price options have higher premiums.

The premium is made up of two broad elements: intrinsic value and time value:

Premium (PM) = intrinsic value (IV) + time value (TV)

6.1.1 Intrinsic Value (IV)

The intrinsic value of an option is the **difference between the strike price and the underlying asset's price**. Call options have intrinsic value when the strike is lower than the underlying asset price. Put options possess intrinsic value if the strike is greater than the underlying's cash price. Intrinsic value can never be negative; it is either positive or zero.

Intrinsic value (IV) = Strike price – Underlying asset's current market price

There has to be some intrinsic value for an option to be worth exercising. An option with zero intrinsic value is not worth exercising at expiry. Intrinsic value can also be thought of as the 'minimum' value that an option can have. An option either has or does not have intrinsic value.

From the above example, for ABC the 500 calls have an intrinsic value of 50p – they must be worth at least 50p because they enable 550p shares to be purchased at 500p.

In the above example, both the 500 and 525 strikes have intrinsic value. If the price remained at 550p at expiry, holders of both those options would exercise them because they allow the holders to buy the asset at a cheaper price than the current market price. All options that have intrinsic value at expiry will be exercised. As the premium is not refundable, the amount paid for the option is not a factor in determining whether to exercise. The holder will realise any intrinsic value, which will then be used to offset the cost of the premium. If the intrinsic value is greater than the premium paid, the holder will make a net profit and the writer will make a net loss.

An option with intrinsic value is described as being **in-the-money (ITM)**. An option with no intrinsic value is described as being **out-of-the-money (OTM)**. An option with an exercise price that equals, or is close to, the underlying asset price is described as being **at-the-money (ATM)**. Sometimes options that are significantly in-the-money are described as **deep in-the-money** options. Similarly, options that are significantly out-of-the-money are described as **far out-of-the-money** options.

Exercise 7

Here is a summary of the terms for a CALL option:

Status of a call option	Definition
In-the-money	Market price > exercise price
At-the-money	Market price = exercise price
Out-of-the-money	Market price < exercise price
Break-even point	Market price = exercise price + premium

Try to complete the same table for a PUT option:

Status of a put option	Definition
In-the-money	
At-the-money	
Out-of-the-money	
Break-even point	

The answers can be found in the Appendix at the end of this chapter.

6.1.2　Time Value (TV)

In the ABC plc example, the 550, 575 and 600 strikes have no intrinsic value, yet a premium still has to be paid. The 500 and 525 strikes have intrinsic value, but the premium exceeds the intrinsic value.

The time value is simply the excess above the option's intrinsic value, ie, the difference between the premium and intrinsic value:

$$TV = PM - IV$$

Why should an option buyer pay more than its intrinsic value? The answer is simply that the price of the underlying asset can move during the lifetime of the option. There is always a possibility that the price can move beyond any given levels by the time of expiry, resulting in potential profits, or losses, for traders. The time value reflects the possibility, or probability, that the price can move beyond any given strike, thus making it worth exercising, and is the price paid for that uncertainty.

The example on the following page illustrates the intrinsic and time values of ABC plc options.

Example 13

ABC plc current share price is 550p. The premium for March options, and their intrinsic and time values, are as follows:

Strike	Call PM	Call IV	Call TV	Put PM	Put IV	Put TV
500	70	50	20	18	0	18
525	49	25	24	23	0	23
550	37	0	37	35	0	35
575	25	0	25	47	25	22
600	19	0	19	67	50	17

The call IV is the share price minus the strike, and the balance is the time value (TV).

The put IV is the strike minus the share price, and the balance is the TV.

Exercise 8

If a call option has a strike price of 234p, the current price of the underlying share is 256p and the option premium is 40p, calculate the intrinsic value and, thus, the time value of the option.

The answer can be found in the Appendix at the end of this chapter.

6.1.3   Main Determinants of an Option's Premium

The two elements that make up the option premium are intrinsic and time values. The intrinsic value can be determined quite simply: the difference between the underlying price and the strike price for in-the-money (ITM) options, or zero for out-of-the-money (OTM) options. **The price of the underlying asset is a major influence because it determines the amount of intrinsic value**.

The time value can be calculated as that part of the option's premium that is not intrinsic value. So, the time value reflects the uncertainty (probability) of an option being exercised. But who or what determines how much time value there should be at any moment?

There are three major factors that determine the amount of time value – all of them are to do with uncertainty. The greater the uncertainty, the greater the time value.

Time to Expiry

A longer-dated option will have more time value than a near-dated one with the same strike. The price of the underlying can move over a greater range in one year than in one week. This means that there is more uncertainty associated with an option with one year to expiry, so the time value will be greater. Looked at another way, **the holder has more time for the option to work in his favour** (and would be prepared to pay more), whilst **the writer is at risk for a longer time** and would need to be paid more for that risk.

If an option with one year to expiry must have more time value than one with one week to expiry, it stands to reason that the time value in an option gradually 'leaks away' as expiry approaches (traders usually talk about the **erosion of time value**, or '**time decay**'). As expiry approaches, there is generally less uncertainty about whether a particular option will be worth exercising. On expiry, there is no uncertainty left. At that stage, either the option will be exercised, or it will not. If the option is OTM at expiry, IV=0 and TV=0, then it will not be exercised. If it is ITM, the holder will exercise to realise the intrinsic value, and there is no possibility of making any more, so TV=0.

The rate at which the time value erodes over the life of the option is not linear (see graph below). **The erosion speeds up as expiry approaches.**

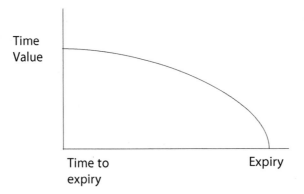

Erosion of time value works against the holder. If an investor buys an option today, and other factors (such as the underlying price and volatility) remain constant, it will be worth less next week. If the investor closed next week, he would crystallise a loss. **Erosion must, therefore, work in favour of the writer.** Providing that other factors remain constant, an option writer could sell an option today and close out next week at a lower price, crystallising a profit.

The Distance Between the Strike and the Underlying Asset

Remember that the time value reflects the uncertainty about whether an option is likely to be exercised on expiry.

In-the-money options (especially deep in-the-money options) have a high probability of exercise. There is less uncertainty about the outcome, so there is less time value.

Out-of-the-money options (especially far out-of-the-money options) have a high probability of being abandoned. There is less uncertainty about the outcome, so there is less time value.

At-the-money options must, therefore, **have the highest amount of time value** because that is the strike where most of the **uncertainty exists**.

Volatility

The more volatile the price of an asset, the greater the uncertainty, so the higher the time value and, hence, the premium. **If the price of an asset is prone to large movements, holders have a higher chance of making a profit and writers are at greater risk.**

Volatility, therefore, has a major impact on the option premium because of its effect on the time value and the price of an option.

However, there are three types of volatility to be considered:

1. **Historic volatility** – this represents how volatile the asset has been in the past, and can be measured accurately because we know what the price movements have been. It is only of limited value in pricing an option because there is no guarantee that the same volatility will prevail in the future.
2. **Future volatility** – in pricing an option, or deciding whether an option is worth buying or selling, it would be incredibly useful to know what the volatility of the asset was going to be. Unfortunately, nobody can predict future volatility perfectly.
3. **Implied volatility** – as it is impossible to predict future volatility, traders must effectively take a view on it. This is implicit when options are traded. If volatility is a component of an options premium, by buying and selling options the market forms a collective view about what is likely to happen in the future.

The actual figure for implied volatility is derived from options pricing models. Perhaps the best known of these is the **Black-Scholes model**, named after its authors Fischer Black and Myron Scholes, two American economists who created the algorithm in 1973. Inputs such as volatility, strike price, underlying price, time to expiry and cost of carry are needed by pricing models in order to compute the premium. If the current option premium is known, the volatility figure can be adjusted (the others being fixed at any moment in time) until the premium calculated by the model is the same as the current price in the market. In other words, by working backwards through the model, it is possible to calculate the volatility implied by the premium.

Different option pricing models are better suited to differing requirements. For example, the Black-Scholes model can only be used to price European exercise options. Another, known as the **binomial pricing model**, is more appropriate for pricing American-style options. Adjustments to models will also need to be made to take into account the differences between options on futures and options based upon actual underlying assets, and to take into account dividends when addressing equity-based assets.

6.1.4   Other Factors Determining the Option Premium

For some types of options, the prices of calls and puts are affected by interest rates and dividend yields.

An example of an option on a physical would be an option on an individual company's shares. If the interest rate rises, the buyer of a call, who effectively keeps his money in the bank, earns more interest. The call writer, who has his money in the shares, is disadvantaged. It is only fair that writers should charge more if rates rise.

From this it is a simple step to see the impact of dividends. If dividends rise relative to interest rates then call writers can afford to charge slightly lower premiums.

For the writers of puts, who hold cash as cover, higher interest rates mean they can charge slightly lower premiums.

6.1.5 Summary: The Impact on Option Prices as Determinants Change

Now that we have seen the factors that affect the option premium, we can summarise the impact of a change in those factors on call and put premiums. The following table is a summary of how call and put prices change as the factors that affect the premium option vary:

Factor	Call premiums	Put premiums
Price of underlying rises	Rise	Fall
Time to expiry rises	Rise	Rise
Volatility rises	Rise	Rise
Exercise prices rises	Fall	Rise
Interest price rises:		
Options on physicals	Rise	Fall
Options on futures [Note]	Generally unchanged	Generally unchanged

Obviously, the opposite reaction applies to decreases!

Note: If interest rates rise, the cost of carry rises, impacting the futures price as well as the incentive to hold cash.

6.2 The Put/Call Parity Theorem

Learning Objective

3.6.2 Calculate a theoretical option using put/call parity to identify arbitrage opportunities; application of the put/call parity theorem; adjustment for cost of carry; limitations in accuracy; identification of arbitrage opportunities; reversal and conversion arbitrage trading strategies

Whilst there is no absolute fair value for an option's premium, there is a connection between the call and put premiums for the same strike on the same underlying asset. Call and put premiums must be fair in relation to one another (for any given price of the underlying), otherwise arbitrage opportunities present themselves. The put/call parity theorem(s) define(s) the relationship between call and put prices and the price of the underlying asset.

The following put/call parity formula applies to all options at expiry and to options on futures at all times:

$$C - P = S - K$$

where:

C	=	**C**all premium
P	=	**P**ut premium
S	=	Underlying price (**S**pot or ca**S**h price/futures price if the option is on a future)
K	=	Stri**K**e price

Example 14

If the futures price is 100.95, the strike price is 100 and the call option on the future's premium is 1.07, the price of the put option on the future can be calculated:

$C - P = S - K$
$1.07 - P = 100.95 - 100$
$1.07 - P = 0.95$
$P = 1.07 - 0.95$
$P = 0.12$

As long as three of the variables are known, the value of the missing variable can be calculated by simply rearranging the formula.

Exercise 9

If the futures price is 101.5, and the premium for a call with a strike of 110 is 12, what is the premium for a put with the same strike?

The answer can be found in the Appendix at the end of this chapter.

For options on futures the underlying asset is the future itself (the right to buy/sell a future on the asset). Costs of carry do not need to be taken into account because the futures price already includes them. However, the formula for put/call parity needs to be adjusted to take account of the costs of carry for options on the underlying asset, when it is not a future or a forward, and therefore has a possible income flow (such as a share dividend or bond coupon payment) that is paid before the option expires.

The formula becomes:

$$C - P = S - \frac{K}{(1+r)^{\wedge}t}$$

where:

C, P, S and K are the same as above.
r = annual risk-free interest rate.
t = time to expiry (in years).

This is the formula used for individual equity options and equity index options.

Example 15 _____

ABC plc share price = 600. The put premium for the 500 strike is 7. The option expires in three months and risk-free interest rates are currently 6% pa.

The call premium for the 500 strike should be:

$$C - P = S - \frac{K}{(1+r)^{\wedge}t} \quad \text{where } r = 0.06 \text{ and } t = 0.25 \text{ years}$$

$$C - 7 = 600 - \frac{500}{(1 + 0.06)^{\wedge}0.25}$$

$$C - 7 = 600 - \frac{500}{1.014674}$$

$$C - 7 = 600 - 492.77$$

$$C - 7 = 107.23$$

$$C = 107.23 + 7$$

$$C = 114.23$$

Note that at expiry t = 0, so the formula becomes C – P = S – K.

_____

Exercise 10 _____

If shares in XYZ plc are currently trading at 410p, and the premium for the 400p call option that expires in two months is 25p, what is the premium for the 400p put that expires at the same time? Interest rates are currently 3% pa.

The answer can be found in the Appendix at the end of this chapter.

_____

The above formulae are more accurate for European-style options than for American-style options. This is because American-style options have the added complication that they can be exercised early.

If the call and put premiums are not consistent with put/call parity, they are mispriced and arbitrage is possible. The key arbitrage trades are (assuming that the options are options on futures):

- **If the call is relatively cheap, then buy the call, sell the put and sell the future**. The combination of buying the call and selling the put creates a synthetic long futures position. This is closed out by selling the future to lock-in an arbitrage profit. This trade is termed a **reversal**.
- **If the put is relatively cheap, then buy the put, sell the call and buy the future**. The combination of buying the put and selling the call creates a synthetic short futures position. This is closed out by buying the future to lock-in an arbitrage profit. This trade is termed a **conversion**.

6.3 Delta (Δ)

Learning Objective

3.6.3   Understand how delta is used in hedging a cumulative position

3.6.4   Calculate the sensitivity of the option premium to changes in price by applying delta values to cumulative positions

---

One of the factors which can change the premium during the lifetime of an option is movement in the price of the underlying. However, **the premium does not always move by the same amount as the underlying asset.**

The delta of an option is a measure of the sensitivity of the option's price to changes in the price of the underlying asset. Simplistically, it can be calculated by measuring the change in an option premium brought about by a small change in the price of the underlying. This would be done using option pricing models such as Black-Scholes.

Simplistically, delta (Δ) $= \dfrac{\text{change in option premium}}{\text{change in price of underlying}}$

The delta will lie somewhere between 0 and 1. For example, if the change in price of the underlying was 20p, and perhaps the option increased by 12p, this would give a delta of 12/20 = 0.6.

A delta of 0 means that the premium is totally insensitive to small changes in the price of the asset. This will be the case for options that are far out-of-the-money.

A delta of 1 means that the premium will change by exactly the same monetary amount as the underlying. This will be the case for options that are deep in-the-money.

The sign of the delta enables us to distinguish between calls and puts.

*   **Call deltas are positive** – because the premium will rise when the price of the underlying rises.
*   **Put deltas are negative** – because the premium will fall when the price of the underlying rises.

Example 16

ABC plc share price = 575.
The 625 call has a delta of 0.30 and a premium of 26.
The 525 put has a delta of –0.30 and a premium of 24.

If the share price rises to 585, using delta we can approximate the new call and put premiums:

The share price has risen by 10.

The delta of the call is 0.30, so the change in premium will be 10 x 0.3 = 3 (ie, the call premium will rise from 26 to 29).

The delta of the put is –0.30, so the change in premium will be 10 x (–0.30) = –3 (ie, the put premium will fall from 24 to 21).

As seen, the delta for a deep in-the-money call option would be +1, and for a deep in-the-money put would be –1.

The delta for a far out-of-the-money call or put would be zero. Generally, an at-the-money option will have a delta of approximately 0.5, +0.5 for a call and –0.5 for a put.

Furthermore, the underlying physical asset and long futures will always have a delta of +1 and short futures will have a delta of –1.

As an option approaches its expiration, its delta will approach zero. The longer to expiration, the slower the decline, but, as an option's expiry date gets closer, the change in delta will increase.

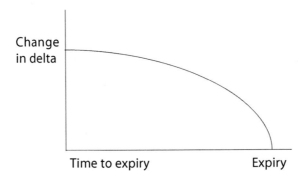

Summary of Deltas

Instrument	Delta
Physical asset or future of a deep ITM call	+1
ATM call	+0.5
Far OTM call or a far OTM put	0
ATM put	–0.5
Deep ITM put	–1

6.3.1 Delta Value of Cumulative Positions

Deltas can also be used to measure the sensitivity of a portfolio containing futures/underlying, calls and puts. The delta calculated for a portfolio of positions is known as the **cumulative delta**.

In order to measure the cumulative delta of a combined portfolio, the deltas of the individual positions within it need to be added together. The cumulative delta then gives the overall sensitivity and directional bias of a portfolio. The directional bias is obtained by taking account of long and short positions (+ for long and – for short). This is best illustrated by looking at an example.

Example 17

Investor A is short an ATM put.

The net delta position is $(-1) \times (-0.5) = +0.5$

This is arrived at by taking the number of positions (1) and assigning a negative to it because it is a short position. This –1 is then multiplied by the delta of an at-the-money put of –0.5.

The result is that, if the price of the underlying rises by 10, Investor A's position improves by 5. The price of the put would have decreased, thus showing a profit on the trade. Obviously, a decrease in the underlying price would show a loss.

Example 18

Investor B is long five ITM calls with a delta of 0.7.

Investor B's net delta is $(+5) \times (+0.7) = +3.5$

If the price of the underlying rises by 1, Investor B's position improves by 3.5. The price of each of the calls would have gone up by 0.7 and he has five of them.

Example 19

Investor C has the following portfolio on the same underlying:

Position	Delta	Comments
Long 10 futures	1.00	
Short 3 calls	+0.30	OTM call
Long 4 puts	–0.65	ATM call
Short 5 puts	–0.15	OTM put
Long 8 calls	0	Far OTM call

The cumulative delta is:

(+ 10)	x	(+1.00)	=	+10.00
(–3)	x	(+0.30)	=	–0.90
(+ 4)	x	(–0.65)	=	–2.60
(–5)	x	(–0.15)	=	+0.75
(+8)	x	(0)	=	0.00
				+7.25

A very bullish position – currently equivalent to being long over seven futures.

Cumulative deltas can be useful to gauge what is required to hedge a portfolio. A portfolio that has a cumulative delta of 0 is insensitive to price movements in the underlying asset – it is a hedged position, often referred to as **delta neutral** or **delta hedged**.

Taking example 19 above, the cumulative delta was +7.25. In order to delta hedge, positions with a cumulative delta of –7.25 need to be added, eg, sell seven futures and buy a put with a delta of 0.25.

It is also useful to note that such delta hedging only hedges against price risk; other risks associated with time decay, volatility and basis still remain. Delta is also a dynamic measure so, as time passes, or the price of the underlying asset changes, the delta will change.

Exercise 11

You have the following position in the same underlying asset:

Short four futures
Short three at-the-money calls
Long six deep-in-the-money puts

What is your cumulative delta?

The answer is in the Appendix at the end of this chapter.

6.4 Other Greek Measures

Learning Objective

3.6.5 Analyse derivatives positions and hedging strategies by using the following greeks: delta; gamma; theta; vega; rho

In addition to delta, which was explained in the previous paragraph, there are several other **greeks** measuring the relationship between an option's price and changes in the price of the underlying asset, as well as over time.

6.4.1 Gamma

Gamma is the measure of how delta changes (the rate of change of delta) with respect to movements in the price of the underlying. It is small when the option is either deep in-the-money, or far out-of-the-money. It is at its greatest when the option is at-the-money, especially when the option is close to expiry. Traders will monitor the impact of gamma on the premiums of options. Short-dated ATM options are more volatile than longer-dated ones, and these differences may present an opportunity for trading profits. Asset managers also use gamma in their dynamic hedging strategies. As indicated, a portfolio can be delta neutral. The delta would have to be monitored and perhaps re-balanced because of the impact of gamma on the portfolio delta.

Since gamma is the measure of changes in delta, it represents the required **adjustments** to any hedges associated with a single option's position or a portfolio of options. It represents the size of these adjustments.

For option holders, the changes in gamma usually correspond to profitable trades, ie, the required adjustments to the delta hedge of the underlying asset will result in a profit. For example, if an investor has a long position on a call option on an individual share, as the share's price rises the option's delta will increase, as measured by gamma, and the investor will sell the **adjustment** or **change to delta** at a higher price. Therefore, when one has a long position on an option or a net long position in an option portfolio, one is said to have a positive gamma indicator or simply **positive gamma**. The opposite is true when one is an option writer or holds a net short option portfolio.

6.4.2 Vega

Vega is a measure of how a 1% change in implied volatility affects an option's price. Vega is always positive for long options positions – both calls and puts. It is greatest for at-the-money options. The further an option goes in- or out-of-the-money, the smaller vega will become. Time increases the effect of changes in volatility upon an option's value. Therefore, vega is higher for long-dated options than short-dated options, and falls as an option approaches its expiration date. Vega can change even if there is no dramatic change in the movements of the underlying asset's price; it is affected by any change in expected volatility.

Vega is useful since it measures an option's or option portfolio's sensitivity to both market sentiment (expected volatility) and current market conditions. Many traders/investors use vega as the key measure of profitability of their option positions, since if they are delta neutral they are trading on an asset's volatility and not on a specific direction, therefore vega tells them how well their positions are performing relative to current market conditions.

6.4.3 Theta

Theta is the measure of the rate of decline of an option's value due to the passage of time. Theta represents how much an option's value will change as one day passes and its underlying asset's price remains steady. Theta can also represent the **time decay** on the value of an option. If all other factors are held constant, then an option will lose value as time moves closer to its maturity.

The measure of theta quantifies the risk that time imposes on options, since they have an expiration date and in most cases are only exercisable for a certain period of time. Time has importance for option traders on a conceptual level more than a practical one.

Theta and Option Positions

- **Long calls and long puts always have negative theta**.
- **Short calls and short puts always have positive theta**.

Theta is highest for at-the-money options and gradually decreases as an option moves further in-the-money or out-of-the-money.

Theta (time decay) would increase sharply as an option approaches its expiration and can severely undermine a long option holder's position, particularly if volatility is also decreasing at the same time. This is because **theta is higher when either volatility is lower or there are fewer days to expiration**.

Theta is used as a factor in combination with gamma and vega in determining trading strategies, since it represents the change in an option's fair value per day. As a percentage of an option's value, theta increases as expiration gets closer. Therefore, if vega is falling a trader is more likely to sell an option that is a few days from expiration rather than one that is six months away.

6.4.4   Rho

Rho is the measure of changes in an option's value due to a change in interest rates. Rho measures how much an option's value will change from a 1% change in market interest rates.

Rho is the least used of the Greek measures, since the relationship between an option's price and interest rates is fairly stable. Also, the chances that an option's value will change dramatically, due to a rise or fall in interest rates, are very low.

The impact of interest rates on an option's price is based on the **cost of carry** associated with holding the underlying asset relative to the option. The interest cost of buying the underlying asset is priced into the option's premium. While other Greek measures, such as delta, are 0.5 for an ATM option, rho is normally in the range of 0.04–0.02 for the same option.

An increase in interest rates will increase the value of calls and decrease the value of puts, while a drop in interest rates will have the opposite effect. The longer the time to expiration, the higher an option's rho. At-the-money and in-the-money options have relatively higher rho.

6.5   Premium Payment

For the majority of options contracts, the buyer of the option is requested to pay the premium immediately. The seller of the option will receive the premium into his broker's account on the morning of the next business day.

At the point of trading, the seller's broker becomes liable for any margin required by the clearing house. This is collected when the market value of the underlying instrument moves against the seller (known as marking-to-market). Both the broker and the clearing house make the margin collection, with respect to the selling client and broker respectively. For example, if the mark-to-market shows the option to be further in-the-money, the seller will need to deliver margin to his broker and onto the clearing house to represent the worsening of his position.

However, the margining of options positions is made more complex because some option premiums are payable **futures style**. Such premiums are not payable immediately, but are paid during the life of the contract through margining. Certain financial options on ICE, such as bond and interest rate options, are futures style.

The following table summarises the margin requirements for options positions:

Position	Initial margin	Variation margin
Equity Index and Single Stock Options		
Long positions	No	No
Short positions	Yes	No
Bond and STIR Options		
Long positions	No	Yes
Short positions	Yes	Yes

7. Order/Instruction Flow and Order Type

In an **open outcry market**, the exchange floor is split into designated sections, traditionally known as **'pits'**, where individual futures or options products are traded. Orders are initially received by a floor booth belonging to the broker and are transmitted to the trader in the pit. Traders stand in their pits and trading takes place face-to-face. To maintain price transparency, orders are shouted out (backed up by hand signals) so that all participants have an equal opportunity to trade.

In a **screen-based market**, orders are placed directly onto an electronic order book via traders' computer terminals. This obviously eliminates the need to have a trading floor. Orders will take their place in the relevant buy/sell queue (determined by price and time of placement) where they will await a matching transaction, or they will match against orders that are currently in the system. Depending on whether they are market or conditional orders, they may be executed immediately or remain stored in the queue.

The order will move up or down the queue as a result of trading and the placing of other orders.

European exchanges are now generally screen-based, whereas trading floors still exist in the US; however, all the major American exchanges have adopted electronic trading in parallel with open outcry.

7.1 Trade Execution and the Nature of Orders

Learning Objective

3.7.1 Understand how exchange-traded orders are processed: acting as principal, agent or in dual capacity; how clients, brokers and exchange members are linked; principles of order flow on electronic and open outcry markets; opening, closing and cross trades; liquidity measures: volume and open interest; audit trail

7.1.1 Principles of Order Flow

In a traditional **open outcry** system, customer orders specify:

*   the asset
*   whether it is a buy or sell order
*   the size of order (number of contracts or lots)
*   the expiry month, and
*   price conditions (if any).

The order is passed by telephone, fax or by electronic means to the edge of the trading floor, where a booth clerk passes or signals it to the trader in the pit. Many pit traders execute orders for clients as well as for their own institution.

The details of any trade executed are then passed back by the trader to the clerk, who confirms back to his office and enters details of the trade onto a matching system; this allows trades to be matched with the floor counterparty so that any discrepancies can be resolved before the trades are registered at the clearing house.

In **screen-traded** systems (ICE's Universal Trading Platform), order flow is more straightforward. Orders are input and then executed and reported by the system. There is no need to match trade details afterwards with a counterparty, as the trades are already 'matched' when the order book links together a buyer and a seller.

7.1.2 Principal and Agency Functions

Exchange members can execute a trade in one of two capacities, either as principal or as agent.

Acting as **principal** means that the member is carrying out the trade **on his own behalf** and will be subject to profits and losses on those trades. In other words, when dealing as a principal, the member firm is dealing for their **own account** and therefore they will benefit from, and incur, any profits or losses from that position themselves.

Acting as **agent** means that the firm is carrying out the trade **on behalf of clients**, ie, acting as broker. So an **agency order** is one arranged by a brokerage on behalf of its client. This may give the client the advantage of anonymity in the arranged transaction. The trade will be registered in a client account (see notes on trade registration in Section 8) and the client will be responsible to the member for profits/ losses resulting from it.

The ability of the member to act as **either principal or agent** in any transaction is known as '**dual capacity**'. In other words, a member is allowed to trade for both its own account as well as execute its clients' orders. It is argued that clients benefit from this, since it allows the member firm to obtain better prices when executing market orders for clients, in addition to the extra insight that members can pass along as advice to clients. But some would argue that it also increases the possibility of a conflict of interest, when both client and member are looking to trade the same instrument at the same time.

Cross trading is when a brokerage firm matches a buy order of one customer against the sell order of another, when one is non-competitive (that is, the customer has not specified a specific price). On US exchanges, this practice is permissible only when executed in accordance with the Commodity Exchange Act, Commodity Futures Trading Commission (CFTC) regulations, and the rules of the exchange.

7.1.3   Opening Trades

Opening trades create a position in the market and so incur rights or obligations. They will be subject to profits/losses arising from subsequent price movements. They can be opening purchases or sales.

7.1.4   Closing Trades

Closing trades are trades that offset an existing long/short position (established through an opening purchase/sale) in the market. They extinguish any existing rights or obligations. A closing transaction is the point at which profits/losses on the contract are crystallised.

They can be closing sales or purchases.

7.1.5   Volume and Open Interest

Both of these are measures of a derivatives contract's liquidity.

Volume is usually reported for each product and its expiry month; it shows the cumulative number of contracts traded so far each day.

Open interest shows the **total number of contracts** for any delivery month that **remain open**. Open positions are contracts that will either be closed out before expiry or taken to delivery. As most contracts will be closed out before expiry, it is an **important indicator of the contract's liquidity**.

NB: Open interest is the sum of all open long positions OR the sum of all open short positions, NOT the sum of both.

7.1.6   Cross Trades

As noted above, a member of an exchange is said to have dual capacity if he is able to trade as a principal and arrange trades as an agent. This dual capacity will enable the member to enter into **cross trades**, sometimes referred to as **matching orders**. A cross trade is a situation where the member:

- has a buyer and a seller for the contract at a given price, or
- is willing to deal with a client as principal.

The member can effectively conduct the transaction without taking the trade into the market. However, for the purposes of price transparency and to allow other traders the opportunity to trade at the given price, the order needs to be executed within the market.

There are strict rules that need to be adhered to prior to the exchange accepting a cross order; for example, in an open outcry market cross trades must be verified and signed off by exchange officials (pit observers) when the order is executed. An exchange's rules will state whether cross trades are permitted and what reporting conditions apply.

7.1.7 Audit Trail

An audit trail is a record of a transaction. To assist in the resolution of disputes and to promote confidence in an exchange, it is important to be able to trace a trade from start to finish and vice versa.

7.2 Order Types

Learning Objective

3.7.2 Understand the typical range of orders placed in derivatives markets and the reasons for using them: market order; limit order; spread order; scale order; market if touched order; opening and closing orders; good 'til cancelled; immediate or cancel/fill or kill order; stop, stop limit and guaranteed stop orders; day orders

While particular exchange systems have specific names for the types of orders they accept, the following types of order are typical of those placed in derivatives markets. They can be used on their own or combined with others as appropriate.

- **Market Order** – this is an order to buy/sell immediately. It does not stipulate a price and will be executed at the best price currently available in the market. A buy order will **hit** the ask price, a sell order will **hit** the bid. A market order is guaranteed to be filled.
- **Limit Order** – such an order stipulates a required price level. If the trade can be executed at a better price than stated, the client will be **filled** at the improved price. The broker is not allowed to take the difference. Execution is not guaranteed, as the market might not reach the required price.
- **Spread Order** – the simultaneous purchase and sale of futures or options is executed for a specified price difference.
- **Scale Order** – a 'stepped' order when a gradual entry/exit from a position is needed.
- **Market If Touched (MIT)** – a combination of a limit order and a market order. Initially, the trade specifies a limit. If the market trades at or through the price, the order becomes a market order and will be executed at the best prevailing price.
- **Opening Order** – an order, with or without a stipulated price, which is to be executed during the official opening period of the market, usually the first two minutes of trading. If the order cannot be filled during that period, it is cancelled.
- **Closing Order** – as above, but executed towards the end of the day.
- **Day Order** – an order that automatically expires if it is not executed on the day that it is placed.

- **Limit or Market on Close (MOC)** – will be executed at the stipulated price during the day, or else it will be executed at the best available price towards the end of the day, usually within the last five or ten minutes of trading. It is guaranteed to be filled.
- **Stop (Loss) Order** – this is designed to limit trading losses. A stop is primarily used to close out a position if the price moves against the trader. The stop is triggered when the market trades at the stipulated price. However, there is no guarantee that the order will be filled at the stop price. In volatile markets it might not be possible to obtain that price, so it can be filled at any price once it is triggered.
- **Stop Limit Order** – as above, but this order stipulates two prices within which the stop order operates. Once the stop price is reached, a stop-limit order becomes a limit order that will be executed at a specified price (or better).
- **Guaranteed Stop** – a facility offered by some brokers that guarantees the stop price to a client (perhaps the firm is willing to take the position at that price). The broker will probably charge more for this service.
- **Good 'til Cancelled (GTC)** – this really is an instruction accompanying an order and defines the period of validity for the order. A GTC order is firm until the client specifies otherwise. In the real world, most orders are **good for the day (GFD)** and will be cancelled if the order remains unfilled at the close of trading.
- **Fill or Kill (FOK)** – this means execute the whole quantity of the order if market conditions permit, otherwise cancel the whole order if the former cannot be achieved. They are often referred to as **immediate or cancel** orders.

When brokers enter client orders they will occasionally make mistakes. Some exchanges allow members to correct genuine mistakes by requiring the brokerage firm to submit a correction declaration. Depending on the exchange's policy and rules, the erroneous trade may possibly be reversed. The exchange will check to ensure that the client is not disadvantaged.

8. Trade Registration

Learning Objective

3.8.1 Understand the processes involved in trade registration, input, matching and allocation including: differing requirements of electronic and open outcry markets; assignment to house, segregated or non-segregated accounts; reasons for allocating a trade to an account; use of give-up agreements; risk implications

Once a deal has taken place, the position needs to be allocated to the relevant account. The trade may have been executed for the firm itself (and may, therefore, be allocated to the firm's principal account), or on behalf of a client (and may, therefore, be allocated to a client account). The details of the trade will be reported into the administration system that is used by the exchange, such as ICE Clear for ICE London or in the case of the Dubai Mercantile Exchange their DME Direct system. These systems will ensure that the trade inputs are matched; in other words, that both a purchase and a sale exist on the same terms. This process is particularly important when the exchange uses open outcry, where there is scope for more human error than an electronic order-matching system.

8.1 Client Accounts

As mentioned above, trades may be executed by the firm for itself or on behalf of a client. As a result of this, the trades will be assigned to one of three types of account:

1. **House** – for all proprietary trades of the clearing member.
2. **Segregated** – for trades that the member firm is registering on behalf of a 'segregated' client. In the event of the member firm's default, these positions will be protected against having to meet the defaulting firm's liability.
3. **Non-segregated** – client trades that are not segregated and therefore are not protected in the event of the firm's default.

Note that most exchanges and major market regulators require their member firms to ensure that all client assets are placed in **segregated** accounts. The client benefits from such accounts in that, should the member firm have financial problems, their funds will be protected and can only be used to meet their commitments. Member firms cannot use funds from segregated accounts to meet any of their own, or other, client margin or other financial commitments.

The decision as to whether to use a non-segregated account, when permitted by the exchange or market regulators, is the client's and not the member firm's.

8.2 Pre-Registration/Allocations/Give-Ups

Pre-registration involves a member firm indicating that a deal they are doing should be allocated or **given-up** to a second member. This is also described as an **allocation**.

Give-ups are the sending of a trade to another member of the exchange. The member to whom the trade is given-up is said to be performing a **give-in**. Both parties to an allocated transaction risk the other not fulfilling their obligations. A give-up trade is allocated to the give-in on ICE; this is done by ICE Clear.

Give-up trades are mainly performed in order to separate the execution and the clearing function. Hence, a customer might wish to trade (execute) through one exchange member but state that the trade should be given up to the customer's usual clearing broker. This keeps one clearing relationship between the customer and the clearing broker. Give-ups are sometimes also undertaken because of shortages of trading staff at a give-in firm, or to preserve anonymity where a give-up firm is helping another member build up a position.

Example 20

For example, member firm ABC executes, confirms and matches a trade which it pre-registers, notifying the system that the trade should be allocated to another member firm (DEF).

ABC gives-up the trade to DEF. In turn, DEF will claim the trade, which will be registered to DEF as a house, segregated or non-segregated transaction.

9. Market Transparency, Trade Reporting and Monitoring

Learning Objective

3.9.1 Understand the purpose, process and responsibilities of trade reporting including: dissemination of information from exchanges to quote vendors; constituents of exchange price feeds and display screens; advantages of transparency to investors; monitoring volume and open interest

9.1 Trade Reporting

In order to regulate the activities of their member firms satisfactorily, derivatives exchanges need to know what trades have been executed by their members. To this end, they may require members to **trade report** the transactions they have been involved in. The exchanges specify the **time limits** within which these trade reports must be submitted, and the member firms could be subject to disciplinary action if they fail to adhere to these limits.

The electronic nature of the trading system provided by exchanges such as ICE means that trade reporting is largely automatic. It is only block and basis trades that need to be reported into the exchange.

On ICE, **block** trades must be reported to the exchange within five minutes of verbal agreement being reached, under normal market conditions. Those block trades that are dependent on the execution of a transaction in another instrument or when market conditions are considered 'exceptional', must be reported within 15 minutes, while all basis trades must be reported within 15 minutes of the time the trade was organised.

9.2 Price Transparency

In order for investors to have confidence in the exchange, they must know that prices are determined fairly. For an exchange, investor confidence is vital because its income is primarily derived from fees charged on the contracts traded.

Price transparency is a central part of investor confidence and refers to the availability of up-to-date trading information for anyone who wishes to receive it. This transparency is generally provided by the exchange feeding the prices to members and to quote vendors such as Reuters and Bloomberg.

9.2.1 Constituents of Exchange Price Feeds

The exchange disseminates the trade reporting information through a price feed to its members. Real-time price and trade information via the feed is made available to quote vendors (eg, Reuters and Bloomberg) so that investors at large can see the information on their price screens.

The price screens will generally include the following information:

Buying and Selling Prices

The best buying price (bid – often shown by the letter **B**) and offer price (selling price – often shown by the letter **A** for ask) will constitute the bid/offer spread in the market.

The screens are designed to report all data that traders and investors wish to know. This will include volume traded and open interest (as at the close of the previous business day), plus price information showing the opening price, the closing price (again, as at the close of the previous business day), the price of the last trade, and the day's high and low prices, all shown by delivery month. This data is made available both via real-time price feeds and on a delayed basis.

Delivery Month Codes

Each futures expiry month has its unique identifier.

January	F	April	J	July	N	October	V
February	G	May	K	August	Q	November	X
March	H	June	M	September	U	December	Z

For example, Z 4245B 4246A = current bid/ask for December future.

9.3   Monitoring Volume and Open Interest

It is important for any exchange to publish accurately its open interest so that all market observers and investors can make judgements in respect of their positions and trading strategies. To this end, markets such as ICE and Eurex set down procedural rules as to how members of the market should report open interest on a daily basis back to the exchange(s). In the case of ICE this is effected by the use of ICE Clear, through which all members report their holdings in respect of their ongoing client positions. These details are provided to interested parties via information vendors.

This is separate from the open interest that may be recorded in omnibus accounts at the clearing houses. It falls to every client to be aware of their position(s) where they are holding long or short contracts, and to instruct their clearing brokers carrying their positions where contracts are to be closed, matching purchases against sales. Sometimes systems will exist operationally to effect these close-outs automatically. If a client failed to manage the open interest on their account properly, it may lead to unwanted delivery situations.

If the client's position were to become excessive, there is a danger of the client breaching his credit limit with the broker when prices move against him. However, as will be covered in more detail in Chapter 5, the clearing system provides a mutual guarantee structure.

9.4   Wholesale Trading

Exchange for Physical (EFP) is a technique (which originated in the commodity markets) whereby a position in the underlying asset is traded for a futures position. In financial futures markets, the EFP bypasses any cash settlement mechanism that is built into the contract and substitutes physical settlement. EFPs are used primarily to adjust underlying cash market positions at a low trading cost. An EFP by itself will not change either party's net risk position materially, but EFPs are often used to set up a subsequent trade which will modify the investor's market risk exposure at low cost. It is occasionally called **Against Actuals (AA)**.

Exchange for Swap is similar to EFP and is a technique used by many banks to avoid taking physical delivery of a commodity. The process involves a dealer taking on the bank's futures position into its own account and swapping the commodity's return for an agreed funding rate.

Both of these are part of the wholesale trading facilities that most exchanges offer, such as ICE. One of the main advantages of both EFP and EFS is that they eliminate any risks associated with trading in the Central Order Book.

Appendix

Answers to the exercises included in this chapter.

Answer to Exercise 1

The investor has a loss 6425 – 6550 = 125 index points on each contract.

125 x 2 = 250 ticks.

250 ticks x £5 = £1250 per contract.

£1250 x 6 contracts = £7,500 loss.

Answer to Exercise 2

The put options will be worth exercising, each gaining 6500 – 6475 = 25 index points. However, the investor's option cost 15 index points, so the overall gain is 25 – 15 = 10 index points.

10 index points x £10 x 7 contracts = £700

Answer to Exercise 3

While the put will be exercised against the fund manager, since the index is 10 points lower than the strike price, the fund manager still has a profit of 8 per option (18 – 10).

8 index points x $10 x 20 puts = $1,600.

Answer to Exercise 4

The fair value of a future with 45 days to delivery would be:

Cash price	£750.00
Finance £750 x 0.03 x (45/365)	2.77
Storage £750 x 0.005 x (45/365)	0.46
Fair value	£753.23

Answer to Exercise 5

The fair value of the FTSE 100 future with 91 days to delivery would be:

Cash index = 6500

Interest rate = 0.5%

Dividend yield = 2.5%

Fair value = cash price x interest rate $(1 + (0.005 \times (91/365)))$ – dividend points (see below).

Dividend yield conversion: FTSE 100 dividend yield = 2.5%

Conversion to dividend points = 6500 x 0.025 = 162.5

= 162.5 points per year * (91/365) = 40.51 points

Fair value of the future = 6500 x $(1 + (0.005 \times (91/365)))$ which equals 6508.103 – 40.51 = 6467.80

Answer to Exercise 6

Cash price	=	£104.30
Finance costs £104.30 x (0.0025 – 0.015) x (2/12)	=	(0.22)
Fair value	=	£104.08

Answer to Exercise 7

Status of a put option	Definition
In-the-money	Market price < exercise price
At-the-money	Market price = exercise price
Out-the-money	Market price > exercise price
Break-even point	Market price = exercise price – premium

Answer to Exercise 8

The option allows the investor to buy a share at 234p that is currently trading at 256p. This is equivalent to saving 22p, and this is the intrinsic value.

Since premium = intrinsic value + time value

Given the premium of 40p and the intrinsic value of 22p from above: 40p = 22p + time value

Rearranging this equation gives:

Time value = 40p – 22p = 18p

Answer to Exercise 9

Using C – P = S – K

12 – P = 101.5 – 110

12 – P = – 8.5

P = 12 + 8.5

P = 20.5

Answer to Exercise 10

The put premium can be found by solving the following equation:

$C - P = S - \dfrac{K}{(1+r)^{\wedge}t}$ where r = 0.03 and t = 2/12 or 0.16667 of a year

$25 - P = 410 - \dfrac{400}{(1 + 0.03)^{\wedge}0.16667}$

$25 - P = 410 - \dfrac{400}{1.004939}$

25 – P = 410 – 398.03

25 – P = 11.97

25 – 11.97 = P

P = 13.03

Answer to Exercise 11

				Δ
Short 4 futures	–4	x	1	–4
Short 3 ATM calls	–3	x	0.5	–1.5
Long 6 deep ITM puts	+6	x	–1	–6
Cumulative delta				–11.5

End of Chapter Questions

1. Identify the three categories of exchange membership.
   Answer reference: Section 1.2

2. At what time and how many ring trading sessions does the LME have per day?
   Answer reference: Section 2

3. For market participants, what are the benefits of EFP transactions?
   Answer reference: Section 2

4. What is the fair value of the future?
   Answer reference: Section 5.3

5. Describe contango and backwardation.
   Answer reference: Section 5.4

6. Why is cash and carry arbitrage named as such?
   Answer reference: Section 5.7.1

7. What is the main difference between futures and options costs?
   Answer reference: Section 6

8. Why should an option buyer pay more than its intrinsic value?
   Answer reference: Section 6.1.2

9. What is the function of a stop (loss) order?
   Answer reference: Section 7.2

10. Why are give-up trades mainly performed?
    Answer reference: Section 8.2

Chapter Four
OTC Derivatives

This syllabus area will provide approximately 13 of the 80 examination questions

1.   General Introduction

So far the focus has been on exchange-traded derivatives rather than over-the-counter (OTC) or off-exchange derivatives.

OTC derivatives are extremely popular for hedging, speculation and arbitrage, principally because their contracts are not standardised and therefore can be constructed around the unique needs of their users. This is despite the fact that only recently a Central Counterparty (CCP) and Trade Reporting procedure has been established for these contracts. The European Market Infrastructure Regulation (EMIR) was created to provide greater stability in the derivatives market in the EU.

As seen in the previous chapters, exchange-traded derivatives have standardised contract specifications that may not precisely meet the hedging or speculative needs of the investor. In the OTC market, the derivatives can be precisely tailored to the needs of the investor. The OTC markets also provide confidentiality in that the only market participants aware of the deals that have been completed are the two counterparties, plus anyone else they care to inform. By comparison, the exchange-traded derivatives markets are much more transparent, with the exchanges providing details of all prices and volumes traded in order to assist in the price-formation process and to build confidence and liquidity.

The value of underlying instruments traded in the OTC markets is much larger than that traded on exchanges. Major OTC products include swaps and swaptions, forward rate agreements (FRAs), caps, floors, collars and a range of credit derivatives.

2.   Forwards, Forward Rate Agreements (FRAs) and Contracts for Difference (CFDs)

Learning Objective

4.1.1   Understand the differences between the range of underlying assets, key characteristics, investment implications and applications of: forward contracts; forward rate agreements (FRAs); contracts for difference; spread betting

4.1.2   Analyse the mechanisms for OTC derivative pricing and the relationship with the underlying cash prices together with the significance of contributing factors: spot and forward rates; cash flow analysis and the zero curve; the role of interest rates and yields; other factors affecting pricing

2.1   Forwards

A **forward contract** is an OTC transaction in which delivery of the commodity/asset is deferred until a date in the future that is specified in the contract. Although the delivery is made in the future, the price is determined on the initial trade date.

Forward contracts are traded on a wide variety of assets such as currencies, commodities and equities.

The forward price that is agreed by the buyer and seller is determined by a number of factors, such as the interest rate differential between the two currencies, in the case of an FX forward. For commodities, these factors would include the current interest rate, the cost of financing should the commodity be purchased today, and storage costs. Equity forward prices take into account the differential between the current interest rate and the equity's dividend yield.

These factors are key to reducing arbitrage opportunities, the same way as in futures' prices.

Example 1

A French company has a series of future yen payments over the next 12 months and is concerned that the euro will weaken against the yen, thus making their materials more expensive. In order to lock in its cost now, the company can enter into a series of EUR/JPY forward contracts that will allow it to set the exchange rate today for its future payments. This is done through FX forwards contracts where the company buys yen against the euro, for specific future dates at rates that are agreed today.

Since this is an OTC transaction, the company can arrange the amounts and dates exactly to match the payments it has to make to its Japanese supplier. The forward contracts' rates will be based on the current FX spot rate and the interest rate differential between euros and yen. Since yen interest rates are slightly lower than euro rates over the period, the yen will be at a slight premium to the euro, thereby making yen more expensive in the forward FX market.

Example 2

A food company is concerned that the forecasts of a drought will result in a significant reduction in this year's cocoa harvest. Since the company has several key production dates, exchange-traded cocoa futures are not an option. Therefore, it calls its broker and arranges a series of cocoa forward contracts, where it agrees to buy set amounts at set dates at prices agreed upon today. The cocoa forward's price will be determined by today's market price of a tonne of cocoa, plus any adjustment for storage costs and the current interest rate for the forward's duration.

Forwards are similar to futures contracts as they are legally binding agreements to make or take delivery of a specified quantity of a specific asset at a certain time in the future for a price that is agreed today. They are usually traded off-exchange (OTC) but can also be traded on-exchange, eg, the London Metal Exchange (LME) lists forward contracts. They may not be marked-to-market daily or, if they are, then the resulting profits are not paid out until maturity and if they are cleared by an exchange's clearing house any losses must be paid to that clearing house. Forwards are, therefore, settled only on the delivery date.

Most forwards, however, are OTC contracts, usually with banks. Outright forwards are a common product traded in the foreign exchange (FX) market. Corporations, institutional investors and banks themselves use forwards to manage their FX transaction risks. If an organisation is importing or exporting goods (or investing) in a foreign currency, they can use forwards to protect against adverse currency movements. Forward contracts are also used to lock in the price of physical commodities, such as energy, metals and foodstuffs (see the example above).

In the physical markets, an airline might use forward prices on jet fuel to lock in one of their major costs. They would agree a price today for delivery in a future month.

Forwards are derivatives – the future price agreed for a forward is based on the spot price of the underlying asset; in the case of a currency it would be adjusted for the interest rates in the relevant currencies. The main advantages of forwards compared with futures (which are always, by definition, exchange-traded) are:

- flexibility (details such as size and date)
- wide range of underlyings
- easy to access – forwards are available from most commercial banks.

Their main potential disadvantages are counterparty risk, cost and, in some cases, liquidity. With exchange-traded futures, counterparty risk is reduced considerably by novation through the central clearing house.

2.2 Forward Rate Agreements (FRAs)

Learning Objective

4.1.3   Calculate the price and net settlement amount of a forward rate agreement

A **forward rate agreement (FRA)** effectively enables a company to fix an interest rate in advance. It enables a borrower or lender to take a view on whether rates are rising or falling. There is no principal amount actually borrowed or lent, but a cash flow arises from the difference between the interest rate fixed at the outset (the fixed rate) and the level of benchmark rate at a point of time in the future (the floating rate). The FRA pays out the interest rate difference for a predetermined future period on an agreed principal amount. The benchmark rate most often used is ICE LIBOR.

Therefore an FRA is effectively an agreement to buy or sell an interest rate which is fixed today and which will be revalued against prevailing market rates, using a benchmark rate:

- starting on an agreed future date
- for an agreed future period
- based on an agreed principal amount (a notional amount, ie, used for the calculation but not actually transferred).

The party that pays the fixed rate is the buyer of the FRA, and the party that receives the fixed rate and pays the floating rate is the seller of the FRA.

An FRA is settled on the date when the FRA period starts. In an FRA the settlement amount is subject to **discounting**. This happens because the FRA payment takes place at the beginning of the FRA period rather than following market convention for other instruments, and paying at the end, or on maturity. The discounting is applied at current market rates, and represents a deduction for the interest which would accrue if the amount paid were to be deposited from the date of payment through to the end of the FRA period.

The benchmark rate, eg, ICE LIBOR, ie, the floating-rate value, is determined on the first day of the FRA period and will then apply through to the agreed maturity. The difference between the level of the benchmark rate and the pre-agreed fixed rate will give rise to a **net settlement amount** calculated using the following formula:

$$\text{Notional Principal Amount} \times \frac{(\text{ICE LIBOR} - \text{FRA rate}) \times \dfrac{\text{days in FRA period}}{\text{days in year}}}{\left(1 + \left(\text{ICE LIBOR} \times \dfrac{\text{days in FRA period}}{\text{days in year}}\right)\right)}$$

The period over which interest is calculated is known as the **calculation period**. The length of this as a proportion of a year is known as the **day count fraction**. All day counts are taken from, and including, the first day of the calculation period up to, but excluding, the last day. The denominator in the day count fraction – days in year – is taken as either 365 or 360, depending on the market convention; for example, both euro and dollar use 360, and sterling uses 365.

The calculation of the FRA settlement amount can result in a positive or a negative figure. The amount is transferred from seller to buyer if ICE LIBOR is higher than the FRA rate (negative) and from buyer to seller if ICE LIBOR is lower than the FRA rate (positive).

Example 3

A company knows that in one month's time it will need to borrow €15 million for a period of six months. The company treasurer is concerned that interest rates might rise in the next month, thereby making its borrowing more expensive. He wants to fix the future borrowing rate today, even though the money isn't needed for a month.

He enters into a forward rate agreement whereby he buys an FRA on €15 million to start in one month's time to run for a period of six months, at a rate of 5.4%. It is agreed that in one month's time the 11.00am fixing of ICE LIBOR, for a six-month maturity, will be used as the benchmark rate.

Suppose that the ICE LIBOR fixing is 5.55%. The seller of the FRA will therefore pay the company 0.15% (the difference between the 5.4% rate agreed and the 5.55% subsequently fixed) on €15 million, for a period of six months.

There is no exchange of principal between these two parties. Instead, the company will borrow the €15 million from its usual lending bank, or some other source, at the prevailing market rate of 5.55% (plus any lending margin which it negotiates with its bank).

The net settlement amount is:

$$€15,000,000 \times \frac{(0.0555 - 0.0540) \times 182/360}{1 + (0.0555 \times (182/360))} = €11,064.54$$

Alternatively, suppose that interest rates had fallen and the ICE LIBOR fixing was 5.25%. The company would have to pay the seller 0.15% on €15 million for six months. However, the actual borrowing from the bank would be at only 5.25% plus margin. The net effect is, therefore, still that the company borrows at 5.40% plus lending margin.

Therefore, a fall below 5.40% does not benefit the company as it must pay the seller the difference but conversely, any rise above 5.40% is offset by the receipt of the difference from the seller.

The FRA described in the previous example is known as a 1 v 7 FRA. This means that it covers a future period which begins one month from today and ends seven months from today.

FRA quoted rates are based on the **forward/forward rate**; for example, the quoted rate of a 1 v 7 FRA is based on the six-month starting in one month's time; that is the definition of a forward/forward rate. To calculate this you need the current one-month and seven-month reference rates (usually ICE LIBOR).

$$\text{FRA quoted rate} = r_{FRA} = \frac{(r_2 n_2 - r_1 n_1)}{n_{FRA}(1 + r_1 n_1 /365)}$$

where:

n_1 is the number of days from the dealing date or spot date to the settlement date
n_2 is the number of days from the dealing date or spot date to the maturity date
r_1 is the spot rate to the settlement date
r_2 is the spot rate from the spot date in the FRA contract period
n_{FRA} is the number of days in the maturity date
r_{FRA} is the FRA rate.

Therefore, if the one-month UK rate is 5.55% and the seven-month rate is 5.85%, what is the price of a 1 v 7 GBP FRA?

$$1 \text{ v } 7 \text{ GBP FRA} = \frac{(5.85\% \times 214 - 5.55\% \times 31)}{183 \times (1 + (5.55\% \times (31/365)))} = 5.87\%$$

or:

$$1 \text{ v } 7 \text{ GBP FRA} = \frac{(10.7985)}{183.8626} = 5.87\%$$

Since FRAs are traded in the over-the-counter market, they can be tailor-made to suit a hedger's exposure, since the notional amount, future period, currency and reference rate are flexible. As mentioned above, FRAs are quoted giving the deferred period first, then the notional maturity. Therefore, a 2 v 5 FRA is one for a three-month rate that starts two months in the future.

A series of FRAs that cover future three-month interest rates is similar to a series of three-month interest rate futures contracts, if they both are in the same currency and have the same reference or underlying interest rate. A key difference is that, by being an OTC derivative, the details of the FRA are flexible.

2.3   Contracts for Difference

Contracts for difference (CFDs) allow investors to benefit from the capital gains from a particular underlying index, stock, currency or commodity without having to actually physically own or pay for it.

The profit or loss is determined by the difference between the prices at which the investor buys and sells the contract and the contract amount. The investor can profit from predicting the correct movement in the underlying asset's price, either up or down, without having to buy or sell the actual asset.

The key difference between CFDs and more traditional trading is that CFDs do not buy or sell the underlying asset, but trade on its price movement.

Investors using CFDs have one key decision to make – do they think the underlying asset is going to go up or down? If they get it right, they will win; if they get it wrong, they will lose. The key feature of CFDs is that they do not have a set maturity, and, since they are OTC contracts, the contract's specification ranges from the asset to the amount negotiated between the buyer and seller.

CFDs are **cost-efficient**, in that an investor buying a CFD on a share does not have to pay stamp duty, nor the broker's fee that is normally associated with a share transaction. CFDs also allow investors who are bearish on a share an easier way to profit from the fall in a share's price, rather than physically going short of a share.

CFDs are based on margin trading, so an investor can **leverage** their position. Most brokers require a **margin deposit** of 10–30% of the contract's value. This allows investors to increase their risk, based on the size of their initial investment. But many contracts include an automatic **stop loss order** as part of the contract, which minimises the risk of a large loss. Most CFDs are nominally intra-day trades, since those that are held overnight normally incur interest charges.

CFDs do not have an expiry or maturity date like options or futures. As opposed to having an expiry date, a CFD is effectively renewed/rolled over at the close of each trading day if desired. An investor can keep their position open indefinitely, as long as there is enough margin in their account to support the position.

Example 4

An investor is bearish on company ABC plc shares. They are currently trading at 145p. The investor decides to sell a contract for difference on 5,000 shares at that price. The investor's broker requires a 15% margin or £1,087.50.

$$5,000 \times 145p = £7,250$$
$$£7,250.00 \times 0.15 = £1,087.50$$

Just before closing, ABC's shares have fallen to 137p. The investor decides to end the CFD, realising a profit of £400.

$$5,000 \times 137p = £6,850$$
$$£7,250 - £6,850 = £400$$

This is a return of 36.8% on the investment.

The two key differences between spread betting and contracts for difference are that the latter do not have a fixed maturity/expiration date and that spread betting in the UK is considered gambling and therefore is treated differently as far as tax is concerned, since CFDs are subject to capital gains tax.

3. Foreign Exchange (FX) Forwards and Swaps

Learning Objective

4.2.1   Analyse the purpose, risks, benefits and costs of foreign exchange forwards and swaps

The FX spot market involves the exchange of two currencies very soon after the date of transaction. For most currency transactions in the wholesale market this is T+2.

The market is used by customers with a need to exchange one currency for another. This will often be because of an underlying transaction, for example, the import or export of goods or services, or the purchase or sale of investments.

Suppose that the GBP/USD spot rate is 1.3450/55.

The size of the spread between the bid price ($1.3450) and the ask or offer price ($1.3455) will depend on the size of the transaction and the importance of the customer relationship.

Small clients might face a spread wider than 2¢. On deals with large corporates or interbank transactions the spread might be as low as 5 'pips' or 0.0005 of a dollar. (A pip is the smallest price increment in a currency. They are similar to 'ticks' in the futures markets. In the above example, in GBP/USD, a move from 1.3450 to 1.3451 is one pip). Thus, for interbank deals, after a five point/pip move, the GBP/USD spot prices might be quoted as 1.3455/60 from its original rate of 1.3450/55.

Spot foreign exchange facilities are provided by most commercial banks.

Remember that in foreign exchange, one currency is quoted in terms of another currency. Therefore, in the quote shown above, sterling (GBP) is the base currency – the first currency quoted, by FX market convention, is the base or action currency, while the dollar is being quoted in terms of sterling.

- **1.3450 is the bid for GBP** – this means that the quoting bank will buy sterling and sell dollars at this rate, since it is cheaper: £1,000,000 costs $1,345,000.
- **1.3455 is the offer for GBP** – here the quoting bank will sell sterling and buy dollars. At this rate sterling is more expensive: £1,000,000 costs $1,345,500.

Note that in most cases the amounts traded are also based on set amounts of the base currency.

Take the case of a UK consultancy firm that has a contract in the European Union and will be receiving payments in euros over the next six months. It might want to lock-in the exchange rate for these payments now by entering into a forward contract. A forward contract is simply a deal between two participants to agree now the rate at which a certain amount of foreign currency will be exchanged at some pre-agreed date in the future. In this case, the UK company would buy GBP and sell euros, using forward contracts that would match the dates that it receives euros payments.

These forward contract rates are quoted over-the-counter by banks. The quotation is based on applying a margin to the spot quotes to arrive at a forward rate. Any FX contract that matures one day beyond the normal spot date (T+2) is considered a forward deal. For the major currencies, forwards, or **outright**

forwards as they are known, can have maturities out to five or ten years. But note that the longer the maturity, the less liquid the market.

Example 5

Spot GBP/EUR is	1.2415/1.2420
1-month is	1.2395/1.2405
3-month is	1.2350/1.2365
6-month is	1.23085/1.24010

In the above example, the margin applied to the spot rate is a **discount to the base currency – GBP**. A discount indicates that the base currency (sterling, in the above example) is becoming cheaper relative to the euro. As a result, the forward points are subtracted from the spot rate, so that in the forward deal the pound will buy less euros (the bid column), and the euro holder will also pay less to get the same number of pounds (the ask column).

When quoting forward points, it is the market convention that, when the forward point decreases, the bid increase is greater than the offer's increase as in the example above – the one-month forward points would be quoted as 20/15, then they would be subtracted from the spot rate. Remember, in this case, it indicates that the base currency, GBP, is at a **discount** and the traded currency, the euro is at a **premium**, based on their relative interest rates.

In the above example the GBP/EUR forward points would be quoted as:

- 1- month   20/15
- 3-month   65/55
- 6-month   130/110

When the forward points quote increases, the base currency is at a premium in the forward market and the points would then be added from the spot rate. This is described as a **forward delivery premium**.

The banks will calculate the necessary premium or discount considering the relevant short-term interest rates of the two currencies.

The key advantage of forward contracts is certainty.

As well as commercial users, the forward market is used extensively by speculators, for example, hedge funds and the proprietary trading desks at investment banks. Since forward rates are based on the interest rate differential between the two currencies, the FX forward market is used to speculate on expected changes in the difference between these two interest rates. These are done using **FX swaps**, which entail buying one currency spot and selling it at a future/forward date at the same time. Therefore any movements in the forward points, which are based on the interest rate differential between the two currencies, will be the basis for any profits or losses on such a trade.

Speculators on the movements in spot rate mainly take spot or outright forward positions.

3.1 Interest Rate Parity

We have seen that the forward rates of exchange are linked to the spot rate by applying a discount or premium. The factor that links spot rates is the relative interest rate between the two currencies.

The link between spot and forward rates is based on the principle of arbitrage. Put simply, if the forward rate quoted is not in line with relative interest rates, there would be an opportunity to make a guaranteed profit by borrowing funds and entering into a forward foreign exchange contract. This is the theory of **interest rate parity**.

The link between relative interest rates and the forward foreign exchange rate can be summarised as follows:

Higher interest rate currency = discount in the forward foreign exchange market
Lower interest rate currency = premium in the forward foreign exchange market

When calculating forward foreign exchange rates for periods of less than one year, we have to take into account the different day count conventions of the different currencies' money markets. For example, both the euro and dollar use an Actual/360 day count, while sterling uses Actual/365.

4. Interest Rate Swaps and Swaptions

Learning Objective

4.3.1 Analyse the purpose, key characteristics and valuation of interest rate swaps and swaptions: types of swap agreements: vanilla, basis, coupon, index and currency; interest calculations (compared to bond markets)

A **swap** is an OTC derivative, where two counterparties exchange one stream of a cash flow against another. These payment streams are called the **legs** of the swap. The cash flows are calculated over a **notional principal/asset amount**.

For example, a straightforward interest rate swap (a so-called **plain vanilla swap**) involves one party exchanging a floating interest rate obligation for another party's fixed-rate obligation. The floating rate will be determined on the swap's **reset date**. For example, for a fixed versus six-month floating swap, the reset date will be every six months. Once the floating rate is determined, the swap will start accruing interest as of its **effective date**.

The plain vanilla interest rate swap, based on an agreed notional principal sum, will specify a particular start date and run for a set period. The swap will specify particular periods at the end of which the cash flow exchanges will take place; this is known as the swap's **payment date**.

With the agreement of both parties, and after an evaluation or **mark-to-market** of the swap's value, either party can initiate action to cancel or end the swap after an agreed payment. When this happens, all calculations of accrued interest are based on the swap's **termination date**. This is the date that the swap officially ceases to exist.

For example, a three-year plain vanilla interest rate swap might be arranged with quarterly payments based on a principal sum of £6 million, effective from 1 January 2015, exchanging a fixed interest rate for a floating interest rate based on ICE LIBOR (the London Interbank Offered Rate). The first payment under the swap will be at the end of March 2015, the second at the end of June 2015 and so on.

At each payment date a net payment will be made between the two participants based on the difference between floating rate (such as ICE LIBOR or the Fed Funds rate) and the fixed rate on the underlying principal sum for the quarter. If ICE LIBOR exceeds the fixed rate, the difference will be paid to the party that is due to receive ICE LIBOR and pay the fixed interest. The payments will be made in the opposite direction if ICE LIBOR is less than the fixed rate.

A **swaption** is an arrangement where a buyer pays an up-front sum for the right to enter into a swap agreement by a pre-agreed date in the future. In other words, the buyer of a swaption has the option to enter into a swap. The concept is the same as we saw for options earlier.

Large corporations and other institutions use these interest rate swaps and swaptions to manage risk and, potentially, take advantage of cheaper and more appropriate funding. The arrangements are facilitated by financial institutions. It is a wholesale market not open to the private investor.

As they are OTC instruments, swaps come in a variety of forms. In addition to fixed-for-floating swaps (as illustrated above), there are also floating-for-floating swaps. These are alternatively referred to as 'basis swaps' and might enable a borrower to swap six-month ICE LIBOR rates for three-month ICE LIBOR rates. Basis swaps are considered in more detail shortly. As well as these interest rate swaps that are based on a single currency, there are also currency swaps (where there is an exchange of currency, as well as interest) and equity index swaps.

Currency swaps were one of the earliest types of swap. A currency swap is an agreement to exchange a series of specified payments denominated in one currency for a series of specified payments that are denominated in another currency.

In a currency swap, the parties exchange the principle amounts of two different currencies at the start of the agreement, giving each the use of the other currency. They then make the interest payments to each other on the principle during the life of the swap. The combination of interest rates vary with each swap agreement, they can be for one party to pay a fixed rate, while the other pays a floating rate in the different currencies, or they can both pay a fixed rate to each other or both pay a floating rate.

One of the first examples was between the World Bank and IBM in 1981. IBM wanted to borrow US dollars and the World Bank wanted to borrow Swiss francs and German marks. However, because the World Bank was already a frequent issuer of European currency debt and IBM was not, the rarity value meant IBM could borrow Swiss francs and German marks more cheaply. So, IBM borrowed Swiss francs and German marks, the World Bank borrowed US dollars and they entered into a swap – the result being that they both saved money on their borrowings.

Currency swaps have continued to develop. It is possible to enter into currency swaps that exchange:

- fixed interest in one currency for floating interest in another currency
- fixed interest in one currency for fixed interest in another currency
- floating interest in one currency for floating interest in another currency, or
- floating interest in one currency for fixed interest in another currency.

An illustration of the potential benefit of a currency swap is provided on the following page.

Example 6

A UK company might expect to receive a stream of US dollars from exports over the next five years. It needs to convert US dollars into sterling. Rather than use a series of separate forward foreign exchange transactions to achieve this, it could instead use a currency swap. The series of US dollar flows are considered as a package and, in the swap, the company agrees to pay these flows to a counterparty over the five years, in return for a series of sterling cash flows. This would be a fixed-fixed currency swap without principal exchanges. The UK company has protected itself against its UK income being eroded by exchange rate movements depreciating against the US dollars. Conversely, if exchange rates improve, it will see no benefit.

As seen above, the uses of currency swaps include potentially reducing the cost of borrowing and replacing unpredictable future cash flows (due to exchange rate movements) with predictable cash flows agreed in a swap.

In an **equity swap** (or index swap), two counterparties agree to exchange the return on an equity index, or a specified basket of shares, for a fixed or floating rate of interest. This enables the creation of a synthetic portfolio of shares without the need to buy all of the individual underlying shares and incur the transaction costs for doing so. See Section 6.10 for more on this.

A fixed/floating swap (as described above) is also known as a **coupon swap**. An alternative is a floating/ floating swap, known as a **basis swap** or **index swap**, in which each of the two payment streams is based on a floating rate. For example, an organisation might pay three-month ICE LIBOR and receive six-month ICE LIBOR. A basis swap might also be a currency swap (see below) – for example, paying three-month ICE LIBOR in one currency and receiving six-month ICE LIBOR in another. The term 'basis swap', therefore, covers a range of possibilities.

For example:

- single-currency swap from one period ICE LIBOR to another period ICE LIBOR
- single-currency swap from ICE LIBOR to an overnight interest rate
- single-currency swap from ICE LIBOR to another interest rate, such as a commercial paper rate
- cross-currency swap from a floating-rate in one currency to a floating-rate in another currency.

5.   Caps, Floors and Collars

Learning Objective

4.4.1   Calculate the likely outcome of implementing caps, floors and collars: purpose and construction; risks, benefits and costs

Various OTC option-based products are offered by banks to their customers, some of which can be constructed from straightforward options. Caps, floors and collars are commonly employed with regard to interest rates.

A **cap** is an option product which can be used to protect the cost of a floating-rate borrowing over a series of settlement periods. Suppose that a borrower has a five-year loan which he rolls over every three months at the three-month ICE LIBOR then current. He can buy a five-year cap which will put a maximum cost on each of the rollovers. Whenever the rollover rate exceeds the cap strike rate, he receives the difference. Suppose the strike rate on the cap is 1% and ICE LIBOR is set at 1.2%. Then, at the end of the three-month interest rate period, the purchaser of the cap will receive 0.2% accrued over the three-month period. Whenever the rollover rate is lower than the cap strike rate, nothing is paid or received. The settlement for a cap is paid at the end of the interest period, exactly as for a swap.

Floors are options that enable the buyer to demand a minimum rate of interest paid on a deposit, regardless of a fall in the prevailing rate of interest. Floors can be used to protect the income on a floating-rate investment by putting a minimum return on each rollover. Whenever the rollover rate is lower than the floor strike rate, the buyer receives the difference. Whenever the rollover rate is higher than the floor strike rate, nothing is paid or received. The settlement mechanics for a floor are analogous to those for a cap.

Collars are contracts that incorporate both a cap and a floor. For a borrower, a cap provides a fixed worst-case level of interest but allows the customer to pay the market rate if this turns out better. A collar allows the customer to pay a better market rate in the same way, but only down to a certain level. Beyond that level the customer must pay interest at another fixed best-case level. In return for this reduced opportunity, the customer pays a lower premium for the option.

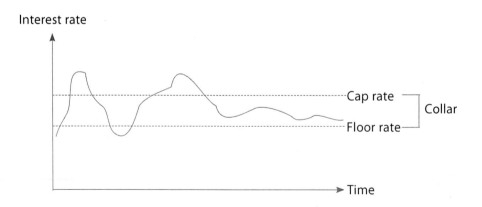

Collars can be constructed so that the two premiums – the premium paid to buy the cap and the premium received when a floor is sold – net zero. This is referred to as a **zero-cost collar**.

Example 7

Suppose City plc is a floating-rate borrower that fears rates rising.

It has borrowed £100 million for three years at ICE LIBOR plus 0.25%. City plc can buy a cap (an OTC option) so that, if rates go above its specified rate (say 6%), the bank from whom it bought the cap (Cap Bank plc) will pay City plc compensation. If it had capped the whole £100 million and in year two rates were 8%, City plc would pay 8 + 0.25% (£8.25 million) to its lending bankers but receive 8 − 6% (£2 million) from the Cap Bank. During the term of the cap, the worst rate that City plc can pay is 6% plus 0.25%.

If the premium City plc were quoted was too high for it, it might finance this by selling a floor to Cap Bank plc or to another bank.

Caps, floors and collars tend to be the preserve of the wholesale participants and are arranged by the large banks.

6. Other Types of Swaps

Learning Objective

4.5.1 Analyse the key features and risk/reward trade-offs of other types of swap instruments including investment applications and relationships to other markets: asset and total return swaps; amortising, accreting and rollercoaster; inflation; dividend; constant maturity; arrears; forward start; overnight index (OIS); mark-to-market (MTM)

There are several types of swaps in common use other than the interest rate and currency swaps previously mentioned. Here we will describe the variety of products and types of swaps that are traded in the OTC market. At the end of the chapter, some of the operational complexities that arise are considered.

6.1 Asset and Total Return Swaps

An **asset swap** is a swap that can be used to change the interest rate exposure or currency exposure of an investment. The swap itself can be straightforward. The term asset swap is used to denote the reason for doing the swap, and is also used for the whole package of the asset and the swap together.

An investor might, for example, buy a floating-rate note (FRN) and also transact a swap to receive a fixed interest rate and pay ICE LIBOR. The result would be a synthetic fixed-rate investment. Or, in reverse, he might create a synthetic FRN by buying an underlying fixed-rate investment while paying fixed and receiving floating in the swap.

The advantage of such a structure is that the investor is then able to choose the underlying asset according to such criteria as availability, credit quality, liquidity and competitive pricing. The choice of whether to invest in fixed or floating rate can be separated from the choice of asset.

Example 8

An investor wishes to buy a ten-year floating-rate note issued by the government (because he wants the highest credit rating possible) but no such issue exists. He can instead buy a ten-year government fixed-rate bond and swap it.

Even if such an FRN does already exist, it might be that the synthetic structure using the swap achieves a slightly better yield, if the two markets are not exactly in line.

In a **total return swap**, one of the legs pays the total return on a particular financial asset, ie, the total benefit that would have arisen from holding that asset, including all interest payments, fees and capital appreciation. This amount could be negative if the security's value has fallen rather than risen.

For example, the swap could be linked to the value of a particular bond. In this case, one party would pay the other the total increase in value of the bond from the start of the swap to the end of the swap (or receive the total fall in value) and also pay the value of any coupons received on the bond over the life of the swap. The other leg of the swap would typically be a floating-rate interest such as ICE LIBOR.

Example 9

A UK pension fund wishes to invest in Eurozone shares quickly.

One way to do this is to become the receiver of a total return swap (TRS) that has a portfolio of Eurozone shares as the underlying instrument.

The price of the TRS will roughly be the same as the cost of a long position of the underlying share portfolio for the pension fund (the TRS buyer), whilst the seller is financing the position.

The pension fund will receive any increase in the value of the Eurozone share portfolio (underlying asset), whilst the seller will receive any fall in the share portfolio's value.

6.2 Amortising, Accreting and RollerCoaster Swaps

An interest rate swap is often used by a company to convert the interest rate risk on a borrowing, eg, from floating rate to fixed rate. Suppose that the underlying borrowing arrangement with a bank involves paying the loan back in instalments during its life (an **amortising loan**). In this case, the swap needs to be amortising also, to match the loan pattern; the notional principal on which the swap payments are based will decrease over the life of the swap.

Other patterns could also be used. For example, the notional principal in the swap might be designed to increase (an **accreting swap**) rather than decrease. Or it might rise and fall repeatedly, in line with seasonal borrowing requirements (a **rollercoaster swap**).

6.3 Inflation Swaps

An inflation swap involves an exchange of cash flows, with one or both of its legs calculated with reference to an inflation index. It provides investors with protection against rising prices on a notional principal or an asset's future value. An investor who wants protection from rising prices agrees to pay a fixed amount based on the expected rate of inflation.

The swap payments are based on benchmarks such as the Retail Prices Index in the UK, the Eurozone's Harmonised Index of Consumer Prices, or the US Consumer Price Index. Maturities normally range from five to 30 years for inflation swaps.

6.4 Constant Maturity Swaps

A constant maturity swap (CMS) allows the purchaser to fix the base of received flows on a swap.

The floating leg of a basic interest rate swap is typically reset against a published index, such as LIBOR. The floating leg of a constant maturity swap is fixed against a point on the swap curve on a periodic basis.

It is an interest rate swap where the interest rate on one leg is reset periodically, but with reference to a market swap rate rather than ICE LIBOR. The other leg of the swap is generally ICE LIBOR but may be a fixed-rate or, potentially, another constant maturity rate.

CMSs can either be single-currency or involve two currencies. The prime factor for a CMS, therefore, is the shape of the forward implied yield curves.

6.5 Arrears Swaps

In a plain vanilla interest rate swap, the floating interest rate is observed at the start of a period, and paid at the end of that period. In an arrears swap, however, the floating rate is observed and paid at the end of the period.

For example, in a LIBOR-in-arrears swap with semi-annual resets, the three-month ICE LIBOR rate from time t_{may} to t_{august} is used to calculate the coupon payment at time t_i.

6.6   Forward Start Swaps

A forward start swap is one that is agreed today, but the exchange of funds takes place at a future date. It is often priced as two partially offsetting swaps – both starting today, but one ending on the deferred start date of the forward swap. For example, a one-year swap and a five-year swap could partially offset to create a four-year swap, starting in a year's time. Forward start swaps are also known as **deferred start swaps** or **delayed start swaps**.

6.7   Overnight Index Swaps (OISs)

An **overnight index swap (OIS)** is a fixed/floating swap (or basis swap) where the floating index (or at least one of them) is an overnight interest rate, eg, a swap to pay 5% fixed for three months and receive the overnight interest rate recorded each day.

In this case, the overnight benchmark interest rate used is not, say, overnight ICE LIBOR, which is the rate at a particular time of day. Instead, the benchmark used is a published overnight index, such as Fed funds effective for USD. This is the average of the overnight interest rate throughout a given day, weighted by the volume of business transacted in the market at that rate. The equivalent published indices for sterling and the euro are SONIA and EONIA respectively. Some OISs use a tom/next interest rate rather than an overnight interest rate (by buying or selling a foreign amount settling tomorrow and then doing the opposite – selling or buying it back settling the day after).

In order to avoid the expense and administration of many payment transfers, the floating-rate payment is not physically paid each day. Rather, it is accumulated and paid, say, each month. Because this effectively delays the payment, the daily interest rate fixings are compounded to calculate the actual payment, rather than simply added together.

An OIS might be used, for example, by a bank that lends money for three months at a fixed rate but funds itself in the overnight market. The swap described above – pay 5% fixed for three months and receive the overnight interest rate – would hedge the interest rate risk.

Although OIS means 'overnight index swap' in general, it usually refers to a USD OIS in particular. Similarly, although 'TOIS' means 'tom/next indexed swap' in general, it usually refers to a USD TOIS in particular.

The OIS market has grown dramatically in volume. Some of the instrument's various advantages and uses are as follows:

- Liquidity requirements and interest rate risk can be managed separately. Suppose, for example, that a bank wishes to borrow for one year to ensure liquidity but would prefer to fund itself overnight from the point of view of interest rate risk. It can take in a one-year borrowing and transact a one-year OIS to pay the OI and receive one-year fixed.
- An OIS can be used in arbitrage strategies. For example, a dealer might borrow funds repeatedly in the overnight market, lend for, say, a three-month term, and pay fixed/receive the OI in an OIS.

- Credit risk can be reduced significantly. Rather than lend money for one year, a dealer can transact an OIS to pay the OI and receive one-year fixed, and at the same time lend money for only one day in the overnight market and then roll over this overnight cash loan repeatedly for a year. The credit risk on the rolling overnight loan is far smaller than the credit risk would be on a one-year loan. This separates the interest rate decision from the balance sheet decision. The same could be done with a traditional term swap, say for one year against three-month ICE LIBOR, but an overnight credit risk is clearly less than a three-month one and leaves the dealer with greater flexibility in his lending decisions.

- Conversely, an investor can use an OIS for an asset swap, whereby he invests in an attractively priced long-term investment but swaps the income to the overnight rate (receive the OI and pay the fixed in the OIS).

6.8   Mark-to-Market (MTM) Swap

A mark-to-market swap is one where settlements are calculated by revaluing the swap (ie, marking it to market) regularly and paying or receiving the mark-to-market loss or gain since the previous settlement. The benefit of this is that it removes, at each settlement date, any credit risk that has built up.

The effect is the same as closing-out the existing swap, settling its current value, and putting in place a new swap at the current swap rate for the remaining life of the original swap. This can be done for a single-currency swap or a cross-currency swap (an FX resettable swap).

An **FX resettable swap** has the characteristics and structure of a basic currency swap and an MTM swap. This includes the fact that all payment dates must be set so that they are business days for both currencies, to avoid any mismatch of payments. Also, as is the case with most basic FX swaps, there will be an exchange of principals at the beginning and end of the swap.

6.9   Commodity Swaps

Learning Objective

4.5.2   Analyse the key features, risk/reward trade-offs and investment applications of commodity forwards and swaps

A commodity swap involves paying or receiving a cash flow that is determined by the price or returns of a specific commodity. This type of swap has become increasingly popular given the significant volatility in both the supply and demand for most commodities. The users of this type of swap are increasingly interested in hedging their risks. This ranges from airlines, who want to lock in one of their major costs – jet fuel – to farmers and other agricultural producers, who are looking for a stable income flow from their production.

A **fixed-for-floating commodity price swap** is one whereby one party periodically pays to the other the cash value of an agreed quantity of the underlying commodity multiplied by a fixed price, and the other party in return periodically pays the cash value of an agreed quantity multiplied by a floating price, indexed to current commodity prices. With this swap there is no exchange of the commodities. This is analogous to a fixed/floating interest rate swap.

Example 10

An aluminium producer makes regular sales of aluminium and receives the market price for his sales of aluminium. He believes that the aluminium price is going to fall over the next 12 months and wishes to hedge against this risk. He therefore undertakes a swap to receive, from a swap counterparty, an agreed fixed aluminium price each month, based on an agreed quantity of aluminium. At the same time, he agrees to pay that counterparty each month the market price for aluminium, which is then current, based on the same quantity. He will continue to sell aluminium to his customers in the usual way, as the swap is a completely separate transaction from the underlying physical aluminium sales.

The net effect is that the producer will receive an approximately fixed price for his aluminium sales. The two swap parties will need to agree on an aluminium price index for the purpose of the swap settlements. This index will not necessarily be exactly the same as the price received by the producer from his customers from time to time, so that he will be left with a basis risk, but the two should move closely in line. The timing of the swap settlements might also not be exactly the same as for the physical sales, but again, the producer will be better protected than if he had not hedged at all.

* Aluminium price

A **commodity price-for-interest swap** is one whereby the value of a fixed amount of the specified commodity is exchanged for a floating-rate interest payment (usually related to ICE LIBOR) or a fixed-rate interest payment.

Commodity swaps can involve any commodity if a producer wishes to fix the net price he will receive over time, a user wishes to fix the net price he will pay over time, or a speculator wishes to take a view on the price over time. Some particular areas in which such swaps are transacted are:

- bullion swaps (gold, silver, platinum and palladium)
- energy swaps (crude oil, natural gas and gasoline).

6.10 Equity, Volatility, Variance and Dividend Swaps

Learning Objective

4.5.3   Analyse the key features, risk/reward trade-offs and investment applications of equity forwards, swaps and swaptions: volatility; bullet; variance

Equity swaps are swaps whose payments on one or both sides are linked to the performance of equities or an equity index. They are sometimes used to avoid withholding taxes, obtain leverage, or enjoy the returns from ownership without actually owning equity.

This type of swap allows an investor or fund manager to exchange the returns on an equity investment (an individual share, a basket or index) for a return on another non-equity or equity-based investment. Its returns are strictly based on the relative volatility of an individual share or index.

The simplest type of equity swap is a **bullet** swap in which all payments are made at maturity.

Example 11

Investor A swaps $10 million at ICE LIBOR + 0.05% (ICE LIBOR + 5 basis points) against the return of the Hang Seng index over six months. Investor A would receive from investor B any percentage increase in the Hang Seng applied to the $10 million notional (if the Hang Seng declined over the year, not only would investor A receive nothing from investor B, but investor A would have to pay investor B the value of the fall in the index, thus synthesising an actual investment in that index).

Let's assume that in six months' time ICE LIBOR is 5.5% and also assume a swap tenure of precisely 180 days. If that is the case, then the floating leg payer/equity receiver (investor A) would owe (5.5% + 0.05%) x $10,000,000 x 180/360 = $277,500 to the equity payer/floating leg receiver (investor B).

If over the same period the Hang Seng had risen from 23,100 to 25,250 or 9.3%, investor B would have to pay investor A 9.3% of $10 million = $930,000. But if over that same period the Hang Seng had fallen to 22,100 or by 4.3%, investor A will have to pay investor B a total of $707,500 ($430,000 due to the drop in the index and $277,500 for the ICE LIBOR leg of the swap).

A **variance swap** takes the concept of an equity swap beyond the movement in equity prices. A variance swap allows an investor to hedge or speculate on the future price movements of an underlying asset, which can be a currency, interest rate, commodity or index. In a variance swap, one side's payment will be linked to the realised variance – the price movements of the specific asset over the life of the swap. These prices are recorded on a daily basis, and are most commonly based on the asset's closing price. The other side of the swap will pay a fixed amount, which is agreed up-front.

The main attraction/advantage of a variance swap is that it provides pure exposure to the **volatility** of the underlying asset's price as opposed to straight call or put options, which may require delta hedging. It is for this reason that variance swaps are more widely used in the equity markets than volatility swaps. The profit/loss of a variance swap depends solely on the difference between implied and actual volatility.

A **dividend swap** is a swap that consists of a series of fixed payments, which might be based on current interest rates, while the other series of payments is based on the future dividend payments from an individual share, or group of shares or an equity index. Unlike other equity-related swaps, dividend swaps are based solely on the actual dividend payments, without taking into account the underlying share price or index's level.

The holder of the fixed leg will pay their counterparty a pre-designated fixed payment at each interval. The other party – the holder of the floating leg – will pay their counterparty the total dividends that were paid out by a selected underlying, which can be a single company, a basket of companies, or all the members of an index. The payments are multiplied by a notional number of shares, which is agreed when the swap is first entered into.

Like most swaps, the contract is usually arranged such that its value at signing is zero. This is accomplished by making the value of the fixed leg equal to the value of the floating leg – in other words, the fixed leg will be equal to the average expected dividends over the term of the swap. Therefore the fixed leg of the swap can be used to estimate market forecasts of the dividends that will be paid out by the underlying.

6.11 Property and Environmental Swaps

Learning Objective

4.5.4 Analyse the key features, risk/reward trade-offs and investment applications of environmental and property swaps

Environmental swaps (also known as 'Debt for Nature' swaps) are usually debt swaps, which allow the debtor country (usually a less developed country) to have the amount of its debt reduced by the amount that it spends on key environmental projects. These swaps can be structured on a bilateral or tripartite basis. In the bilateral type of swap, the borrower has its debt reduced directly by the creditor for the amount that has been spent on the pre-agreed environmental issue. In a tripartite-based swap, a third party, such as an international organisation, pays the creditor for the amount that the borrower has spent on the environmental project. One of the main purposes of this type of swap is to reduce the debt problems of poorer countries while promoting conservation/environmental issues.

Property swaps are a variation on a total return swap, where the return/payment of one side is linked to the returns (rental income and/or appreciation in value) of a specific property or group of properties or a development. In return, the buyer of the property return will pay a pre-agreed interest rate. While most property swaps are used by investors to gain exposure to the property sector without the cost of physically buying the properties, this type of swap has become popular as a way of making houses affordable in a rising property market.

6.12 Zero Coupon Inflation Products

A **zero coupon inflation product** is a standard derivative product based on an inflation rate. The underlying asset is a single price index (inflation measure) such as the CPI in the US or the RPI in the UK.

It is called a zero coupon product or swap because there is only one financial flow, at the end, without any intermediate coupon. At the maturity date there is a swap of a fixed amount against a floating amount.

This type of product allows market participants to:

- hedge against /speculate on future inflation fluctuations
- evaluate inflation linked securities, including asset swapping treasury inflation protected securities (TIPS) and other securities
- hedge against central bank credit tightening policies (due to the fact that central banks will tighten monetary policy to fight rising inflation).

7. Credit Derivatives

An area of derivative products that has grown significantly in recent years is that of credit derivatives. These are instruments whose value depends on agreed credit events relating to a third-party company, for example, a credit downgrading of that company, or an increase in that company's cost of funds in the market, or a default, or bankruptcy. The purpose of such derivatives is to enable an organisation to protect against unwanted credit exposure, by passing that exposure on to someone else. Credit derivatives can also be used to increase credit exposure, in return for income.

7.1 Credit Default Swaps (CDSs)

Learning Objective

4.6.1   Analyse the key features, risk/reward trade-offs and investment applications of credit default swaps: credit events: credit default swaps: basic, index and basket; credit-linked notes; agreements including compensation and settlement

In a credit default swap (CDS), the party buying the credit protection makes a periodic payment (or pays an up-front fee) to the other party. In return, it receives an agreed compensation if there is a credit event relating to some third party or parties.

Credit events are typically defined to include a material default, bankruptcy, significant fall in an asset's value or debt restructuring for a specified reference asset. If such a credit event occurs, the seller makes a predetermined payment to the buyer, and the swap then terminates.

What can be considered a credit event?

- **Default** – failure by the reference asset (assets) to make specific debt or other reference payments as defined in the default swap agreement (see below).
- **Significant fall in asset price/value** – most common in basket-based swaps, the swap contract will have a clearly defined valuation level for a specific or basket of assets. Once its/their value falls below this level, the buyer can trigger the swap payment agreement.

- **Bankruptcy** – once the reference asset files for, or is forced into, bankruptcy, most default swaps are automatically triggered for final payment.
- **Debt restructuring** – if the reference asset or its creditors initiate debt restructuring that will change the status or priority of the default swap buyer's asset, if included in the swap agreement, the buyer will receive payment.
- **Merger or demerger** – any change in the owner status or independence of the asset or company is considered a credit event, as is any significant change in the asset ownership structure.
- **Certain government actions**.

The definition of a credit event is determined in the **agreement** made between the counterparties to the transaction at the time of the trade. The agreement, which is usually based on the ISDA's Master Agreement, will also clearly define the responsibilities and process for notification of a credit event; this is normally done by the buyer or its agent. It also includes the details of the settlement procedures. This is, in effect, an option, and the periodic payments are effectively an option premium.

There are three types of credit default swaps:

- **Basic** – based on a specific asset as reference to the credit event. The reference asset is usually the asset or at least is the pricing guide to the obligation that can be delivered, if that is part of the swap agreement.
- **Index** – based on the movements of an index, either a debt-related or equity/market-based index; the buyer will most likely purchase protection if the underlying index falls below a certain level. This type of CDS is closely related to a total return swap (see the next section).
- **Basket** – based on the default of a basket of securities, such as a portfolio of several airline debts. The terms of this type of credit default swap could be based on the first to default, or any number within the basket to trigger the credit event. The number of securities in the basket can range from three to 20. The greater the number in the basket, the higher the initial premium, given the wider insurance provided.

If a default should occur, the agreed **compensation** is settled by a cash payment or physical delivery.

- **Cash settlement** – this is effected by paying a sum of money in compensation. This might, for example, be determined by the level at which a reference asset (such as a bond issued by the underlying third-party company) trades after the default.
- **Physical settlement** – this is where the buyer of the risk pays the full value of the principal against delivery of the defaulted asset. This could be a specific asset agreed in advance (reference asset or obligation) or any financial obligation of the given issuer, eg, a bond or a derivative contract.

Every credit default swap includes the trigger points and notification procedures, such as who has the right to do so, time limits and payment schedules. In most cases, the buyer has exclusive notification/ exercise rights, while some swaps have an automatic notification trigger, under certain predefined events. As with all other OTC products, these can be **customised** to meet the buyer's demands or the nature of reference asset or assets.

Most credit default swaps are priced using the **reduced-form pricing approach**, in which the credit event process is modelled directly into the swap's price based on the probability of the credit event occurring. The most widely used measure of the probability is what is known as the default swap or asset swap spread, which is the premium being paid to investors over ICE LIBOR or another reference rate to hold the asset. The ongoing premium payments made by the purchaser of the default swap are based on this spread, and most likely change on an ongoing basis over the duration of the swap.

Example 12 _____

ABC Bank has a portfolio of airline leases and is concerned that higher fuel prices will hurt airline profits. It buys a basket credit default swap that is based on a portfolio of aircraft leases for five airlines from a hedge fund. The terms of the basket swap define a trigger credit event when the second of the airlines applies to restructure their leases. When this occurs, ABC Bank notifies the hedge fund of the trigger; it receives the remaining payments due from all of the leases and the hedge fund now owns the leases and is directly exposed to the five airlines.

7.1.1 Credit-Linked Notes

A credit linked note (CLN) is a form of funded credit derivative. It is structured as a security, with an embedded credit default swap allowing the issuer to transfer a specific credit risk to credit investors. The issuer is not obligated to repay the debt if a specified event occurs. This eliminates a third-party insurance provider. Under this structure, the coupon or price of the note is linked to the performance of a reference asset. It offers borrowers a hedge against credit risk, and gives investors a higher yield on the note for accepting exposure to a specified credit event.

Example 13 _____

A bank lends money to a company, and at the time it issues a credit-linked note, which is bought by investors. The interest rate on the note is determined by the credit risk of the company. The funds the bank raises by issuing the note are invested in high-quality, low-risk bonds.

If the company remains solvent, the bank is obliged to pay the note in full. But, if the company goes bankrupt or is unable to repay the loan, the note-holders/investors become the company's creditors and take on the original loan. The bank in turn gets compensated by the returns on less-risky bond investments funded by issuing credit linked notes.

7.2 Credit Spreads

Learning Objective

4.6.2 Analyse the key features, risk/reward trade-offs and investment applications of credit default options; credit default obligation and synthetics

In a credit spread option, a credit spread is first defined as the difference between the yield on a particular asset (eg, the yield on a particular bond issued by a company) and some agreed benchmark (eg, a swap rate or government treasury bond yield for the same maturity as the bond).

A strike rate is then set for this spread. In the case of a put option, the option buyer then pays a premium up-front and receives any difference between the actual spread and the agreed strike if the spread rises above that strike.

Example 14

Bank A lends cash to Company XYZ for five years and then wishes to protect against the credit risk of Company XYZ. Bank A purchases a credit spread put option, where the credit spread is defined as the difference between the yield on a particular bond issued by company XYZ and the yield on a Treasury bond. If the spread rises above an agreed level (the strike), Bank A receives an agreed compensation from Bank B to offset the deterioration in its own asset (its loan to Company XYZ).

Credit spread options are designed to hedge against (for the buyer) or capitalise on (for the seller) changes in credit spreads, ie, differences in their respective yields. A reference security is selected and strike spread and maturity are set. The pay-off is based on whether the actual spot or market spread at the exercise date is over or under the spread on the reference security. The transaction may be either based on changes in a credit spread relative to a risk-free benchmark (eg, ICE LIBOR, gilts or US treasuries) or changes in the relative spread between two credit instruments.

Credit spread options may be structured as an American or European option.

The buyer of a credit spread option would be looking to protect, or hedge, against a widening of the spread between the two securities. If a fund manager holds a large position in a non-EU government debt, he might buy a credit spread option with EU government debt as a reference to protect the portfolio from a deterioration in the fund's holding debt's price in the short term, if elections are expected shortly.

Example 15

A fund manager had a €50 million position in a ten-year non-EU government bond that yields 7%. The manager is confident that the position has good long-term potential, but is concerned that the upcoming elections might cause short-term spreads to widen. Currently ten-year EU government debt is yielding 4.75%.

The fund manager can buy a three-month €50 million spread option on the 7% non-EU government debt versus a 4.75% EU government bond; the fund's bond is currently trading at a 2.25% spread to its EU benchmark.

The fund manager can lock in the 2.25% spread by buying the credit spread option. It is a European-style option. In three months' time, if the spread has widened beyond 2.25%, the fund will receive the equivalent payment that will effectively lock in that spread.

7.2.1 Option Adjusted Spreads

As we have discussed earlier, we know that any bond's yield is typically comprised of two components:

1. The risk-free return on a similar benchmark security, such as government bonds.
2. A premium above the yield on that benchmark security that compensates an investor for that specific bond's associated credit risk.

This premium is referred to as its yield spread or simply 'spread'. For bonds with embedded options (for example, callable or puttable bonds), this spread must be adjusted to account for the fact that the bond's embedded options may change the expected cash flows of this bond.

For example, if a bond is repaid before it matures, its interest payments cease and principal is returned earlier than the bond's maturity. This option-adjusted measure is referred to as **option adjusted spread (OAS).**

An OAS is the yield spread which has to be added to a benchmark yield curve to discount a security's payments to match its market price, using a dynamic pricing model that accounts for these embedded options.

The option adjusted spread helps investors compare a fixed-income security's cash flows to reference rates, while also valuing embedded options against general market volatility. By separately analysing the security's two components – the bond and the embedded option – analysts can determine whether the investment is worthwhile at a given price. The OAS method is more accurate than simply comparing a bond's yield to maturity to a benchmark.

The OAS takes into account two types of volatility facing fixed-income investments with embedded options: changing interest rates (which affect all bonds) and prepayment risk. The shortfall of this approach is that estimates are based off historical data, but are used in a forward-looking model. For example, prepayment is typically estimated from historical data, and does not take into account economic shifts or other changes that might occur in the future.

OAS's are model-dependent. This concept can be applied to a mortgage-backed security, or any other bond that has an embedded options (such as being callable or that allows for early repayment), or any other interest rate derivative or option

In the context of an MBS or callable bond, the option relates primarily to the borrower's right to refinance the debt at a lower interest rate. These securities must therefore pay higher yields than any non-callable debt, and their values are more fairly compared by OAS than by yield. OAS is usually measured in basis points (bp).

7.2.2   Credit Default Options and Other Instruments

A **credit default option** is an option or obligation to buy protection (payer option) or sell protection (receiver option) on a credit default swap based on a specific reference credit with a specific maturity. The option is usually a European-style option, meaning that it is exercisable only at one date in the future at a specific strike price defined as a coupon on the credit default swap.

Credit default options on single credits are extinguished upon default without any cash flows, other than the upfront premium paid by the buyer of the option. Therefore buying a payer option does not provide protection against an actual default, but only against an increase in the credit spread (higher interest rate/lower price for that single credit). This may explain why these options are very illiquid and therefore less popular. Another key feature is that their prices are usually based on very high implied volatilities. A put option that makes a pay-off if the issuer of a specified reference asset defaults is called a default option.

Collateralised debt obligations (CDOs) are a type of structured asset-backed security (ABS) whose value and payments are derived from a portfolio of fixed-income underlying assets. CDOs' securities are split into different risk classes, or tranches, where 'senior' tranches are considered the safest securities. The interest and principal payments are made based on seniority, therefore the junior tranches pay a higher coupon payment (and interest rate) and are quoted at lower prices to compensate for their higher default risk.

A few analysts and investors are concerned that CDOs, other ABSs and other derivatives spread risk and uncertainty about the value of the underlying assets more widely, rather than reducing risk through diversification. The onset of the 2007/08 credit crunch gave substantial support to this point of view. In fact, before the credit crunch, all of the credit rating agencies failed to adequately account for these large risks (this can be seen in the case of the nationwide collapse of housing values) when rating CDOs and other ABSs.

CDOs vary in structure and underlying assets, but the basic principle is the same. To create a CDO, a corporate entity is constructed to hold assets as collateral and to sell the packages of cash flows to investors.

The following is an example of how a typical CDO is constructed. A special purpose entity (SPE, more commonly referred to as a special purpose vehicle or SPV in European markets) acquires a portfolio of underlying assets. Common examples of the types of these underlying assets include mortgage-backed securities, commercial real estate bonds and/or corporate loans. The SPE then issues bonds (CDOs) with different tranches, and the proceeds are used to purchase the portfolio of underlying assets. The senior CDOs, since they pay a higher price, are paid from the cash flows from the underlying assets before the junior securities and equity securities. Losses are first borne by the equity securities, next by the junior securities, and finally by the senior securities.

The risk and return for a CDO investor depends directly on how the CDO and its tranches are defined, and only indirectly on the performance of the underlying assets. In particular, the investment depends on the assumptions and methods used to define the risk and return of the tranches. CDOs, like all other asset-backed securities, allow the originators of the underlying assets to pass credit risk to another institution or to individual investors. Thus investors must understand how the risk for CDOs is calculated. The issuer of the CDO, typically an investment bank, earns a commission at time of issue and earns management fees during the life of the CDO.

A **collateralised bond obligation (CBO)** is a derivative security that creates an investment-grade bond from a pool of junk bonds (high-risk). These junk bonds are typically not investment grade, but, because a CBO includes a pool of several types of credit-quality bonds together, they offer enough diversification to be considered 'investment grade'.

In other words, a CBO is a type of asset-backed security that is composed of the receivables/payments from junk bonds. Issuers of CBOs package and sell their receivables on bonds they own to investors in order to reduce their default risk. Returns on CBOs are considered to be a lower risk than the individual bonds backing them. This is based on the view that it is unlikely that all or even most of the junk bonds will default. They are similar in structure to a **collateralised mortgage obligation (CMO)**, but different in that CBOs represent different levels of credit risk, not different maturities.

A **synthetic CDO** is a form of collateralised debt obligation (CDO) that invests in **credit default swaps (CDSs)** or other non-cash assets to gain exposure to a portfolio of fixed-income assets, as opposed to a basic (or cash flow) CDO which is backed by a portfolio of underlying assets. As with basic CDOs, synthetic CDOs are typically divided into credit tranches based on the level of credit risk assumed. Initial investments into the CDO are made by the lower tranches, while the senior tranches may not have to make an initial investment.

All tranches will receive periodic payments based on the cash flows from the credit default swaps. If a credit event occurs in the fixed income portfolio, the synthetic CDO and its investors become responsible for the losses, starting from the lowest-rated tranches and working up. Synthetic CDOs can offer extremely high yields to investors. However, investors can also be responsible for much more than their initial investments if several credit events occur in the reference portfolio.

Synthetic CDOs were first created in the late 1990s as a way for large holders of commercial loans to protect their balance sheets without actually selling the loans and potentially harming client relationships. They have become increasingly popular because they tend to have shorter life spans than cash flow CDOs.

8. OTC Options

As seen earlier, an option is defined as a contract whereby one party has the right to complete a transaction in the future (at a previously agreed amount, date and price) if he so chooses, but is not obliged to do so. This party is known as the buyer of the option, or option holder. The counterparty, the option seller or writer, has no choice, therefore he must complete the transaction if the first party wishes, but he cannot do so otherwise.

For the **buyer**, an option is, therefore, similar to a forward deal, with the difference that he can subsequently decide whether or not to exercise or complete the transaction.

For the **seller**, it is similar to a forward deal with the difference that he does not know whether or not he will be required to fulfil his obligations. Clearly, the contract will be delivered only if it is advantageous to the option buyer.

In return for this flexibility awarded to the option buyer, he must pay an up-front premium to compensate the option seller for the latter's additional risk.

As with other derivative contracts, such as forwards, options can be used to hedge an existing position or future commitment, as well as for speculation.

8.1 OTC Options Products

Learning Objective

4.7.1 Analyse the key features, risk/reward trade-offs and investment applications of OTC option products: main types: European, American, Bermudan, Asian; key differences between exchange-traded and OTC instruments; exotics: Asian, lookbacks and variants, ratchets/cliquets; clearing, settlement and delta-based collateral

4.7.2 Understand the purpose, requirements of and process of premium payment: when paid; credit exposure; the collateral process

The three most popular exercise styles of options that are available are:

- European
- American, and
- Bermudan.

With a **European** option, the holder can exercise the option only on the expiry date. With a three-month option, for example, he can choose only at the end of three months whether or not to exercise.

An **American** option, however, allows the holder to choose to exercise at any time between the purchase of the option and expiry. The premium is normally higher for American options, if all other specifications of the option are the same.

European and American options are both available everywhere; the terms are technical, not geographical.

Bermudan options lie between European and American (as Bermuda lies between Europe and America). A Bermudan option can be exercised on any of various specified dates between original purchase of the option and expiry. Bermudan style is also occasionally known as **mid-Atlantic** or **pseudo-American style**.

With both American and Bermudan options, it is possible for the option to allow for partial exercise on a number of occasions within the total amount of the option.

Here are some more exotic OTC options structures:

An **Asian** option (or average rate or average price option) is a cash-settled OTC option that pays the difference between the average rate of the underlying (calculated on predetermined fixings of an agreed reference rate) and its price at expiration.

The volatility of an averaged rate is lower than the volatility of the rates from which the average is calculated, and so average rate options are cheaper than standard European options.

An **average strike option** is one whose strike price is set at the expiration date to be the average rate of the underlying over the life of the option. This is compared with its final value at expiry. The option can be exercised for physical delivery, or cash settled against the underlying price at maturity.

As with an average rate option, average strike options are cheaper than standard European options.

A **cliquet** or **ratchet** option is a series of at-the-money options, with periodic settlement, resetting the strike value to the price level at that time. The option locks in the difference between the old and new strike and pays it out as profit. The profit can be accumulated until final maturity, or paid out at each reset date.

A **lookback** option is a call or put option whose strike price is not determined until the option is exercised. At the time of exercise, the holder can exercise the option at any underlying price that has occurred during the option's life. In the case of a call, the buyer will choose the lowest price, and in the case of a put, the buyer will choose the highest price. The premium on such options tends to be high since it gives the buyer great flexibility, and the writer has to take on a lot of risk.

The two most widely used and accepted models for option pricing are the Black-Scholes and Binomial models. The key factors that both use in calculating an option's premium are:

- strike price
- underlying asset's price
- time to expiration
- underlying asset's volatility
- risk-free interest rate.

An option's premium rises:

- as its time until expiration increases
- as the volatility of the underlying asset rises
- the greater its intrinsic value (ie, for calls: the lower the strike price versus the asset's current market price and for puts: the higher the strike price versus the asset's current market price).

The following, known as the **greeks**, are measures of the changes in an option's premium over its life:

- **Delta** is the ratio comparing the change in the price of the underlying asset to the corresponding change in the option's price or value. It is sometimes referred to as the hedge ratio. The closer an option is to being in-the-money, the closer delta is to 1. Delta has a range of zero to one. Delta reflects the change in value of option position/change in value of the underlying. Note that, while delta for calls is positive, it is negative for puts.

Example 16

A call on BP shares has a delta of 0.6; if BP shares fall by 50p in a trading day, the corresponding call will lose 30p from its premium/value, owing to the fall in the underlying shares.

Example 17

A EUR put/USD call with a delta of −0.3 will see its value rise as the EUR falls. Therefore, if EUR/USD falls by 0.5% in a day, the put's value will rise by 0.15% due to the movement in the spot rate.

- **Gamma** is the rate of change for delta with respect to the underlying asset's price. Mathematically, gamma is the first derivative of delta and is used when trying to gauge the price of an option relative to the amount by which it is in- or out-of-the-money. When an option being measured is deep in- or out-of-the-money, gamma is small. When the option is near-the-money, gamma is largest. Gamma is most extreme for short-dated (those close to expiration), near-the-money options. Gamma reflects the change in delta of option position/change in value of the underlying.
- **Vega** is the change in an option's value for a 1% change in implied volatility. Vega is positive for long call and put positions. It is also greatest for longer and at-the-money options.
- **Theta** is a measure of the rate of decline in the value of an option due to the passage of time. Theta can also be referred to as a measure of the time decay on the value of an option. If everything is held constant, then the option will lose value as time moves closer to the maturity of the option. The measure of theta quantifies the risk that time imposes on options, as options are only exercisable for a certain period of time.

For more on this subject, see Chapter 3, Sections 6.3 and 6.4.

While OTC options lack the central clearing house and settlement/payment process that exchange-traded options have, the market does have a standard procedure for premium payments. The general rule is that the buyer will pay the premium on either the next business day or T+2 at the latest (the latter being the general rule for OTC FX options). The OTC market is now developing Clearing House structures and capabilities under EMIR.

Since the sole credit risk exists for the option holder/buyer, in certain cases banks/brokers who have purchased options from clients may require collateral payments as the option moves closer in-the-money (its value increases). An accepted benchmark for these payments is related to the option's delta.

8.2   FLEX Options

Learning Objective

4.7.3   Understand the purposes, key features and risk/reward trade-offs of flexible exchange (FLEX) options, including how they differ from standard exchange-traded and OTC options

---

FLexible EXchange (FLEX) options combine the benefits of customisation of an OTC product with the advantages of being listed on an exchange. FLEX options allow investors to customise key contract terms, including expiration date, exercise style and exercise price, and to take advantage of expanded position limits. See also Chapter 1, Section 3.6.

FLEX options differ from standard exchange-traded options since they offer a wide degree of flexibility. FLEX options, unlike ETD options, do not have standardised strike prices, expiration dates or contract sizes.

While they provide the same degree of choice, FLEX options do not have the same credit/counterparty risk associated with other OTC options. Since they are listed on an exchange, they have the same clearing house protection as any other ETD product.

9.   Structured Products

Learning Objective

4.8.1   Understand the purpose of structured products and how they utilise embedded derivatives to achieve a specific risk/return profile: callable and puttable bonds; convertible bonds; index-linked notes; capital protected products

Options are written on a vast range of underlying instruments, including bonds. A straightforward bond option is thus a call or put on a particular bond. For example, a fund manager or bond dealer might use a call or a put to take a view on a bond, in the same way as he might by buying or selling the bond in the cash market.

A **callable bond** is a bond with a call option embedded in it. The call can be exercised by the issuer of the bond which, under certain circumstances defined for that particular bond – for example on certain dates (such as coupon dates) and at a certain strike price (often higher than par) – allows the issuer to buy back the bond. This in effect allows the issuer to redeem the bond early, which he might do if interest rates fall so that he can issue a new bond instead, to finance himself more cheaply.

A **puttable bond** is a bond with a put option embedded in it. The put can be exercised by the holder of the bond, again under certain circumstances defined for that particular bond – on certain dates, and at a certain strike price (often lower than par). This, in effect, allows the holder to insist on early redemption of the bond, which he might do if interest rates rise so that he can buy a new bond at a higher yield.

A **convertible bond** is a bond with an option exercisable by the bondholder to convert the bond into something else, usually equity in the issuing company. Again, there would be conditions attached: certain dates on which this would be exercisable and a fixed number of shares for a given face value of the bond. The holder will exercise this right if the shares become sufficiently valuable.

Example 18

ABC plc requires £15 million in ten-year funding for an expansion project. It has decided to raise this amount by issuing a convertible bond. In doing so, it can reduce the yield required by investors, owing to the fact that the bond will include an option or warrant that will allow the bondholders to covert the bond into ABC's shares at a pre-defined price. It also avoids having to issue new shares and diluting current shareholders' stake in the company.

Today ABC's shares are trading at 105p, and ten-year bond yields on corporate bonds of similar credit standing are 4.9% (which is 25bp above the ten-year UK government bond).

ABC's convertible bond will have a 4.75% yield along with a conversion clause that allows bondholders to convert this bond into the equivalent amount of ABC shares at a conversion rate of 130p, after five years.

The net result is that the company is able to save 15bp on its interest payments, whilst bondholders are able to profit if the company is successful and its share price rises.

When valuing convertible, callable and putable bonds you must remember that you must value both the bond itself and its embedded option or warrant, in most cases, a call, in that it allows the bondholder to exchange the bond for the company's shares or demand repayment before its maturity, while a put allows the borrower to repay the bond early. How this can be valued is discussed in Section 7.2.1 of this chapter.

An **index-linked note** is an instrument whose return is determined by a specific index. This index could be an equity index, which can be based on the performance of a single share, or a basket of shares, or a market index, such as the FTSE 100 or S&P 500 index or, for a bond/debt instrument, an inflation index such as CPI (consumer prices index) or RPI (retail prices index). For example, for UK-issued index-linked gilts in 1981, both the semi-annual coupon payments and their redemption value were linked to the UK retail prices index.

An **equity-linked note** is a debt instrument whose yield is determined by the performance of an equity product. A company might link the return of its debt to the performance of its share price as a method of lowering the base interest rate.

A **capital protected product** (which is also known as a **capital protected borrowing**) is generally associated with the purchase and holding of shares or other financial securities, such as single warrants. This type of financial product allows an investor to borrow money or obtain credit to purchase shares or other types of financial securities. These shares and financial securities purchased then become security for the loan. Under the terms of the financial product, if the shares or financial securities fall in value below their purchase price the purchaser can transfer the shares or securities back (a put option), or surrender them to the lender to meet all outstanding obligations under the loan (a limited recourse loan). Therefore, the purchaser/investor is guaranteed a minimum price/value for the shares/securities that are part of the capital protected product. In effect, it is a loan with an embedded put option for the financed securities.

Capital protected loans, generally, have higher interest rates and/or additional fees.

Capital protected borrowings include arrangements where an investor uses shares or other financial securities as security for borrowing money or obtaining credit, and those shares or other financial securities are protected from a fall in their value.

10.   Master Agreements

Learning Objective

4.9.1   Understand the potential impact of credit exposures on OTC positions and the documentation designed to protect against counterparty risk: purposes and protocols of ISDA documentation; master agreement including main areas of content; confirmation; credit support annex documentation

The recognition by swap participants of the need for a means to reduce potential disagreements by developing standardised documentation was instrumental in the International Swaps and Derivatives Association (ISDA) becoming chartered in 1985.

Generally, the aims of the ISDA documentation are to:

- provide standard market terms to encourage growth and confidence in OTC products
- minimise the administration needed to support transactions
- help to facilitate cross-border trading.

10.1   ISDA Master Agreements

A **master agreement** provides a single umbrella framework within which all relevant OTC deals between two parties can be transacted. A key advantage of this is that all individual transactions can be brought together to form part of the master agreement. This means that, in the event of a counterparty becoming insolvent or going into default, it is possible to close-out all transactions covered by the master agreement rather than relying on cross-default or other provisions to close-out transactions individually.

Once the master agreement is in place, each deal still needs to be confirmed in the usual way. It is not necessary to repeat the legal terms and conditions when confirming each transaction, as these have already been covered in the master agreement. Most importantly, the master agreement allows for all the deals to be netted in the event of a default, rather than considered separately. This is important to provide protection for the non-defaulting party against selective default and termination.

The master agreement is negotiated between the two parties on the basis of a standard printed contract, and is legally binding once signed by both parties. It provides mutual protection for both parties. No specific references are made in the agreement to individual transaction terms. To enable a degree of flexibility, there is a schedule to the master agreement to allow for specific provisions to be determined by the counterparties.

The most important of the issues dealt with by the master agreement are:

- **termination events**, ie, generally external circumstances outside the control of the parties, eg, changes in tax law or illegality, which can allow deals to be terminated early by one of the parties affected

- **events of default**, ie, events which are generally the fault of one of the two parties, eg, failing to pay an amount due or bankruptcy, which can allow all outstanding deals to be terminated early by the other party
- **netting** (important for credit risk and, as explained in Chapter 10 on finance and regulatory issues, for capital adequacy purposes). The master agreement covers two types of netting:
  - ○ **payment netting** (netting of amounts due in the same currency on the same day in the ordinary course of business), and
  - ○ **close-out netting** (netting of all amounts due between the parties upon early termination by valuing all transactions and converting amounts due to a single termination currency for settlement). This is a key part of the documentation. When negotiating documentation with a counterparty, it is vital to ensure that close-out netting will in fact be supported by the courts. In some legal jurisdictions, this is not necessarily the case. Banks must, therefore, seek legal opinions from all relevant jurisdictions when negotiating.

The specific terms of each deal are set out in a supplement to the master agreement, called a **confirmation**. Each confirmation refers to the master agreement and is governed by the terms agreed between the parties in that contract. This enables the confirmation to be considerably shorter than it otherwise would have been. If there is a conflict between something contained in the confirmation and the master agreement, the confirmation takes precedence for that deal.

If a master agreement has not yet been agreed and signed between the parties, the general terms of the published contract (ie, without any variations as may be agreed in the schedule) apply. This will generally protect both parties as to how their rights and obligations will be legally interpreted. There is some risk, however, that in the event of default this interpretation may depend on the legal jurisdiction of each party. It is, therefore, best practice to have the master agreement negotiated and signed between the parties as quickly as possible.

10.2 Credit Support Annex (CSA)

In response to the growing concern over the counterparty credit risk associated with longer-term OTC derivative contracts, ISDA has included as part of its documentation procedures that allow counterparties to periodically reduce this exposure by including a **Credit Support Annex (CSA)** as part of an ISDA agreement.

For example, Company A enters into a ten-year interest rate swap, as a fixed-rate payer, with one of its main banks. As market rates fall, in favour of the bank and against Company A, the **mark-to-market** profit on the swap represents a loss to Company A and a profit for the bank. This in turn increases the bank's risk exposure to the company, since it has a loss on this swap position. One way that the bank can reduce its risk exposure created by the swap is to enter into a Credit Support Annex (CSA) or Collateral Support Document (CSD), which contains the details of the conditions and procedures by which collateralisation will occur.

A Credit Support Annex is a legal document that regulates and defines the criteria for collateral payments (credit support) for OTC derivative transactions. It is one of the four parts of an ISDA contract. A CSA defines the rules and conditions under which collateral is transferred between the counterparties to the derivative contract. Its main aim is to mitigate the credit risk arising from the **out of-the money** or mark-to-market loss of a derivatives position.

The CSA defines the procedures/rules by which a swap or other longer-term OTC derivative transaction is marked-to-market and the credit support (collateral) is paid. This credit exposure develops from the unrealised loss (out-of-the-money) position that one counterparty holds, based on current market prices.

The CSA defines the timing (how often), the minimum transfer allowed and the type of collateral accepted for these transfers. All CSAs require an ISDA agreement to be in place.

In addition to setting the timing of the MTM, the CSA will also include key procedural details such as setting:

- the **threshold amounts** – which is the unsecured credit exposure that one counterparty is prepared to accept before making a collateral request; this is usually set at a relatively low level, in order to reduce credit risk
- **minimum transfer amounts** – the minimum amount of a collateral request; any collateral transfer below this amount is not permitted; it is designed to prevent frequent and unnecessary calls of collateral, as well as avoid the costs involved with small transfer payments
- the valuation percentage or **haircut** – the discount that is applied to the collateral's market value; this protects the collateral receiver from falls in the collateral's value in the period between collateral calls; the higher the quality of the collateral, the lower the haircut.

The **Collateral Support Document (CSD)** is very similar to a CSA, in that it contains the timing and procedure for the mark-to-market (MTM) of the contract. Once the new valuation has been agreed, the counterparty with the negative MTM valuation will transfer the change in value to the counterparty with the positive MTM.

10.3 Protocols

A protocol is the term used to describe the set of documents, such as master agreements, that are widely used by market participants that define the procedures associated with specific financial transactions and the responsibilities of each counterparty.

They are useful, in that these agreements set out all of the legal requirements and are regularly updated, when necessary. For example, the ISDA set out several protocols after the euro was introduced, to ensure an easy transition for those existing transactions such as currency swaps that were originally denominated in euro members' old national currencies, so that euro-based settlement could take place.

These protocols cover a wide range of transactions. The use of these is not restricted to the ISDA. The Federal Reserve has also issued these, when required.

There are protocols that define the most basic aspects, such as the particular nature of a swap. The specific definition of each type of swap can be found earlier in this chapter.

11. Collateral Management

Learning Objective

4.10.1   Understand the purpose and application of collateral management: quality of collateral: volatility, creditworthiness, liquidity; acceptable types of cash and non-cash collateral; credit lines; valuation and pricing; thresholds and haircuts; delivery, return and minimum transfer amount (MTA)

Collateral is something of value. The main types of collateral that are accepted include cash, bank guarantees, certificates of deposit, government bonds or negotiable (ie, tradeable) securities, such as equities with special agreement since they are not accepted by several major exchanges.

Collateral is held against the risk of default by a counterparty. It is important that the collateral is an asset that is easy to liquidate in the case of default.

Collateral management is the process that allows market participants to reduce the counterparty credit exposure that arises from longer-maturity OTC derivative contracts, such as swaps and options.

If a bank considers that the credit risk incurred by trading with a particular counterparty is too great, or has already reached the credit limit in place, then it may ask for collateral from the counterparty in order to continue trading with it.

Cover for initial margin can be also provided using collateral rather than cash.

A bank ensures that it has the most up-to-date and accurate measure of its **credit exposure** to a counterparty by ensuring that its operations area processes all **deal tickets** and **term sheets** (a non-binding agreement which sets out the basic terms and conditions under which an investment or trade will be made; a term sheet is usually used as a template to develop a more detailed legal document) on a timely basis.

The bank assesses the size of the risk it is taking in making the transaction and requires that the counterparty places with it collateral to that value, either at the same time as dealing or beforehand. Typically, the arrangement will allow for the bank to ask for more collateral subsequently (this is known as the **delivery amount**) if the value of the existing trade or collateral falls during the life of the deal. It might also return some collateral if the value of either the collateral or the trade rises; this is known as the **return amount**.

The amount associated with either normally has a pre-agreed minimum, the **minimum transfer amount**. This is useful in reducing the cost and number of transfer payments between the bank and its counterparty during the contract's existence.

The bank ensures that the amount of collateral reflects both the current risk associated with the counterparty's possible default to the transaction, and the current value of the collateral it holds by having its operations area conduct regular **mark-to-market valuations** of both the transaction and the collateral it currently holds. This enables the bank to manage its exposure to the counterparty, since the counterparty's potential loss is the cost that the bank would incur if the counterparty defaulted and it had to close out the transaction in the market. This will ensure that, at any given time, the bank has the amount of risk collateral required; this is referred to as the **threshold amount** for the transaction.

If either the risk increases and/or the value of the collateral falls, the counterparty will be required to deposit more collateral with the bank. As an extra insurance, most banks will require more collateral than the current risk requires to ensure that they are fully covered at all times. This practice is similar to the amount of margin that exchanges require. For example, suppose that a bank transacts a straightforward interest rate swap with a counterparty, whereby the bank is paying fixed and receiving floating. At the time of the transaction, there is no immediate credit risk. This is the same as saying that the mark-to-market value of the swap at that moment is zero – the threshold amount. Ignoring transaction and legal costs, if the counterparty were to go bankrupt immediately, the bank could instantly replace the transaction by an identical transaction with another counterparty.

However, if the market moves so that swap fixed interest rates rise slightly, the bank could only replace the transaction at a slight loss if the counterparty defaulted. At this point, if the bank has an arrangement in place to do so, it can ask the counterparty to transfer some collateral to it – the **delivery amount**. Depending on the agreement with the counterparty, this will be a specified percentage of the potential loss, the maximum percentage being 100% of the loss. Any collateral called by a bank would normally be held in a third party account and not the company's own account. This is to protect the depositing counterparty's assets from being used to meet any liabilities of the holding bank (eg, in the case of bankruptcy). If the counterparty then goes bankrupt, the bank can try to use this collateral to offset the loss. In practice, the extent to which it can do so depends on the documentation governing the transaction and the collateral (this is known as the **dispute resolution clauses**), the law governing each, and the legal jurisdiction of each of the two parties. The bank is nevertheless generally in a stronger position than it would be without the collateral.

Collateral of this nature is often called margin, and asking for collateral, or more collateral, is **making a margin call**. It may be that the bank subtracts or assigns a reduced value to the collateral's market value. This is known as a **haircut**. The size of the haircut reflects the bank's perceived risk of holding the specific asset. In other words, it is applied to protect against any potential movements in the market and potential changes in the collateral's value which might arise before there is time for extra collateral to be transferred from the counterparty. The size of this haircut is directly related to the minimum threshold amount and the price volatility of the collateral.

Depending on the transaction's agreement, collateral or a margin might be called for by either party (ie, by whichever party is currently in mark-to-market profit from whichever party is currently in loss) or by the higher credit-rated party. The agreement may be that margin calls can be made daily, weekly or monthly, or only at the time of an event such as an interest settlement.

The quality of collateral varies. The best is cash in the currency of the risk, which will not vary in value. The next best is generally a government security in that currency; although the value of it will vary with the market, thereby requiring margin calls to be made, there is generally no significant credit risk.

It is important to note that it is the bank's/broker's decision as to what types of securities are acceptable as collateral. Their relationship with the client and the specific regulatory rules they are subject to are major factors. Also, the types of acceptable collateral vary among different clearing houses. Generally speaking, lower-quality assets, such as junk bonds and illiquid shares/equities, are not acceptable forms of collateral.

In general, the issues to be considered regarding the quality of collateral are the volatility in its value, its creditworthiness, and its liquidity (ie, the ease with which it can be sold if necessary in the event of a counterparty default).

Swaps are sometimes transacted on the basis of mutual collateralisation. This involves both counterparties depositing collateral at the start of the transaction. A party is then obliged to add further collateral subsequently, either because of an increasing loss, or because its credit rating falls.

There must be a benchmark pricing source agreed for marking the transaction to market. For convenience, this benchmark might be an exchange-traded price or accepted market published price, such as LIBOR. For example, a swap involving an equity index might use the closing futures market price for the index.

In summary, management of collateral requires that the bank does the following:

- marks the transaction to market on a regular basis
- monitors the value of the collateral (if necessary, converted to the same currency as the mark-to-market value of the transaction)
- makes margin calls and returns as appropriate
- checks that margin calls have been received
- makes transfers to the counterparty in response to any margin calls it makes against the bank
- pays interest on any cash collateral according to whatever has been agreed.

12. Trade Processing Services

Learning Objective

4.11.1 Understand the key features of the main platforms and mechanisms used for trading and settling OTC derivatives: Bclear, SwapClear; MarkitSERV; SwiftNet FpML; TriOptima; ICE LINK; AffirmXpress

With more and more funds including hedge funds using OTC derivatives and in Europe with the support of the UCITS III Directive expanding the range of permissible investments to include derivative instruments, the use of OTC derivatives has become widespread.

Since these instruments are relatively complex, this has increased the importance of having an efficient operational infrastructure that allows market participants to effectively monitor their position and manage their risk.

Regulators are greatly concerned about the operational as well as the legal, regulatory and financial risks posed by the growing use and complexity of OTC derivatives. This was highlighted during the credit crunch and was focused upon with great interest by regulators subsequently. There is therefore a great deal of scope to apply superior electronic processing and confirmation processes to improve the post-trade and downstream processes attached to OTC derivative instruments.

For example, the very large global custodian banks whose clients include both traditional and hedge fund managers are institutions that are very exposed to operational risks in this field. Therefore they are now leading efforts to improve the processing, servicing and valuation of OTC derivatives of all kinds. They, together with investment banks, have embarked upon building derivative-processing platforms.

The original systems were built by the prime brokerage arms of the investment banks in order to help them structure transactions for hedge funds. Such platforms invariably contain detailed information about the components of various instruments, but there was plenty of scope for enhanced functionality. They were not always designed to handle the trade capture and asset-servicing challenges set by today's more complex OTC derivative instruments, the prime area of concern being valuation and risk management.

OTC derivatives range from simple futures and vanilla swaps to credit default swaps and synthetics. The developing of a range of systems that is able to manage the specific risks associated with each, as well as being tailored to fit each organisation's dealing and client-servicing structure, is a significant challenge.

Many specialist trade confirmation services such as the Depository Trust and Clearing Corporation's DTCC Deriv/SERV and others have been adopted throughout the industry, and there is a great deal of potential amongst both the financial and commodity OTC derivative arenas for ongoing systems improvement. In parallel with this chapter, the development of standard ISDA documentation with their master agreements and term sheets will lead to the requirement to review every element of documentation for every derivative transaction by both client and counterparties.

The derivative markets have seen a significant increase in both trading volumes and the number of different types of products traded. One of the key developments that has helped volumes increase, whilst limiting costs and making deal processing more efficient, is electronic processing. This covers a wide range of electronic trading platforms to a number of electronic processing and clearing services. Some electronic processing platforms have direct links with a number of trading platforms, which allows trade execution direct feeds to straight-through processing (STP) tools.

The following are brief descriptions of the better-known electronic services that are currently available in the derivatives market.

12.1 MarkitSERV

MarkitSERV is a new company that combines Markit's (Markit Wire) and the Depository Trust & Clearing Corporation's (DTCC) electronic trade confirmation and workflow platforms that will provide a single gateway for OTC derivative trade processing. The strategic partnership was first announced in July 2008 and received regulatory approval in September 2009 from the UK Financial Services Authority (FSA) and the US Department of Justice.

Jointly owned by DTCC and Markit, MarkitSERV combines the DTCC Deriv/SERV and Markit Wire trade confirmation platforms to cover all major asset classes including credit, interest rate, equity and commodity derivatives. It will connect multiple market participants and execution venues to downstream processing platforms such as DTCC's Trade Information Warehouse for credit default swaps (CDSs). It will also connect to various central counterparty platforms for interest rate swaps and CDSs, in collaboration with the DTCC Trade Information Warehouse (TIW).

MarkitSERV also connects dealers and their clients to central clearing counterparties (CCPs), trade repositories and third-party administrators. MarkitSERV also connects dealers and buy-side institutions to central clearing counterparties, trade repositories and electronic swap markets.

MarkitSERV's main aim is to increase greater co-operation within the industry over infrastructure to accelerate the adoption of electronic trade confirmation and reduce risk in the OTC derivative markets.

12.2 SwapClear

SwapClear was launched in September 1999 to provide clearing for basic interest rate swaps and was the first service designed by LCH.Clearnet to meet the needs of the OTC derivatives market. In clearing swaps, LCH.Clearnet becomes the central counterparty to each half of the OTC trade.

In effect, SwapClear provides the clearing house function to the OTC derivatives markets. It offers the interbank swap market a facility to free-up credit lines, reduce risk and use capital. SwapClear also gives banks the ability to net multiple OTC swaps in an efficient multilateral agreement, as LCH.Clearnet becomes the central counterparty.

SwapClear is not an STP processing system. Before a swap is registered with SwapClear, the bank must have already confirmed and processed the swap with its original counterparty. The benefits of the system are realised after the swap has been received, since SwapClear provides an automated facility that marks-to-market swaps and collateral, and allows for net payment of margin requirements per currency.

The service is for clearing members of SwapClear. If one of the original parties is not a clearing member, then the chain is longer. For example, if neither party is a clearing member, each original contract is replaced by two new contracts: one between that original party and a clearing member, and another between the clearing member and LCH.Clearnet. The clearing member takes collateral from the non-clearing dealer on whose behalf it has cleared, in the same way that LCH.Clearnet has taken margin from the clearing member.

To be a SwapClear clearing member (SCM), an organisation must:

* be an LCH.Clearnet shareholder
* contribute to LCH.Clearnet's default fund
* meet minimum resource requirements
* make regular financial reports to LCH.Clearnet
* maintain adequate systems and records, and employ operations staff with adequate expertise in swaps.

To be a SwapClear dealer, other than a clearing member, an organisation must:

* be a principal in wholesale market transactions

- be a SWIFT user
- have (or be a fully guaranteed subsidiary of an entity that has) a credit rating of BBB or better.

Both counterparties to a swap transaction must be SwapClear dealers for the transaction to be registered through SwapClear.

Confirmations between the two parties are matched through Accord (SWIFT's own confirmation matching system) or another compatible matching system. Once both parties have agreed the transaction and agreed to clear it through SwapClear, the details are submitted to LCH.Clearnet via SWIFT. LCH.Clearnet will only accept confirmed transactions, which encourages the use of automatic matching facilities.

The products cleared through SwapClear include a wide range of swaps and FRAs:

- Interest rate and zero coupon, single currency basis, compounding swaps:
  - EUR, USD and GBP swaps up to 50 years
  - AUD, CAD, CHF, JPY, SEK up to 30 years
  - CZK, DKK, HKD, HUF, NOK, NZD, PLN, SGD and ZAR up to 20 years.
- Overnight interest rate swap – CHF, EUR, USD and GBP up to two years.
- Variable notional swaps – EUR, USD and GBP swaps up to 50 years.

The benefits of SwapClear are:

- a reduction in credit risk through effective multilateral netting and margining of exposures, freeing up bank credit lines for further business
- a reduction in regulatory capital requirements through the Capital Requirements Directive (CRD) Annex II exemption, removing the need for banks to calculate counterparty risk requirements
- initial margin offsets between swaps and interest rate and government bond futures and options positions traded on ICE
- a reduction of operational risk through the centralisation and standardisation of processes providing post-trade straight-through processing
- a reduction in operational and administrative costs.

12.3   The Depository Trust & Clearing Corporation (DTCC)

The DTCC (Depository Trust & Clearing Corporation) provides a matching service (**Deriv/SERV**) for OTC derivatives, which is used in post-trade processing. The service requires mainframe-to-mainframe connections between the DTCC and each firm.

Deriv/SERV is a global service offering focused on automating the entire life cycle of OTC derivatives. This includes front-office trade affirmation, automated confirmation and matching, payment processing, and a trade warehouse. The service offered includes:

- **Omgeo, OASYS –** is a screen affirmation platform that allows traders and front-office staff to affirm credit derivative trades from multiple inter-dealer brokers (IDBs) at the point of trade. The platform allows immediate trade affirmation of brokered transactions. It also supports credit derivatives, including single-name and index credit default swaps (CDSs), and tranched index swaps.

- **Omgeo Central Trade Manager (Omgeo CTM)** – provides a platform for the central matching of cross-border and domestic transactions automating the trade confirmation process across several asset classes, such as equities, fixed income, repurchase agreements (repos), exchange traded derivatives and synthetic equity swaps.
- **Matching and confirmation** – Deriv/SERV provides automated matching and confirmation for OTC derivatives contracts, including credit, equity and interest rate derivatives.
- **Payments** – Deriv/SERV provides payment matching and bilateral netting services, providing greater accuracy and straight-through processing.
- **Trade information warehouse** – the warehouse comprises a comprehensive database containing the most up-to-date record of each contract, as well as a processing component that standardises and automates 'downstream' processing over a contract's life cycle, which can extend over five years or more.

In addition, the DTCC (which is currently the largest global securities processing service), through its subsidiaries, provides post-trade clearance, settlement, custody and information services for a wide range of cash market and derivatives equities. The National Securities Clearing Corporation (NSCC) subsidiary, which acts as a central counterparty, provides trade guarantees, netting and risk management services for equity and debt transactions from all US stock exchanges and markets. The Depository Trust Company (DTC) subsidiary has custody of, and provides asset servicing for, millions of securities issues of issuers from the US and over 60 other countries. The DTC serves as a major clearing house for institutional post-trade settlement.

Many market participants have designed direct links between their internal MIS systems to the DTCC to increase efficiency, reduce operational risk and provide better service for their clients.

12.4 SWIFTNet FpML

SWIFT, the financial industry co-operative payment system, has developed SWIFTNet FpML, which allows users to send and receive secure messages and OTC derivative trade confirmations and advice via their SWIFTNet system.

This is a real-time matching and exception service for handling FX, money market and OTC derivative confirmations. Its main goal is to enhance the efficiency of the user's STP of OTC derivative contracts.

SWIFTNet FpML is accessible via SWIFT's secure IP network. It also provides a long-term archival service for all trades processed through the system, which will be held for one year after their maturity. FpML is widely recognised as the standard of choice among ISDA members for communicating information electronically.

The service is geared to work with users' existing processing systems and is available to all SWIFT members. Its key benefits are:

- reducing operational risk
- lowering costs
- ease of access via graphical user interface (GUI) and application programming interface (API)
- increasing straight-through processing (STP)
- reducing settlement risk.

12.5 TriOptima

TriOptima is a private financial software and service technology company that has developed a software product that helps its clients reduce the capital, credit and operational costs and centrally manage its counterparty risk that are associated with their OTC derivative portfolio. The service, triReduce, produces proposals to terminate a package of deals through its **unwind cycle**.

The service requires the client to supply triReduce with selected portfolio information. Once the service has sufficient information, it generates proposals of possible deals that can be terminated to reduce the bank's exposure, thereby reducing the capital required as well as the other operational costs of maintaining a large portfolio of derivative contracts.

Its **triResolve** platform is used to manage counterparty exposure. It is a network platform that provides its users with counterparty exposure management services that include portfolio reconciliation of OTC derivative portfolios, margin call management and dispute resolution.

Its **triBalance** service goes one step further, in that it enables its users to reduce their counterparty risk associated with a wide range of OTC contracts, by 'in effect' netting their counter party exposure with other TriOptima users.

Its **triCalculate** platform, is its new centralised risk analytics service, that provides a web-based service that produces price and risk calculations to evaluate and manage its user's centralised counterparty analysis.

The service produces proposals for each type of OTC derivative contract supplied. It requires portfolio information from a number of market participants. It is available to any willing subscriber. Its current client list includes 70 of the largest banks in the OTC derivatives market.

12.6 Financial Products Markup Language (FpML)

FpML (financial products markup language) is an open source industry-standard protocol developed for the electronic dealing and processing of OTC derivatives communications. It is based on XML (extensible markup language), the standard meta-language for describing data shared between software applications. The purpose of FpML, which is available free, is to automate the flow of information across the entire derivatives network, independent of the underlying software or hardware infrastructure supporting the activities related to these transactions. FpML provides the standard data content and structure to exchange derivatives transactions electronically. While it is an open data standard, it is not an application nor an electronic dealing or processing service. It is the standard that many of the services cited in the previous section, and most participants in the derivatives markets, use.

The following is a list of the main products that are currently covered by FpML applications:

1. **Interest rate derivatives** – interest swaps, swaptions, FRAs, caps and floors, inflation swaps, and bullet payments.
2. **Foreign exchange** – foreign exchange swaps, spots, forwards, and FX options.
3. **Credit** – single-name credit default swaps, credit default swap indices and baskets.
4. **Equity** – equity swaps, equity options, variance swaps, and total return swaps.

12.7 ICE Link

ICE Link (formerly known as T-Zero) is an electronic credit derivatives trade matching and processing services provider. It provides trade information and novation of credit derivative transactions on a T+0 basis, which meets industry targets set by the ISDA Board Oversight Committee (IBOC).

12.8 BClear

Bclear is an electronic trading processing service provided by ICE for OTC equity and commodity derivative contracts. The service is available to members of the London derivatives market and processes a wide range of individual equity, equity index, commodities and financial derivative contracts. It has expanded to commodity derivatives.

13. Control Processes

Learning Objective

4.11.2 Understand the main control processes in trading and processing OTC instruments: order placement, deal tickets and term sheets; trade validation and confirmation; reconciliation processes: internal and external; cash flow/asset movement instructions and control processes; profit and loss reporting and position management; risks of weak controls and spreadsheet environments; close out or maturity instructions

13.1 The Importance of Controls

The efficient administration of all transactions is essential. In the case of derivatives, the risks arising from inefficiency are potentially greater because derivatives are geared, therefore the full risk of any trade can be significantly more than the initial transaction.

There is no set structure that organisations apply for the administration of their derivatives business. For example, the structure in a bank will generally be different from that within a fund management company. There will be many factors involved, including:

- **volumes of transactions** – the market players will undertake many more transactions, particularly if it is a market-maker, so they will tend to have more specialist areas within the overall operations area
- **range and complexity of products** – an end-user such as a fund manager is likely to be involved in a narrower range of products, so will require a narrower range of expertise
- **valuations and risk monitoring** – both market-makers and end-users need to have efficient systems that value all existing positions, as well as measure all of their associated risks
- **reporting** – while the regulatory reporting requirements for the fund manager may be less onerous and less frequent than for a bank, both will have to report their respective positions on a regular basis.

In some organisations the structure of the operations area is along product lines; in others it cuts across product lines and is organised along process lines instead, eg, by domicile of the counterparty or by complexity of the deal. Within derivatives operations, particularly in major market participants, there is also often a split between OTC and exchange-traded instruments. Within a bank, there is often a front office, a middle office, an operations department (what used to be called the 'back office') and a risk management area. Which processes are performed in which area can vary from bank to bank. Hence it is better to concentrate on the processes themselves. No matter how the operations area is organised, the key objectives are efficiency, flexibility, security and control.

13.2 The Process Flow

The processes which follow an OTC derivatives transaction, many of which are common to all financial transactions, are as follows.

13.2.1 Trade Capture and Verification

Since most trades are automatically input into the system in the dealing room, the details of the transaction must be verified by the middle office by the end of the trading day. Trade entry must follow the deal immediately, because any delay means that market risk and credit risk are not being monitored correctly, and because in turn it delays the confirmation and settlement process.

The same problems arise if trades are booked incorrectly. For example, if the sale of an equity index call is booked as a purchase, not only will the trader's position be incorrect, so will the bank's risk report. This type of error will also result in the bank paying the premium, as well as not being able to monitor that it has in fact received the premium from its counterparty. The error will also cause a failed settlement.

The late or incorrect booking of trades, particularly where exacerbated by poor controls, can result in a wide range of potential problems including:

- inaccuracies in evaluating risk, managing positions and investment decisions
- late-settlement-related interest payments and fees owed to counterparties
- operational losses through funding and timing difficulties, eg, late receipt of sales proceeds can create knock-on delays in settling other trades
- poor-quality client servicing, eg, inaccurate or late reports
- rule breaches, leading to fines or disciplinary action taken by exchanges and/or regulators
- reputational loss, including loss of trading/research opportunities with certain counterparties, and negative impact on client and stakeholder relationships.

Similar risks can arise through reliance on spreadsheets, which are very accessible and familiar to many people, but nevertheless proven to distort our perceptions of efficiency, accuracy and utility. When replaced by expertly programmed and tested software designed to work as part of a bigger system, spreadsheets are often found to be much slower to run, and highly susceptible to bugs and human error.

13.2.2 Position-Keeping and Profit and Loss Analysis

Positions must be monitored for risk control and the profit and loss calculated.

The extent to which position-keeping is a responsibility of the front office or of the operations area varies between organisations. Clearly, it is of prime importance to the dealer to monitor their own position, as that is what gives rise to their profit or loss. Most dealers are now able to monitor their current position using a real-time position system.

However, the role of checking for risk management purposes should fall outside the dealing area. Most major houses have a product control team or similar unit that performs this function. Again, using electronic position-keeping, this area is able to ensure that each dealer and the trading area as a whole remains within their respective individual, product and area limits at all times. Any positions that are above their limit should be reported. Failure to maintain up-to-date and reconciled end-of-day positions between the dealing room and product control team could result in losses from unreported transactions or positions in excess of risk management limits.

13.2.3 Confirmation and Documentation

The details of the trade and any documentation to be used are agreed. It is important that these be agreed between the operations areas of the two parties, independently of the dealers, to reduce the risk of either fraud or unauthorised dealing on the part of the dealer.

A confirmation sets out the terms and conditions of an individual transaction at the point of trading; it is a written representation of the verbal contract (the trade) and is evidence that the transaction has occurred. Once it has been signed by both parties, there is no possibility of dispute over the trade's terms and conditions. It is important that there is a reference on the confirmation to the date of the master agreement. The confirmation incorporates the ISDA definitions appropriate to that trade.

Historically, the key difference between the administration of OTC transactions and that for exchange-traded contracts concerns the documentation relating to the trades. As there are no standard terms for OTC contracts, unlike for a listed product on an exchange, both counterparties to an OTC transaction were required to ensure that the trade is recorded on the terms that both dealers agreed at the time of the trade. However, for those counterparties with high mutual trading, a master confirmation can be agreed upon. This provides a general framework for each type of transaction's confirmation. Its use improves the speed of the confirmation process, thus avoiding later settlement and risk management problems that arise when incorrect position records are encountered or with late or missed payments.

But the financial crisis of 2008 highlighted the problem of counterparty credit risk in the OTC derivatives market. In response to this, in order to ensure that government funds would not again be used to bail out the financial industry, in order to prevent a further market collapse, the EU introduced a series of regulations that requires that all OTC derivative trades are reported to a Trade Repository (TRS) as well as a central counterparty, thus reducing counterparty credit risk and operational risks.

The details of all trades must be reported no later than the working day following the conclusion (modification or termination) of the contract.

The reporting obligation applies to derivatives contracts, which are entered into on or after the date of entry into force (16 August 2012) of EMIR and to those contracts that are already outstanding on that date.

EMIR reporting requirements do not apply to individuals nor do they extend to non-EU counterparties. However, in the case of an EU counterparty under EMIR dealing with American counterparties (or from other jurisdictions) the equivalent Dodd-Frank or other OTC derivative reporting requirements would apply to the other side of the transaction.

A master confirmation represents the market consensus as to how a product is expected to work and sets out the standard definitions and terms for that product on either a global or regional basis. It allows thereafter for the exchange of what is called a 'transaction supplement', which has only the trade-specific details of the individual transaction. The transaction supplement merely has to reference the fact that it is written under the terms of the master confirmation and so in most cases it is shorter than a normal confirmation.

Similarly Markit has been responsible for achieving consensus in the credit market in the same way as ISDA and, by publishing standard terms, has allowed market participants to reference those terms much in the same way as if they had executed a specific master confirmation.

Any disagreements must be identified, reported and resolved immediately, and if a confirmation, or acknowledgement of a confirmation, is not received from the counterparty within a prescribed time, escalation procedures must be in place.

Market regulators, such as the SEC and FCA, have been significant in bringing down the number of outstanding or 'unconfirmed' confirmations. A key part of this goal has been ensuring that market participants do not allow any confirmations to remain 'outstanding' for more than 30 days.

In addition, Markit, a provider of a fully electronic trade processing service, also provides as part of its service a standardised confirmation. Its confirmation services, with links to DTCC and Markit Wire, provide an STP-standard confirmation for a wide range of OTC products.

13.2.4 Settlement

At the time of the trade and/or subsequently, there will be one or more settlements to be made, which must be monitored, calculated, netted if appropriate, and settled.

The settlement process in OTC derivatives is more complex than with cash instruments. With cash instruments there is often only one fixed settlement date; the amount to be settled is fixed, and this amount can be calculated as soon as the deal has been transacted. With OTC derivatives, apart from the premium paid up-front for an option, this is often not the case. For example:

- A cap has a series of potential settlement dates; all, some or none might involve a settlement.
- An American option can be exercised at any time until expiry.
- The settlement amount on a fixed/floating swap cannot be calculated until the floating rate has been set.
- The fact that a payment is necessary and the specific amount related to a credit default swap is determined should the predefined credit event occur.

Timely trade processing can help avoid the risks that can arise through late settlement.

13.2.5 Reconciliation

All the cash flows passing across the bank account which arise from the transaction must be compared with the expected cash flows and any discrepancies investigated.

13.2.6 Collateral Management

If collateral is required on one or both sides to the deal, its market value must be monitored frequently, as must the current value of the deal, so that the collateral requirement can be adjusted accordingly.

13.2.7 Risk Management

The trade will give rise to both market risk and credit risk. Although the responsibility for monitoring these does not usually fall within the operations area, the operations area is a vital link in ensuring that the data used for the risk analysis is updated both quickly and accurately.

13.3 Benefits of Straightforward Trade Processing

Learning Objective

4.11.3 Understand the benefits of processing on straightforward OTC markets

In recent years, the OTC derivatives market has seen a dramatic increase in the number of exotic structured products in different underlying instruments tied to interest rates, currencies, credit, commodities and equities being traded. The recent financial crisis, which some claim can be traced back to the proliferation of such exotics, has exposed fundamental systemic issues in risk management, compliance, operations and technology.

The combination of increased regulation and internal policies for increased and improved risk management has provided extra incentives to improve straightforward and central clearing of a wide range of OTC trades.

The key areas of improved trade processing include:

- trade automation
- document management
- process connectivity
- risk management.

The following are the key benefits of straightforward and central clearing of OTC derivative trades. The individual nature of specific contracts is the key reason why some OTC derivatives have been more popular in adopting a centrally cleared procedure.

1. **Reduced counterparty credit evaluations and ongoing credit exposure monitoring** – by using a central counterparty or clearing house, straightforward and central clearing in OTC markets facilitates 'counterparty anonymity' and reduces the need for credit evaluations of individual counterparties on an ongoing basis. That separation of price and credit risks has long been recognised as a significant benefit of organised futures exchanges and fast, straightforward and central clearing of OTC trades.

2. **Transparency and consistency of pricing for margin and funds settlements** – the use of agreed and established sources for mark-to-market prices to calculate any payment obligations for any centrally cleared OTC derivative trade reduces the risks of any payment or pricing dispute between trade counterparties. The fact that the same contract price is applied to all like positions and accounts also reduces operational risks by establishing an efficient mechanism for monitoring and ensuring compliance with margin requirements. This also reduces the possibility of any disputes over collateral valuation.

3. **Monitoring of multilateral exposures and correlation risks** – central clearing and straightforward OTC trade processing allows each counterparty to evaluate more effectively all of the risks faced by individual market participants. In other words, it can function in part as a 'delegated risk manager', since it provides a central and current monitoring of all of the exposure to individual counterparties across a wide range of OTC contracts. This delegated monitoring capability is, of course, limited to the OTC positions cleared through the trade process and does not take into account non-derivatives positions. As such, counterparty credit risk monitoring is not a substitute for internal or outsourced enterprise-wide risk monitoring.

4. **Default resolution** – the rule is that most OTC-cleared derivatives that have been settled using a central process are trades that are more easily offset or unwound following a clearing member default.

5. **Default risk mutualisation and loss allocation** – if a derivatives dealer or large end-user incurs losses on an OTC derivatives contract in excess of any collateral posted, the remaining financial resources of the firm are all that remain to cover the open payment obligation. In other words, dealers backstop their obligations with their own capital. If the swap participant incurs correlated losses that erode its capital base rapidly, the firm itself could default. Clearing default funds financed by clearing members are economically equivalent to 'industry mutuals' in the traditional insurance arena. In such mutuals, all participants make initial contributions. A large loss by any individual member in excess of its margin is then covered by payments from the mutual. As long as risk exposures are imperfectly correlated across clearing members and positions, a smaller amount of total risk capital must be collected from individual members to achieve a given desired level of risk coverage *vis-à-vis* a situation when all members had to provide their own risk capital to cover each of those potential losses in isolation.

End of Chapter Questions

1. How is an FRA used?
   Answer reference: Section 2.2

2. Describe the theory of interest rate parity.
   Answer reference: Section 3.1

3. What is the main purpose of an interest rate swap?
   Answer reference: Section 4

4. What are floors?
   Answer reference: Section 5

5. What is the benefit of an MTM swap?
   Answer reference: Section 6.8

6. Name six types of credit event.
   Answer reference: Section 7.1

7. What are the key factors used to calculate an option's premium?
   Answer reference: Section 8.1

8. Why might a company use an equity-linked note?
   Answer reference: Section 9

9. What is SwapClear?
   Answer reference: Section 12.2

10. Historically, what is the key difference between the administration of OTC transactions and that for exchange-traded contracts?
    Answer reference: Section 13.2.3

Chapter Five
Clearing

5

This syllabus area will provide approximately 7 of the 80 examination questions

1. The Definition and Purpose of Clearing

1.1 Clearing and Risk

Learning Objective

5.1.1 Understand the process of clearing, the risks involved and how these can be reduced: market, settlement, currency and counterparty risks; eligibility and credit standing of counterparties; implications of default; mutual offset system; principal to principal; guarantee

Clearing is the process by which exchange-traded derivatives trades are confirmed and registered. Registration is with a **clearing house** that becomes legal counterparty to every transaction. The legal process whereby the clearing house becomes the counterparty to all trades is called **novation**. This involves substituting the clearing house as the buyer to every seller and the seller to every buyer. Hence every original exchange contract becomes two new contracts; the original contract no longer exists.

Any **currency risk** that exists for clearing members with regard to settlement is minimal, since as a member of a clearing house and exchange it must maintain an account in the clearing house's currency. Any currency risk that does arise from the clearing process arises from the exchange rate movements between the member's home currency and that of the exchange's, for the amounts of their net daily margin payments.

This central counterparty structure removes almost all **counterparty risk (credit risk)** from all clearing members operating within the market. The only counterparty risk faced by clearing members is with the clearing house itself, not with each other.

In addition, the clearing house will monitor all open positions and will facilitate the settlement process by acting as the intermediary with respect to the close-out and delivery of futures contracts and the exercise and assignment of options contracts. In the rare case of default, the clearing house faces one day of **market risk**, since all members must pay a daily margin payment which is based on their net position's profit/loss relative to the previous day's price movement.

On the rare occasion that the margin payments do not cover the net position's loss, all clearing houses, such as LCH.Clearnet or ICE Clear Europe, for example, maintain a **default fund**, which is cash that is paid in by its members. In order to ensure that the fund is sufficient, the clearing house runs a wide range of stress tests, so that the fund's size meets worst case estimates of the market's volatility. Note that this fund only covers default by members directly to the clearing house.

One of the major advantages of having such a clearing system, therefore, is that it greatly reduces counterparty risk. The clearing house guarantees the financial performance of the contract and, as long as the clearing house is backed by substantial financial resources, and is thus highly creditworthy, market users and investors can have a high degree of confidence in the system. Another advantage is that contracts become very easy to trade, with the clearing house making it easy to close-out a trade by taking an equal and opposite position – because both long and short positions are novated to the clearing house as central counterparty, the previous position is effectively closed.

Settlement risk – the risk that an expected payment of cash or a security will not be made on time or at all – is another risk associated with the delivery/clearing process. The establishment of a **netting system/agreement** is an effective method of minimising this kind of risk.

One extension of the clearing process is a **mutual offset system**. This is an agreement between two exchanges that allows trades executed on one exchange to be booked and cleared through another. Such an agreement exists between the CME and the Singapore Exchange (SGX) for a few of the contracts that are traded on both. Two of these contracts are the Eurodollar and Euroyen TIBOR futures.

In a **principal-to-principal system**, such as that operated by ICE Clear Europe, the clearing house guarantees the performance of trades done by its members on the exchanges that it serves. The guarantee does not extend to members' clients or non-clearing exchange member firms. As a result, it will implicate the broker as long as the broker is an ICE Clear Europe member.

Major Exchanges	Clearing Houses
ICE London	ICE Clear Europe
LME	LME Clear
Turquoise Derivatives	EuroCCP, LCH.Clearnet, EMCF, x-clear
ICE Futures	ICE Clear Europe
CME Group (CBOT, CME and NYMEX)	CME Clearing
OneChicago	CME Clearing or Options Clearing Corporation (OCC) depending on membership
Philadelphia Stock Exchange (PHLX)	Exchange's clearing house
Eurex	Eurex Clearing AG
Euronext Derivatives (European exchanges)	LCH Group and Euroclear
Mercado Español de Futuros Financieros (MEFF)	Exchange's clearing house
Singapore Exchange (SGX)	SGX-DC (exchange's clearing house)
Osaka Securities Exchange (OSE)	Exchange's clearing house
Brazilian Mercantile & Futures Exchange (BM&F)	Trades are cleared through the BM&F clearing house
Dubai Mercantile Exchange (DME)	NYMEX clearing house
NDCEX National Commodity & Derivatives Exchange Ltd (India)	Trades are processed via the exchange's clearing house, physical delivery through its Depository Clearing System, while margin payments and cash settlement are via an approved clearing bank

Major Exchanges	Clearing Houses
South African Futures Exchange (Safex), part of the Johannesburg Stock Exchange (JSE) Group	Exchange's clearing house
Shanghai Futures Exchange (SHFE)	Exchange's clearing house

Recently there has been a similar shift to establishing a central counterparty (CCP) and a formal trade reporting procedure for OTC derivative contracts. The main reason for this is to provide greater stability in the market, by reducing counterparty credit risk and ensuring better risk management. The EMIR is the regulatory guideline for this clearing and margin structure for the EU derivatives market.

1.2 The Structure of the Clearing System

Learning Objectives

5.2.1 Understand the role played by the clearing house in the clearing process and the relationship between the clearing house, clearing members and non-clearing members: trade reporting, confirmation, matching, registration and novation; use of payments systems

The different tiers that make up the clearing system at the exchange level are the clearing house, the clearing members and the non-clearing members. The clearing members themselves can be general clearing members or individual clearing members, which means respectively that they clear either:

- for themselves, for direct clients and for other exchange members, or
- for just themselves and direct clients.

The clearing house is typically owned by its members or by the exchange whose contracts it clears, or both. There are different models. For example, in the case of the Options Clearing Corporation (OCC) in the US, the clearing corporation is jointly owned by several exchanges. On the other hand, the Chicago Mercantile Exchange's clearing house is a division of the exchange itself. ICE Clear Europe is owned by exchanges and clearing members. The tiers are:

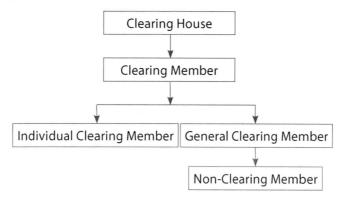

To illustrate its different tiers and the clearing process, it is useful to look at a typical trade and the individual steps involved. The example that follows highlights the systems and procedures that are used when a trade initiates on ICE, for which ICE Clear Europe acts as the clearing house.

As mentioned in Chapter 3, Section 9.1, the first part of the clearing process is trade reporting or registration. For most exchanges, such as ICE, its electronic trading system automatically reports a trade, once it happens, to the Universal Clearing Platform (UCP). Once this takes place, the clearing process begins.

Example 1

Step 1. The trade

Mr X. Ample is a client of ABC Ltd, a member firm of ICE. He places a market order. ABC Ltd will act as broker, executing the trade on the ICE exchange. ABC Ltd is not a member of ICE Clear Europe.

Any trade executed needs to be reported to and registered with the clearing house (ICE Clear Europe). The trade will need to be registered via a clearing member, and ABC Ltd has an agreement with a general clearing member, KMM Ltd, a firm which is a member of both the exchange and ICE Clear Europe.

Step 2. Confirmation and matching

ABC Ltd will pass details of the trade to KMM Ltd (its clearing member) who will input the details into the confirmation and matching system (known as UCP, used by ICE) where it will wait until the counterparty to the ABC Ltd trade enters the equal and opposite details into the system.

Step 3. Registration

Once matched, KMM Ltd registers the trade with ICE Clear Europe (via UCP), giving details of the type of account the trade is assigned to. The account will either be in a segregated, 'client' account, or within the non-segregated 'house' account.

Step 4. Novation

At the point of registering the trade with ICE Clear Europe the contract is novated, resulting in ICE Clear Europe becoming counterparty to two new transactions – one with KMM Ltd and the other with ABC Ltd's original counterparty. The original contract between ABC Ltd and its counterparty no longer exists. In effect, ABC Ltd (a non-clearing firm) has committed KMM Ltd (its clearing member) to a transaction with ICE Clear Europe (the clearing house).

ICE Clear Europe guarantees the performance of the contract to its immediate counterparty, the clearing member – KMM Ltd in the above example. This is known as a 'principal-to-principal' guarantee.

ICE Clear Europe will call on KMM Ltd for any subsequent payments (margin) on the contract as necessary. KMM Ltd, as a clearing member, will pay any margin due through the Protected Payments System (PPS) – a system used by ICE Clear Europe in conjunction with several leading banks, which will automatically debit members' bank accounts. KMM Ltd will collect any payments from ABC Ltd, its customer. ABC Ltd will in turn call on any payments from its customer, Mr Ample. Each party has a principal-to-principal relationship with the other.

When Mr Ample decides to close the position, the same process takes place. Note that ABC Ltd will not have to go back to the original counterparty because the original contract no longer exists. As the contract is standardised, the offsetting trade simply cancels out the trade previously registered with the clearing house, thus cancelling any delivery obligations.

Note also that the clearing house does not give any guarantees to Mr Ample, the client. Mr Ample and his broker (ABC Ltd) have a risk on each other defaulting, as does ABC Ltd and the clearing member (KMM Ltd). So, although the system substantially reduces the risk of default, it does not eliminate it along the whole system.

1.3 Guarantee

Learning Objectives

5.3.1 Understand the backing arrangements in place in the event of a member default, and how they are utilised: margin and collateral; default guarantee fund; mutual and independent guarantees

As noted earlier, clearing houses operate a principal-to-principal guarantee based on a mutual guarantee structure. There are many clearing houses and their models differ.

As an example, the supporting financial resources pertaining to LCH.Clearnet in London are provided as follows:

- **Initial margins** are collected from clearing members in the form of cash (in various currencies) and acceptable securities and other collateral.
- In the event of a **member default** the clearing house would first utilise the **margin monies and collateral placed by the defaulting member**.
- The major tranche of financial support which is next in line is the **member default fund**, which is a pool of units and to which every clearing member contributes in cash (interest-bearing) according to the volume of its clearing activities. The amount that members are required to deposit is reviewed and adjusted normally every three months. See Section 1.5.1. Hence, for example, a member default occurring in swaps clearing is also supported by the fund provided by those firms involved in futures or equity clearing. As a result of this, the system is known as a **mutual guarantee system**. An **independent guarantee system** would not have a collective default fund.
- The next level of support is provided by an **insurance policy** from an insurance company.

1.4 Prime Brokers

Learning Objectives

5.3.2 Understand the services offered by prime brokers as they relate to: trade execution, settlement, custody and asset servicing; client services: global custody, stock lending, reporting; value-added services: introduction, advisory and consulting services

A prime broker's role in relation to derivatives is that it is primarily responsible for the following:

- Efficient and best execution of all trades.
- Ensuring confirmation of client trades through the required trade documentation.
- Settlement of trade cash flows, to provide cash financing or securities lending as pre-agreed and when needed.
- Providing custody and safekeeping of all assets, as well as any risk management systems that the client may require.
- Keeping clients aware of all issuer correspondence, such an annual meetings and corporate actions.

A prime broker can provide a number of services for its client; these include:

- Clearance and settlement of trade in global markets.
- Central custodianship of assets, and using consolidated positions for the extension of leverage.
- Financing multiple currencies, as required.
- Stock borrowing capabilities to support trade strategies.
- Integrated web reporting of positions, activities and performance.
- Hedge fund consulting services.
- Facilitating communication between sales, trading and research.

In addition, certain prime brokers provide additional **value-added** services which may include some or all of the following:

- **Capital introduction** – a process whereby the prime broker attempts to introduce its hedge fund to qualified hedge fund investors who have an interest in exploring new opportunities to make hedge fund investments.
- **Office space leasing and servicing** – certain prime brokers lease commercial real estate and then sublease blocks of space for hedge fund tenants. These prime brokers, typically, provide a suite of on-site services for clients who utilise their space.
- **Risk management advisory services** – the provision of risk-analysis technology, sometimes supplemented by consulting by senior risk professionals.
- **Consulting services** – a range of consulting and advisory services, typically provided to start-up hedge funds, and focused on issues associated with regulatory establishment requirements in the jurisdiction where the hedge fund manager will be resident, as well as in the jurisdiction(s) where the fund itself will be domiciled.

Given the wide range of services and different types of clients that prime brokers deal with, from large hedge funds and companies to individual investors, the regulation of prime brokers is the responsibility of a number of agencies. In the UK, they are regulated by the FCA and the MiFID regulation, while in the US both the Federal Reserve and the Securities and Exchange Commission (SEC) monitor their activities.

1.5   Exchange-Cleared OTC Products

Learning Objectives

5.2.2   Understand the benefits of centralised OTC clearing and how this is achieved in the major OTC markets

The increased concern over counterparty risk combined with exchanges' desire to expand and diversify has led to exchanges offering clearing facilities and guarantees to a range of OTC derivatives.

One such clearing facility is ICE's **Bclear**. Once an OTC is agreed, its details can be submitted into Bclear and the OTC trade is replaced with an exchange contract. Bclear provides clearing of a wide range of individual and index equity, commodity and other financial futures and options. These include contracts on all of the major European indices and a few key US indices, plus many individual equities, as well as bond and short-term interest products.

One of the few restrictions on the OTC contracts that can use Bclear is based on volume or trade size. This varies for specific contracts, but most have a minimum trade size to use Bclear.

The CME Group's **Clearing360** provides a similar if somewhat more restricted service for OTC interest rate derivative contracts and FX option block trades. Access to Clearing360 is restricted to firms that act as principal or agent for the OTC trades. These include hedge funds, major banks, prime brokers and proprietary trading firms.

Rather than simply clearing the OTC trades, Clearing360 substitutes the OTC FRAs and interest rate swaps with corresponding futures contracts.

Eurex also provides clearing of OTC block trades, EFP, EFS and Vola trades (bilateral volatility trades which involve OTC options and the off-exchange purchase or sale of the underlying futures contract) using its **Eurex OTC Clear** system.

The main advantage of having an OTC derivative cleared or substituted by an exchange's clearing house is that it **eliminates any counterparty risk**. This is particularly attractive for longer-term contracts. Once the OTC contract is cleared, it is subject to the same requirements, such as margin payments and delivery procedures, as any other exchange-traded derivative.

Centrally cleared OTC products are executed and delivered in a similar process to exchange-traded products. For any type of delivery to take place, both counterparties must be exchange members and have either a direct or indirect clearing relationship with the respective clearing house.

Unlike exchange-traded contracts, the clearing house does not assign or match buyers to sellers, but it does monitor and guarantee that delivery is made on both sides of the trade. The trades are executed between two counterparties and delivery takes place using the respective clearing system.

1.5.1   Clearing Fund

The clearing fund is a pool of funds contributed by clearing members for use in case of default, for both exchange-traded and OTC contracts that are cleared by the clearing house.

Every clearing member is required to contribute to the clearing fund. The required amount is based on a risk assessment using each clearing member's level of uncovered risk, which is based upon the trading activity. This risk-based payment is reviewed on a regular basis: for example ICE exchange recalculates each clearing member's payment on a monthly basis; other exchanges reassess these payments on a quarterly basis.

The clearing fund will be used should a clearing member default in the delivery process. The fund is used only after any margin or other related funds have been utilised.

The main types of collateral that are accepted by these clearing funds are:

- cash (EUR, USD, GBP, CHF, JPY, SEK, DKK, NOK)
- bonds to be deposited with the clearing house, valued at market, haircuts applied upon maturity.

UK	Gilts
US	Treasury bills and bonds
Germany	Bunds
France	OATs, BTFs (bills of up to one year to maturity), BTANs (1–6-year notes)
Italy	BOTs (bills of up to one year to maturity), BTPs (bonds), CCTs (floating rate notes)
Japan	Japanese government bonds (JGBs)

Most exchanges, such as the CME Group have several categories of accepted collateral (in their case they have four categories) and based on the collateral asset's risk, it applies a valuation 'cap' or discount on their face value ranging from zero to 75%.

The LME applies a similar 'haircut' on certain types of collateral, using a 5 key point methodology.

2. Margin

Learning Objective

5.4.1 Understand the purpose of margin, its various types, and how margin payments are paid or collected: reduction of counterparty credit risk; initial, variation, intra-day and maintenance margin; advantages and risks of house, client segregated and non-segregated accounts; clearing house and broker margin; flow of margin

5.4.6 Understand methods of margining centrally cleared OTC products and their implications: calculation of exposure; what margins are applied; payment of margin

2.1 Introduction

In guaranteeing contracts, the clearing house is taking on a substantial risk, especially on those contracts which have a **contingent liability**, such as futures contracts and written options. A contingent liability is one where a loss might arise but it is not possible to be certain of its amount – the outcome is contingent upon the price of the underlying asset.

In order for any clearing house to protect itself there are a number of steps that it might take:

- It only permits to become clearing members firms that meet (and continue to meet) its membership and financial criteria. This is the first line of defence – the quality of its membership.
- It only deals directly with clearing members, all of whom have the most onerous financial resources requirements.
- The next line of defence is its margining system, where margin is best defined as the cash (or equivalent) deposited with the clearing house to cover the risk of the clearing member defaulting on its position.

- It relies on its own financial resources and perhaps operates *inter alia* a default fund; it has lines of credit with a consortium of major banks; and it has insurance policies.

The underlying reason for requiring margin payments is to support the guarantee provided by the clearing house, in other words to **reduce or eliminate any counterparty credit risk**. This is the underlying purpose of an efficient margin system.

Margin is collected in two ways: **initial margin** is largely collected when a position is first established, and then **variation margin** may be collected as that position worsens. Margin is demanded by the clearing house separately for the house accounts maintained by the clearing member (which will include any non-segregated client positions) and the segregated client accounts. As an example, ICE Clear Europe will demand margin from each type of account separately, on the basis of the **net positions** in that account.

SPAN, which stands for **Standard Portfolio ANalysis of risk**, is the leading system used to calculate daily margin requirements, and has been adopted by most of the leading futures and options exchanges. It uses a set of algorithms to determine a portfolio's daily risk. The SPAN margining system measures and determines the risk and therefore the daily margin requirement based on the entire portfolio, rather than on each specific open position. It allows both futures and options to be included together when calculating a portfolio's risk. SPAN has the capacity that allows for both inter-maturity and inter-commodity spreads.

One of the first exchanges to use SPAN was the CBOT, which is now part of the CME Group. SPAN's ability to measure across a wide range of products and contracts allows clearing members more efficient use of their capital, as it often implies lower margin requirements.

Placing client positions within the house account as **non-segregated clients** may provide a cash flow benefit to the clearing firm, because any credit positions will effectively offset any debit positions. These benefits would be lost if the client's account was segregated.

However, the client is obviously facing an additional risk if they are non-segregated. If the firm were to default they would potentially lose out.

These margin demands are made of the clearing member, and for LCH.Clearnet and ICE Clear Europe any cash payments are drawn directly from a bank account held by that member. This process (mentioned earlier) is known as the **Protected Payments System (PPS)**, and the accounts are referred to as **PPS accounts**. Note that no cash call would be made for initial margin if the clearing member were covering initial margin requirements by an acceptable form of collateral and sufficient value of that collateral was already in place.

For the **clients** of the clearing member, the financial rules set by the Financial Services Authority require the margin demanded by the clearing member to be **at least as much** as that being demanded by the clearing house, in order to avoid the need to retain more financial resources.

The concept and protection provided by margins has started to be applied to a select group of exchange-cleared OTC products. The two types that have been most popular to date have been contracts for difference (which are mainly cash-settled) and certain types of energy contracts. In both cases, the clearing house will swap the OTC contract with an exchange-based equivalent. It can then apply its standard margin requirements to the position, and normal payments and procedures are then followed.

2.2 Types of Margin

There are basically two types of margin: **initial** and **variation** margin.

2.2.1 Initial Margin

Learning Objectives

5.4.2 Understand how initial margin is calculated and the factors that exchanges take into account when calculating initial margin: systems – SPAN and STANS; spreads: spot and offset margining; purpose, nature and use of offsets; effect of volatility

Initial margin is a good faith deposit (perhaps in the form of collateral rather than cash), lodged with the clearing house against potential liabilities on an open position. It is returned when the position is closed out.

Initial margin is calculated by the clearing house in respect of clearing members' positions using whatever system it has adopted (see the notes on SPAN margining below). The clearing member similarly calculates margin with respect to its clients, and may demand a higher rate of margin (known as **broker margin**) from its client.

Once a client's trade has been executed, the clearing member or broker that holds the client's account will put the trade in the client's segregated or non-segregated account (depending on its relationship with the client), and at the same time collect the initial margin that is required.

Note that if the new trade was the purchase of an option, no initial margin is collected; instead the premium payment will be collected from the client's account. The reason for this is that buying an option is not a contingent liability transaction. The maximum loss an option buyer will have is the up-front premium payment.

Initial margin seeks to protect the clearing house (and in turn the broker) from the worst-case loss a position could potentially incur in one day. The actual initial margin rate per contract will be set by looking at the recent **price volatility of the contract** and will be determined by the clearing house following consultation with the exchange.

Example 2

For example, by continually monitoring market prices, ICE Clear Europe calculates that the most the price of the FTSE futures contract could move in one day is 300 points. Given the tick size and tick value, this could mean a potential loss of £3,000 per contract on the day on long/short open positions. So the initial margin rate will be set at £3,000 per contract for both the buyer and seller of a future. If the volatility changes up or down, the initial margin requirement may be changed.

Scan risk applies no additional charge for inter-month spread risk. The scan risk calculation assumes that a long position in one month exactly offsets a short position of the same amount in a different month. In contrast, SPAN does apply an Inter-Month Spread Charge to each spread in the portfolio to cover this risk.

The ICE Clear US Risk Department selects an Inter-Month Spread Charge Method for each commodity using three methods: the first method where no additional charge is added, the second applies a charge based on a single rate, while the third tier method applies a charge that is based on three tiers that are based on the spread's maturity.

In order to account for the fact that deep out-of-the-money options may present more risk to the portfolio than the scanning range covers, SPAN creates a Short Option Minimum Margin. Each commodity is assigned a Short Option Minimum Charge by the ICE Clear US Risk Department. All short options, puts and calls, are totalled and multiplied by the appropriate short option charge.

The result is the Short Option Minimum Margin.

The Short Option Minimum Margin is not a charge to be added to the portfolio risk. Instead, it is the absolute minimum margin assessed to a portfolio. The margin calculated under SPAN is compared to the Short Option Minimum Margin and the larger number is taken to be the portfolio's margin. Thus, the Short Option Minimum Margin acts as an absolute floor on the margin amount for the portfolio. Information on Short Option Minimum Margins is distributed each day with the parameters that accompany the risk arrays.

Example 3

Since SPAN applies a minimum charge rate for each commodity, if it has a minimum charge of $100, then a portfolio that is short 10 option contracts will be charged $1,000.

Initial margin is re-computed every business day and effectively called first thing in the morning before markets open. After the market has opened, if there is a sudden jump in the volatility, and the clearing house is no longer comfortable with the amount of initial margin held – indeed, if the initial margin amount is exhausted – it can call for an extra **intra-day margin** which is taken immediately from the clearing members via their PPS accounts.

Initial margin can be provided in **cash** or covered by acceptable **non-cash collateral**. Clearing houses have different rules on the forms of acceptable collateral they will accept. As one might expect, the lists of collateral published by ICE Clear Europe, OCC and the CME Group are rather longer than those of smaller clearing houses. See Section 2.5.

As stated earlier, the system used to calculate initial margins for futures and options positions is known as **SPAN** or its UK variant used by LCH.Clearnet, known as **London SPAN**. Other clearing houses may use methods other than this, some risk-based and some self-developed. Another well-known method is the **Theoretical Intermarket Margining System (TIMS)**, which was invented and used by the Options Clearing Corporation. However, in August 2006 the OCC implemented its new **STANS** system **(System for Theoretical Analysis and Numerical Simulations)**, which is more sophisticated. All these three systems are portfolio approaches that examine the risk of futures and options positions in the same portfolio and work out the worst scenario from a standard set of scenarios in order to reflect fairly the risk of the clearing house. See Section 2.4 for more on SPAN, STANS and TIMS.

Spreads involve more than one position across different delivery months in the same contract (a trader perhaps being long a June FTSE 100 future and short a September FTSE 100 future). The initial margin will be substantially lower than normal in this case because the two positions largely offset each other, and the price movements of each month, although not perfectly, do tend to correlate in their movement. These are known as **intra-commodity spreads**. Spreads also exist between different instruments that always exhibit correlation in their price movements. These are called **inter-commodity spreads** and apply to such contracts as ICE Futures Gas Oil and ICE Futures Brent Crude Oil.

Therefore, most exchanges take into account the offsetting nature of these positions when setting the margin requirements. The net result is a reduction in the margin required for the two spreads mentioned above. For example, CBOT, which is now part of the CME Group, has a comprehensive list of the offset that is applied to spreads margin due to their reduced risk. It depends on the particular contract and varies from $25 to as much as $110 per contract.

As a contract nears its expiry date, its **volatility can increase**. If physical delivery is required in final settlement of the contract, then only those position-holders who wish, or may wish, to take delivery should maintain their open contracts in the market. Others should close out or roll their positions forward to later delivery months. Therefore, as delivery for that product draws near, the clearing house may wish to minimise the speculative and delivery pressures by increasing the initial margin (this is known as a **spot month margin**).

This occurs in order to ensure that those position-holders contemplating taking the contract to delivery either have the underlying asset to deliver or have allocated adequate funds to effect settlement. It will also force any less well-capitalised speculators out of the market, thereby reducing short-term speculative pressures.

2.2.2   Variation Margin

Learning Objective

5.4.3   Calculate variation margin based on marking to market

Exchanges establish settlement prices every business day in order to provide the price yardsticks for calculation of **mark-to-market** variation margin and valuation of positions at the end of the day. This procedure is normally conducted at the end of the trading period, so the daily settlement price is also referred to as the **closing price**. However, some markets do not use the closing price, particularly those that have a global pricing influence (such as the LME), or markets that are in operation for most of the 24-hour day.

The **closing range** is a measure of the range or spread of prices that are quoted during a specified time just before daily trading ends. Each exchange has its own criteria for determining the closing range; most have different time frames for different contracts and they are usually longer for commodity contracts compared to financial contracts.

Example 4 below explains the standard criteria used by ICE on its futures contracts to arrive at daily settlement prices for each delivery month.

Example 4

A time is specified at which the daily settlement price is calculated (eg, the close of trading for that day), and the two minutes up to this time are known as the **settlement range**. The first 90 seconds of the settlement range allows the market supervision department to monitor spread levels. Generally, the daily settlement price is then simply the weighted average traded price during the final 30 seconds of the settlement range. However, market supervision has the flexibility to adjust the daily settlement price if the calculated price is not deemed to be a fair reflection of the market price.

At the close of each trading day all positions are **marked-to-market**, based on the daily settlement price. The profit/loss on the day is measured and must be paid to/received from the clearing house as variation margin by the following day by the clearing members. The same procedure applies between clearing members and their customers by exactly the same process in turn. In this way, profits and losses accruing to positions are accounted for every day.

Variation margin, which must be paid in cash (cleared funds) in the currency of the contract, is calculated as:

> **Variation margin = ticks moved on the day (today's closing price – yesterday's closing price) x the contract's tick value x number of contracts of the open position.**

Example 5

An investor is long 20 December Euroyen (TIBOR) Futures on the SGX. The contract closing price is 99.7750, down from its previous closing price of 99.7825. The contract's minimum price fluctuation is 0.0025, which equates to a tick value of JPY 250,000. The investor will have JPY 37,500 debited from their account, for the day's variation margin for this position.

JPY 37,500 = 0.0075 (today's price movement) x JPY 250,000 (tick value) x 20 (number of contracts of the open position)

Note: For this contract the Singapore Exchange has a minimum price movement of 0.0025 or JPY 625. This is based on the contract's specification, where 1 tick or 1.0 price movement equals JPY 250,000. Therefore, a price movement of 0.0025 = JPY 625 (JPY 250,000 x 0.0025).

Exercise 1

A trader goes short five FTSE 100 futures at 6540 and, at the end of the day, the daily settlement price is 6570. What is the variation margin payable?

The answer can be found in the Appendix at the end of this chapter.

As noted earlier, each clearing member has at least one bank account to which ICE Clear Europe has access via a direct debit system so that variation margin payments can be transferred. These are the **Protected Payments System (PPS)** accounts.

Exercise 2

A trader has a position of being long 20 LME three-month tin futures at $18,950 and at the end of the day the daily settlement price is $18,980. What is the variation margin flow for this position?

The answer can be found in the Appendix at the end of this chapter.

2.2.3 Maintenance Margin

This is an arrangement between member and client and is not operated by the clearing house. Usually a member firm will expect a client to deposit more than the initial margin. This provides a safety cushion for the member and allows for the payment of some variation margin without referring back to the client every day. Once the credit **breaches a preset limit (trigger/maintenance level)**, the member will issue a **margin call (trigger margin)**, expecting the client to replenish the account to the original amount. This practice is common in the United States.

For example, if the initial margin for a long gilt futures contract on ICE is set at £5,000 per contract, a broker/clearing member might require that its client deposit an additional 25% of that amount as a maintenance margin. This will ensure that the member is protected from any possible losses, should the client be unable to meet any variation margin payments, particularly in volatile markets.

The level of maintenance margin is usually set at 25–50% of the initial margin payment of any new positions.

2.3 Price and Position Limits

Learning Objective

5.4.4 Understand the purpose of settlement price limits and position limits including: key features and differences; who imposes limits; the effects of their application; action in the event of breach

2.3.1 Price Limits

These are **circuit breakers** imposed by the exchange that place limits to absolute price movements on the contract on any day. If the limit is breached (limit up/limit down), trading in the contract halts for a few minutes. The idea is that, at a time when markets are subject to extreme price movements, a trading halt gives participants time to calm down and take a more reasoned view about trading conditions. However, it does not always work.

While some exchanges do not have any **standing price limits** on most derivatives contracts, others do. For example on ICE there are no price limits for the long gilt contracts, while there are for their Japanese government bond futures – of JPY2 from the Tokyo Stock Exchange closing price.

Others have **scaled price limits**. The CME Group has several down-price limits on most of its equity index futures, starting at 5% down to 20% down (each requiring a longer time before trading can resume). Also CME Globex has a 5% either-direction price limit on all of its equity contracts.

The National Commodity and Derivatives Exchange (NCDEX) also has scaled daily price limit rules. While the price limit depends on the specific contract and ranges from +/– 4% for its gold futures to +/–6% for several of its agricultural/soft contracts, such as robusta coffee, once that limit has been breached, trading resumes after a 15-minute cooling-off period, and the price limit is increased by 50%. So for example, the new price limit for gold would be +/–6%. But if that limit is broken, trading will be ended for that day.

An exchange's electronic systems also operate price limits to make sure that orders entered on to the system are within an allowed spread around the prevailing market price. If orders are entered outside this price spread, they are rejected. This should lessen the possibility of errors on entry.

2.3.2   Position Limits

It is always possible for someone to try and corner the market in any asset by building up large derivatives positions. This would give them the power to manipulate short-term price movements to their advantage. Position limits attempt to prevent this from happening. With this in mind, many exchanges do have position limits when contracts approach their maturities. For example, the CME Group has established a limit during the last ten days of trading for treasury futures and the last five days for their wheat contracts. Less liquid markets have established stricter limits, such as in Kuala Lumpur, where the Kuala Lumpur Stock Exchange (KLSE) has a position limit of 10,000 contracts per open position for its composite index future, for the future's entire life.

Similarly, for credit risk reasons, a clearing house or broker may impose position limits on a clearing member firm or client respectively, such that only a position of a certain size may be carried. An example of this is the Mercado Español de Futuros Financiaros (MEFF)'s open position limit (OPL), which limits a member's open position to one that would require a theoretical extraordinary margin that is 20% of the member's shareholder's funds. Such a position limit is based on credit risk, rather than market manipulation concerns.

2.4   Methods of Determining a Margin

Learning Objectives

5.4.5   Understand methods of margining involving delta and SPAN and their implications: application of delta; SPAN: scenario risk analysis; STANS: portfolio-based margining; effect of price change in the underlying; net liquidation value

Exchanges have developed several different programs to calculate the initial and variation or daily margin requirements for all new and existing futures and options positions. The two most common are SPAN (described in Section 2.1) and TIMS.

The level of variation/daily margin required for an existing position is determined by the **change in the price of the underlying asset**.

For **futures**, there is a direct relationship, therefore a 3% rise in the price of gold in the cash market will have a similar effect on the margin required for those short gold futures, since the future's price will rise at least that amount.

For **options**, the relationship between price changes in the underlying and its effect on an option's value is more complex, given the characteristics of an option. As explained in Chapter 3, Section 6.3, an option's **delta** is used to measure the sensitivity of an option's price to changes in the price of the underlying asset. Since an at-the-money option has a delta of 0.5, a 3% rise in the price of its underlying asset will result in an approximate 1.5% rise in the value of the option. Remember, however, that this is only one of the factors that will influence the option's price; any changes to its volatility and time decay will also be taken into account.

2.4.1 Standard Portfolio Analysis of Risk (SPAN)

SPAN (Standard Portfolio ANalysis of risk) is a **scenario-based risk program** used for calculating daily margins. It was originally developed by the CME Group, which then permitted LCH.Clearnet (previously used by ICE) to adapt its specifications to produce London SPAN. It has also been licensed by the CME Group for use by many other clearing houses.

Essentially, SPAN looks at the impact on a position of futures and options contracts if the price and volatility of the underlying asset changes by set amounts. Its parameters include the initial margin rate (known as the **scanning range**) and the percentage volatility movement.

SPAN is based on the estimation of the liquidation value of a position or portfolio using several **scenarios** representing changes in market conditions. There is a set of scenarios for each contract, which is updated on a daily basis, to reflect current market conditions.

SPAN scenarios include the following factors:

- possible changes of the underlying asset's price
- changes in the underlying asset's price volatility
- the impact of time on an option's value.

Although it draws heavily upon complex options pricing theory, SPAN itself is based upon an extremely simple set of arithmetic equations, and it is this simplicity that is perhaps the key element of the program's success. SPAN considers a total of 16 risk scenarios, when estimating the maximum loss that might be incurred from one position from one trading day to another. This is the basis for the clearing house's initial and variation margin requirements.

It separates the total position of the clearing member into **individual portfolios**, eg, all gilt futures and options in one portfolio, and FTSE 100 futures and options in another.

For each portfolio, the clearing house will set its maximum scanning range; for the FTSE 100 – say, a 300-point price movement, up and down – as well as a change in the volatility – say, a 30% rise or fall. It then applies 16 scenarios with price and volatility moving up and down by varying degrees and measures the impact on the position, eg, price up 1/3 of range and volatility up 30%. A **charge for inter-month spreads** is added, as delivery months within one instrument do not exhibit perfect correlation between each other. A **credit** is given for **inter-commodity spreads** (where permitted by the clearing house), recognising the correlation of price movements between different contracts because gains in one instrument will often offset losses in another. SPAN also recognises the additional risk of **spot delivery months** and adds a **charge** for this. Finally, it chooses the largest resulting negative number. This then becomes the **initial margin requirement**.

In a futures contract there are only price movements to consider, so the initial margin tends to remain the same unless the scanning range is changed.

Options positions (and combined futures and options positions) will be affected by changes in volatility as this is the most important element in pricing options, so the initial margin needed to maintain a position is likely to change daily. For options positions, SPAN uses deltas to calculate the equivalent number of futures to quantify any potential offset.

SPAN produces an overall initial margin requirement for the member, covering all of the contracts registered in the member's name at ICE Clear Europe. If a member has registered positions in both house and client accounts, it must simultaneously meet a separate requirement for each account.

2.4.2 Theoretical Intermarket Margining System (TIMS) and System for Theoretical Analysis and Numerical Simulations (STANS)

The Theoretical Intermarket Margining System (TIMS) was launched in 1986 and has been approved for use by the OCC and is also used by several other exchanges. TIMS uses a portfolio-based margining methodology and is particularly well suited for measuring the risk of mixed portfolios (those containing physicals, futures and options).

TIMS uses an option pricing model to identify the risks of options on a specific underlying asset which have different strike prices and maturities, and provides for offsets between positions in different, but highly correlated, underlying assets.

It bases its total margin calculation for each position on calculating two margin components: the premium margin and the risk margin. The sum of these is the total margin. The premium margin is the market value of a particular position at the close of trading. It represents the daily change or price movement. The risk margin uses an option pricing formula to measure the potential change in the position's value, assuming the assessed maximum probable intra-day price movement (using forecasts of implied volatility).

TIMS is a more complex methodology than SPAN, but one that is considered to be well-suited for use in these mixed portfolios, given its use of the option pricing model, stress testing, implied volatility and correlation modelling.

As noted earlier, in August 2006 the OCC implemented STANS – a proprietary risk margining system based on a more modern approach to measuring risk. This new approach requires more sophisticated statistical methods, more complex calculations and greater computing power than TIMS, and addresses certain shortcomings of the TIMS model, particularly with respect to correlations in price movements and the modelling of extreme events.

STANS generates a set of 10,000 hypothetical market scenarios that incorporate information extracted from the historical behaviour of each individual security as well as its relationship to the behaviour of other securities. Scenarios are generated for more than 7,000 risk factors, including a broad range of individual equities, exchange-traded funds, stock indices, currencies and commodity products.

Although the OCC continues to use TIMS for several risk management functions, it relies on STANS for the critically important purpose of assessing clearing member margin requirements. According to the OCC, the STANS model provides margin calculations that are more precise, more realistic, and more consistent across portfolios, which should improve the financial stability of the derivatives markets and produce capital efficiencies beneficial to investors.

Both SPAN and TIMS were designed to measure the market risk associated with derivatives.

2.4.3 Net Liquidation Value

Because margin requirements are based on the net positions held by the member firm, and there may be a variety of positions held at a given time, the calculation of the total margin amount due or to be received is based on the **net liquidation values (NLVs)** of the constituent parts of the portfolio. This allows for the profits showing on a portion of a member firm's positions to offset the losses of other positions in its portfolio, resulting in one net payment.

2.5   Acceptable Collateral

Cover for initial margin can be provided using collateral rather than cash. The following is the full list of assets that some of the major clearing houses accept as payment for initial margin from their members:

- **Cash** in most major currencies (sterling, euros, US dollars, Swiss francs, Swedish krona, Danish krone, Norwegian kroner and Japanese yen). Most national exchanges accept cash deposits at approved banks in their local currency.
- **Bank guarantees** from an approved bank in an approved form.
- **Certificates of deposit** (denominated in £ sterling and US dollars).
- **Government debt** (bills, bonds and notes) from the following 14 countries: the UK; Germany; Italy; the Netherlands; Sweden; Austria; the US; France; Spain; Belgium; Canada; Australia; Finland; Denmark.

However, it is important to note that:

- undated bonds are not acceptable
- the bonds must be denominated in the currency of the issuing country
- Swiss bonds are not acceptable
- collateral is also marked-to-market daily and is subject to a published 'haircut', which means that the full market value is not credited; this has become more common after the downgrading of several government bonds on the list
- the securities that are used as collateral are lodged with depositories and custodians that are acceptable to the specific clearing house.

2.6   Credit Lines

Although it is uncommon, some exchanges allow their members to extend credit to their clients to cover margin requirements. Deals requested in excess of a specified credit line will be rejected by the exchange member firm. These so-called **credit lines** will be subject to the regulatory rules specifying the circumstances in which lending money to clients is acceptable. For example, the FCA has rules on customer borrowing; under FCA rules, credit may be extended for up to five days without a formal written loan agreement.

Credit lines, which are used by customers to finance their derivatives trading, are not allowed by the ICE markets for their financial products.

2.7   Collateral Management

Collateral is the name for the assets that are used as a guarantee or as security for the credit line or loan. Collateral reduces the exchange member's credit risk from the client to whom they have extended the credit line.

Collateral management is the process that allows market participants to reduce the counterparty credit exposure that arise from longer-maturity OTC derivative contracts, such as swaps and options.

For example, Company A enters into a ten-year interest rate swap, as a fixed rate payer, with one of its main banks. As market rates fall, in favour of the bank and against Company A, the **mark-to-market** profit on the swap represents a loss to Company A and a profit for the bank. This in turn increases the bank's risk exposure to the company, since it has a loss on this swap position.

One way that the banks can reduce the risk exposure created by the swap is to enter into a Credit Support Annex (CSA) or Collateral Support Document (CSD), which contains the details of the conditions and procedures by which collateralisation will occur.

A **Credit Support Annex** is an agreement relating to the credit support/collateral management of longer-term derivatives transactions. It is one of the four parts of an ISDA contract. A CSA defines the rules and conditions under which collateral is transferred between the counterparties to the derivative contract. It main aim is to mitigate the credit risk arising from the 'out-of-the-money' or mark-to-market loss of a derivatives position. See Chapter 4, Section 10.

The **Collateral Support Document (CSD)** is very similar to a CSA, in that it contains the timing and procedure for the mark-to-market (MTM) of the contract. Once the new valuation has been agreed, the counterparty with the negative MTM valuation will transfer the change in value to the counterparty with the positive MTM.

This process is very similar to the daily margin process that all exchange clearing houses go through with their members.

In addition to reducing counterparty risk, collateral management can also improve capital usage, increase the potential number of transactions that can be undertaken with an individual counterparty, and reducing dealing spreads.

In addition to setting the timing of the MTM, the CSA will also include key procedural details such as setting:

* the **threshold amounts** – which is the unsecured credit exposure that one counterparty is prepared to accept before making a collateral request. This is usually set at a relatively low level, in order to reduce credit risk
* **minimum transfer amounts** – the minimum amount of a collateral request; any collateral transfer below this amount is not permitted. It is designed to prevent frequent and unnecessary calls of collateral, as well as avoid the costs involved with small transfer payments;
* the valuation percentage or **haircut** – the discount that is applied to the collateral's market value; this protects the collateral receiver from falls in the collateral's value in the period between collateral calls. The higher the quality of the collateral, the lower the haircut.

See also Chapter 4, Section 11.

Appendix

Answer to the chapter exercises.

Answers to Exercise 1

Sold at	6540
Less: current cost of purchase	(6570)
Loss in index points per contract	(30)

Variation margin payable = 30 index points x £10 per index point x 5 contracts = £1,500.

Answers to Exercise 2

Bought at	$18,950
Daily settlement price	$18,980
Profit	$30

Variation payable to the trader = $30 per tonne x 5-tonne contract size x 20 contracts = $3,000.

End of Chapter Questions

1. What is clearing?
   Answer reference: Section 1.1

2. What is novation?
   Answer reference: Section 1.1

3. A prime broker's role in relation to derivatives is that it is primarily responsible for what?
   Answer reference: Section 1.4

4. What is the main advantage of having an OTC derivative cleared or substituted by an exchange's clearing house?
   Answer reference: Section 1.5

5. Every clearing member is required to contribute to the clearing fund. Upon what is the required amount is based?
   Answer reference: Section 1.5.1

6. What is a contingent liability?
   Answer reference: Section 2.1

7. How does a spot month margin reduce short-term speculative pressures?
   Answer reference: Section 2.2

8. At what level of the initial margin payment of any new positions is maintenance margin usually set?
   Answer reference: Section 2.2.3

9. What assets do some of the major clearing houses accept from their members as cover for initial margin?
   Answer reference: Section 2.5

10. What is a CSA?
    Answer reference: Section 2.7

Chapter Six
Delivery and Settlement

This syllabus area will provide approximately 5 of the 80 examination questions

1. Delivery and Settlement – Futures

1.1 Introduction

Even though most futures positions are closed out before expiry, the conceptual basis of these contracts is that delivery can take place. Hence mechanisms must be in place to ensure that this can happen. The clearing house will manage and define rules and procedures, in conjunction with the exchange, to govern the delivery process.

As seen in Chapter 5, Clearing, the clearing house becomes the legal counterparty (via the process known as novation) after the trades have been confirmed and registered. The clearing house guarantees the performance of the trades carried out by its members and substantially reduces counterparty risk.

As buyer and seller to each contract, when a futures contract proceeds to delivery, the clearing house manages the contract delivery of open contracts between clearing members and may enable the delivery of documents to represent the underlying assets (such as 'warrants' used in the metals market operated by the London Metal Exchange).

For example each LME warrant represents one lot of a specific type/grade of metal. The buyer of the metal (or holder of the warrant) presents this to a LME listed warehouse and upon receipt of the warrant, it will deliver to the holder the precise amount and grade of metal that it represents.

1.2 Closing Contracts

Learning Objective

6.1.1   Understand the purpose of closing contracts compared with rollover or delivery, and the main methods for performing close-outs

Holders of futures contracts have three choices:

1. to close out the contract before expiry, or
2. to roll the position forward by closing out the existing position and simultaneously establishing a new position in a new quoted month, or
3. to proceed to delivery.

Closing out the contracts before delivery will avoid the need to make or take delivery and enables the holder to realise any profit or loss arising on the position. Once the contracts have been closed out, the holder/seller no longer has any market exposure, as opposed to when a futures position is rolled over, which in effect, if it is a full rollover, changes the position's maturity, but not its risk. Most exchanges have a specific rollover date (normally five to eight trading days before the contracts mature) which in effect shifts the exchange's price reference to the new contract.

While any gains or losses will be realised when a contract is closed out or delivered, the decision to close it out provides the holder/seller with more flexibility, since he can do it at any time up to its maturity. Also it may be cheaper, since it allows the holder/seller to realise any profits or losses, without incurring any delivery/storage charges that would occur if the contract went through its delivery process.

In order to relinquish any obligations in the market, a close-out instruction must be given by the client. This instruction determines which long position (or part-position) to close out against which short position (or part-position).

For clients holding various positions in a particular contract (ie, both long and short positions held 'gross'), there are various common methods for performing close-outs:

- **First-in, first-out (FIFO)** – close out the oldest long position against the oldest short position.
- **Last-in, first-out (LIFO)** – close out the most recent trade (long or short) against the oldest position (long or short).
- **Maximum profit** – close out an equal number of long and short positions to realise the maximum amount of profit.
- **Maximum loss** – close out an equal number of long and short positions to realise the maximum loss.

Positions can be designated to be left open, for instance if they are part of a specific strategy.

There are other close-out methods that are used, and it is also possible to provide manual instructions to close-out specific positions. A position which has been closed out and effectively no longer exists is described as being **flat**.

If a position is closed out incorrectly or in error then it is possible to **bust the settlement**. This is the term used for reversing the closing action and reopening a position.

1.3 Physical Delivery or Cash Settlement

Learning Objective

6.1.2 Understand the purpose, key features and differences between cash settlement and physically delivered contracts: factors used in ascertaining the invoice amount; warrant delivery; differences between financial and commodity products

6.1.3 Understand the importance and implications of the delivery of open contracts at expiry and the significance of the short position: purpose of open contracts; financials versus commodities; avoidance of delivery – reasons and methods; seller's choice of delivery time and method; underlying asset delivery to the clearing house; relevance of first notice day, last notice day and delivery day or period

6.1.4 Understand the processes for physical delivery including: exchange delivery settlement price (EDSP) and the factors affecting its value; auction process; calculation of the invoice amount on a physically settled contract

As seen in the previous section, the rationale for closing out a contract is to avoid the need to take or make delivery of the underlying asset. For those contracts that have not been closed out and remain open at expiry, the exchange rules define what assets, in terms of quality and quantity, may be **delivered** in final settlement of exchange contracts.

For example, the LME defines in its rules the brands, origins and warehouses that are acceptable as good delivery against each of its metals contracts, and ICE Futures similarly defines delivery points and deliverable grades for its deliverable gas oil contract.

The LME uses a **warrant-based system** that allows for easy delivery, since its approved warehouses are located around the world. This system is known as **LMEsword**. This allows the LME to accommodate metal producers that have excess supply at times. In this aspect, it becomes the **market of last resort**.

LMEsword is a secure electronic transfer system for LME warrants which are to be held in a central depository. All LME warrants are produced to a standard format with a barcode. Warehouse companies issuing these warrants ensure that the details are known to LMEsword, which acts as a central database, holding details of ownership, and is subject to stringent security controls. The ownership of LME warrants can be transferred between LMEsword members in a matter of seconds, and all rent payments are automatically calculated.

LMEsword brings a number of benefits, particularly in administrative efficiency, by removing the physical transfer of warrants and simplifying the manual operations involved. It also reduces the number of times a warrant has to be passed by hand, as warrants no longer need to be physically transferred from owner to owner every time the material is bought or sold. Warrants are immobilised in a depository.

For physically deliverable futures contracts, the underlying asset changes hands. The exchange stipulates the **last trading day** for the contract, at the end of which the closing price is established. In the case of the ICE markets, this is known as the **Exchange Delivery Settlement Price (EDSP)**. At expiry, the exchange rules define what assets, in terms of quality, quantity and location, may be finally delivered.

The delivery process then begins for all open positions.

Futures sellers give notice declaring their intention to deliver the asset to the clearing house. This is known as a **tender notice** – they are 'tendering' for delivery. It then assigns those assets to futures buyers, usually on a random basis. If there is any flexibility allowed in the contract, the futures seller has the choice of what, where and when to deliver – this is referred to as **seller's choice**.

The **timetable** for the tender process varies between contracts. Sometimes there is only one notice day and tenders are all processed together (an example is the Euro-Bund future on Eurex). On other contracts there may be a longer period starting with a **first notice day** and ending with a **last notice day** (such as the long gilt, cocoa and robusta coffee futures on ICE). The underlying asset is then delivered on the **delivery day**.

These are the first two steps of four main stages that are part of ICE's delivery procedure:

1. The seller or holder of the short futures position advises ICE Clear Europe/ICE market of their intention to deliver the underlying asset.
2. ICE's Universal Clearing Platform (UCP) then matches sellers to buyers on a random basis. UCP is also used for trade and position management following the transaction providing daily position management. But it then feeds the positions and margin requirements to ICE Clear's ECS.

The next two steps in the delivery process are discussed in the following sections of this chapter:

3. ICE Clear Europe calculates the invoice amount and notifies the seller and buyer.
4. The seller delivers the underlying asset as instructed to the clearing house and receives the invoice amount. The buyer makes the invoice payment to the clearing house and receives delivery of the underlying asset.

As the above-mentioned examples show, whether the physical delivery is for financial or commodity contracts can be significant. For both, the seller must ensure that, whether it is 30-year US Treasury or South American soya beans, he must deliver the correct quantity and quality as specified in the contract. But, as the LMEsword system shows, for the most part the delivery process for commodities can be more involved and sometimes more expensive.

For both, however, the delivery process ensures that the buyer receives what he has paid for and that it is available to him, whether it be JGBs deposited in his Tokyo brokerage account, or a warrant giving him access to corn.

1.3.1   Invoice Amount

For physically delivered contracts the futures buyers will receive an invoice for the asset and have to pay the amount stated in the invoice. The formula is:

EDSP x scale factor x number of contracts

The **scale factor** converts the price quote to reflect the total value of the assets being delivered, as in the following example.

Example 1

The EDSP for Brent crude is $45 per barrel. Contract size is 1,000 barrels. Because the price is quoted in barrels, and each contract is for 1,000 barrels, the scale factor is 1,000.

The invoice amount for five contracts might be:

$$\$45 \times 1{,}000 \times 5 = \$225{,}000$$

The EDSP is unlikely to be the price originally agreed. Suppose the buyer went long at $40.70. By paying $45.00, he is paying more than the agreed price. But remember that the buyer will already have received variation margin through the lifetime of the contract and that profit will be in his account.

So, in net terms, the actual price paid is the agreed price of $40.70 per barrel.

As seen earlier in Chapter 3, the invoice amount for a bond futures contract is slightly more involved. It is given by the following equation:

(EDSP x price factor x scale factor x number of contracts) + accrued interest

There are two additional elements in this equation. The **price factor** is used to convert the EDSP based on the notional bond to the equivalent EDSP for the bond actually being delivered. The **accrued interest** reflects the fact that the EDSP is quoted clean (ignoring the accrued interest implicit within the bond at the point of delivery).

Exercise 1

What would be the invoice amount for the following delivery of ICE London's long gilt future?

Five contracts when the EDSP for the contract is £98.50, the price factor of the bond being delivered is 1.12142 and the bond has accrued interest of £4.54 per £100 nominal. The scale factor is 1,000.

The answer can be found in the appendix at the end of this chapter.

1.3.2   Cash Settlement – Contracts for Difference

Learning Objective

6.1.5   Understand the processes, merits and limitations of cash settlement of contracts for differences

With cash-settled contracts there is no exchange of the underlying asset. There is an exchange of funds representing profits and losses on the contract.

The key **advantage** of cash settlement over physical delivery is that cash settlement avoids the need for the asset to be delivered, and the consequent need for precise specification of quantity, quality and location. Cash settlement also allows contracts to be based on non-deliverable underlying assets, such as short-term interest rate deposits, or the FTSE 100 and S&P 500 equity indices.

As variation margin payments will have already been made or received daily during the life of the open position, the only element required to settle the trade is the payment of the last day's variation margin against the EDSP (being the final price for the contract month); this satisfies the delivery obligations.

But in some cases, cash settlement is seen as a **disadvantage**. This is the case in some bond index futures, such as ICE London's EuroMTS government bond index future, which is based on the price of several euro government bonds and does not provide for pricing factors that allow for delivery of a specific bond that is a component of the index. This is due to the fact that this future is exclusively cash-settled but, as mentioned below, there is a possibility that its price is vulnerable to manipulation.

There is concern that cash settlement for this contract, since it is based on an index, may be vulnerable to manipulation by market participants in some cases. In addition, it also carries risks, in that trading activity on the underlying market during the EDSP period is likely to be affected by the activity of particular market participants who are seeking to obtain price convergence at the EDSP between offsetting bond and futures positions. Such participants might typically seek to achieve this by unwinding their bond positions during the EDSP period at prices which they anticipate will contribute to the calculation of index figures, which will, in turn, be used to determine the final EDSP.

1.4 Exchange Delivery Settlement Price (EDSP)

Learning Objective

6.1.4   Understand the processes for physical delivery including: exchange delivery settlement price (EDSP) and the factors affecting its value; auction process; calculation of the invoice amount on a physically settled contract

As seen, the Exchange Delivery Settlement Price (EDSP) is the ICE Europe market's term for a future's closing price.

The EDSP (or equivalent on other exchanges) is very significant, as it is the sole price at which all outstanding futures (bought and sold) will be closed. In setting the EDSP, the exchange must use an openly declared mechanism that will prevent any price manipulation. The resulting price must be fair, and truly representative of spot prices.

Note that many contracts are cash-settled and, by definition, physical delivery does not apply (examples are STIR and stock index futures and options). The EDSP process is still of fundamental importance, however, as the EDSP effectively becomes the final price at which variation margin changes hands. Some exchanges have contracts which offer the option of cash settlement instead of settlement by physical delivery (eg, ICE Futures Brent crude oil).

The EDSP could be subject to manipulation and needs to be a fair reflection of the underlying asset at expiry. As a result, the exchange will endeavour to avoid manipulation by following the procedures outlined in Chapter 5, Section 2, Margin, for establishing the daily settlement prices.

ICE uses a variety of techniques across its various contracts. The flagship contract, the ICE EURIBOR short-term interest rate (STIR) future, depends upon an EDSP price that is supplied by the European Banking Federation (ie, the price view of some 40-plus banks). Whatever technique is used to determine the EDSP by an exchange, it must be fair and reflect as accurately as possible the price status in the underlying market. It must also be free from manipulation. Exchanges keep such matters under close supervision, together with the regulators. For example, the procedure for establishing the EDSP for the FTSE 100 futures and options contracts on ICE London was changed for the November 2004 expiry. Previously, a price-averaging system, based on actual trades over the last 20 minutes of trading on the morning of the last trading day, had been used. This was replaced by a system that derives the EDSP from an intra-day auction.

The new system ensures that, at expiry, potentially substantial trading activity in the underlying shares is channelled into a mechanism where there is opportunity for aggregate supply and demand to be matched efficiently. Every share in the FTSE is included within parallel auctions, all of which last for no more than 15 minutes. By doing this, the exchange knows that the EDSP is being based upon the very latest information from the market as to where each share price (and hence the overall index itself) lies. Similar approaches are used by derivatives markets in Germany and the US.

ICE London uses a completely different technique for its long gilt futures contract. The EDSP of this contract is the market price of the contract at 11.00am on the second business day prior to settlement, unless notice is given on the last notice day, when it is the price prevailing on the last trading day. The invoice amount with respect to the deliverable gilt is calculated by a price factor system, with an adjustment for any coupon interest accruing as at the settlement day.

2. Delivery and Settlement – Options

Learning Objective

6.2.1 Understand the processes and implications of the exercise of options, the assignment of obligations, abandonment and expiry: purpose of assignment of obligations; instigating an assignment notice; receiving an assignment notice; abandonment; which options are most likely to be exercised before expiry; exercise at expiry; European, American and Bermudan options; action upon exercise; reasons for assignments; effect of assignment; advantages to the investor; probability of assignment

Assignment is the process of requiring option sellers to perform their obligations. For example:

- A seller of an equity call would be obliged to sell the shares at the option's strike price.
- A seller of a bond call would, potentially, become the short to a bond future at the option's strike price.

2.1 Exercise of Physically Deliverable Options

A European-style option can only be exercised at expiry, whereas an American-style option can be exercised over a set period up to the expiry date. However, remember that even American-style options are unlikely to be exercised until the expiry date approaches, because the holder will prefer to sell the option and realise the time value that adds to the option's premium. The same is also true for Bermudan-style options, despite the fact that they can be exercised at certain specified dates before expiration, like American-style options, their holders will receive more if they sell at a date close to the expiry date.

Furthermore, an option-holder will only exercise an option if it is **in-the-money (ITM)**, with the exercise itself either realising a profit or reducing the loss on the open trade.

If the option-holder decides to exercise a profitable (ITM) option, he notifies his broker. The broker will then fill in an **exercise notice** that is delivered to the **clearing house** (by the deadline) via the **clearing member**. Notice how with options, unlike futures where the seller commences the delivery cycle, it is the buyer (holder or owner) who exercises his right and starts the process.

On receipt of the exercise notice the clearing house will select (**assign**), at random, an option writer (seller or short) and send them an **assignment notice**. The assignment notice is the formal notification that the terms of the contract must be fulfilled. The transaction then becomes a **cash market transaction** and is subject to the normal trading costs, such as commissions.

Example 2 _____

On exercise of an ICE equity call option contract on the shares of a UK company, both the holder and the writer will receive contract notes, and the holder will have to pay commission on the value of the shares, as well as Stamp Duty Reserve Tax (SDRT) and Panel on Takeovers and Mergers (PTM) levy. The trade will settle through the UK equity cash market settlement mechanism (Euroclear UK & Ireland Limited) on the normal equity settlement timetable of T+3.

2.2   Exercise of Cash-Settled Options – Contracts for Differences

The process is effectively to transfer the intrinsic value of the option from the writer to the holder.

Example 3 _____

If an investor exercises one FTSE call option with a strike at 6450 when the EDSP is 6530, since the contract size is £10 per point he will receive:

$$(6530 - 6450) \times £10 = £800$$

Remember, for options which have futures-style premium payment (as with all ICE markets), variation margin will have accounted for most of this, and only the final day's variation margin will change hands.

But if this were an OTC option, the option-holder would most likely receive the full amount upon its exercise.

2.3   Exercise of Options on Futures

If these are exercised, the process is as above, except that the holder and writer will be assigned a long/ short futures position at the strike price. As a result of the option being exercised, the open interest in the underlying futures contract will increase by the number of exercised options.

2.4   Abandonment and Cabinet Trades

If the holder decides not to exercise, the option lapses and the writer's obligation ceases.

Holders tend to wait until the last possible moment before abandoning the option. They would abandon options that are out-of-the-money, or slightly in-the-money but not worth exercising when transaction costs are taken into account.

Sometimes traders prefer to close out the position for a nominal amount – a **cabinet trade** – in order to crystallise a loss for tax or accounting purposes. If an investor wants to set losses against current or future capital gains, documentation is required.

2.5   Automatic Exercise

Learning Objective

6.2.2   Understand the significance of automatic exercise: purpose of automatic exercise; options that may be subject to automatic exercise; reasons for clearing houses to adopt automatic exercise; benefits to members and holders of long positions; prevention of automatic exercise

---

ICE Clear Europe operates an automatic exercise facility (for ICE and ICE Futures) whereby it will **automatically exercise any option that is sufficiently in-the-money at expiry**. This reduces the paperwork and also means that participants need not worry about forgetting to exercise.

The trigger for automatic exercise is when the price of the underlying asset is at or above a certain level for a call or at or below a certain level for a put – in other words, when the option is **in-the-money** at its expiration enough to cover any delivery cost associated with exercising the option.

Capped-style options are those which are subject to automatic exercise. They have an established profit cap; once the underlying asset's price has moved beyond that cap and the option is in-the-money at expiration, it will be subject to automatic exercise.

Note, there are exercise fees to be paid, so, if an investor does not want the option exercised, a **suppression notice** must be filed with the clearing house.

2.6   Early Exercise of Options

It is possible to exercise American-style options before their expiry. The decision to exercise early is the responsibility of the holder and not the clearing house. The clearing house will assign the contracts to writers at random.

Normally, it is not rational to exercise an option before its expiry. Exercising realises the intrinsic value of the option and not its time value. It makes more sense to sell the option to capture the time value as well. However, for some types of options (eg, equity-based) there are times when it will be feasible to exercise early. This requires three criteria:

1. **American-style** – European-style options cannot be exercised before expiry.
2. **Deep-in-the-money** – the option must have intrinsic value.
3. **Close to expiry/short-dated** – there must be very little time value left.

With equity options there are sometimes good reasons to exercise early, because the owner can then take up dividend rights pertaining to a stock/share, or be able to obtain voting rights.

Answer to the chapter exercise.

Answer to Exercise 1

The invoice amount is given by the equation:

(EDSP x price factor x scale factor x number of contracts) + accrued interest

where:

EDSP	=	£98.50
Price factor	=	1.12142
Scale factor	=	1,000 (the long gilt contract has a notional value of £100,000 nominal and with the EDSP based on £100 nominal it must be scaled up by 1,000)
Number of contracts	=	5
Accrued interest	=	£4.54 x 1,000 x 5 = £22,700 (the accrued interest must reflect £100,000 nominal per contract)

Invoice amount = (98.5 x 1.12142 x 1,000 x 5) + 22,700 = £574,999

End of Chapter Questions

1. Why must delivery mechanisms be put in place for futures?
   Answer reference: Section 1.1

2. In terms of closing, what are the three choices open to holders of futures contracts?
   Answer reference: Section 1.2

3. What is meant by the term 'bust the settlement'?
   Answer reference: Section 1.2

4. Why does the LME use LMEsword?
   Answer reference: Section 1.3

5. What is the key advantage of cash settlement over physical delivery?
   Answer reference: Section 1.3.2

6. Why would cash settlement be seen as a disadvantage?
   Answer reference: Section 1.3.2

7. For what reason is the EDSP so important?
   Answer reference: Section 1.4

8. On receipt of an exercise notice, what does a clearing house do?
   Answer reference: Section 2.1

9. What is a cabinet trade?
   Answer reference: Section 2.4

10. What triggers an automatic exercise?
    Answer reference: Section 2.5

Chapter Seven
Portfolio Research and Construction

This syllabus area will provide approximately 7 of the 80 examination questions

7

1. Introduction

Research is a key part of investing and portfolio construction. The first section of this chapter provides a brief review of the main sources of market information and context of their content. It is key that all investors and portfolio managers have access to and clearly understand both the information provided and its purpose, to ensure that they use all the information and analysis they receive, in the right context.

Portfolio construction and management is an ongoing process, and one that involves risk/return assessment. Sections 3 and 4 examine the key elements of this assessment.

2. Market Information and Research

2.1 Information and Communication

Learning Objective

7.1.1 Understand how to access and use regulatory, economic and financial communications: news services; government resources and statistics; broker research and distributor information; desk research; regulatory resources

Individual investors and portfolio managers have access to a wide range of financial communication that ranges from macro-economic news, and a company's financial results, to official and privately produced research and forecasts.

Technology has made available to most investors market information that at one time was available only to traders and brokers on an exchange's trading floor or in a bank's trading room. Today, any investor with a mobile phone and/or the internet has access to current market data and news via a wide range of online news services, such as Thomson Reuters, Bloomberg, the BBC and the Financial Times, as well as to recent prices using an exchange's website. While many charge a subscription fee for the most up-to-date prices and analysis, all provide up-to-date news and economic releases.

Since most government departments and the Bank of England (as well as most other major central banks) maintain their own websites, investors have easy access to the most current statistics and official forecasts. Both also produce more in-depth analysis and reports that can be downloaded from their website and are also available in print.

While most of the major investment brokers, fund managers and banks distribute market information and research, many do so, on a priority basis. That is, their premium clients usually get this information first and in full detail. This is usually followed by summaries that are posted to their public websites. It is important to remember that most of this information and research is based on the source's opinion, rather than hard-and-fast facts. Many financial regulators require that most forecasts, asset-specific analysis and investment recommendations carry a clear notice that they are just that, ie, the broker's opinion. Many regulators also require the firm to list any financial interests it has with the assets discussed in the research. This is done solely for investor protection.

2.2   Market Research and Reports

Learning Objective

7.1.2   Understand the different types, uses and availability of research and reports: fundamental analysis; technical analysis; volatility in underlying sector: benchmark and relative; sector-specific reports

Fundamental analysis is about using real data to evaluate a security's value. Although most analysts use fundamental analysis to value stocks, this method of valuation can be used for just about any type of security. Fundamental analysts attempt to study everything that can affect the security's value, including macro-economic factors – such as the overall economy, current interest rates and industry conditions – along with company-specific factors, such as its financial condition, competitiveness (such as products, market standing and research programmes) and management, or, in the case of bonds, factors like government policies, policy constraints and credit ratings.

The aim of fundamental analysis is to determine a value that an investor can compare with the security's current price, with the aim of deciding what sort of position to take with that security (underpriced = buy; overpriced = sell or go short). This method of securities analysis uses a completely different approach from technical analysis.

Example 1

If a US-based portfolio manager, who holds a significant amount of EU shares, is concerned that the euro might weaken, one method of research would be fundamental analysis, which would entail measuring and comparing the key economic statistics and interest rates between the US and EU. This will give an indication of whether the dollar will strengthen against the euro and whether the portfolio manager should hedge his EUR/USD exchange rate risk.

When assessing individual shares, this method uses a company's financial statements, looking at its revenues, earnings, future growth, return on equity, profit margins and other data to determine its underlying value and potential for future growth. In terms of stocks, fundamental analysis focuses on the financial statements to determine the company's intrinsic value.

Technical analysis is a method of evaluating securities by analysing the statistics generated by market activity, such as past prices and volume. Technical analysts do not attempt to measure a security's intrinsic value, but instead use charts and other tools to identify patterns that can suggest future activity. Just as there are many investment styles on the fundamental side, there are also many different types of technical traders. Some rely on chart patterns, others technical indicators and oscillators, and most use some combination of the two. In any case, technical analysts' exclusive use of historical price and volume data is what separates them from their fundamental counterparts. Unlike fundamental analysts, technical analysts don't worry whether a stock is undervalued – the only thing that matters is a security's past trading data and what information this data can provide about where the security might move in the future.

Sector-specific reports are produced by a wide range of sources, from investment advisers, brokers, fund managers and independent research firms. These reports can combine both fundamental and technical-based analysis as part of their recommendations. Their main purpose is to cover a specific asset sector, such as global car companies or a specific credit ranking of corporate bonds.

Those reports that have more of a technical base usually include analysis on the price movements of a specific asset relative to its sector, a specific **benchmark** and/or the overall market. A key basis of these types of reports is the **relative price volatility**, since many portfolio managers find this useful when assessing an asset's price, and/or when evaluating the derivatives that are based on that asset.

The main purpose of these types of reports is to give an assessment and forecast for the sector and asset class covered by the report, and in most cases to provide a ranking and recommendation for each of the companies or assets covered by the report.

2.3   Securities and Derivatives: Influences and Relationship

Learning Objective

7.1.3   Assess key factors that influence derivatives markets and sectors: responses to change and uncertainty; volume, liquidity, and nature of trading activity in domestic and overseas markets; volatility; risk-based regulations and restrictions

The value and therefore the price of all derivatives is based on and has a close relationship with the **price of its underlying security**. If this were not true, the markets would be full of arbitrage opportunities. While these opportunities do exist in certain conditions, they do so for only a short period and are relatively small, since the markets are efficient.

Securities and derivatives respond in the same way to change and uncertainty. In many cases, derivatives might seem to be the first to react, for example to increased uncertainty, which results in higher volatility in their price and will result in an increase in the price of options on that market or security; however, any difference will be small and short-lived.

All of the key factors that influence a security's price, such as trading volume, liquidity, news announcements and market sentiments, will have the same effect on the related derivatives price. The recent advances in communication and inter-market dealing have ensured that both markets move together.

3.   Portfolio Construction

3.1   Main Types of Portfolio Risk

Learning Objective

7.2.1   Analyse the main types of portfolio risk and their implications for investors: systemic risk; market or systematic risk – asset price volatility, currency, interest rates, commodity price volatility; investment horizon; liquidity, credit risk and default; counterparty risk

Almost all investments carry a certain level of risk. The following is a description of the main types of risks that an investor has to deal with regarding their portfolio.

3.1.1   Systemic Risk

Systemic risk is the risk that **affects the financial system as a whole** – as opposed to any specific asset – and is therefore likely to affect all investments. Systemic risks tend to be beyond the power of most investors to predict, and often of the portfolio manager to protect against; however, some types of investment are more vulnerable to systemic risk than others.

Systemic risk is the risk of collapse of an entire financial system or entire market, as opposed to risk associated with any one individual asset, sector or component of a system. It can be defined as 'financial system instability, any potential catastrophe, that is caused or exacerbated by idiosyncratic events or conditions in financial intermediaries'. It refers to the risks associated with the interdependencies within a system or market, where the failure of a single participant or number of participants can cause a cascading failure, which could potentially bankrupt or bring down the entire system or market.

3.1.2   Market Risk

Market risk is the risk that the value of an individual asset or an entire portfolio will decrease due to the change in value of the market risk factors. It is also known as systematic risk and is one that cannot be diversified away.

The four standard market risk factors are: stock prices, interest rates, foreign exchange rates, and commodity prices. The associated market risks are:

*   **Equity risk** – the risk that stock prices and/or the implied volatility will change.
*   **Interest rate risk** – the risk that interest rates and/or the implied volatility will change.
*   **Currency risk** – the risk that foreign exchange rates and/or the implied volatility will change.
*   **Commodity risk** – the risk that commodity prices (eg, corn, copper, crude oil) and/or implied volatility will change.

3.1.3   Investment Horizon

Investment horizon refers to the total length of time that an investor expects to hold a specific security or portfolio. It is used to determine an investor's income needs and desired risk exposure, which is then used to aid security selection.

As one's investment horizons increase, some riskier assets, such as equities, have a higher risk-adjusted return than fixed-income securities and cash. For shorter investment horizons, equities become the riskier asset class, because they carry higher levels of volatility.

An individual's investment horizon depends on when and how much money will be needed for a specific time frame, and this horizon influences the optimal investment strategy. As a rule, the shorter an investor's horizon, the less risk he should be willing to accept.

3.1.4   Liquidity, Credit Risk and Default

Liquidity can mean both the amount of cash in a portfolio, or, in connection with a specific investment, how easily it can be sold and converted into cash at or at least close to its current market price. If a specific type of investment or market is illiquid, this means that it is hard to sell the investment quickly for a fair price; in such cases there is little that an investor can do. Problems of illiquidity can be normal for certain investment classes (such as property that can be hard to sell in poor markets), or they can arise suddenly, because of a particular event. For example, when Northern Rock first had its problems, other banks and financial institutions were unwilling to lend it funds, even in the overnight market. It eventually had to receive government support, to ensure that it was able to raise funds.

An illiquid market can result in a significant reduction in mark-to-market profits or even greater losses, if the investor is unable to sell an asset at what is the published price.

Credit risk and default is the risk that the issuer of a security defaults, that is, he cannot repay the capital, and/or (in the case of a fixed-interest security) the interest, as it falls due. While investors and portfolio managers use an issuer's credit rating as a measure of the likelihood of this, there are no absolute guarantees.

The lower a debtor's credit rating, the higher the yields demanded by investors to buy its debt. Therefore, investors are compensated for the increased risk of default through higher returns. A prime example of this is the higher yield that investors have demanded on Greek, Spanish, Portuguese and Italian government bonds compared to German government bonds, due to their 'higher risk' or 'lower creditworthiness' among EU government debt.

3.1.5   Counterparty Risk

Counterparty risk (also referred to as credit risk) is the risk that your counterparty in a trade or transaction cannot honour its obligation to you. For example, you have bought an OTC equity put option on a specific share. The company announces an unexpected profit warning and its share price collapses and the mark-to-market value of your put option increases sharply, which has introduced significant counterparty risk since the trade is on the OTC market and you have to rely on the counterparty to fulfil his obligation.

Basically, it is the potential loss from the possibility that any trade counterparty will not be able to meet their obligations. Note that counterparty risk exists only for OTC positions that are profitable to your portfolio.

3.2 Investment Allocation and Mitigating Portfolio Risk

Learning Objective

7.2.2 Understand the core principles used to mitigate portfolio risk: correlation; diversification; active and passive strategies; hedging and immunisation

7.2.3 Understand the key approaches to investment allocation for bond, equity and balanced portfolios: asset class; geographical area; currency issuer; sector; maturity

There are a number of ways that a portfolio manager can reduce a portfolio's risk. Here are the main principles that are currently used.

3.2.1 Diversification

Diversification within a portfolio can be achieved through a number of ways, one of which is to reduce risk by investing in a broad exposure to different characteristics within the asset class. This can be based on:

- asset classes
- geographical areas
- sectors
- currencies
- maturities.

Spreading investments across a wide range of available **asset classes**, eg, cash, bonds, equities, commodities and other assets, is a starting point for most portfolio managers.

Further diversification can be achieved by spreading the portfolio's exposure to a specific asset class across various **geographical areas**, eg, UK equities, European equities and/or emerging markets equities. The same is true for **bonds**: to reduce the portfolio's risk, a manager may invest in bonds, both government and corporate, from a number of countries. Since credit risk is a factor for bond investments, the portfolio manager, subject to his investment guidelines and restrictions, may also invest in a range of bonds based on their different **credit rating** and **maturity**, the latter of which will help reduce the portfolio's risk to a rise in inflation in a specific country.

Sector diversification such as spreading equity and bond exposure across different sectors, eg, banking and utilities, can help reduce the risk of a downturn in any particular area.

Investing in different **currencies** can also help to limit the risks of any unfavourable exchange rate movements. This may be particularly useful if the client is based overseas.

3.2.2 Correlation

But you might ask, given the increased integration of the global economy and financial markets, how can a portfolio manager judge how to construct a diversified portfolio? One of the most popular tools is to measure the **correlation** between the potential assets. Correlation is a measure of how the returns/performance of two assets' returns are related, or move together over time. The most common measure used is the **correlation coefficient**, which is a measure of how well trends in the predicted values follow trends in the actual values in the past.

The correlation coefficient is always a number between minus one and one. As the relationship between the predicted values and actual values increases, so does the correlation coefficient. A perfect fit gives a coefficient of +1.0 (perfect positive correlation) or –1.0 (perfect negative correlation). In other words, assets with a high level of correlation (close to +1) tend to move in the same direction at the same time. Assets with a low correlation (close to 0) tend to move independently of each other. Assets with strong negative correlations (close to –1) tend to move in opposite directions.

Assets with a low or negative correlation are attractive to investors, in that, when one asset is performing badly, the other asset is hopefully rising in value. When constructing a diversified portfolio, the manager will choose investments that hopefully will do well and which are independent, at least to some degree, from one another – that is, their movements are not dependent on the same factors, time or conditions as the other investments that have been chosen. For example, if the profits of companies in a specific sector have not been affected by higher inflation and therefore higher interest rates, holding shares in that sector would be a good way to diversify from shares that are interest-rate-sensitive, such as consumer goods shares or bonds.

Correlation coefficients are therefore useful to portfolio managers in two ways.

* By choosing assets with a **low correlation coefficient**, he can reduce the portfolio's risk, by constructing a well-diversified portfolio.
* When a portfolio manager identifies an attractive investment asset, but for whatever reason it is too expensive or restricted or illiquid, he can try to find an attractive alternative by using an asset that has a **high correlation coefficient** (which means that their returns are highly related).

3.2.3 Active and Passive Strategies

Other measures that a portfolio manager might use to mitigate risk are again dependent on his investment guidelines. He might take an **active** strategy – one that involves the constant monitoring of the performance of the individual assets within the portfolio, to use as a basis for the ongoing buying and selling of the portfolio's investments. This is mainly used by those portfolio managers that have the goal to outperform a specific index or benchmark.

The opposite is an investment strategy that involves very limited ongoing buying and selling actions. **Passive** investors will construct an investment portfolio based on the view of long-term appreciation and limited maintenance. Unlike active investors, passive investors buy a security and typically don't actively attempt to profit from short-term price fluctuations. Passive investors instead rely on their belief that in the long term the investment will be profitable. Portfolio managers who use this strategy do not have to worry about short-term price movements that might handicap their performance. Index-tracking is often referred to as a passive strategy.

3.2.4 Hedging and Immunisation

Two other ways to reduce portfolio risk are hedging and immunisation. **Hedging** involves entering into a contract that either reduces part or all of the risk associated with any adverse price movements in a specific asset or holding within the portfolio. For example, if the portfolio manager is concerned that the portfolio's base currency will appreciate and therefore reduce the returns from its foreign assets, he might hedge the currency risk using forward FX contracts.

Immunisation is the process where the portfolio manager tries to match most of the maturities and expirations within the portfolio with any future commitments. This type of investment strategy is most popular with bonds and currency swaps. For example, a bond portfolio is said to be immunised when its composition is set to produce a target rate of return, regardless of any changes in bond prices or market interest rates.

3.3 The Use of Derivatives in Portfolio Management Strategies

---

Learning Objective

7.2.4   Understand the main purposes and applications of derivatives in portfolio management strategies and styles: indexing/passive management; active/market timing; passive-active combinations; growth versus income; immunisation; long, short and leveraged; contrarian; yield enhancement

---

The following is a description of how derivatives can be used as part of the most popular portfolio management strategies.

3.3.1 Indexing/Passive Management

Passive management or indexing requires the construction of an equity portfolio to track, or mimic, the performance of a recognised equity index.

Indexation is undertaken on the assumption that securities markets are **efficiently priced** and cannot therefore be consistently outperformed. Consequently, no attempt is made to forecast future events or outperform the broader market.

Given the wide range of exchange-traded and OTC derivatives that are based on specific financial indices, their use for this type of portfolio management strategy is easily recognisable. For example, Euronext alone lists a wide range of both futures and options on European equity indices.

For portfolio managers using this strategy, using these derivatives not only perfectly matches that specific strategy, since the contract's underlying asset is the same, but also allows them to both reduce their trading-related expenses and increase their trading efficiency, since it is easier to buy/sell an index future or option than to trade the individual shares that are index components.

3.3.2 Active/Market Timing

In contrast to passive portfolio management, active/market timing strategies seek to outperform a predetermined benchmark over a specified time period by employing fundamental and technical analysis to assist in the forecasting of future events and the timing of purchases and sales of securities.

The **active manager's** goal is to **exploit market inefficiencies** by purchasing securities (shares, bonds or commodities) that are undervalued, or by short selling securities that are overvalued. Either of these methods may be used alone or in combination. **Market timing** is closely related, since it is based on a concept whose goal is to deal at specific market prices when a security is considered to be mispriced.

Here again, the trading efficiencies and wide range of derivatives available to portfolio managers make their use a key part of this investment management strategy. For example, news is released on a specific commodity such as gold; outside of normal trading hours a portfolio manager can use either ETD futures or an OTC forward to take advantage of any price movements, to either establish a new position or hedge an existing holding. Once the market timing position has been established, the fund manager can take time to decide whether to alter any cash positions during normal trading hours.

3.3.3 Passive-Active Combinations

After describing active and passive management, it should be mentioned that active and passive investment strategies are not mutually exclusive. Index trackers and actively managed portfolios can be combined in what is known as **core-satellite management**. This is achieved by indexing a portion of the portfolio, say 70–80%, to reduce its risk of underperformance, and then by actively investing the remainder in a number of individual securities, known as the satellites.

As mentioned in the previous sections, portfolio managers can use derivatives for both aspects of the strategy. For example, for the passive portion of the portfolio, the manager can simply buy a range of index-based futures or forwards, while on the active trading side the portfolio manager can use options, such as writing calls on a bond or share that he considers to be overvalued. This could be easier and more cost-efficient if this was a short selling active strategy.

3.3.4 Other Management Strategies

The wide range of derivatives fits all of the other portfolio management strategies that are commonly used. One of the main characteristics of derivatives (one that is directly related to their increased risk) is that they allow their users to **leverage up** their risk, since most require only a fraction of the contract's face value. Therefore, any portfolio management strategy whose purpose is to increase or leverage its risk is one where derivatives are well suited.

Selling options, particularly when their prices are inflated by high volatility, would be particularly attractive to a portfolio management strategy that holds a **contrarian** view. Since a contrarian strategy is based on the view that certain crowd behaviour among other investors has led to an exploitable mispricing of a specific security, the portfolio manager who holds this view can take advantage of the premium associated with the mispriced options, as part of the strategy.

3.3.5 Yield Enhancement

Derivatives can be used to improve a portfolio's performance and its yield in a number of ways. They are most commonly used during times when volatility is expected to fall, ie, when investment managers are expecting the markets/specific assets to trade within a trading range.

When they hold this view, and if their investment guidelines allow, one common yield enhancement strategy is to sell covered calls. By selling an out-of-the money call on an asset that is held in the portfolio, the portfolio receives the premium, and if, as expected, the underlying asset trades within a range, or at least its price does not reach the call's strike price, the portfolio will continue to hold the asset in addition to receiving the option's premium.

4. Assessing Portfolio Risk and Return

Learning Objective

7.2.5   Assess portfolio risk and return using the following measures: holding period return; total return and its components; standard deviation; volatility; covariance and correlation; risk-adjusted returns; benchmarking

The following is a review of the main methods used to measure a portfolio's risk.

4.1   Holding Period Return, Money-Weighted Return, Time-Weighted Return

The three most common methods used to measure portfolio performance are:

*   holding period yield – sometimes referred to as total return
*   money-weighted rate of return
*   time-weighted rate of return.

The **holding period yield** or **return** simply measures how much the portfolio's value has increased over a period of time and expresses it as a percentage. It suffers from the limitation of not taking into account the timing of cash flows into and out of the fund, and so it is not a particularly useful measure for most investment funds. Instead, the money-weighted and time-weighted rates of returns are used.

The **money-weighted rate of return** is used to measure the performance of a portfolio that has had deposits and withdrawals during the period being measured. It is also referred to as the internal rate of return of the fund.

The standard money-weighted return measurement used in the UK is the Modified BAI Method and the formula for calculating it is:

$$\text{Vend} = \text{CFi} \, (1+r) \text{wi}$$

where:
Vend = value at the end of the measurement period
CFi = cash flow i
i = number of cash flows (ie, deposits and withdrawals) during the period
r = rate of return
w = weighting of cash flow i

One of the main drawbacks of this method is that to calculate the return is an iterative process and so is a more time-consuming calculation than other methods.

The **time-weighted rate of return** (TWRR) removes the impact of cash flows on the rate of return calculation. This method is established by breaking the investment period into a series of sub-periods. A sub-period is created whenever there is a movement of capital into or out of the fund. Immediately prior to this point, a portfolio valuation must be obtained to ensure that the rate of return is not distorted by the size and timing of the cash flow.

The TWRR is calculated by compounding the rate of return for each of these individual sub-periods, applying an equal weight to each sub-period in the process. This is known as unitised fund performance.

The formula for TWRR is:

$$\text{TWRR} = [(1 + \text{RSP1})(1 + \text{RSP2})........(1 + \text{RSPn})] - 1$$

where:
RSPn = the percentage return during a sub-period.

Example 2

An investment portfolio was valued at £1,000 at the beginning of January and grows in value to £1,200 by 15 January. On the following day it received an inflow of £250; at the end of the month it was valued at £1,500.

Using TWRR, a percentage return is calculated for each separate period as follows:

Period 1: $r = \dfrac{1,200}{1,000} - 1 = 0.20$

Period 2: $r = \dfrac{1,500}{1,450} - 1 = 0.034$

TWRR = $[(1 + 0.20) \, (1 + 0.034)] - 1 = 1.2408 - 1 = 24.08\%$

4.2   Standard Deviation

The standard deviation of a set of data is simply the **square root of the variance** and is the most commonly used measure of dispersion.

Although the variances and standard deviations of both ordered raw and frequency distribution data can be calculated quickly and easily by using a scientific calculator, it is useful to understand how to work through their calculation. In summary, the steps you should take in making these calculations manually are as follows:

1. Obtain the arithmetic **mean**.
2. Obtain the set of **deviations** from the mean.
3. **Square** each deviation.
4. **Divide** the sum of the squared deviations by the number of observations to obtain the **population variance**.
5. Take the **square root of the variance** in each case to obtain the standard deviation.

To ensure precision in the calculation of the variance and standard deviation, statistical rules require a slight change to the formula if measuring a **sample**. The limitations of small data sets include the fact that they may not provide a representative picture of the population as a whole, and so sampling error may arise. As a result, a slight adjustment to the standard deviation formula is made by reducing the number of observations by one.

The formulas for both calculations are expressed as follows:

Population standard deviation = $\sqrt{\dfrac{\Sigma\,(x-\bar{x})^2}{n}}$

Sample standard deviation = $\sqrt{\dfrac{\Sigma\,(x-\bar{x})^2}{n-1}}$

In effect, by taking the square root of the variance, the standard deviation represents the average amount by which the values in the distribution **deviate from the mean**. With sufficiently large data, the pattern of deviations from the mean will be spread symmetrically on either side, and if the class intervals are small enough the resultant frequency distribution curve may look like a cross-section of a bell, ie, a bell-shaped curve.

Statistical analysis shows that in a normal frequency distribution curve:

*   approximately two-thirds or 68.26% of observations will be within one standard deviation either side of the mean
*   approximately 95.5% of all observations will be within two standard deviations either side of the mean
*   approximately 99.75% of all observations will be within three standard deviations of the mean.

Normal Frequency Distribution Curve

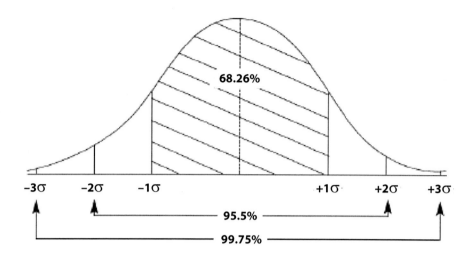

Data does not always conform to a normal pattern, and is then referred to as skewed. If the peak of the curve is to the left of centre it is said to be **positively skewed** and, if to the right, **negatively skewed**. Most long-run distributions of equity returns are positively skewed. That is, equity markets produce more extreme positive and negative returns than should statistically be the case – a phenomenon known as **kurtosis** – but these extreme positive values far outweigh the negative ones.

4.3   Risk-Adjusted Returns

Having calculated how a portfolio has performed, the next stage is to compare its performance against the market as a whole or against other portfolios. This is the function of risk-adjusted performance measurements, of which there are four main methods in use, outlined in Sections 4.3.2 to 4.3.5 below.

4.3.1   Benchmarking

Portfolio performance is rarely measured in absolute terms but in relative terms against a predetermined benchmark and against the peer group. Once a portfolio has been constructed, therefore, the portfolio manager and client need to agree on a realistic benchmark against which the performance of the portfolio can be judged. The choice of benchmark will depend on the precise asset split adopted, and should be compatible with the risk and expected return profile of the portfolio.

Where an index is used, this should represent a feasible investment alternative to the portfolio constructed. As an example, if the portfolio consists largely of smaller growth stocks with an international scope, the appropriate benchmark index to use would be the FTSE AIM All-Share index.

In addition, indexed portfolios are also evaluated against the size of their **tracking error**, or how closely the portfolio has tracked the chosen index. Tracking error arises from both underperformance and outperformance of the index being tracked.

It is essential that the portfolio manager and client agree on the frequency with which the portfolio is reviewed, not only to monitor the portfolio's performance but also to ensure that it still meets with the client's objectives and is correctly positioned given prevailing market conditions.

4.3.2 Sharpe Ratio

The Sharpe ratio measures the return over and above the risk-free interest rate from an undiversified portfolio for each unit of risk assumed by the portfolio: risk being measured by the standard deviation of the portfolio's returns.

The ratio is expressed as follows:

Sharpe ratio = $\dfrac{(R_p - R_f)}{\textbf{standard deviation of the portfolio}}$

where:
R_p = return on the portfolio.
R_f = risk-free return.

The higher the Sharpe ratio, the better the risk-adjusted performance of the portfolio and the greater the implied level of active management skill. The Sharpe ratio provides an objective measure of the relative performance of two similarly undiversified portfolios.

4.3.3 Treynor Ratio

The Treynor ratio takes a similar approach to the Sharpe ratio but is calculated for a well diversified portfolio. As the portfolio's return would have been generated only by the systematic risk it had assumed, the Treynor ratio therefore **divides the portfolio's return over and above the risk-free interest rate by its Capital Asset Pricing Model (CAPM) beta** (the measure of its relative volatility or risk versus the market).

The ratio is expressed as follows:

Treynor ratio = $\dfrac{(R_p - R_f)}{\beta_p}$

where:
R_p = return on the portfolio.
R_f = risk-free return.
β_p = beta of the portfolio.

Once again, the higher the ratio, the greater the implied level of active management skill.

4.3.4 Jensen Measure

The Jensen measure of risk-adjusted portfolio returns is employed to evaluate the performance of a well-diversified portfolio against a **CAPM benchmark** with the same level of systematic risk as that assumed by the portfolio. That is, the CAPM benchmark beta is the same as that of the portfolio.

The ratio is expressed as follows:

Jensen measure = $\quad R_p - R_{capm}$

where:

$R_p \quad$ = return on the portfolio.

R_{capm} = return predicted by CAPM.

The Jensen measure establishes whether the portfolio has performed in line with its CAPM benchmark and, therefore, lies on the **security market line (SML)** or whether it has out- or underperformed the benchmark and is, therefore, positioned above or below the SML. The extent of any out- or underperformance is known as the portfolio's **alpha**.

4.3.5 Information Ratio

The information ratio compares the excess return achieved by a fund over a benchmark portfolio to the fund's **tracking error**. Its tracking error is calculated as the standard deviation of excess returns from the benchmark. The tracking error gives us an estimate of the risks that the fund manager takes in deviating from the benchmark.

The ratio is expressed as follows:

Information ratio = $\quad \dfrac{ER}{SER}$

where:

ER $\quad$ = arithmetic mean of excess returns.

SER $\quad$ = standard deviation of excess return from the benchmark.

A fund's performance may deviate from the benchmark owing to the investment manager's decisions concerning asset-weighting. If the fund outperforms, the ratio will be positive, and if it underperforms it will be negative. A high information ratio is therefore a sign of a successful fund manager.

End of Chapter Questions

1. What is fundamental analysis?
    Answer reference: Section 2.2

2. What is technical analysis?
    Answer reference: Section 2.2

3. What is the price of all derivatives based on?
    Answer reference: Section 2.3

4. Describe systemic risk.
    Answer reference: Section 3.1.1

5. What are the four standard market risk factors?
    Answer reference: Section 3.1.2

6. What term is used to describe the total length of time that an investor expects to hold a specific security or portfolio?
    Answer reference: Section 3.1.3

7. How would you use immunisation?
    Answer reference: Section 3.2.4

8. On what assumption is indexation undertaken?
    Answer reference: Section 3.3.1

9. What are the three most common ways to measure portfolio performance?
    Answer reference: Section 4.1

10. What is the purpose of the information ratio?
    Answer reference: Section 4.3.5

Chapter Eight

Trading, Hedging and Investment Strategies

This syllabus area will provide approximately 12 of the 80 examination questions

CISI
CHARTERED INSTITUTE FOR
SECURITIES & INVESTMENT

1. Introduction

A structured product, also known as a market-linked product, is generally an investment strategy that is based on derivatives, such as futures, options and to a lesser extent swaps.

Given the variety of products that are considered to be structured products, there is no single, uniform definition of the term. They can include a combination of an underlying asset and a single derivative or a strategy that includes a number of different contracts or derivatives, such as a range of options or series of futures contracts.

As such, structured products were created to meet an investor's specific needs that cannot be met from the standard or underlying financial instruments available in the markets. Structured products can be used as an alternative to a direct investment, as part of the asset allocation process to reduce risk, or to increase one's exposure to an asset or market, or to take advantage of any mispricing that might occur.

We have already looked at individual futures and options trades and their uses as speculative, hedging and arbitrage instruments. In this chapter we will look at how the different types of structured products (a combination of these contracts) can be used.

Remember that **hedging** involves reducing the risk of adverse price movements on an underlying position, **arbitrage** activities take advantage of mispricings, and **speculators** are placing bets on the direction of the price of the underlying asset by taking on new or extra risk.

2. Futures Spreads

Learning Objective

8.1.1   Analyse futures spreads and the scenarios in which they may be appropriate: intramarket spreads; motivations and uses in differing market conditions; situations resulting in profitability/loss

A futures spread trade involves simultaneously buying and selling futures contracts.

Note that in all types of futures or options spreads, or even combination trades, it is always possible to 'leg in' to the strategy by undertaking one half of the trade now and completing the second leg later. Clearly, until the second leg is completed, the trader will be exposed to price risk.

2.1 Intra-Market Spreads

These are trades based on the simultaneous buying and selling of futures with different expiry dates, but on the same underlying asset, for example, selling the June long gilt contract (ie, the long-dated gilt future) and buying the September long gilt contract.

The **motivation** for entering into these intra-market spreads can take a number of forms:

- **Anticipating changes in basis** – it could be that the basis is expected to strengthen or weaken.
- **Reducing risk** – intra-market spreads are less risky than taking an outright position (basis risk is smaller than price risk, but profits will be smaller too).
- **Arbitrage** – where the same underlying product is traded in two different markets and there are price differences; for example, buying SGX Nikkei 225 futures (traded in Singapore) and selling OSE Nikkei 225 futures (traded in Osaka).
- **To 'roll over' an existing hedge** so that it continues further into the future – as would be the case of selling the June natural gas on ICE, to close out an existing long futures position, and then buying the December natural gas future, to continue the hedge for another six months.

2.2   Inter-Market Spreads

These trades are based on simultaneously buying and selling futures on different underlying (but probably correlated) assets, for example, buying September short sterling contracts and selling September long gilt contracts.

The **motivation** for these trades is often that the price relationship between two correlated products has temporarily broken down or has moved outside its normal range. The trade anticipates a re-establishment of a more normal relationship.

They are very popular in interest rate markets where traders take a view on the relationship between long-term and short-term interest rates (the yield curve). The example quoted above is a trade that anticipates a steepening of the yield curve.

These trades are also used as a means of changing asset allocations within a portfolio. A fund manager may be long equities and be looking to reduce the exposure by selling some shares and using the funds to buy bonds. By using the futures market (selling FTSE 100 futures and buying long gilt futures) it is possible to produce the same effect without the need to trade the actual securities. It is usually much faster and less expensive. In the meantime, the fund manager can continue to benefit from dividend income until the securities are sold as needed, and will only unwind the futures positions when he has the required physical portfolio in place.

Note. In differentiating between intra- and inter-market spreads, it is the underlying asset that is important and not the physical location of the futures product.

- **Intra** ('within') = underlying assets are the same.
- **Inter** ('between') = underlying assets are different.

Example 1

An international equity fund manager holds the view that UK shares will outperform French shares over the next few months. To take advantage of this view, he will sell CAC 40 futures contracts and, at the same time, buy the FTSE 100 futures for the same maturity and for the same amount.

If the inter-market spread was established when the December FTSE 100 futures were trading at 6564 and the December CAC 40 was 4738, this spread would be profitable if the fall in the CAC 40 was greater than the fall in UK shares, **or** if the FTSE 100 rose by a greater percentage then the CAC 40.

By using this inter-market spread, the fund manager has reallocated the fund's investments from French to UK equities to take advantage of the view that the UK market will outperform the French market.

The inter-market spread was established by buying the December FTSE 100 future at 6564 and selling the equivalent of the December CAC 40 future at 4738. After two months the December FTSE 100 contract is trading at 6749 and the December CAC 40 contract is trading at 4773; the fund manager would make a profit of £1,850 per FTSE 100 contract and a loss of €350 per CAC 40 contract. After adjusting for the exchange rate, the inter-market spread would show a profit of £1,600 per futures contract.

3.   Hedging Using Futures

Learning Objective

8.2.1   Calculate the number of contracts required to hedge a portfolio of Cheapest To Deliver bonds (CTDs): price factors; highest implied repo rate; understand the basis of adjustment for non-CTD bonds

8.2.2   Calculate the number of contracts required to hedge an exposure to a single equity holding or equity portfolio

Remember that unhedged positions are at risk from changes in the price of the underlying asset. The unhedged position may be a long underlying position or it may be a short underlying position.

Hedgers offset the price risk in the underlying asset by taking an opposite position in the futures market. So, someone long the underlying would sell the equivalent number of futures contracts to hedge the risk (a short hedge). However, although the cash and futures prices are strongly correlated, there is, as we have seen, some flexibility in that relationship. Basis changes will affect the performance of the hedge. This is termed the **basis risk** of the hedge.

If the long gilt futures (or most other bond futures) contract is used to hedge a portfolio of underlying gilts, any risk is limited to the basis risk (assuming that the appropriate number of contracts are entered into). Remember that the long gilt futures contract has a basket of deliverable gilts, one of which is cheaper to deliver than the others (the **Cheapest to Deliver** or **CTD**).

The CTD bond is the deliverable gilt with the highest **implied repo rate**. The futures contract price will be very closely correlated to this CTD bond, and the number of contracts used to hedge is calculated on the basis of holding the CTD bonds in the portfolio, not any other bonds.

The **implied repo rate** is a measure of the funding cost implied in futures prices, which reflect the difference between a bond's cash price and the price of a futures contract.

For many products the number of contracts needed to hedge is simply a matter of dividing the portfolio size/value by the contract size/value. However, with bonds, the price factor of the CTD bond needs to be taken into account. The formula is:

$$\text{Number of contracts} = \text{price factor} \; \times \; \frac{\text{nominal value of CTD portfolio}}{\text{nominal value of the contract}}$$

Example 2

You have a portfolio of CTD bonds with a nominal value of £10,000,000 and a market value of £11,500,000. The price factor is 1.1214645. The contract size of the long gilt future is £100,000, nominal. Number of contracts needed to hedge =

$$1.1214645 \; \times \; \frac{£10,000,000}{£100,000}$$

$= 112.15$

$= 112$ approximately.

Note that if you did not have a portfolio of CTD bonds, the above formula would need to be adjusted. Hedging non-CTD bonds is outside the exam syllabus.

Exercise 1

An investor has sold short CTD gilts with a nominal value of £15 million and a market value of £15.4 million. The price factor is 1.12486. She wishes to hedge the position using long gilt futures. How many contracts are required and should the investor buy or sell the long gilt futures contracts?

The answers can be found in the Appendix at the end of this chapter.

When using futures to hedge an equities portfolio, its **beta** is useful when calculating how many contracts you will need to trade to be fully hedged. **A share's beta is the measure of its relative volatility or risk versus the market**. Therefore a portfolio's beta is the weighted average of the individual betas of the shares that make up the portfolio.

Example 3

If a portfolio has a beta of 1.1 relative to the S&P 500, it means that if the S&P 500 index rises by 10%, that portfolio would rise by 11.0%. In other words, the share portfolio is riskier than the index.

Therefore, if this portfolio has a value of US$8.0 million and the fund manager wants to hedge this portfolio using S&P 500 futures, the portfolio's beta is useful in calculating the number of contracts required to fully hedge this portfolio. At the time the S&P 500 index was trading at 1600. The CME S&P 500 contract's size is US$250 times the index.

Number of contracts = $8.0m/($250 x 1600) = 20
20 x 1.1 = 22 contracts

In the case of short-term interest rate futures, the size/tick value relative to a basis point is the key factor when determining the number of contracts that are required to hedge a specific position.

3.1   Basis, Basis Trading and Basis Risk

Learning Objectives

8.2.3   Calculate the change in value caused by movement in basis, know the implications of basis risk and understand how changes in basis can be used to advantage by an investor

Basis and basis trading were covered in Chapter 3, Section 5.6. Remember that basis is the difference between the cash and futures prices. Basis risk is the risk that the change in futures prices will be different from changes in the cash price. Basis trading is implementing strategies in order to profit from anticipated basis changes.

Example 4

A fund manager has a portfolio of top UK equities, currently valued at £15,000,000. He hedges the portfolio by selling 250 FTSE index futures at 6515. The FTSE 100 currently stands at 6565. A day later the FTSE 100 has fallen by 20 index points and the future has fallen by 16 points to 6499. The outcome for the fund manager is as follows:

1. Unhedged equity portfolio value = £15,000,000

Day 1	Day 2
$£15{,}000{,}000 \times \dfrac{(6565 - 20)}{6565}$ =	£14,954,303

2. Futures profit = 250 x (6515 – 6449) x £10 = £40,000

3. Hedged portfolio value

Day 1	Day 2	Loss
£15,000,000	£14,954,303	£45,697

4. Difference = loss due to change in basis = £5,697

---

4. Hedging Using Options

Learning Objective

8.3.1 Analyse an investor's net long/short position using delta hedging

The four basic options positions (long call, short call, long put and short put) can be used as hedging instruments against an underlying position.

Remember that the efficiency of hedging using options is dependent upon the delta of the options' position mirroring the delta of the underlying position, in other words, creating a delta-neutral portfolio overall.

Broadly, the deltas are as follows:

Position	Delta
Long underlying	+1
Short underlying	–1
Long future	+1
Short future	–1
Long call (deep in-the-money)	+1
Long call (at-the-money)	+0.5
Short call (deep in-the-money)	–1
Short call (at-the-money)	–0.5
Long put (deep in-the-money)	–1
Long put (at-the-money)	–0.5
Short put (deep in-the-money)	+1
Short put (at-the-money)	+0.5

So a long underlying position (delta +1) could be hedged by a short, deep in-the-money call (delta –1) to create a delta neutral portfolio (overall delta = +1 – 1 = 0). Alternatively, it could be hedged by two short at-the-money calls (–0.5 x 2 = –1), or a deep in-the-money long put (–1), or even two at-the-money long puts (–0.5 x 2 = –1).

4.1 Hedging a Long Underlying Position using Options

Learning Objective

8.3.2 Calculate the number of contracts required to hedge a long underlying position by: buying a put option; selling a call option

---

This is best illustrated by an example:

Buy a Put Option

Example 5 ———————————————————————————————

Investor A owns a portfolio of FTSE shares with a current value of £550,000. The FTSE index stands at 6567. He is exposed to a fall in the value of the shares. To hedge the risk he needs an options position that will make a profit if the index falls – for example, a long put position.

If his worries are borne out and the index falls, the loss on the portfolio will be offset by the profit on the put option. Remember that the premium paid on the put will never be refunded, so the hedge has a cost (unlike a futures hedge).

However, if the index were to rise, the long underlying position can still show an overall profit once the cost of the put premium has been recouped.

How many contracts are needed to hedge?

The contract size of a FTSE option on ICE London is the index level x £10 per point.

With the put option exercise price at, say, 6550 (choose the option with the strike price that is closest to the current index level), each contract hedges £65,500 of shares (6550 x £10 per point).

So the number of contracts needed = £550,000 ÷ £65,500 = 8 contracts.

Sell a Call Option

(Also see the notes on covered calls in Section 4.3 below.)

Example 6 ———————————————————————————————

An aluminium producer does not have forward sale agreements for all of its production over the next six months. One way to hedge against a possible fall in the cash price would be to sell calls on the LME's primary aluminium futures. The contract size is 25 tonnes. If the amount of the unsold December production is 100 tonnes, the producer can sell four primary aluminium calls with a strike price of $1,700, its budgeted sale price. By selling this covered call, since the producer has the underlying metal, the premium received will partially offset any price fall that might occur. But if the price rises, the producer will only receive the strike price of $1,700 if the option expires in-the-money.

4.2 Hedging a Short Underlying Position Using Options

Learning Objective

8.3.3 Calculate the number of contracts required to hedge a short underlying position by: selling a put option; buying a call option

The following illustrates how a short position might be hedged:

Buy a Call Option

Example 7

Investor B needs to buy 500oz of gold for June; gold is currently trading at $1,375.00 per oz in the cash market.

The investor is exposed to an increase in gold's price. One way to hedge the risk would be to buy a gold futures call option for June, a position that will make a profit if the price of gold rises. To be fully hedged, investor B will have to buy five calls, since each option has a value of 100oz per contract.

If the price of gold rises, the extra cost of buying it in the cash market will be offset by the profits on the call option. But remember that the premium paid to buy the call will not be refunded, therefore this method of hedging has an initial cost (unlike a futures hedge).

But if the price of gold falls, investor B will be able to buy gold at a lower price and reduce his costs, after recouping the premium paid for the call.

Sell a Put Option

(See the notes on covered short puts in Section 4.3 below.)

It is useful to note the following:

- Unlike a futures hedge, an options hedge will underperform because of the premium paid.
- In contrast to a futures hedge, an options hedge provides flexibility. It allows overall profits to be made if the price of the underlying moves in the investor's favour instead of against him, because the loss on the option is limited to the premium paid.

4.3　Covered Options Positions

Learning Objective

8.3.4　Apply covered calls and covered puts as part of an investment strategy: characteristics and risks; motivation for the writer of a covered short call; motivation for the buyer of a covered short put; calculation of the outcome on expiry; maximum upside and downside; uses in different market conditions

Covered Short Call

A covered short call is sometimes referred to as a **buy/write strategy**. It is constructed by combining a long underlying position with a short call position.

The following example illustrates the potential outcome of a covered short call strategy.

Example 8

An investor is long 1,000 ABC plc shares. Current share price is 407. He sells an ABC plc 425 call for a premium of 11 (each contract is for 1,000 shares).

Analysis of outcome at expiry

If the share price is unchanged at expiry, the option is abandoned. The investor keeps the premium, thereby creating a positive return on investment.

If the share price drops, the premium helps to cushion the fall. The investor is hedged to the extent of the premium. If the fall is less than the premium, the investor is still better off. If the fall is greater than the premium, the investor loses the excess above the premium.

If the share price rises up to 425, the investor will make a profit on the shares and keep the premium (18 on the underlying and 11 on the premium = 29). This is the 'point of maximum profit'. The return on investment would be 18 (425 – 407); since the premium of 11 that was received for the call reduces the initial investment to 396, that return is (425 – 407)/396 x 100 = 4.55% over the period.

If the price rises above 425, the option would be exercised against the investor. He would deliver the share for 425. He has effectively capped his maximum potential profit at 29 (ignoring dividends paid on the shares).

In summary, the **motivation** is to enhance returns in a stagnant market and, at the same time, to partially hedge a long underlying position. If the market remains static, an investor will enhance the return on the asset, since he has collected the option's premium and it will expire unexercised. In a falling market, the premium will reduce the loss, but will not provide a true hedge. In a rising market, overall gains will be limited, since the call will be exercised and any further gains above the strike price will not be realised, since he no longer owns the asset.

Exercise 2

Mr Z holds 1,000 shares in XYZ, with a current price of 215p. He writes a single call option (on 1,000 shares) with an exercise price of 220p and for a premium of 9p. What is the outcome for Mr Z if the price of XYZ shares at expiry is:

a. 194p
b. 208p
c. 230p

The answer can be found in the Appendix at the end of this chapter.

Note that selling call options without owning the asset is known as creating a **'naked' short call position** or **'naked' writing**. This is more of a **speculative position**, where the investor might be happy to sell the asset at that price, based on the outlook that its price will later fall. Again, receiving the premium does raise one's breakeven level, but this strategy has created an open risk that the asset's price will continue to rise.

Covered Short Put

A covered short put position is constructed by selling a put but, at the same time, holding sufficient funds to buy the asset if necessary or already having a short position, such as being short the futures contract then writing/selling a put on the futures contract.

Example 9

ABC plc share price is 407p. An investor leaves the funds (£4,070) on deposit and sells the 400 put for 20p per share.

Analysis of outcome at expiry

If the share price is unchanged at expiry, the option is abandoned by the long and the investor keeps the premium. This increases the return on his funds by the premium retained.

If the share price rises, although the investor is enhancing the return on his funds by the premium received, he has forgone the opportunity to make a profit on the shares he could have purchased. There is an opportunity cost for the investor.

If the share price falls below 400, the option will be exercised against the investor. He will have to buy the shares at 400p. The investor has effectively reduced the cost price of the shares to 400p, less the amount of the premium. That is 380p (400 – 20).

The point of maximum profit is at 400. The investor will make 20 on the premium, plus the interest on the funds, and be able to buy the shares at 400 rather than 407.

In summary, the **motivation** is to enhance the return on funds in a stagnant market and to partially hedge a short underlying position. It is also an attractive method of taking profit on a short position. But it does limit gains on that short position, since, once the put is exercised, the investor no longer has a short position in that asset and therefore will no longer profit from further falls in its price.

Exercise 3 _____

Mrs P enters into a covered short put position on the shares in QRS plc. She writes a 700p put option for a premium of 12p at the time QRS plc shares are trading at 718p. What is the outcome for Mrs P if the price of QRS shares at expiry is:

a. 690p

b. 718p

c. 750p

The answer can be found in the Appendix at the end of this chapter.

Selling put options without having the funds to pay for the asset is known as creating a **naked short put position**. This is a **bearish speculative** position, as it fits the view that the underlying asset's price will bottom out and then recover. The returns of this strategy are enhanced by receiving the put's premium. But once a naked put has been exercised, the risk is the same as any long cash position in that asset.

5. Options Spreads

An options spread involves the simultaneous purchase and sale of options in the same class, ie, calls or puts on the same underlying asset. There are three different types of options spreads that are constructed as follows:

1. **Vertical spread** – buying and selling calls (or puts) with **different strikes**, but the **same expiry**, eg, buy April 200 call and sell April 220 call or buy September 500 put and sell September 550 put.
2. **Horizontal (calendar) spread** – buying and selling options with the **same strike**, but **different expiry** months, eg, buy April 200 call and sell May 200 call or sell September 500 put and buy December 500 put.
3. **Diagonal (diagonal calendar) spread** – buying and selling options with **different strikes** and **different expiry** months.

5.1 Vertical Spreads

Learning Objective

8.4.1   Apply vertical spreads as part of an investment strategy: characteristics and risks; bull call and bear call spreads; bull put and bear put spreads; calculation of the outcome on expiry; maximum upside and downside; uses in differing market conditions

---

Vertical spreads can be split into two basic types: **bull spreads** and **bear spreads**.

In a **bull spread** the investor **buys the lower strike** and **sells the higher strike**: for example, buying the 500 call and selling the 600 call (a 'bull call spread'); or, alternatively, buying the 500 put and selling the 600 put (a 'bull put spread').

The opposite is true for a **bear spread**, where the investor **sells the lower strike** and **buys the higher strike**, for example, selling the 500 call and buying the 600 call (a 'bear call spread'); or, alternatively, using put options by selling the 500 put and buying the 600 put (a 'bear put spread').

All vertical spreads attempt to profit from a directional movement in the underlying. However, unlike an outright purchase of a call or put, spreads are **moderately bullish/bearish** strategies.

Example 10

The current price of ABC plc is 550 and the options available with the quoted premium (PM) at a range of exercise prices are as follows:

Call PM	Strike	Put PM
70	500	18
49	525	23
37	550	35
25	575	47
19	600	67

Rationale

Suppose an investor is bullish on ABC shares. He could buy the 550 call and pay a premium of 37. However, he is moderately bullish and does not think the shares will rise beyond 590 by expiry. So he sells the 600 call at the same time. He receives a premium of 19, which reduces his net outlay to 18. This is known as a 'bull call spread'.

Analysis

If the price remains at 550 or below, both options will expire OTM and be abandoned. The loss would be limited to the net outlay of 18.

If the price rises to between 550 and 600, he would exercise the 550 call and collect the intrinsic value (the 600 call would be abandoned). To make a net profit on the trade, the intrinsic value of the 550 call needs to be greater than 18, his initial net outlay. The breakeven point is 568.

If the price rises beyond 600, both calls are ITM and would be exercised. In effect, the investor would exercise the 550 call and would be obliged to deliver the ABC shares at 600. The profit would be capped at 32 ((600 – 550) – 18). Looked at another way, once ABC shares are above 600, all the extra profit made from the 550 call is taken away by the short 600 call.

All vertical spreads work in a similar way. A bear spread is essentially the other side of a bull spread.

Exercise 4

Mr Z buys a 500 put in ABC plc shares for 18p and sells a 550 put at 35p. What is the outcome at expiry if the price of ABC plc shares is:

a. 490p
b. 530p
c. 575p

The answer can be found in the Appendix at the end of this chapter.

5.1.1   Summary of Vertical Spreads

Bull Call

Motivation	Moderately bullish.
Construction	Buy at lower strike price, sell at higher strike price.
Net premium	Paid out.
Maximum risk	Net premium paid.
Maximum reward	Difference in strike prices less the net premium paid.
Breakeven point	Lower strike price + net premium paid.

Bear Call

Motivation	Moderately bearish.
Construction	Sell at lower strike price, buy at higher strike price.
Net premium	Received.
Maximum risk	Difference in strike prices less the net premium received.
Maximum reward	Net premium received.
Breakeven point	Lower strike price + net premium received.

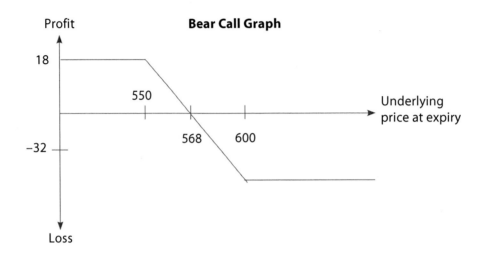

Bull Put

Motivation	Moderately bullish.
Construction	Buy at lower strike price, sell at higher strike price.
Net premium	Received.
Maximum risk	Difference in strike prices less net premium received.
Maximum reward	Net premium received.
Breakeven point	Higher strike price less net premium received.

The shape of the bull put graph will be identical to the bull call graph.

Bear Put

Motivation	Moderately bearish.
Construction	Sell at lower strike price, buy at higher strike price.
Net premium	Paid out.
Maximum risk	Net premium paid.
Maximum reward	Difference in strike prices less net premium paid.
Breakeven point	Higher strike price less net premium paid

The shape of a bear put graph will be identical to the bear call graph.

Exercise 5

Mr Z buys a 500 put in ABC plc shares for 18p and sells a 550 put at 35p. What is the breakeven point and what is the maximum profit on this trade?

The answers can be found in the Appendix at the end of this chapter.

5.2 Horizontal and Diagonal Spreads

Learning Objective

8.4.2 Apply horizontal and diagonal spreads as part of an investment strategy: characteristics and risks; horizontal spreads; diagonal spreads; calculation of the outcome on expiry; maximum upside and downside; uses in differing market conditions

Horizontal spreads are also known as calendar spreads. They are motivated by expected moves in volatility. There are two basic types. The first is based on the view that **volatility will fall**, and involves selling a shorter maturity and buying a longer maturity option on the same asset with the same strike price. This type of spread takes advantage of the fact that short-dated options will lose their time value faster, and therefore react more quickly to a fall in volatility, than the longer-dated option.

Example 11

The GBP/USD spot rate is currently quoted at 1.5850/55, the following options, with ATM strike prices are currently quoted in the market.

Expiration	Call Premiums	Strike Price	Put Premiums
1 month	45	1.3565	50
3 months	130	1.3495	145
6 months	280	1.3065	295
12 months	575	1.24995	585

Rationale

Based on the viewpoint that currency rates will remain steady over the near-term and that the slight premiums the sterling short-term puts have will decrease, an investor will sell the one-month 1.3565 put and buy the six-month 1.3065 put, for a net cost of 245 (the premium of 295 for the six month put less 50 from the sale of the one put). This is known as a horizontal spread.

Analysis

If the GBP/USD exchange rate remains fairly steady and looks set to settle into a trading range, the implied volatility combined with the larger time decay will cause the premium on the shorter-term GBP put to fall faster than that of the longer maturity.

After two weeks, when the premiums of these same options have fallen to, say, 20 for the two-week and 275 for the five-and-a-half month GBP put, the investor will receive a net premium of 10, since he/she is able to unwind the spread and receive a net payment of 255, compared to the initial cost of 245.

The second type of horizontal or calendar spread is based on the view that volatility, particularly short-term volatility, will **rise**. It involves buying a shorter maturing option and selling a longer maturity option, again on the same underlying asset with the same strike price. This strategy is used most often ahead of key announcements, such as companies' earnings reports or central bank meetings, to take advantage of any dramatic short-term moves that may occur from the news.

Exercise 6

An investor holds the view that a company's earnings report is going to be much higher than the market's expectations. Based on this view, he buys a two-week 110p call on its shares for 20p and sells a three-month 110p call at 130p.

If he is right, and the premium on the short-term option goes to 35 and the longer option's is 135p, what is the investor's net profit/loss?

The answer can be found in the Appendix at the end of this chapter.

Diagonal spreads are directional depending on market view. They will be constructed with call options if the investor's view is bullish or put options if bearish by selling shorter-dated options and buying longer-dated and further out-of-the-money options. Diagonals are difficult to compute as, once again, they use differently dated expiries.

Both these strategy types take advantage of the different rates of time decay for options with different expiries. Essentially, the trades are designed to take advantage of changes in volatility.

6. Options Combinations

Learning Objective

8.5.1   Apply long and short straddles and strangles as part of an investment strategy: characteristics and risks; long straddle; short straddle; long strangle; short strangle; calculation of the outcome on expiry; maximum upside and downside; uses in differing market conditions

A combination strategy involves the simultaneous purchase/sale of calls and puts. (Although synthetic positions also involve the use of calls and puts, they will be treated separately.)

The two major strategies are **straddles** and **strangles**. They attempt to profit from a change in the volatility of the underlying asset. Long positions anticipate an increase in volatility and short positions anticipate a decrease. Both strategies will be illustrated using the following example:

Example 12

The current price of DEF shares is 550p and the following options are available:

Call PM	70	49	37	25	19
Strike	500	525	550	575	600
Put PM	18	23	35	47	67

6.1   Long Straddle

Rationale

Suppose an investor was unsure about the direction of movement in the price of DEF shares. Perhaps a major announcement was due. Good news will push the share price higher; bad news will push it lower. By buying a 550 call for 37 he will profit if the price rises, and by buying a put for 35 he will profit if the share price falls. By doing both, a long straddle position is created for a net premium outlay of 72 (37 + 35).

Analysis

If the news was good, and the share price rose to, say, 660 by expiry, the investor would exercise the call (110 intrinsic value) and abandon the put. He has paid 72 for the strategy, giving a net profit of 38. For the strategy to make a net profit, the price has to rise above 622 (550 + 72).

If the news was bad and the share price fell to 500, the investor would exercise the put (50 intrinsic value) and abandon the call. The price move has not been large enough to offset the premium paid. The price would have to fall below 478 (550 – 72) before the strategy showed a net profit.

There is a profit potential on this trade in either direction, as long as the price movement is large enough (high volatility) to overcome the cost of both premiums. The strategy has two breakeven points, an upside and a downside breakeven.

Motivation	Expectation of increase in volatility.
Construction	Buy a call and a put with the same strike and expiry.
Maximum risk	Total sum of premiums paid.
Maximum reward	Unlimited.
Breakeven point	Downside: strike price less total premium paid. Upside: strike price plus total premium paid.

Exercise 7

What is the breakeven range for the buyer of a put and a call on XYZ plc shares, where the 500p call has been purchased for 18p and the 500p put has been purchased for 7p?

The answer is in the Appendix at the end of this chapter.

6.2   Short Straddle

Rationale

Taking the opposite view, an investor who is unsure as to directional movement, but is convinced that the price will not move too far away from the current price, would be looking to sell both call and put, ie, taking a **short straddle** position. This is simply the other side of the long straddle, for example, an investor selling a 550 call for 37 and selling a 550 put for 35.

Analysis

The investor would have received a net premium of 72 (call = 37, put = 35).

If the share price rose, the investor would have the call exercised against him and lose the intrinsic value. As long as this was less than 72, the investor would still be making a net profit. A movement above 622 would produce a net loss.

If the share price fell, the investor would have the put exercised against him and lose the intrinsic value. As long as this was less than 72, the investor would still be making a net profit. A movement to below 478 would produce a net loss.

The point of maximum profit would be at 550. Here, both options would be abandoned and the seller of the straddle would keep the total premium. You can see that there is a profit potential on this trade in either direction, as long as the price movement is not large enough (low volatility) to outweigh the net premium received.

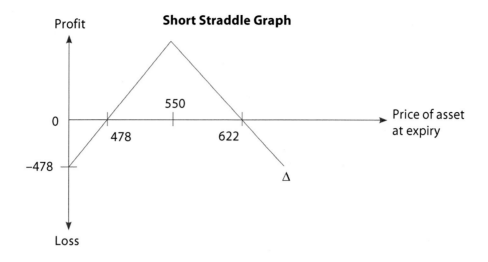

Motivation	Expectation of decrease in volatility.
Construction	Sell a call and a put with the same strike price and expiry.
Maximum risk	Unlimited.
Maximum reward	Limited to the sum of the premiums received.
Breakeven point	Downside: exercise price minus premiums. Upside: exercise price plus premiums.

6.3　Long Strangle

A strangle is a variation of a straddle undertaken for the same purposes, ie, expectation of changes in volatility. For example, buying a 500 put for 18 and buying a 600 call for 19.

The differences between a long strangle and a long straddle are as follows:

- A strangle involves the purchase of a call and a put with the same expiry but different strike prices (normally constructed with the put strike lower than the call strike).
- The premium outlay on a strangle will usually be lower than on a straddle.
- The strategy needs more volatility to succeed.
- The maximum loss on a long position will be crystallised over a range (between the two strike prices) where neither option would be worth exercising.

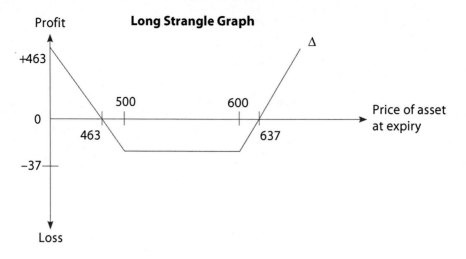

Long Strangle Graph

Motivation	Expectation of large increase in volatility.
Construction	Buy a call and a put with the same expiry but with different strikes.
Maximum risk	Total premium paid. (Call strike price higher than the put.) (If constructed with the call strike lower than the put, this will be limited to the premium less the difference between the strike prices.)
Maximum reward	Unlimited.
Breakeven point	Downside: lower strike price less total premiums paid. Upside: higher strike price plus total premiums paid. (Call strike price higher than the put.) (If constructed with the call strike lower than the put, these will be reversed.)

Exercise 8

What is the breakeven range for the buyer of both a 400 put at 17p and a 450 call for 8p?

The answer can be found in the Appendix at the end of this chapter.

6.4 Short Strangle

A short strangle is the other side of a long strangle strategy. For example, it would be created by selling a 500 put for 18 and selling a 600 call for 19.

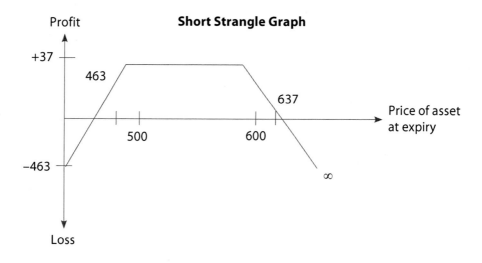

The differences between a short strangle and a short straddle are as follows:

- A short strangle involves the sale of a call and a put with the same expiry but different strikes (normally constructed with the put strike lower than the call strike).
- The total premium received on a strangle will usually be lower than on a straddle.
- The strategy can withstand more volatility before losses are incurred.
- The maximum profit on a short position will be crystallised over a range (between the two strikes) where neither option would be worth exercising against the seller.

Motivation	Expectation of a large decrease in volatility.
Construction	Sell a call and a put with the different strike prices but same expiry.
Maximum risk	Unlimited.
Maximum reward	Total premium received. (Premiums received less difference between the strikes if call strike is lower than the put.)
Breakeven point	Downside: lower strike price minus premiums. Upside: higher strike price plus premiums. (Put strike lower than the call.) (If the call strike is lower than the put, these will be reversed.)

7. Synthetics

Learning Objective

8.6.1 Understand the use of synthetic positions by combining futures and options: characteristics and risks; synthetic long and short futures; synthetic long and short calls; synthetic long and short puts; calculation of the outcome on expiry; maximum upside and downside; uses in differing market conditions

By combining futures and options it is possible to create positions synthetically. There are six basic synthetics that you should be familiar with:

1. **Synthetic long future** = buy a call and sell a put with the same strike and expiry. This position has the same characteristics and risk as **buying a futures contract**. Therefore **maximum loss** would be if the price of the underlying asset went to zero – adjusted for the net premium payment (the difference between the cost of the call and the premium received from the put). The **potential profit** would be the difference between the price of the underlying asset and the call's strike price, at the call's expiration, again adjusted for the net premium payment.

2. **Synthetic short future** = sell a call and buy a put with the same strike and expiry. This position has the same characteristics and risk as **selling a futures contract**. Therefore, **maximum loss** would be potentially unlimited, since, as the price of the underlying asset goes higher, the position's loss also increases – adjusted for the net premium payment (the difference between the cost of the call and the premium received from the put). The **maximum profit** would be if the underlying asset goes to zero; any profit would be the difference between the asset's price and the put's strike price at expiration, again adjusted for the net premium payment.

3. **Synthetic long call** = buy a future and buy a put. (Note this is the same as having a hedged long position.) This position has the same characteristics and risks as **buying a call**. Therefore, the **maximum loss** is the premium paid for the put, adjusted for any difference between the put's strike price and the price of the future. As is the case of any long call position, the **potential profit** is unlimited, after taking into account the premium paid and in this case any difference between the put's strike price and the future's price.

4. **Synthetic short call** = sell a future and sell a put. (Effectively a short call position.) This position has the same characteristics and risks as a **short call**. The **maximum profit** would be the premium, if both the put and the future were sold at the same price and the put is exercised. That would close out the existing short futures position. The **potential loss** is when the future's price rises above the put/short future position, less the premium received for the put. In effect, the potential loss could be significant, if the future's price rises significantly. This type of combination would be used only when the future's price is expected to fall and if current volatility is high, making options expensive.

5. **Synthetic long put** = buy a call and sell a future. (Note this is the same as a hedged short position.) This position has the same characteristics and risks as **buying a put**. Therefore, the **maximum loss** is the premium paid for the put, adjusted for any difference between the put's strike price and the price of the future. As is the case of any long put position, the **maximum profit** after taking into account the premium paid for the call, and in this case any difference between the put's strike price and the future's price, is when the underlying asset's price falls to zero.

6. **Synthetic short put** = sell a call and buy a future. (Effectively a short put position.) This position is in effect the reverse of number 4. Its **maximum profit** is the premium received for writing the call, when the future's price rises, adjusting for any price differential between the two contracts. The **maximum loss** will occur if the future's price falls to zero, less the premium received. This type of position is again popular when one holds a mildly bullish view, to take advantage of current high volatility prices.

The reason for using synthetics might be to create positions that may not be available on the underlying asset. For example, if no futures were available, the investor could create a futures position synthetically, as long as options are available.

However, the main reason for the use of synthetics is **arbitrage**. The put/call parity formula encountered earlier (Chapter 3, Section 6.2) defined the relationship between call and put premiums and the price of the underlying asset. If call and put premiums are out of line with one another, it is possible to lock in riskless profits. This is illustrated in the following examples, both creating synthetic futures.

Example 13

The long gilt future is currently trading at 114.14. The premium of the 114.00 call is 0.45 and the premium of the 114.00 put is 0.39.

What should you do?

Buy the call and sell the put for a net premium outlay of 0.06. This gives you a long futures position (synthetically) at 114.06.

But the actual future is trading at 114.14, so **sell the future** to lock in the difference of 0.08.

The whole trade is known as a **reversal**.

Example 14

The long gilt future is currently trading at 114.14. The premium of the 114.00 call is 0.51 and the premium of the 114.00 put is 0.31.

What should you do?

Sell the call and buy the put for a net premium receipt of 0.20. This gives you a short futures position (synthetically) at 114.20.

But the actual future is trading at 114.14, so **buy the future** to 'lock in' the difference of 0.06.

The whole trade is known as a **conversion**.

Both OTC and exchange-traded derivatives can be used in the wide range of trading strategies discussed in this chapter. Many include both types as part of the same strategy.

The same factors that an investor or fund manager uses when deciding which type of contract to use in a basic position are also used in these strategies. The most basic is: which type of contract best fits the goal of the strategy? If it is a hedge, does the flexibility of an OTC contract better suit the hedge? Or does the extra liquidity and ease of trading an exchange-based product better suit one's goal?

While they are important, they are just some of the many factors that are used when deciding what type of contract is best.

8. Comparison of Exchange-Traded and OTC Hedges

Learning Objective

8.7.1 Analyse the advantages and disadvantages of using exchange-traded versus OTC products in hedging: exposure flexibility versus contract specification; ease/cost of closing OTC transactions versus exchange-traded positions; margins versus collateral processes; counterparty exposure versus centralised clearing; price transparency; best execution; documentation; settlement mechanism

As we have seen in previous chapters, exchange-traded (ETD) and OTC derivatives each have their advantages and disadvantages with respect to speculative and hedging strategies.

The following table gives a summary of these:

	Advantages	Disadvantages
Exchange-Traded	More liquidity. Full price transparency. Counterparty credit risk limited to the exchange's clearing house.	Margin payments required. Standardised contracts.
Over-the-Counter	Flexible contracts to fit any exposure. No margin required, collateral depends on counterparty.	Counterparty credit risk. Limited price transparency. Higher transaction costs.

Note that **best execution** depends more on the client's relationship with their broker. While the increased **price transparency** associated with ETD contracts does give them a slight advantage, in this aspect it is more of a case-by-case basis.

When comparing an OTC to an ETD derivative, any investor has to weigh up the advantages and disadvantages. One of the key advantages of OTC is the flexibility that this type of contract gives to an investor. An OTC derivative can be negotiated and customised to meet the specific needs of an individual investor, including contract amount, maturity/expiration date and contract price. This flexibility is key to OTC derivatives, but there is a trade-off, since OTC derivatives have several disadvantages compared to ETD derivatives.

OTC contracts tend to have more counterparty risk, and less market transparency – this might result in limited liquidity and higher transaction costs.

Since most ETD contracts have standard specifications, their documentation and trade processing and clearing is also fairly standard. In contrast, while some OTC derivative counterparties can have 'netting' and other agreements that will enable them to reduce the associated trade documentation, the fact that the OTC derivatives are individual means that, for most, the trade documentation process is more involved, usually meaning higher transaction and processing costs.

The same is true for settlement agreements/procedures. The fact that the clearing house is the counterparty to every trade means that there are specific and standard delivery procedures for those exchange-traded derivatives that do go to delivery. This again reduces counterparty risk, as well as delivery costs. Recent regulatory changes have increased the level of standardised or 'straightforward' processing of a wide range of OTC derivatives. Several market-based organisations such as the International Swaps and Derivatives Association (ISDA) have established settlement best practices and procedural guidelines for its members to use to improve the settlement time and risk-management of their OTC derivatives exposure.

OTC derivatives' flexibility with regard to contract maturity/expiration also extends to its delivery mechanism. When an OTC derivative is negotiated, either counterparty can include specific delivery arrangements that meet his specific requirements. For example, a buyer of a silver call may have included, as part of the contract agreement, specific details of where the seller will deliver the silver, if the buyer chooses to exercise the call. This flexibility should be priced into the call's premium.

9. Indirect Investments

Learning Objective

8.8.1   Analyse the main types, features, styles and applications of derivatives- based indirect investments: accounts; pooled funds; speculative, guaranteed and synthetic funds; Authorised Funds: retail schemes; onshore and offshore funds; taxation, access and cost considerations

Most investors are unlikely to become involved directly in the derivatives markets, but there are numerous instruments that they do invest in which indirectly involve the use of futures and options.

There are two main routes for most customers wanting to invest in derivatives, accounts and pooled funds.

1. **Accounts**
   A discretionary account operates where the client entrusts money to a regulated firm, which then undertakes to manage the funds according to the client's objectives, perhaps subject to restrictions on the types of instruments that can be used by the manager. Wealthy individuals normally use such funds. The types of derivatives used, and the degree of risk, are agreed as part of the initial agreement that the client signs when the account is established. The key advantage of such accounts is that the client benefits from professional management and oversight. The client also benefits from profits, but is equally liable for losses on the portfolio that can be more than the funds invested.

2. **Pooled Funds**

These are collective investment schemes (CISs) managed by regulated fund management companies on behalf of investors whose money is pooled together and invested. These collective schemes can include derivatives. An investment pool is specific to the US and relates to small, highly regulated funds. The maximum loss to the investor is restricted to the amount they invest. Their main advantage is that, by pooling the funds, **risk is diversified**. The number of investors in a pooled fund is usually small, normally 20–30, and management fees are relatively high.

9.1   Retail Schemes

The most recent regulatory definition of **retail schemes** or **retail investment products** is deliberately broad in range. The current regulatory definition is as follows:

- a life policy
- an exchange-traded unit
- a real estate investment trust
- a stakeholder pension
- a personal pension
- an investment trust
- a security in an investment trust
- a structured capital-at-risk product
- a fund of traded endowments
- an open-ended investment company.

It also includes a 'catch-all' provision: *'any other designated investment which offers exposure to underlying financial assets, in a packaged form which modifies that exposure when compared with a direct holding in the financial asset'*.

A **retail client** is currently defined as someone who is not a professional client or an eligible counterparty (the latter being, broadly, any financial institution or large undertaking). This is not quite the same as a 'consumer' (defined as someone acting for purposes outside his trade, business or profession), although the vast majority of those affected by the new regime will be consumers.

In contrast, the following is a list of the main investment products that under current regulation are not considered to be retail schemes:

- unregulated collective investment schemes (UCIS)
- traded life policy investments (TLPI)
- qualified investor schemes (QIS) and
- certain securities issues by Special Purpose Vehicles/Entities (SPVs), collectively described in the paper as 'non-mainstream pooled investments'.

Investment advisers are permitted to offer these schemes to clients that are defined as:

- certified sophisticated investors
- self-certified sophisticated investors or
- certified high net worth individuals.

9.2 Investment Style of Derivatives-Based Funds

The investment style/objectives of derivatives-based funds vary, but can be categorised by three main types:

1. **Speculative** – highly geared funds investing in derivatives to produce high returns, at a high risk. As seen above, clients cannot lose more than the funds invested.

2. **Guaranteed** – funds that lock in the investor for a minimum period and provide exposure to a market but **guarantee** that, **at worst, the investor will get their money back** (or a preset amount, eg, 95%). Typically, most of the funds will be invested in zero coupon bonds, or cash, with the balance being used to buy options, eg, FTSE put options for an index bear fund. These are low-risk because investors' capital is safe. However, the lock-in periods can be quite long (one to seven years). If after five years an investor only received their money back, the cost is the lost returns he could have received elsewhere, for example bank interest. This is known as opportunity cost. This is also known as a structured fund.

3. **Synthetics** – funds designed to **replicate the performance of an index**. They use the techniques described earlier in this chapter to achieve their objectives. Typically, the funds are invested on risk-free deposit and the relevant numbers of futures contracts (representing the value of the funds) are purchased. Note, even though futures are being used, there is no gearing in these funds.

9.3 Derivatives-Based Funds

As seen, **collective investment schemes (CISs)** are a means of investing money alongside others, benefiting from professional fund management. The prime vehicle is the **unit trust**, which pools funds placed by investors.

There are two types of unit trusts: **authorised** and **unauthorised**. The authorisation comes from the FCA. The significance of authorisation is that it dictates the marketability of the fund to private customers. Authorised unit trusts (AUTs) can be freely advertised and marketed; unauthorised unit trusts cannot.

9.4 Offshore Funds

Investors can invest in CISs established within the UK (onshore funds) or outside the UK (offshore funds). Offshore funds may provide the UK investor with greater choice and may be tax-efficient; however, the regulatory protections may be less substantial and the charges may be higher than in an equivalent UK fund. Most are based in an offshore financial centre, such as Luxembourg, the Cayman Islands or the British Virgin Islands.

9.5 Other Considerations

When assessing the attractiveness of any of these indirect investments, one must consider both their costs and how accessible their funds will be. All providers of these investment products must advise clients of the terms of commitment, ie, if the account or fund has a specific maturity, which means that the client cannot withdraw his funds at all, or only by paying a significant penalty.

The tax treatment of these investments depends upon where the investment is based, as well as the investor's tax jurisdiction.

10.   Application of Derivative Strategies and Funds

Learning Objective

8.9.1   Analyse the relative attractiveness of derivative positions or investments to specific client circumstances: private client investment portfolios; high net worth portfolios; institutional asset managers; corporate treasurers; hedge funds; structured funds; sovereign wealth funds

We have seen that derivatives can be used to reduce risk as a **hedge**, or increase risk as a way of increasing profit – **speculation**. We also know derivatives are **leveraged**, some more than others. The following provides an overview of how different types of clients/investors are most likely to use derivatives.

Private Client Investment/Portfolios

Also widely known as private investors or retail clients, their use of derivatives can range from 'never' and 'for hedging existing investment positions' to 'moderately speculative' depending on their knowledge/ understanding of the markets, as well as their arrangements with their bank/broker. The institutions that execute trades for these clients are bound by the FCA, the EU and the US and other regulators to 'know their customers' and not mis-sell or misrepresent the risk associated with any trades, particularly those that involve derivatives (see Chapter 7). In addition, private clients will find that their speculative use of derivatives may be restricted by their banks/brokers, since they must ensure that clients have sufficient assets/credit facilities to meet all of their obligations, which range from margin calls to the liabilities associated with writing a naked option. There are also regulations that restrict private client use of derivatives, particularly when it is related to self-managed individual pension accounts.

In summary, the use of derivatives by private/retail investors ranges from never, through buying and selling futures and options as a hedge, to moderately speculative, which might include the sale of covered options, to increase returns on their portfolio. Given those restrictions, any positions will be much smaller than other classes of users.

High Net Worth Clients/Portfolios

This classification of client is defined by a wide range of regulations – FCA, MiFID and SEC guidelines, to name a few (see Chapter 9). Also, most banks/brokers have their own in-house parameters that define a client as 'high net worth' – normally a minimum benchmark such as £10 million or €15 million of assets that the client has deposited with the specific institution. While slightly more relaxed, the 'know your customers' rules still apply since, with these sums, the regulators are also concerned about money laundering as well as client protection.

Given their increased assets, this class of client will normally have a wider range of derivative products available for their use. They tend to have a higher risk tolerance, therefore their use of derivatives is more speculative than that of private retail clients. In summary, high net worth clients normally take riskier derivative positions, depending on their wealth; these can sometimes match those of the small hedge funds.

This class of investor will normally be more restricted by the limits placed upon them by their banks/ brokers, who must ensure that they have sufficient funds/credits to cover any margin calls or funds to cover the exercise of any naked written option position held by these clients.

Institutional Asset Managers

Collective investment or fund managers use derivatives to both reduce risk (hedge) and increase it (speculate), as a means to increase the return of their fund. Each will have specific guidelines within which they must operate. While UCITS III has allowed OTC funds to increase their use of derivatives, as long as they report and account for such use and manage it within their guidelines, institutional asset managers, for the most part, will be more conservative in their use of derivatives than hedge fund managers. In summary, while it very much depends on their individual fund's guidelines, most institutional asset managers' use of derivatives will be more speculative than a corporate treasurer's, but less than a hedge fund's.

Corporate Treasurers

Most companies are not in the business of speculating in derivatives as a way of generating profit. Therefore, most corporate treasurers will use derivatives as a hedge in order to reduce risk. Their use of derivatives ranges from buying or selling futures (both financial and commodities) to reduce any price risk associated with their line of business. For example, a mining company might sell copper futures when planning their budget to lock-in the future price they will get for the copper they produce. Corporate treasurers may also buy options, such as FX options, if they are involved in international transactions, in order to reduce any currency risk. In summary, corporate treasurers are most likely to be among the most conservative users of derivatives.

Hedge Funds

As discussed in the previous section, there is a wide range of hedge funds, each with its own goal and risk parameters. Funds' use of derivatives will range from hedging, to reduce risk and lock-in profits, to highly geared speculative positions. Again, their use of derivatives depends on their investment goals and specific guidelines. Recent regulations, such as UCITS III, have made the use of derivatives by OTC funds less restrictive, while also ensuring that these funds report their use properly and remain within their guidelines' limits. In summary, hedge funds can be found along the full spectrum of derivative use, from hedging to highly geared speculative positions, such as naked options writing.

Structured Funds

These funds use a wide range of derivatives, including futures, options and other derivatives, to generate the capital appreciation or higher returns that are associated with these funds. Their use of derivatives is solely for yield enhancement and therefore is almost completely speculatively based. They will use a wide range of derivatives that are related to the index or asset group that the fund's returns are associated with.

Sovereign Wealth Funds (SWFs)

These are pools of money derived from a country's reserves, which are set aside for investment purposes that will benefit the country's economy. The funding for a sovereign wealth fund (SWF) comes from central bank reserves that accumulate as a result of budget and trade surpluses. The types of acceptable investments included in each SWF vary from country to country; these include stocks, bonds, property, precious metals and other financial instruments (which in some cases include derivatives).

Some countries have created SWFs to diversify their revenue streams. For example, the United Arab Emirates (UAE) relies on oil exports for its wealth. Therefore, it devotes a portion of its reserves to an SWF that invests in other types of assets that can act as a shield against oil-related risk.

Some SWFs may be held by a central bank, which accumulates the funds in the course of its management of a nation's banking system; this type of fund is usually of major economic and fiscal importance. Other SWFs are simply the state savings schemes that are invested by various entities for an attractive investment return.

The accumulated funds may have their origin in, or may represent, foreign currency deposits, gold, special drawing rights (SDRs) and International Monetary Fund (IMF) reserve positions held by central banks and monetary authorities, along with other national assets such as pension investments, oil funds, or other industrial and financial holdings. Such investment management entities may be set up as official investment companies, state pension funds, or sovereign oil funds, among others.

The following is a list of the 10 largest SWFs as of February 2016:

Fund's name	Country	Size of fund – USD bn
Government Pensions Fund	Norway	825
Abu Dhabi Investment Authority	Abu Dhabi	773
China Investment Company	China	747
SAMA Foreign Holdings	Saudi Arabia	633
Kuwait Investment Company	Kuwait	592
SAFE Investment Company	China	474
HKMA Investment Portfolio	Hong Kong	442
Government Investment Corporation	Singapore	344
Qatar Investment Authority	Qatar	256
National Social Security Fund	China	236

Appendix

Answers to the chapter exercises.

Answer to Exercise 1

Number of contracts required =

Price factor x $\dfrac{\text{Nominal value of CTD portfolio}}{\text{Nominal value of the contract}}$

Number of contracts needed to hedge =

$$1.12486 \quad \text{x} \quad \frac{£15,000,000}{£100,000}$$

= 168.729

= 169 contracts approx.

Because the investor has short sold the gilts, she should buy 169 long gilt futures.

Answer to Exercise 2

a. There is a loss on the shares of 21p (215p – 194p); however, the option is not exercised, so Mr Z keeps the premium of 9p, resulting in an overall loss of 21p – 9p = 12p per share.

b. There is a loss on the shares of 7p (215p – 208p); however, the option is not exercised, so Mr Z keeps the premium of 9p, resulting in an overall profit of 9p – 7p = 2p per share.

c. The gain on the shares would have been 15p (230p – 215p), but the option is exercised, so Mr Z needs to deliver his shares at 220p, a gain of only 5p (220p – 215p). However, he also keeps the premium of 9p, resulting in an overall profit of 9p + 5p = 14p per share.

Answer to Exercise 3

a. The option is exercised and Mrs P has to pay 700p under the terms of the option. But since she was short of the shares at 718p, that will give her 18p of profit, which, combined with the premium received from writing the covered put, results in a total profit of 30p.

b. The option is not exercised and Mrs P keeps the 12p premium.

c. While the option is not exercised, Mrs P will realise a loss of 32p (the difference between the share's price of 750p and where she is short, 718p). But that will be reduced by the 12p premium that she received for writing the put, which results in a net loss of 20p.

Answer to Exercise 4

a. The 550 put will be exercised, so Mr Z will buy the ABC shares at 550p each and he will be able to sell them for 500p under the terms of the put option he holds. The loss will be 50p, but Mr Z has received a net premium of 17p (35p – 18p), so in overall terms he has lost 33p (50p – 17p).

b. The 550 put will be exercised, so Mr Z will buy the ABC shares at 550p each and he will be able to sell them for 530p on the market. The loss will be 20p, but Mr Z has received a net premium of 17p (35p – 18p), so in overall terms he has lost 3p (20p – 17p).

c. Neither option will be exercised, so Mr Z will keep the net premium of 17p (35p – 18p).

Answer to Exercise 5

This is a bull put spread.

The breakeven will be when the share price reaches 533p. At this price the holder of the 550 put will exercise, so Mr Z will lose 17p (buying shares for 550p that are only worth 533p). However, there is also the net premium receipt of 17p to consider (35p – 18p), so overall Mr Z will break even.

The maximum profit will occur at 550p or above. At 550p, Mr Z will keep the premium of 35p, having spent a premium of 18p on the bought put with the lower exercise – a net profit of 17p.

Answer to Exercise 6

This is a type of horizontal spread.

The investor took the position of buying the shorter-term option and selling a same option with a longer expiration, based on the view that a higher than expected earnings report would result in an increase in short-term volatility.

The initial position of buying the two-week and selling the three-month gave the investor a net payment of 110p per contract (paid 20p and received 130p per contract). After the announcement, the investor was able to unwind the position at a net cost of 100p per contract (received 35p and paid 135p per contract). The net result is a profit of 10p per contract.

Answer to Exercise 7

This is a long straddle, and the breakeven range is the strike plus and minus the two premiums, here 7p + 18p = 25p. So, in this instance the shares would need to fall below 475p (500p – 25p) or rise to above 525p (500p + 25p) to bring about a profit for the investor.

Answer to Exercise 8

The underlying share has to rise above 450 plus the two premiums or fall below 400 minus the two premiums. So the breakeven range is from 375 to 475.

End of Chapter Questions

1. What are inter-market spreads based on?
   Answer reference: Section 2.2

2. When using futures to hedge an equities portfolio, how is its beta useful?
   Answer reference: Section 3

3. Describe basis, basis risk and basis trading.
   Answer reference: Section 3.1

4. What is the motivation for a covered short call?
   Answer reference: Section 4.3

5. How do you create a naked short put position?
   Answer reference: Section 4.3

6. Name the three different types of options spreads.
   Answer reference: Section 5

7. What is the rationale behind a long straddle?
   Answer reference: Section 6.1

8. Identify the six basic synthetics positions.
   Answer reference: Section 7

9. Which main investment products are not considered to be retail schemes under current regulation?
   Answer reference: Section 9.1

10. What is a typical definition of high net worth clients?
    Answer reference: Section 10

Chapter Nine

Investment Selection and Administration

This syllabus area will provide approximately 4 of the 80 examination questions

1. Introduction

When selecting investments and developing a strategy for a client, the most important requirement is a clear understanding of the client's investment goals. That is, are they looking for capital appreciation or income, or some combination of both? Once that is established, additional factors need to be considered, such as the length of time they wish to invest for, and the level of risk they are prepared to take in order to achieve these objectives.

The latter is particularly important when selecting an investment strategy that includes derivatives, since some are highly geared and therefore carry greater risks, but also, many investors do not fully understand how derivatives work and all the risks that are associated with them.

Once these criteria are satisfied, an adviser can then start constructing an investment strategy which they feel is most likely to deliver the investor's desired return.

2. The Advisory Process

The following outlines some of the essential information that all investment advisers must obtain, to ensure that they recommend the most appropriate financial planning and advice for their clients.

2.1 Financial Objectives

Learning Objective

9.1.1 Apply a range of essential information and factors to form the basis of appropriate financial planning and advice for clients: financial objectives; current and future status risk profile; level of knowledge about investments; existing debts and investments

2.1.1 Growth or Income

The client's requirements for capital growth or income need to be established from the beginning to ensure the correct mix of instruments is used and the most appropriate types (cash and/or derivatives) are selected.

For example, an investor who is looking for a stable income from his/her investment portfolio would be more likely to be advised to hold a significant percentage in 'high quality'/lower risk bonds and short-term deposits rather than newly issued small company shares.

2.1.2 Timescale

The length of time the client wishes to invest for is also an important consideration. If they only require an income, then the time period may be open-ended, while clients who require capital growth may need to access some or all of their capital at a point in the future.

As a rule, those clients looking for income are usually not candidates for strategies that involve a large number of derivatives, unless they are investing a significant amount or their required income is in the middle- or long-term future.

When dealing with shorter timescales, you need to consider the liquidity and volatility of the underlying assets. For example, if the client tells you that they need access to some of their capital in the next six months, then investments that are very liquid and of relatively low volatility should be high on the list, to ensure that the capital value is preserved and that the funds are easily accessible.

While most futures and option contracts do have shorter maturities/expirations, it is more the client's time horizon of accessibility to their funds that is a key factor.

2.1.3 Attitude to Risk

Understanding the client's attitude to risk is an extremely important part of the investment selection process when derivatives are involved. A number of different methods may be used to assess how a client feels about investment risk, including questionnaires, software applications and training/investment information.

Question-based assessments generally categorise clients into one of a number of risk classifications, ie, cautious, balanced, aggressive. The combination of the client's objectives, timescale and attitude to risk helps as a guide in electing a suitable choice of investments, both cash and derivatives.

The table below shows some of the possible strategies which reconcile the desire for returns as expressed in the investment objectives and the tolerance for risk.

Investment objective	Risk tolerance	Attitude to risk and possible investments
Income	Cautious	Willing to accept a lower level of income for lower risk. Exposure to high-yield bonds and equities will be low. No derivatives, as well as avoiding any collective investment that uses derivatives.
	Moderate	Seek to balance potential risk with potential for income. Exposure to high-yield bonds and equities will be higher. Use funds that use some yield-enhancement derivative strategies.
	Adventurous	Willing to adopt more aggressive strategies that offer potential for higher income. Exposure to high-yield bonds and equities may be substantial. Willing to include some higher-risk, income-generating derivatives strategies, such as writing naked options.

Income and Growth	Cautious	Seeking maximum growth and income consistent with relatively modest degree of risk. Equities will form a relatively small percentage of the portfolio. Avoid all exposure to derivatives.
	Moderate	Seeking to balance potential risk with growth of both capital and income. Equities will form a significant percentage of the portfolio, with perhaps a 60/40 allocation between equity and bonds. Invest in funds that employ derivatives to hedge specific exposure.
	Adventurous	Able to adopt a long-term view that allows them to pursue a more aggressive strategy. Equities and other indirect holdings and possibly derivatives will form the principal part of the portfolio.
Growth	Cautious	Seeking maximum growth consistent with relatively modest degree of risk. Equities will form the principal part of the portfolio, but no exposure to derivatives.
	Moderate	Seeking to balance potential risk with growth of capital. Equities will form the principal part of the portfolio, and there may be some exposure to indirect holdings such as ETFs and derivatives.
	Adventurous	Able to adopt a long-term view that allows them to pursue a more aggressive strategy. Equities may form the whole of the portfolio, with also the possibility of including leverage instruments such as futures and CFDs.

2.1.4 Investment Knowledge

When advising clients on investing in derivatives, it is extremely important to ensure that the client fully understands how the derivatives work and their corresponding risks. Many financial regulators require all advisers to pass a number of exams, to ensure that they fully understand what they are recommending to clients.

Most regulators and central banks also require that clients acknowledge their understanding of these risks, by signing specific customer agreements, before any derivatives transactions are executed in their account.

2.1.5 Existing Investments and Debts

As part of any introductory process, most investment advisors ask clients to complete an application and information form. One of the key reasons for this, in addition to establishing their investment objectives, is to obtain information about their current financial position. The adviser needs to know of all existing debts and of any other current investments, to ensure that their financial advice meets the client's goals and, most importantly when dealing with derivatives, their risk exposure. It is also key for both tax planning and reporting on the client's portfolio.

2.2 Selecting Suitable Strategies

Learning Objective

9.1.2 Analyse and select strategies suitable for the client's aims and objectives in terms of: investment objectives; risk tolerance; liquidity, trading and ongoing management; mandatory or voluntary investment restrictions; tax and cost considerations

9.1.3 Analyse and select derivatives suitable for a particular portfolio strategy: direct holdings, indirect holdings and combinations; rationale; impact on client objectives and priorities; balance of investments

An adviser needs to be able to analyse a wide range of potentially suitable investment and derivative products, taking into account their client's current holdings, as well as their goals and objectives. The client's needs and demands should be considered in order to match possible appropriate solutions to these needs and demands, in the light of the features of the various investment alternatives. It is not always the case that there is only one possible solution that should be recommended: in many cases there may be a number of possible strategies that should be discussed with the client.

Once an adviser is aware of their client's objectives and **risk tolerance**, he can analyse and suggest an investment strategy. A client's risk tolerance is one of the key factors when selecting derivatives, since many clients do not fully understand them and therefore, maybe be unaware of their total risk. One important decision related to selecting suitable derivatives is whether to have the client **hold derivatives directly**, ie, have a futures account or directly trade equity options, or **invest in an indirect way**, such as through funds that hold derivatives, as part of their holdings. It is important that, no matter which alternative is chosen, the client is aware of the associated risks and costs.

Once the strategies are chosen, the adviser must explain to the client how these strategies will meet their goals. All strategies that include derivatives should have a clear and definable **balance** between cash investments and all derivatives. This is particularly important for combination strategies, whether they include cash and derivatives or two types of derivative contracts.

It is important, in both the initial discussions as well as part of the ongoing communications between adviser and client, that the adviser is aware of the client's **tax status**. This will ensure that the strategy is most efficient given the client's current situation. For example, if a client experiences a dramatic rise in taxable income, the adviser will most likely shift the investment mix, either to defer any income or to bring forward any losses, to ensure that the client receives the most favourable tax treatment.

An adviser should also be aware of any **investment restrictions**, either mandatory or voluntary, that a client has. These could range from ethical issues to risk tolerance ones.

3. Administration and Maintenance

Learning Objective

9.2.1 Apply key elements involved in managing a client portfolio: systematic and compliant approach to client portfolio monitoring, review, reporting and management; selection of appropriate benchmarks to include market and specialist indices, total return and maximum drawdown; arrangements for client communication

9.2.2 Apply measures to address changes that can affect a client portfolio: client circumstances; financial environment; new products and services available; administrative changes or difficulties; investment-related changes (eg, credit rating, corporate actions); portfolio rebalancing; benchmark review

It is important to ensure that the management of a client's portfolio is reviewed on a regular basis. The frequency of review should be agreed with the client and should take into account any changes in the client's circumstances or requirements.

It is also important that the adviser keeps the client updated on the performance of all investments. The reason for this is twofold: first, to ensure that they are up-to-date with the client's goals and objectives, as well as their current circumstances; and secondly to ensure that the client is advised of any significant changes to existing strategies, such as increased volatility in option prices related to a specific event, eg, a takeover announcement for a company, or a significant credit downgrading of a debt issue.

Changes in the performance of the portfolio may also require a **rebalancing of the asset allocation**. For example, a dramatic increase in price volatility in a specific asset class, such as equities, may be suited to a specific derivative strategy, such as selling covered calls on specific shares or an index, that the client holds as part of their portfolio. This could be based on the aim of income enhancement, if the adviser and client hold the view that volatility will fall in the near term, or as an attractive way to take profits.

A key aspect of managing a client's portfolio is the **monitoring** of the recommended strategy's performance relative to current markets. For many clients/investors, this communication is their sole measure of their adviser's performance as to whether their holdings will meet their investment goals.

While a portfolio's composition is based upon the investor's objectives, so should the **benchmarks** and **measure approaches** be related to its composition. Most broad-based portfolios use a systematic measurement approach – that is, one where the portfolio's return is measured against a broad, well-diversified asset mix. But, even when using a broad-based asset mix, its components must have a direct relationship with those in the portfolio. If the client's portfolio is very asset- or derivative-specific, or contains a fairly narrow mix of assets, such as one that holds only financial and bank shares, then a more specific monitoring approach would be required.

Therefore the selection of the appropriate benchmark for the specific portfolio's performance should be agreed between the adviser and client. It is also important that this choice is based upon accepted market practices.

Changes in Client Circumstances

Changes in the client's personal circumstances, such as early retirement or unexpected expenses, can have an influence on the portfolio's structure and might require a review, eg, an increased priority for a regular income instead of capital growth, which might decrease the client's risk tolerance.

When creating a portfolio it is important to consider the client's requirements and ensure that a liquid reserve is built in to cope with any unforeseen events, ie, to make sure that some capital remains accessible in case of an emergency.

Changes in the Financial Environment

Economic changes can impact the portfolio and will require a review to assess their effect and determine a strategy for minimising it. Examples include an increase in the margin requirements by specific exchanges, or changes to the tax treatment of options or swaps and of capital gains.

Another such example is Britain's recent vote to leave the European Union. An investment advisor must assess and advise their clients of both the short and long-term changes that are expected to take place, in light of this decision. This is expected to be an ongoing exercise, given the time frame that the negotiations of Britain's future relationship with the EU will take.

New Products and Services

The introduction of new products into the market can also require a review due to improved charging structures or additional features and benefits that were not offered by the original instrument. As exchanges establish increased alliances and product agreements, specific derivatives might become more cost-effective to trade.

Administrative Changes or Difficulties

If the ongoing management of the portfolio is proving difficult owing to issues dealing with a particular platform, technology or exchange that is proving detrimental to the efficient and timely dealing for the portfolio, then a review may be appropriate.

Investment Related Changes

Changes to the underlying holdings within a portfolio due to a corporate action or the merging of an exchange should trigger a review of the portfolio to ensure that the level of overall exposure to that particular share or specific contract has not altered significantly.

Portfolio Balancing

Portfolio balancing relates to adjustments in the levels of exposure to the various assets, including both cash and derivatives, and should be reviewed as part of the regular portfolio review, or sooner if changes in the economic cycle or financial markets signal that a greater or lesser exposure is required in other areas.

Benchmark Review

A review of the benchmark(s) may be required if it/they are no longer representative of the portfolio's objective or if the portfolio's exposure has shifted, due to a significant change in its assets/derivatives or if a certain number of derivatives have been converted to underlying assets and cash or vice versa.

End of Chapter Questions

1. What is the most important requirement when selecting investments and developing a strategy for a client?
   Answer reference: Section 1

2. Why is knowing what level of risk your client is prepared to take particularly important when selecting an investment strategy that includes derivatives?
   Answer reference: Section 1

3. In what way would timescale be a factor when considering if a client requires only an income or if they require capital growth?
   Answer reference: Section 2.1.2

4. How might you assess how your client feels about investment risk?
   Answer reference: Section 2.1.3

5. Why do most investment advisors ask clients to complete an application and information form?
   Answer reference: Section 2.1.5

6. Why should an adviser be aware of their client's tax status?
   Answer reference: Section 2.2

7. Why is it important that the adviser keeps the client updated on the performance of all investments?
   Answer reference: Section 3

8. What might changes in the performance of a client's portfolio provoke?
   Answer reference: Section 3

9. Why should the selection of an appropriate benchmark for the specific portfolio's performance be agreed between the adviser and client?
   Answer reference: Section 3

10. What type of occurrence might require a review and/or rebalancing of the asset allocation within a client's portfolio?
    Answer reference: Section 3

Chapter Ten
Regulatory Requirements

This syllabus area will provide approximately 5 of the 80 examination questions

10

This chapter covers some of the key aspects and the role of market regulators in relation to derivatives in some of the main markets. It is followed by a review of UK and US regulations and a brief review of the international accounting rules that apply to derivatives.

1. The Scope of Regulation

Learning Objective

10.1.1 Understand in outline the scope of regulation of derivatives markets and related activities in the main developed and emerging economies: UK, USA, Japan and Europe; India, China and South America; passporting and cross-border agreements; business versus investment activity

1.1 Main Market Regulators

Europe	European Banking Authority (EBA)
	European Securities and Markets Authority (ESMA)
	UK – Prudential Regulation Authority (PRA) and Financial Policy Committee (FPC) (part of the Bank of England) and the Financial Conduct Authority (FCA)
Asia	Hong Kong – Securities and Futures Commission (SFC)
	India – Securities and Exchange Board of India (SEBI)
	Singapore – Monetary Authority (MAS)
	Japan – Financial Services Authority (FSA)
	China – China Securities Regulatory Commission (CSRC), China Insurance Regulatory Commission (CIRC) and China Banking Regulatory Commission (CBRC)
US	Federal Reserve (Fed)
	Securities and Exchange Commission (SEC)
	Commodity Futures Trading Commission (CFTC)
Latin America	Argentina – Comisión Nacional de Valores (CNV)
	Brazil – Comissão de Valores Mobiliários (CVM)
	Mexico – Secretaría de Hacienda y Crédito Público (SHCP)

10

The main purpose and aims of regulation, in all markets globally, are to:

- maintain and promote the fairness, efficiency, competitiveness, transparency and orderliness of the securities and futures industry
- promote understanding by the public of the operation and functioning of the securities and futures industry
- provide protection for members of the public investing in or holding financial products
- minimise crime and misconduct in the securities and futures industry
- reduce systemic risks in the securities and futures industry, and
- assist in maintaining the market's financial stability by taking appropriate steps in relation to the securities and futures industry.

1.2   UK and EU

While each country has its own financial regulator (such as the PRA and FCA in the UK), which sets out the rules for all the UK markets, including the derivatives markets, the EU through the Markets in Financial Instruments Directive (MiFID) and European Market Infrastructure Regulation (EMIR), has introduced more extensive rules and regulations regarding the conduct of business and organisational requirements of firms within the financial industry.

While the results of the June 2016 referendum mean that the UK will leave the EU, it will change the relationship between the EU regulators and the UK, but given London's position as a key international financial centre, the level of co-operation is expected to remain strong. Therefore, any changes to current and planned future EU-based regulations that apply to the UK will remain as is, until the details of the final Brexit agreement has been settled.

MiFID specifies that if a firm has been authorised in one member state to provide investment services, this single authorisation enables the firm to provide those investment services in other member states without requiring any further authorisation. This principle was, and still is, known as the **passport**. One of the key aims of MiFID is to provide investor protection rules across the European Economic Area (EEA).

MiFID's passportable activities include:

- investment advice
- some underwriting activities
- operating a multilateral trading facility (MTF)
- investment activities relating to commodity derivatives, credit derivatives and contracts for difference
- investment research, where it is an ancillary service to some other core service.

MiFID applies only to activities in relation to a specified list of financial instruments. These are:

- transferable securities
- money market instruments
- units in collective investment undertakings (UCITS funds)
- derivatives relating to securities, currencies, interest rates or yields, or other derivatives which may be settled physically or in cash
- commodity derivatives that are traded on a regulated market and/or an MTF even if they are physically settled
- over-the-counter (OTC) commodity derivatives with a cash-settled option other than on default or other termination event
- other OTC commodity derivatives which are physically settled, which are not for commercial purposes, and which are similar to other derivatives in certain criteria
- credit derivatives
- financial contracts for difference, and
- derivatives relating to climatic variables, freight rates, emissions allowances or inflation rates or other statistics, and certain other derivatives.

Financial instruments not covered by MiFID include:

- bank accounts
- foreign exchange (unless it relates to the provision of an investment activity or service, for example, buying/selling an option on FX).

A key feature of MiFID is that it improves the passport of regulated firms by clarifying any differences between the home and host markets' regulations. It also sets out a **Capital Requirements Directive (CRD)**, which sets requirements for the regulatory capital a firm must hold. This is to ensure orderly markets and improve client protection.

1.2.1   MiFID II

In April 2014, the European Parliament voted through MiFID II – its new measures will be implemented on 3 January 2018. An overview of the main elements of the proposals is set out below:

- The **scope** of MiFID will be expanded:
    - MiFID will also apply to the advised and non-advised sale of structured deposits by credit institutions.
    - MiFID will apply to all transactions (including spot transactions) in emissions allowances (until now only certain derivative transactions in emissions allowances fell within the scope of MiFID).
    - MiFID II clarifies that the MiFID rules also apply to investment firms and credit institutions selling their own securities at the moment of their issuance when not providing advice.
    - The scope of the existing exceptions for investment firms that deal on their own account will be narrowed. For instance, investment firms that deal on their own account will require a licence if they are a member of a regulated market or MTF.
    - The scope of the existing exceptions for entities active in commodity derivatives trading will be narrowed.
    - Custody of financial instruments will become an investment service. Currently, this is merely an ancillary activity. This means that entities that provide custody services without providing other MiFID services will require a licence.
- The proposals create a **new regime for investment firms based in non-EU/EEA countries**. Pursuant to this regime, investment firms based in non-EU/EEA countries would be able to benefit from a European passport. This requires, among other things, the establishment of a branch in the EU/EEA when offering services to non-professional clients.
- Amendment of the rules regarding **client classification**:
    - The proposals provide that municipalities and other local authorities do not qualify as professional investors.
    - Additional obligations will apply with respect to services offered to eligible counterparties.
- New rules with respect to **investor protection**:
    - Firms giving investment advice will be required to disclose whether the advice is provided on an independent basis, whether it is based on a broad or more restricted analysis of the market, and whether the firm will provide the client with the ongoing assessment of the suitability of the financial instruments recommended. In order to qualify as 'advice provided on an independent basis', the firm must meet certain requirements.
    - Investment firms providing advice on an independent basis or providing asset management services may not receive fees, commissions or other monetary benefits from a third party in relation to the provision of the service to clients.
    - The exception with respect to the Know Your Customer requirement for execution-only business will be narrowed by limiting the categories of financial instruments for which this is permissible.
    - The proposals introduce specific information obligations in respect of bundled products.

10

- The proposals contain additional information obligations with respect to order execution policies.
  - The proposals prohibit the conclusion of title transfer financial collateral arrangements with non-professional clients.
- Additional **corporate governance requirements** will be imposed on investment firms, including requirements with respect to the members of the management board and the supervisory board:
  - The existing requirement to have sufficiently experienced members is expanded: members will be required to commit sufficient time to discharge their duties. The proposals include limits on the number of directorships a person can have at any one time.
  - The proposals require, where appropriate, the establishment of a nomination committee.
  - Investment firms must take into account diversity as one of the criteria for selection of members of the management board and the supervisory board.
- The proposals provide that investment firms must **record** certain telephone conversations and electronic communications (for instance email).
- The proposals introduce new rules with respect to the **infrastructure of trading venues**:
  - A new trading venue is to be provided for the organised trading facility (OTF). This is a trading venue other than a regulated market or MTF which brings together multiple third-party buying and selling interests (an example of an OTF is a broker crossing system). OTFs require authorisation from the regulator. In addition, OTFs must meet certain ongoing requirements that also apply to regulated markets and MTFs, but will also be subject to certain investor protection rules. OTFs may not execute orders against their own capital.
  - The regime for systematic internalisers will no longer be limited to shares, but will also extend to other financial instruments. In addition, the proposals contain additional rules for systematic internalisers.
  - Additional requirements will apply with respect to regulated markets (MTFs and OTFs), including the requirement to provide annual information on the execution quality, more extensive transparency and reporting obligations and rules with respect to data consolidation.
- The proposals introduce rules with respect to **algorithmic trading**: investment firms that engage in algorithmic trading must comply with additional requirements.
- **Mandatory exchange trading of derivatives**: in line with EMIR, MiFID requires that transactions in derivatives that have been identified by ESMA may in principle occur only on a regulated market, MTF, OTF or equivalent third country trading venue.
- The proposals provide for **additional powers for the regulators**: regulators will have the power to require any person to reduce its derivatives position, or, with respect to commodity derivatives, to limit the ability of any person to enter into a commodity derivative. In addition, regulators will have the power to prohibit or restrict the marketing, distribution or sale of particular financial instruments or a type of activity.
- The proposals introduce new rules with respect to **sanctions**: there will be minimum requirements that the member states must implement, including the provision that the maximum penalty must be at least 10% of the total annual turnover in case of a legal entity and €5,000,000 in case of a natural person or twice the amount of benefit derived from the violation.

1.3 Global Regulatory Reforms

In line with the EU's G20 commitments, there have been a number of initiatives both by individual jurisdictions and international bodies. At national level, both the US (Dodd-Frank Act) and Japan passed OTC derivatives legislation in 2011. A proposal by the European Commission (see Section 1.3.1) uses different approaches at times, but is very much in line with the legislation being adopted in other parts of the world. This is essential to ensure there is no regulatory arbitrage.

At international level, the Financial Stability Board set up a work stream in order to address the challenges related to the implementation of the G20 commitments. In addition, the **OTC Derivatives Regulators' Forum** was established to promote co-operation between regulators.

The Committee on Payment and Settlement Systems (CPSS) / International Organization of Securities Commissions (IOSCO) has published guidance on the application of its 2004 recommendations for central counterparties (CCPs) to OTC derivatives, and is now in the process of reviewing these recommendations and preparing recommendations for trade repositories.

Learning Objective

10.2.2   Understand the principles set out in the European Market Infrastructure Regulations (EMIR) and European Securities and Markets Authority (ESMA) regarding: central clearing obligations; central reporting obligations

---

1.3.1   European Market Infrastructure Regulation (EMIR) and the European Securities and Markets Authority (ESMA)

In September 2010, the European Commission published a proposal for regulation aimed at bringing more safety and more transparency to the OTC derivatives market. On 4 July 2012 the European Council adopted the regulation, which is aimed at increasing transparency in derivatives and reducing risk in the OTC derivatives market. Because it is a regulation, member states should have embedded it into national law by the end of 2012; there is no transposition requirement.

The regulation requires:

*   The **clearing of standardised OTC derivative contracts through central counterparties (CCPs)** in order to reduce counterparty risk. This is aimed at preventing the default of one market participant causing the collapse of other market players, thereby putting the entire financial system at risk. To be authorised, a CCP will have to hold a minimum amount of financial resources.
*   The **reporting of all derivative contracts to trade repositories** (ie, central data centres). Trade repositories will have to publish aggregate positions by class of derivatives – thereby offering market participants a clearer view of the derivatives market.
*   The putting in place of certain **risk management procedures** for OTC derivative transactions that are not cleared through a CCP, for both financial and non-financial counterparties.

The **European Securities and Markets Authority (ESMA)** will be responsible for the surveillance of trade repositories and for granting and withdrawing their registration. ESMA will also be responsible for the identification of contracts subject to the clearing obligation, while national competent authorities will be responsible for the authorisation and supervision of CCPs – except in the case of CCPs from third countries, which will have to be recognised by ESMA, provided they meet certain conditions.

If a contract is not eligible for clearing by a CCP, the regulation requires the application of different risk management techniques, including the exchange of collateral and the holding of additional capital.

The regulation will apply to CCPs and their clearing members, to financial counterparties and to trade repositories, as well as to non-financial counterparties and trading venues where so provided.

1.3.2 International Swaps and Derivatives Association (ISDA)

The Operations Steering Committee (OSC) of the International Swaps and Derivatives Association (ISDA) has recently outlined its latest targets to improve the operational infrastructure and regulation of the OTC derivatives industry. The OSC, whose membership includes OTC broker-dealers, buy-side firms and industry associations such as the ISDA, has made a commitment to regulators to increase the number and types of OTC products that will be centrally cleared, such as single-name credit default swaps (CDSs) and overnight index swaps (OISs).

In addition, the OSC has increased its emphasis on collateral management. It has implemented daily reconciliation of all collateralised inter-dealer positions in excess of 500 positions. This should cover 70% of the markets covered.

The group has also set a goal that at least 50% of equity derivatives traded can be matched, processed and cleared electronically. Equity derivatives are the least standardised of all OTC derivatives, making operational standardisation the most difficult.

1.3.3 Other European Initiatives Relating to Derivatives

Other measures relevant to OTC derivatives are planned, notably the revision of the **Capital Requirements Directive** (which sets out requirements for the capital a firm must hold; revisions include differentiation of capital charges between CCP-cleared and non-CCP-cleared contracts), the **Markets in Financial Instruments Directive** (MiFID) (eg, ensuring trading of standardised contracts on organised trading venues, enhancing trade and price transparency across venues and OTC markets as appropriate) and the **Market Abuse Directive** (extending the scope of the Directive to OTC derivatives).

1.3.4 European Regulation on Short Selling

The regulation took effect from 1 November 2012. As a regulation it has direct effect across all member states and does not require any further transposition into national law. Therefore, the rules on short selling have become harmonised across the region. The regulation covers equities, sovereign debt and CDSs.

The following are the key elements of the regulation.

Transparency

Shares

There is a two-tier model of private and public reporting at initial and incremental thresholds, triggered by the size of a net short position of shares:

- A net short of 0.2% or more in the issued share capital of a company admitted to trading on a regulated market of MTF must be **reported** privately to the regulator of the home member state competent authority of the relevant issuer.

- Additional reporting must be made if the short position reaches each 0.1% threshold thereafter. A report must also be made when the firm's net short position falls below the relevant thresholds.
- On reaching 0.5% of the issued share capital, and at each 0.1% threshold thereafter, the net short position must also be reported to the market.

In the UK, this has the effect of applying rules to all shares, rather than just to shares that are subject to rights issues and shares in UK financial sector companies.

Sovereign Debt

The regulation provides a requirement to report to regulators certain net short positions in EU sovereign debt, including CDSs referencing EU sovereign debt obligations. Rather than setting a single threshold for all sovereign issuers or individual thresholds for each sovereign issuer, they are grouped into two categories – taking into account the size of the outstanding issued sovereign debt and the liquidity of the sovereign debt market measured in terms of total turnover.

- An initial reporting threshold of 0.1% (and 0.05% intervals thereafter) applies for the first category of member states, where the total amount outstanding issued sovereign debt is up to €500 billion.
- A reporting threshold of 0.5% (and 0.25% intervals) applies if the total amount of the outstanding issued sovereign debt is more than €500 billion or if there is a 'liquid futures market' for the particular sovereign debt.

Restrictions on Uncovered Positions

From 1 November 2012, a firm that wishes to take an uncovered (or 'naked') short position in particular shares will be required either:

a. to have borrowed sufficient shares to settle the short trade, or
b. to have entered into a binding agreement to borrow those shares, or
c. to have *an arrangement with a third party under which that third party has confirmed that the shares have been located*.

ESMA remarked in its draft technical standards that the 'third party' from whom confirmation of share location must be obtained should be a distinct legal entity from the firm entering into the short sale.

The regulation is marginally less prescriptive in relation to uncovered short/CDS positions in sovereign debt than in relation to shares, in that, if such a position is being used for permitted hedging purposes, the firm concerned is not required to have borrowed, or be able to borrow, securities in order to ensure settlement of that position.

An uncovered short position in sovereign debt is permitted if it is being used to hedge a long position in the debt instruments of an issuer, the pricing of which has a 'high correlation' with the pricing of the sovereign debt. In contrast, firms are not permitted to enter into an uncovered, or 'naked', CDS on sovereign debt unless (according to the recitals of the regulation) there is an 'insurable interest'.

There are exemptions from the above requirements for market-making requirements and primary market operations in respect of sovereign debt. This exemption is notified by market makers with the respective competent authority – who will advise the market maker if they have been prohibited from using this exemption on individual stocks – within 30 days of the notification being submitted. The exemption applies to the financial instruments covered by the regulation (equities, sovereign debt and CDSs) and also to related instruments where they are used in appropriate and related hedging by market makers as part of their market-making activities. Despite market makers being able to take short positions, they are permitted to do so only on the basis that the position is being taken for short periods of time.

1.3.5   US: Dodd-Frank Act

On 15 July 2010, after a lengthy and sometimes contentious legislative process, the US Senate approved the Dodd-Frank Wall Street Reform and Consumer Protection Act (the Act). Title VII of the Act sets forth the new legislative framework for derivatives. See Section 2.7.4 for more details.

As well as the new regulation described in Section 2.7.4, the Act calls upon the Commodity Futures Trading Commission (CFTC) and the Securities and Exchange Commission (SEC) to conduct a joint study of the regulation of swaps and clearing agencies in the US, Asia and Europe and report to Congress within 18 months. If at any time the CFTC or SEC determines that the regulation of swaps in a foreign country undermines the stability of the US financial system, it may, in consultation with the Treasury Secretary, prohibit entities domiciled in that country from participating in swaps-related activities in the US.

1.3.6   Japan

Japan's parliament recently approved a bill that will require some OTC derivatives trades to go through a clearing agency, aiming to cut the risks these contracts pose to the financial system. The Japanese bill includes measures such as requiring some OTC derivatives trades – initially plain vanilla yen interest rate swaps and iTraxx Japan credit default swaps (CDSs) – to be conducted via a clearing agency. Financial institutions and clearing agencies will also be required to store trading records of such derivatives transactions and to submit such data to authorities.

1.4   FCA Principles and COBS

Learning Objective

10.1.2   Apply FCA Principles and Conduct of Business Rules when advising on, trading in or managing derivative-based investments and products for clients: client classification; treating customers fairly; suitability and appropriateness of the transaction/product; best execution; justification and risk warnings

The **Financial Services and Markets Act 2000 (FSMA)** gave the then-regulator, the FSA, a wide range of rule-making, investigatory and enforcement powers in order to meet its **statutory objectives** listed below.

1. Market confidence.
2. Financial stability.
3. The protection of consumers.
4. The reduction of financial crime.

Both the statutory objectives and related Principles of Good Regulation were summarised in three strategic aims for the FSA. These were:

- promoting efficient, orderly and fair markets
- helping retail consumers achieve a fair deal and
- improving its business capability and effectiveness.

As a result of the financial crisis, FSMA was amended by the **Financial Services Act 2012** (usually referred to now as 'the Act'), which requires the new conduct regulator, the FCA, to consider eight principles when carrying out its work. These are a supplement to the above-mentioned strategic aims of the old FSA.

The eight principles are:

- Efficiency and economy.
- Proportionality.
- Sustainable growth.
- Consumer responsibility.
- Senior management responsibility.
- Recognising the differences in the businesses carried on by different regulated persons.
- Openness and disclosure.
- Transparency.

The FCA's statutory objective is that relevant markets work well.

It also has three operational objectives, which are:

- To secure an appropriate degree of protection for consumers.
- To protect and enhance the integrity of the financial system.
- To promote effective competition in the interests of consumers.

Underlining the operational objectives are the following three broad outcomes:

- Consumers get financial services and products that meet their needs from firms they can trust.
- Firms compete effectively with the interests of their customers and the integrity of the market at the heart of how they run their business.
- Markets and financial systems are sound, stable and resilient with transparent pricing information.

In order to meet its objectives, the FCA has included the eight principles in its regulatory text (generally referred to as the **FCA Handbook**, or just the Handbook). Firms working within the regulated financial services industry are restricted to those which the FCA **authorises**, and to those exempt from the need for authorisation because they are classified as designated professional bodies (DPBs).

1.4.1   FCA Principles for Businesses

The FCA's Conduct of Business Sourcebook (COBS), which replaced the FSA's sourcebook, still includes 11 key Principles for Businesses, which authorised firms must observe. The Principles apply with respect to the carrying on of regulated activities, activities that constitute dealing in investments as principal, ancillary activities in relation to designated investment business, home finance activity, insurance mediation activity and accepting deposits, as well as the communication and approval of financial promotions. If a firm breaches any of the Principles that apply to it, it will be liable to disciplinary sanctions.

The 11 Principles for Businesses are:

1. **Integrity** – a firm must conduct its business with integrity.
2. **Skill, care and diligence** – a firm must conduct its business with due skill, care and diligence.
3. **Management and control** – a firm must take reasonable care to organise and control its affairs responsibly and effectively, with adequate risk-management systems.
4. **Financial prudence** – a firm must maintain adequate financial resources.
5. **Market conduct** – a firm must observe proper standards of market conduct.
6. **Customers' interests** – a firm must pay due regard to the interests of its customers and treat them fairly.
7. **Communication with clients** – a firm must pay due regard to the information needs of its clients and communicate information to them in a way which is clear, fair and not misleading.
8. **Conflicts of interest** – a firm must manage conflicts of interest fairly, both between itself and its customers, and between customers and other clients.
9. **Customers: relationships of trust** – a firm must take reasonable care to ensure the suitability of its advice and discretionary decisions for any customer who is entitled to rely upon its judgement.
10. **Clients' assets** – a firm must arrange adequate protection for clients' assets when it is responsible for them.
11. **Relations with regulators** – a firm must deal with its regulators in an open and co-operative way and must disclose to the FCA appropriately anything relating to the firm of which the FCA would reasonably expect notice.

1.4.2   Treating Customers Fairly

It should be apparent from a reading of COBS that a general theme of overriding fair play runs through them; this is coupled with a recognition that there is often an information imbalance between the firm and its customers (since the firm is usually more expert in its products and services than its customers).

This theme is reinforced through the FCA's **Treating Customers Fairly (TCF)** initiative. This was originally launched by the FSA in response to some work it undertook in 2000–2001, to look at what a 'fair deal' for customers should actually mean. FCA defines six 'consumer outcomes' to explain to firms what it believes TCF should do for its consumers.

1. Consumers can be confident that they are dealing with firms where the fair treatment of customers is central to the corporate culture.
2. Products and services marketed and sold in the retail market are designed to meet the needs of identified consumer groups and are targeted accordingly.
3. Consumers are provided with clear information and are kept appropriately informed before, during and after the point-of-sale.

4. When consumers receive advice, the advice is suitable and takes account of their circumstances.
5. Consumers are provided with products that perform as firms have led them to expect, and the associated service is both of an acceptable standard and as they have been led to expect.
6. Consumers do not face unreasonable post-sale barriers imposed by firms to change product, switch provider, submit a claim or make a complaint.

A key part of the FCA's approach is that all advisers adhere to its 'Good practice in your behaviour' policy. All advisers should ensure that treating customers fairly is a core part of their business, by following these practices:

- making sure the fair treatment of customers is a crucial part of their business philosophy
- remembering that treating customers fairly is their responsibility and that it cannot be delegated away
- if they use a compliance consultant, ensure the consultant's advice is evaluated and applied with their knowledge of their customers and the issues in their business
- ensure their own knowledge, training and competence is up-to-date
- making themselves aware of changes in the market and
- being conscious of regulatory changes that may affect them or their business.

If a firm does not treat clients fairly or adhere to the **best execution** rule, or if it sells **inappropriate** or **unsuitable** products to investors, the poor results/performance that these clients will receive will result in their using other firms, thereby damaging the firm's reputation and in the long run its overall performance.

1.4.3 Information Requirements: the Nature and Risks of Investments

Firms carrying on MiFID business, or equivalent third country business, must provide clients with appropriate information in a comprehensible form about:

- the firm and its services
- designated investments and proposed investment strategies; including appropriate guidance on, and warnings of, risks associated with investments in those designated investments or in respect of particular investment strategies
- an explanation of leverage and its effects and the risk of losing the entire investment
- volatility of the price and any limitations on the available market for such investments
- where the client has entered into contingent liability transactions, that they might assume additional obligations additional to the cost of acquiring the investments
- margin requirements or similar obligations applicable to certain investments
- execution venues
- costs and associated charges.

This is to ensure that the client is reasonably able to understand the nature and risks of the service and of the specific type of designated investments that are being offered and to take investment decisions on an informed basis.

Firms carrying on non-MiFID business with or for a retail client in relation to derivatives, warrants or stock-lending activity must also provide the information quoted above.

1.4.4 The Conduct of Business Rules (COBS)

Firms are subject to the FCA's COBS Sourcebook if they carry on any of a range of activities from an establishment maintained by them or their appointed representative in the UK.

The activities that are covered are:

- accepting deposits
- designated investment business
- long-term insurance business in relation to life policies
- activities relating to the above.

Under MiFID, the client classification rules (see the following section) were changed. As a result, firms may find that COBS rules apply to some of their activities when previously they did not – because some of their clients now fit into different categories, and are entitled to the different levels of protection that go with these categories. For example, a characteristic of some of the COBS rules introduced by MiFID is that they extend protection from retail clients only, to professional clients.

Certain of the COBS rules are disapplied for specific types of regulated activity such as executing orders on behalf of clients, dealing on their own account and receiving and transmitting orders. For example, a range of COBS rules are disapplied, in certain cases, for firms carrying on eligible counterparty business. These include:

- a large part of **COBS 2** – the Conduct of Business obligations
- much of **COBS 4** – communicating with clients (including financial promotions)
- **COBS 6.1** – provision of information about the firm, its services and its remuneration
- **COBS 8** – client agreements
- **COBS 10** – appropriateness (for non-advised services)
- certain parts of **COBS 11** – best execution, client order handling and use of dealing commission
- parts of **COBS 12** – labelling of non-independent research
- **COBS 14.3** – information relating to designated investments, and
- **COBS 16** – reporting requirements to clients.

This exemption is of particular interest to firms undertaking derivatives trading, as they have the option to classify themselves as ECPs, thereby removing the need to comply with certain COBS requirements such as best execution and the appropriateness requirements.

1.4.5 Client Categorisation

A firm is required to categorise or classify its clients if it is carrying on designated investment business. MiFID lays down rules as to how client categorisation has to be carried out for MiFID business. For non-MiFID business, the FCA uses the same client categorisation terminology, but the rules on how the categories must be applied are modified in some cases. When a firm provides a mix of MiFID and non-MiFID services, a firm must categorise clients in accordance with the MiFID requirements, unless the MiFID business is conducted separately from the non-MiFID business.

COBS defines a **client** as someone to whom a firm provides, intends to provide, or has provided a service in the course of carrying on a regulated activity; and, in the case of MiFID or equivalent third country business, anything which is an 'ancillary service'. The term includes potential clients. In addition, in relation to the financial promotions rules, it includes a person to whom a financial promotion is communicated, or is likely to be communicated. Clients of a firm's appointed representative or tied agent are regarded as clients of the firm.

Client Categories

Under COBS, clients may be categorised as:

1. a retail client
2. a professional client, or
3. an eligible counterparty.

The categories are relevant principally in terms of the level of protection afforded them: retail clients receive the highest level of regulatory protection.

New clients must be notified of how the firm has classified them. They must also, before services are provided, advise them of their rights to request recategorisation and of any limits in their protections that would arise from this.

1. A **retail client** is any client who is not a professional client or an eligible counterparty. The term 'customer' means retail clients and professional clients.
2. **Professional clients** may be either elective professional clients, or per se professional clients. (An **elective professional client** is one who has chosen to be treated as such. **Per se professional clients** are, generally, those which fall into any of the following categories – unless they are an eligible counterparty, or are categorised differently under other specific provisions:
   - an entity required to be authorised or regulated to operate in the financial markets
   - 'large undertakings' – companies whose balance sheet, turnover or own funds meet certain levels
   - governments, certain public bodies, central banks, international/supranational institutions and similar, and
   - institutional investors whose main business is investment in financial instruments.
3. Finally, COBS contains a list with the types of clients that can be classified as **eligible counterparties (ECPs)**, including financial institutions such as central banks, investment firms, pension funds and governments. The list of ECPs is to a certain extent identical to the per se professional client; however, the ECP category is narrower as it does not include large undertakings. A client can only be categorised as an ECP for three types of business:
   - executing orders, and/or
   - dealing on own account, and/or
   - receiving and transmitting orders.
   This means that if the same ECP wants to engage in other types of business, such as investment management or investment advice, it would have to be classified as a per se professional client.

A firm must implement appropriate written internal policies and procedures to categorise its clients. A firm must make a record of the form of each notice provided and each agreement entered into. This record must be made at the time that standard form is first used and retained for the relevant period after the firm ceases to carry on business with clients who were provided with that form.

Recategorisation of Clients

As explained earlier, many of the COBS rules do not apply when the client is an eligible counterparty; the result of this is that the ECP will not benefit from the protections afforded by these rules. Having said that, the majority of ECPs are large firms who are very familiar with the financial markets, or are themselves large players in the financial markets, and would not need such protections anyway.

Some ECPs, however, would rather have more protection by voluntarily asking to opt down a client category and become **elective professional** or even **retail clients**. Firms must allow eligible counterparties to request recategorisation, so as to benefit from the different protections afforded to retail clients or professional clients (as applicable).

Alternatively, as long as certain conditions are met, a professional client may opt up and be treated as an **elective eligible counterparty**, and a retail client may be treated as an **elective professional client**. The firm must give a clear written warning to the client of the lost protections, to which the client must agree in writing.

Recategorisation may be carried out for a client on a general basis; or on more specific terms, for example in relation to a single transaction only. A firm can place a client under a different classification for different financial instruments that they may trade/undertake transactions in.

1.4.6   Best Execution

The rules on best execution apply to MiFID and non-MiFID firms and business. The best execution rules under COBS require firms to execute orders on the terms that are most favourable to their client. Specifically, they require that firms take all reasonable steps to obtain, when executing orders, the best possible result for their clients taking into account the **execution factors**. These factors are:

- price
- costs
- speed
- likelihood of execution and settlement
- size, nature or any other consideration relevant to the execution of an order.

Best execution is, therefore, not merely how to achieve the best price. Any of the other factors mentioned above should be considered and, depending on the criteria or characteristics, could be given precedence. For some transactions, for example, the likelihood of execution could be given precedence over the speed of execution.

The obligation to deliver the best possible result when executing client orders applies in relation to all types of financial instruments. Given the differences in the structures of financial instruments, it may be difficult to identify and apply a uniform standard of and procedure for best execution that would be effective and appropriate for all classes of instruments. Therefore, best execution obligations should be applied in a manner that takes into account all the different circumstances associated with the particular types of financial instruments.

Although best execution is not merely how to achieve the best price, for retail clients, firms must take account of the **total consideration** for the transaction, ie, the price of the financial instrument and the costs relating to execution, including execution venue fees, clearing and settlement fees, and any fees paid to third parties. When a firm could execute the client's order on more than one **execution venue**, the firm must take into account both its own costs and the costs of the relevant venues, eg, different exchanges, in assessing which will give the best outcome. Its own commissions should not allow it to discriminate unfairly between execution venues, and a firm should not charge a different commission or spread to clients for execution in different venues if that difference does not reflect actual differences in the cost to the firm of executing on those venues.

Firms are required to establish an **order execution policy** to enable them to obtain the best possible results for their clients. For each class of financial instrument the firm deals in, this must include information about the different execution venues where the firm executes its client orders, and the factors that will affect the choice of venue used.

Whenever a firm receives a **specific instruction** from a client, it must execute the order as instructed.

Firms may **aggregate** their own-account deals with those of a client, or aggregate two or more clients' deals, only if:

- this is unlikely to disadvantage any of the aggregated clients
- the fact that aggregation may work to their disadvantage is disclosed to the clients, and
- an order allocation policy has been established which provides (in sufficiently precise terms) for the fair allocation of transactions. This must cover how volume and price of orders will affect allocation; it must also cover how partial allocations will be dealt with.

When an aggregated order is only partly executed, the firm must then allocate the various trades in order with this allocation policy. When firms have own-account deals in an aggregated order along with those of clients, it must not allocate them in a way which is detrimental to the clients.

Unless the client instructs otherwise, a firm which receives a **client limit order** for shares listed on a regulated market and which cannot immediately execute it under the prevailing market conditions must make the limit order public (in a manner easily accessible to other market participants) immediately so that it can be executed as soon as possible.

1.4.7   Suitability

The COBS rules on the suitability requirements apply:

- when firms make personal recommendations relating to designated investments
- when firms manage investments.

A firm must provide a retail client with a **suitability report** if it makes a personal recommendation to the client, where the client:

- acquires a holding in, or sells all or part of a holding in:
  - a regulated collective investment scheme
  - an investment trust, either directly or through an investment trust savings scheme
  - an investment trust where the shares are to be held in an ISA which has been promoted as the means for investing in one or more specific investment trusts, or

- buys, sells, surrenders, converts or cancels rights under, or suspends contributions to, a personal pension scheme or a stakeholder pension scheme, or
- elects to make income withdrawals or purchase a short-term annuity, or
- enters into a pension transfer or pension opt-out.

The report must be provided when, or as soon as possible after, the transaction is effected or executed. The report must, at least, specify the client's demands and needs, explain any possible disadvantages of the transaction for the client and why the firm has concluded that the recommended transaction is suitable for the client.

In order to make a **suitability assessment**, a firm should establish, and take account of, the client's:

- investment objectives
- knowledge and experience in the investment relevant to the specific type of designated investment or service
- level of investment risk that he can bear financially that is consistent with his investment objectives.

In order to do so, a firm should gather enough information from its client to understand the essential facts about him. It must have a reasonable basis to believe that, bearing in mind its nature, the service or transaction:

- meets his investment objectives
- carries a level of investment risk that he can bear financially, and
- carries risks that he has the experience and knowledge to understand.

In terms of assessing the client's knowledge and experience, the firm should gather information on:

- the types of service/transaction/investment with which he is familiar
- the nature, volume, frequency and period of his involvement in such transactions/investments, and
- his level of education, profession or relevant former profession.

Firms are entitled to rely on the information the client provides, unless it is manifestly out-of-date, inaccurate or incomplete. If a firm does not obtain the information it needs to assess suitability in this way, it must not make a personal recommendation to the client or take a decision to trade for him.

A firm is entitled to assume that a client classified as a **professional client** in respect of MiFID or equivalent third-country business, for certain products, transactions or services, has the necessary experience and knowledge in that area and that the client is able financially to bear any related investment risks consistent with their investment objectives.

1.4.8   Appropriateness (Non-Advised Sales)

The rules on non-advised sales apply to a range of MiFID (and some non-MiFID) investment services which do not involve advice or discretionary portfolio management. Specifically, they apply to:

- firms providing MiFID investment services other than the provision of personal recommendations or the managing of investments

- firms arranging deals, or dealing, in warrants and derivatives for retail clients, when the firm is, or should be, aware that the client's application or order is in response to a direct offer financial promotion
- firms which assess appropriateness on behalf of other MiFID firms.

When a firm provides one of these services, it must ask the client for information about their knowledge and experience in the investment field of the specific type of product or service offered or demanded so that it can assess whether the product/service is appropriate. In assessing appropriateness, the firm:

- must determine whether the client has the experience and knowledge to understand risks involved
- may assume that a client classified as a professional client for certain services/products has the necessary knowledge and experience in that field for which it is classified as a professional client.

Firms do not need to reassess appropriateness each time if a client is engaged in a series of similar transactions or services, but they must do so before beginning to provide any new type of service. If a client was engaged in a course of dealings of this type before 1 November 2007, the firm may assume that they have the necessary experience and knowledge to understand the risks. Note, this does not mean, however, that the other criteria may necessarily be deemed to have been met.

Circumstances when Assessment is Unnecessary

Firms are not required to ask clients to provide information or assess appropriateness if:

- the service is execution-only, or for the receipt and transmission of client orders, in relation to 'particular financial instruments' (see below) and at the client's initiative and
- if the client has been clearly informed that the firm is not required to do so in this particular case, and that they will, therefore, not get the benefit of the protection under the rules on assessing suitability, and
- the firm complies with its obligations regarding conflicts of interest (see Principle 8 of the Principles for Businesses).

The 'particular financial instruments' mentioned above are:

- shares listed on a regulated market or an equivalent third country market
- money market instruments, bonds or other forms of securitised debt (providing that they do not have embedded derivatives)
- holdings in UCITS funds, and
- other investments meeting a definition of 'non-complex' investments.

A financial instrument is 'non-complex' if:

- it is not a derivative
- there is sufficient liquidity in it
- it does not involve liability for the client that exceeds the cost of acquiring the investment, and
- it is publicly available and comprehensive information is available on it.

In regard to derivatives, therefore, it can be seen that assessment will always be necessary.

Obligation to Issue Risk Warnings

If a firm believes, based on the above assessments, that a product or service contemplated is not appropriate for the client, it must warn them of that fact. It may do so in a standardised format. Further, if the client declines to provide the information the firm needs to assess appropriateness, the firm must warn them that it will then be unable to assess the product/service's appropriateness for them (and again it may do so in standard format).

If the client then asks the firm to proceed regardless, it is up to the firm to decide whether to do so based on the circumstances.

1.4.9 The New UK Financial Services Regulatory Structure

In the UK between 2001 and 2013, the Financial Services Authority (FSA), a quasi-judicial body, was responsible for the regulation of the financial services industry. While its board was appointed by the Treasury, it operated independently of government. It was a limited company and was fully funded by fees charged to the financial services industry.

Due to perceived regulatory failure of the banks during the financial crisis of 2007–2008, the UK government decided to restructure financial regulation and abolished the FSA. On 19 December 2012, the Financial Services Act 2012 received royal assent, abolishing the FSA with effect from 1 April 2013. Its responsibilities have been split between two new agencies: the Financial Conduct Authority (FCA), and the Prudential Regulation Authority (PRA), which is part of the Bank of England.

Financial Conduct Authority (FCA)

The FCA's main goal is to ensure that there is fair competition among financial firms and that they all are sound. While it reports to Parliament, it, like the FSA, is funded by the firms that it regulates. In light of its structure and goals, it is more focused on maintaining a healthy and competitive retail financial industry.

The FCA focuses on:

- **conduct** – for the market to thrive, firms must behave ethically, stick to the rules and meet regulatory standards
- **competition** – it encourages healthy competition between firms to keep the market buoyant and help grow the economy
- **reducing market abuse** – firms need to have procedures to help them identify and stop market abuse, such as insider dealing and share price manipulation.

The FCA's responsibility covers all UK financial markets, including the derivatives markets, and therefore it works closely with its EU counterparts and is active in the implementation of MiFID II and all other international regulations.

Prudential Regulation Authority (PRA)

The Prudential Regulation Authority (PRA), which is part of the Bank of England, is now the United Kingdom's prudential regulator for deposit-takers (banks, building societies and credit unions), insurers and designated investment firms. It derives its responsibilities and its powers from the Financial Services and Markets Act 2000 (as amended by the Financial Services Act 2012) (the Act), and the relevant EU Directives for which it is a competent authority.

Its main focus is to ensure that all companies that are part of any aspect of the UK-based financial markets are financially sound. While it is not the PRA's role to ensure that no firms fail, it is its responsibility to ensure that, should this happen, it does so in a way that avoids any major disruption to the supply of critical financial services.

Therefore, both its authority and involvement in the regulation of the derivatives markets is mainly on an indirect basis.

The two supervisory units run their own risk mitigation programmes and firms have two separate sets of mitigating actions to address.

Financial Policy Committee (FPC)

The Financial Policy Committee (FPC) is part of the Bank of England and is modelled on the Monetary Policy Committee (MPC). It was established on 1 April 2013, as a new body, and is charged with the primary objective of identifying, monitoring and taking action to remove or reduce systemic risks to the UK's economy. Its main focus is on the macro-economic and financial issues that may threaten the economy's long-term growth prospects. The Committee will address any risks it identifies by passing on its concerns to the PRA, which will be obliged to act. Unlike the PRA and the FCA, the FPC will not have direct regulatory responsibility for any particular types of firm.

1.5 European Regulators

1.5.1 The European Banking Authority (EBA)

The European Banking Authority (EBA) is a regulatory agency whose activities include conducting stress tests on EU banks with the goal of increasing transparency within the European financial system, and identifying weaknesses in banks' capital structures. The EBA has the power to overrule any national regulators if they fail to properly regulate their banks, and it can prevent regulatory arbitrage, which should allow banks to compete fairly throughout the EU.

1.5.2 The European Securities and Markets Authority (ESMA)

The European Securities and Markets Authority (ESMA) is one of the three European Supervisory Authorities. Its main role is to establish an EU-wide financial markets overseer by first assessing risks to investors, markets and financial stability, and then composing a single rulebook for EU financial markets, promoting supervisory convergence among EU members and directly supervising credit rating agencies and trade repositories. A single rulebook will enhance the EU's single market by creating a level playing field for investors and issuers across the EU.

1.5.3   Member Regulators

Cyprus – Cyprus Securities and Exchange Commission (CySEC)

CySEC is the financial regulatory agency of Cyprus, and was launched in 2001. When Cyprus became an EU member state in 2004, CySEC became a part of MiFID regulation, which granted firms registered in Cyprus access to all European markets. However, joining the EU and adopting the euro has caused significant changes to Cyprus' financial structure, since it had been considered a tax haven. This, in turn, has caused some major policy changes by CySEC.

France – Autorité des Marchés Financiers (AMF)

The AMF is an independent public body which regulates and monitors the participants and products of France's financial markets, with its main focus on the Paris Bourse and Euronext Paris Matif. It safeguards investments in financial products and maintain orderly financial markets. It also carries out investigations and issues sanctions for any violation of its rules and ensures that investors receive all required information and provides a mediation service to assist them in disputes.

Germany – Federal Financial Supervisory Authority (BaFin)

BaFin is an independent financial regulatory body that supervises all aspects of the German financial system. It supervises around 2,700 banks, 800 financial services institutions and 700 insurance companies, and ensures that their financial condition of solvency and liquidity are met. BaFin ensures that Germany's securities and derivatives markets operate in accordance with the Securities Trading Act, including the prevention of insider trading and other market abuses, such as price and market manipulation. BaFin also has a wide range of enforcement powers.

Netherlands – Netherlands Authority for the Financial Markets (AFM)

The AFM is the financial services regulator for the Netherlands, and its role and the way it operates is comparable to that of the SEC in the US. It is the sole regulator of all Dutch financial markets. It was set up in 2002 by legislation which significantly expanded its responsibilities to cover all financial products, including savings, investments, loans, insurance and accounting.

Spain – Comisión Nacional del Mercado de Valores (CNMV)

The CNMV is the independent agency responsible for the regulation of securities markets in Spain. The reforms that established the CNMV in 1988 defined its powers and responsibilities, and were key to establishment of a regulatory framework that would meet EU standards. The aim of the CNMV is to ensure the stability and transparency of Spain's financial markets, protecting investors and insuring that brokers and intermediaries behave correctly.

1.6   Non-EU European Regulators

Switzerland – Swiss Financial Market Supervisory Authority (FINMA)

FINMA is the Swiss financial regulator. It is an independent body with responsibilities including the supervision of Swiss banks, insurance companies, stock exchanges, futures exchanges, securities dealers, and financial intermediaries. FINMA is responsible for combating money laundering and, where necessary, it conducts financial restructuring and bankruptcy proceedings.

1.7 Asian Regulators

1.7.1 China

The **China Securities Regulatory Commission** (CSRC) is a ministerial-level public institution that was created by China's first comprehensive securities law, which became effective on 1 July, 1999, which granted it the *'authority to implement a centralised and unified regulation of the nationwide securities market in order to ensure their lawful operation.'* The CSRC oversees China's centralised securities supervisory system, its powers include the regulation and supervision of securities issuers, as well as to investigate, and impose penalties for, *'illegal activities related to securities and futures.'* It governs all securities exchanges and futures markets activity within the People's Republic of China and its functions are similar to that of the Securities and Exchange Commission in the United States.

1.7.2 Hong Kong

The **Securities and Futures Commission** (SFC) of Hong Kong is the independent statutory body charged with regulating the securities and futures markets in Hong Kong. The SFC is responsible for ensuring the orderly functioning of Hong Kong's securities and futures markets, to protect investors and to promote Hong Kong as an international financial centre and a key financial market in China. Even though it is considered to be a branch of the government, it is run independently under the authorisation of the laws relating to securities and futures.

The **Hong Kong Monetary Authority** (HKMA) is Hong Kong's currency board and its de-facto central bank. The HKMA is responsible for regulating and supervising banking business and the business of taking deposits in Hong Kong. It is also responsible for the authorisation of licensed banks, restricted license banks and deposit-taking companies in Hong Kong, which are collectively known as authorised institutions.

1.7.3 India

The **Securities and Exchange Board of India** (SEBI) is the regulator for the stock exchange and all other securities markets in India. It was granted its statutory powers on 12 April 1992 through the SEBI Act, 1992. The board plays a key role in maintaining stable and efficient financial and investment domestic markets by creating and enforcing effective regulation in India's financial marketplace. India's SEBI function is similar to that of the U.S. Securities and Exchange Commission.

1.7.4 Philippines

The **Securities and Exchange Commission** (SEC) is an independent government regulatory agency that is charged with supervision over the corporate sector, capital market participants, the securities and investment instruments market. Created on 26 October, 1936 by the Securities Act, the SEC is tasked to regulate the sale and registration of securities, exchanges, brokers, dealers and salesmen. Subsequent laws have been enacted to broaden the commission's mandates and powers and in recent years, to give greater focus on the SEC's role in domestic capital market development, by fostering good governance and enhancing investor protection.

1.7.5 Singapore

The **Monetary Authority of Singapore** (MAS) is Singapore's central bank as well as its financial regulatory authority. It administers all of the regulations that pertain to money, banking, insurance, securities and the financial sector in general, as well as currency issuance.

1.7.6 Sri Lanka

The **Central Bank of Sri Lanka** (CBSL) was established in 1950 and is responsible for the conduct of monetary policy in Sri Lanka and also has wide supervisory powers over the banking sector and the domestic financial system. Its main role is regulating the domestic banking system, to ensure that it is stable and a favourable environment for investors and borrowers. As key aspect of its goal of financial system stability is FX rate management as well as working with the other domestic regulators.

2. Principal Differences between EU and US Regulations

Learning Objective

10.2.1 Understand the role of European regulation on EU derivative markets including the UK: MiFID and the Transparency Directive; clients' money; clients' accounts; margining practices; unregulated markets; access to overseas markets; access to overseas clients

2.1 MiFID and the Transparency Directive

The FCA is the independent body that regulates the financial services industry in the UK. Regulations have been fully discussed in Section 1.4.

Since the UK has a major international financial market, the FCA works closely with other regulators to improve the market standards. Since the UK is part of the EU, approximately 70% of the FCA's policies are based on EU initiatives, particularly the **Financial Services Action Plan**. Two of the key parts of this are **MiFID** and the **Transparency Directive (TD)**. MiFID has been discussed in Section 1.2.

The TD is designed to enhance transparency on EU capital markets by establishing minimum requirements on periodic financial reporting and on the disclosure of major shareholdings for issuers whose securities are admitted to trading on a regulated market in the EU. The directive also deals with the mechanisms through which this information is to be stored and disseminated.

The TD distinguishes between the concepts of home and host member state regulation, allowing the issuer's home country regulator to impose more stringent disclosure requirements than those set out in the directive, but restricting the host competent authority from doing the same.

The TD establishes disclosure requirements on an ongoing basis about issuers who have securities admitted to trading on a regulated market situated or operated within the EU for investors who invest in these securities.

There are three broad areas covered under the directive:

1. The minimum content of annual, half-yearly and interim management statements.
2. The notification requirements of both issuers and investors in relation to the acquisition and disposal of the major holdings in companies.
3. The method of disseminating and storing the information covered in 1 and 2 on a pan-European basis.

2.2 Clients' Money and Clients' Accounts

The rules relating to the custody and safeguarding of client money and client assets are contained in the **Client Assets Sourcebook (CASS)**. They exist to ensure that firms take adequate steps to protect those client assets for which they are responsible.

Within CASS, the requirement to segregate client money from a firm's own money is aimed at ensuring that, if the firm fails, that money will not be used to repay its creditors. Usually this is done by ensuring that it is placed promptly in a separately designated client money account with a bank and ensuring that the bank treats it as separate from the firm's own.

CASS, in general, applies to every firm, with some specific exemptions (see Section 2.2.4). CASS applies directly in respect of activities conducted with, or for, all categories of client, ie, retail clients, professional clients and eligible counterparties. CASS was substantially updated for the MiFID changes that took effect from 1 November 2007.

CASS 6 contains the custody rules that apply when a firm holds financial instruments of a client in the course of MiFID business and when it is safeguarding and administering investments in the course of non-MiFID business.

CASS 7 (client money and distribution rules) applies to a MiFID investment firm either when:

- it holds client money in the course of its MiFID business or in respect of any investment agreement entered into, or to be entered into, with or for a client, or
- in the course of non-MiFID business, it opts to comply with the MiFID client money rules.

There are a number of circumstances when the client money rules will not apply, for example, where money is held in connection with a **delivery versus payment (DVP)** transaction (unless the DVP does not occur by the close of business on the third business day following the date of payment of a delivery obligation) or where it becomes due and payable to the firm. Bank deposits are also exempted.

2.2.1 Regulatory Developments

In 2009 the FSA published a consultation (in CP10/9, Enhancing the Client Assets Sourcebook (CASS)) proposing a number of policies to enhance the protections offered by CASS in response to issues highlighted by the global financial crisis and a number of insolvency appointments – most notably that relating to the insolvency of Lehman Brothers International (Europe) (LBIE). Although the UK client asset regime has performed relatively well in facilitating the early return of client assets and money (compared with some overseas jurisdictions), the failure of LBIE and the financial crisis in general highlighted a number of issues relating to existing market practices.

The consultation focused on the following, which became rules:

- **Re-hypothecation of client assets** – creating a requirement that all prime brokerage agreements will contain a disclosure annexe which will highlight relevant definitions and the contractual limit on re-hypothecation. These are provisions in the contract which apply when a firm can 'use' its clients' assets in specified circumstances.
- **Increased reporting to clients** – the FCA will require daily reporting on client money and assets holdings to all prime brokerage clients.
- **Holding client money with group banks** – restricting the placement of client money deposits held in client bank accounts within a group to 20%. This will limit the amount by which a client is exposed to group credit risk.
- **Prohibiting the use of general liens in custodial agreements**.
- **Creating a new 'controlled function' with specific responsibility for client money and assets**.
- **Introducing a client money and assets return (CMAR)** – this return will be reviewed and authorised on a monthly basis for medium-to-large firms and twice a year for small firms.

2.2.2   Due Diligence and Establishment of Client Bank Accounts

Firms that do not deposit client money with a central bank must exercise all due skill, care and diligence in the selection, appointment and periodic review of the credit institution, bank or qualifying money market fund where the money is deposited and the arrangements for the holding of this money.

Firms must make a record of the grounds upon which they satisfy themselves as to the appropriateness of their selection of a credit institution, a bank or a qualifying money market fund.

2.2.3   The Requirement to Reconcile

Reconciliation of Client Assets

Firms must keep such records and accounts as necessary to enable them at any time and without delay to distinguish safe custody assets held for one client from safe custody assets held for any other client, and from the firm's own assets.

CASS 6.5 sets out the obligations of firms to perform internal and external reconciliations. Broadly, reconciliations should be made 'as often as necessary' to ensure the accuracy of a firm's records and accounts, between its internal accounts and records and those of any third parties by whom those safe custody assets are held. If possible, they should be done by someone who has not been involved in the production or maintenance of the records being reconciled.

If the reconciliation shows a discrepancy, the firm must make good (or provide the equivalent of) any shortfall for which it is responsible. If another person is responsible, the firm should take reasonable steps to resolve the position with that person.

Firms must inform the FCA without delay of any failure to comply with the reconciliation requirements, including reconciliation discrepancies and making good any such differences.

Reconciliation of Client Money

Firms must keep such records and accounts as necessary to enable them at any time and without delay to distinguish client money held for one client from client money held for any other client, and from their own money.

CASS 7.6 sets out the obligations of firms to perform both internal and external reconciliations.

2.2.4   The Exemptions from CASS

CASS does not apply to, *inter alia*:

*   Investment companies with variable capital (ICVCs)
*   incoming EEA firms other than insurers, for their passported activities
*   UCITS-qualifying schemes
*   a credit institution (eg, a bank) under the Banking Consolidation Directive, in relation to deposits held
*   coins held for the value of their metal
*   money transferred under title transfer collateral arrangements
*   money held in connection with a delivery versus payment transaction (unless payment does not occur after three business days), or
*   money due and payable to the firm.

CASS does not apply where a firm carries on business in its name but on behalf of the client when that is required by the very nature of the transaction and the client is in agreement.

The custody rules [CASS 6] do not apply if a client transfers full ownership of a safe custody asset to a firm for the purpose of securing or otherwise covering present or future, actual contingent or prospective obligations.

Specific rules within CASS may be disapplied depending on the nature of a firm's activities; the details are set out within the individual rules.

2.3   Margin Practices

The **initial margin requirement** is the amount required to be collateralised in order to open a position. Thereafter, the amount required to be kept in collateral until the position is closed is the **maintenance requirement**. The maintenance requirement is the minimum amount to be collateralised in order to keep an open position. It is generally lower than the initial requirement. This allows the price to move against the margin without forcing a margin call immediately after the initial transaction. On instruments determined to be especially risky, however, the regulators, the exchange or the broker may set the maintenance requirement higher than normal or equal to the initial requirement to reduce their exposure to the risk accepted by the trader.

When the margin posted in the margin account is below the **minimum margin requirement**, the broker or exchange issues a **margin call**. The investors now either have to increase the margin that they have deposited or close out their position. They can do this by selling the securities, options or futures if they are long and by buying them back if they are short. But if they do none of these, then the broker can sell his securities to meet the margin call.

The amount of **variation margin** is determined by the exchange and the clearing house where exchange-traded contracts are settled – such as LCH.Clearnet in the UK.

2.4 Access to Overseas Markets

Investors can undertake derivative contracts on any regulated market, provided that they have suitable arrangements set up with agents in each country (ie, bank, securities account, broker-dealer).

Subject to meeting local regulatory requirements, investors are not prohibited from undertaking derivatives contracts just because they are not domiciled in that country.

2.5 Access to Overseas Clients

UK-authorised and -regulated firms are permitted to engage with overseas clients. However, what is key is where the legal agreement is signed and where the relationship exists. This will determine the extent of the conduct of business requirements of the host state. However, there may still be some local regulatory requirements that exist even though no business services are conducted in the home country, but rather are carried out in the UK. The firm will have to classify the client and also undertake the appropriate Know Your Customer requirements, adhere to the FCA's conduct of business rules on suitability and appropriateness, and also provide the client with relevant information about the firm, its charges and risk warnings.

2.6 EU Regulators

The details of EU regulation have been discussed in Sections 1.1 and 1.5 and here is a short review.

The EU regulation on the OTC derivatives markets that established central counterparties (CCPs) and trade repositories (TRS) that operates in parallel with individual National Regulatory Authorities (NRA), is covered by the European Market Infrastructure Regulation (EMIR).

EMIR was introduced to improve the transparency and reduce some of the risk associated with the OTC derivative markets that contributed to the financial crisis of 2007–08. EMIR also establishes common organisational, conduct of business and prudential standards for all CCPs and other trade repositories.

The EMIR requires that all those who enter into any form of derivative contract, including interest rate, foreign exchange, equity, credit and commodity derivatives, to:

- report every derivative contract that they enter to a trade repository
- implement new risk management standards, including operational processes and margining, for all bilateral over-the-counter (OTC) derivatives ie, trades that are not cleared by a CCP, and
- clear, via a CCP, those OTC derivatives subject to a mandatory clearing obligation.

EMIR has tightened up various operational areas of OTC derivatives operations, including confirmations, collateral management, portability, reconciliations, dispute resolution and portfolio compression. ISDA terms and protocols continue to operate between transacting counterparties as they have done for over 35 years. ISDA therefore operates in parallel with EMIR.

European Market Infrastructure Regulation (EMIR)

EMIR introduced:

- Reporting obligation for OTC derivatives – the aim is to establish greater transparency within the OTC derivatives market, since it requires that all trades are registered with a trade repository (TRS).
- Central counterparties (CCPs) for all OTC derivative trades – the aim is greater market safety by reducing both counterparty credit and operational risks.

The scope of EMIR is that it applies to all types of OTC derivatives. It applies both to financial firms who use OTC derivatives but also to non-financial firms that have large positions in OTC derivatives. It also applies to CCPs and trade repositories.

2.7   US Regulators

Learning Objective

10.2.3   Understand the role of the Securities and Exchange Commission (SEC) in the regulation of derivatives: regulated investments; regulated exchanges

10.2.4   Understand the role of the Commodity Futures Trading Commission (CFTC) and the National Futures Association (NFA): NFA-delegated functions including 'screening and registration of all firms and individuals who want to conduct futures-related business with the public'; regulated investments; regulation of other entities; dispute resolution

10.2.5   Understand the prohibitions of CFTC Part 30 (Foreign Futures and Segregation of Customer Funds)

One of the key differences between EU/UK versus US regulations is their different regulatory approach. While EU and UK regulators very much follow **outcomes-** or **principles-based approaches**, such as MiFID, their US counterparts follow the **rules-based approach**.

Rules-based regulation is based on strict, clearly defined but inflexible **one size fits all** rules that must be followed. In contrast, **principles-based** regulation allows for flexibility and judgment, as broadly based guidelines/standards are the norm. Principles-based regulation means less reliance on detailed, prescriptive rules, relying more on high-level **principles** and objectives to set the standards by which regulated firms must conduct business.

A good example of this can be seen from the EU's introduction of MiFID, which allows individual member authorities to opt out of certain aspects of the regulations, if they see fit, while the introduction of the **Sarbanes-Oxley Act** in the US is very much in line with its more rules-based approach. This act sets out strict regulations on how a company manages its derivatives use and exposure as well as reporting it. These regulations are strict requirements for any company that wishes to list its shares on a US exchange.

The fallout from this act has seen US exchanges lose listings of international companies to UK and European exchanges, owing to their different regulatory environment.

2.7.1 The Securities and Exchange Commission (SEC)

Although a major regulator of US securities markets, the SEC has a limited role in the regulation of derivatives markets. The SEC regulates the following:

1. Options on currencies undertaken on exchanges (ie, currency options on PHLX).
2. Options on individual stocks.
3. Options on stock indices.
4. The Chicago Board Options Exchange (CBOE) – a major centre for equity-based options.
5. The International Securities Exchange (ISE) – the world's largest equity options exchange.

Note, the SEC does not regulate any futures products or exchanges.

2.7.2 The Commodity Futures Trading Commission (CFTC) and National Futures Association (NFA)

The **Commodity Futures Trading Commission (CFTC)** regulates all on-exchange derivatives transactions that are not covered by the SEC. It regulates all futures products and exchanges (including PHLX) and all of the options not covered by the SEC (including currency options on the CME).

It draws its powers from the Commodities Exchange Act and is also responsible for overseeing the **National Futures Association (NFA)**. The NFA is a self-regulatory organisation registered by the CFTC and was formed in 1982.

The CFTC has delegated powers to the NFA to oversee firms operating in the derivatives industry and, as such, is similar to the UK's FCA in this particular regard.

The NFA provides regulatory programmes that safeguard the integrity of the derivatives markets. It is a not-for-profit organisation, financed exclusively from membership dues and fees and assessments paid by users of the futures markets. Every firm or individual who conducts business with the public on any US futures exchange is required to be registered with the CFTC and be a member of the NFA. The key part of the process is the registration and clearing process that the NFA requires. The NFA has approximately 4,200 members and 50,000 associate members (salespersons employed by NFA member firms).

CFTC Part 30

Within the CFTC rules, CFTC Part 30 specifies that it is illegal to trade with US customers on a US exchange without the relevant authorisation from the NFA, unless the trade is conducted via an NFA firm. Non-US firms are prohibited from dealing with US customers on any non-US exchange, unless they trade via a US-registered firm or have been granted exemption. Firms are prohibited from trading non-US products for US customers, unless the products have been approved by the CFTC.

The above restrictions are designed to give US customers an adequate level of protection.

Part 30 Exemption

Non-US firms can seek exemption from Part 30, but only in respect of derivatives trades on non-US exchanges.

To obtain the exemption, UK firms regulated by the FCA must agree to the following:

- Funds from US clients must be placed into segregated accounts, ie, all clients' funds are subject to the Client Money Rules.
- All US customers must sign two-way risk disclosures.
- To abide by Recognised Investment Exchange (RIE)/Designated Investment Exchange (DIE) rules and FCA Conduct of Business rules.
- Must provide the FCA with information and access to records that may be required under Part 30. The FCA can then provide these to the CFTC.
- Must consent to join the NFA arbitration scheme.
- Must agree to jurisdiction in the US under the Commodity Exchange Act.

Note that not all US citizens are automatically considered as US customers. While all US citizens living within the US are considered as US customers, those living abroad are not automatically classed as US customers under this rule.

2.7.3 Commodity Futures Modernization Act 2000

Learning Objective

10.2.6 Understand the Commodity Futures Modernization Act 2000 and the principles governing trading of single stock futures in the US: physical delivery or cash settlement; market regulators; restrictions

The Commodity Futures Modernization Act (CFMA) is seen as a major step forward in the creation of a flexible structure for the regulation of futures trading, by formalising an agreement between the Commodity Futures Trading Commission (CFTC) and the Securities and Exchange Commission (SEC) to repeal the 18-year-old ban on trading single stock futures, as well as providing legal guidelines for the OTC derivatives markets.

The law, reauthorising the CFTC for five years, also clarifies the Treasury Amendment exclusion and specifically grants the CFTC authority over retail foreign exchange trading.

One of the key changes of this law was that it legalised trading in single stock and narrowly defined stock-index futures under the joint jurisdiction of the SEC and CFTC.

A **single stock future (SSF)** is a futures contract on an individual share. An SSF has a set maturity and amount of shares, and most of those traded in the US on the OneChicago exchange are settled through **physical delivery**.

In addition to those traded in the US, SSFs are also traded in the UK, Spain, and India.

2.7.4 Dodd-Frank Act

On 15 July 2010, after a lengthy and sometimes contentious legislative process, the US Senate approved the Dodd-Frank Wall Street Reform and Consumer Protection Act (the Act). Title VII of the Act sets forth the new legislative framework for derivatives.

10

The Act creates an extensive new regulatory framework for swaps and security-based swaps, **capturing substantially all derivatives transactions that previously were exempt from regulation under the CFMA.**

The Act contemplates **mandatory clearing and trading** on regulated facilities for many derivatives contracts, with an exception for non-financial end users.

Swap dealers and major swap participants are subject, among other things, to **capital and margin requirements**, **business conduct rules** and **special duties** in their dealings with governmental entities, Employee Retirement Income Security Act (ERISA) and governmental plans and endowments. While many end users will not be directly regulated, they often will be affected indirectly as their counterparties become subject to new requirements, in particular with respect to margin rules.

Other significant provisions include the **swaps 'pushout' rule**, **collateral segregation** and **real-time swap transaction reporting requirements**, **position limits** and **large trader reporting**, and the **application of the securities laws to security-based swaps.**

Significant uncertainties remain to be clarified in rulemaking proceedings.

As part of this ongoing process, as of May 2013, the SEC adopted the following updates under Title VII:

*   joint rules with the CFTC regarding the definitions of swap and security-based swap dealers, and major swap and security-based swap participants
*   rules relating to mandatory clearing of security-based swaps that establish a process for the clearing agencies to provide the SEC with detailed information covering the security-based swaps that the clearing agencies plan to accept for clearing
*   joint rules with the CFTC regarding:
    *   the definitions of the terms 'swap', 'security-based swap', and 'security-based swap agreement'
    *   the regulation of mixed swaps, and
    *   security-based swap agreement record-keeping
*   rules that establish standards for how clearing agencies should manage their risks and run their operations.

Swaps and Security-Based Swaps

The Act aims to sweep the universe of previously unregulated derivatives into the new regulatory framework, and divides this universe into two broad categories:

1. **Swaps** – the term 'swap' is defined broadly and includes options, swaps and other transactions based on rates, commodities, securities, debt instruments, indices, quantitative measures and other financial or economic interests, subject to certain exceptions. Building upon the definition of previously exempt swap agreements under Section 206A of the Gramm-Leach-Bliley Act, the Act brings previously unregulated derivatives into the new framework. Swaps are subject to CFTC jurisdiction. Swaps do not include security-based swaps, as discussed below.
2. **Security-based swaps** – swaps based on individual securities or loans, on narrow-based securities indices, or on events affecting individual issuers of securities or issuers of securities in a narrow-based securities index. Security-based swaps are subject to SEC jurisdiction.

The Act seeks to establish **parallel rules** for swaps and security-based swaps. **Mixed swaps**, which combine features of swaps and security-based swaps, are to be regulated jointly by the CFTC and SEC. Parties seeking to list or trade novel derivatives products having both commodities and securities features may petition the CFTC and SEC for a determination of the product's regulatory status. The CFTC and SEC are required to consult and co-ordinate with one another (and with the federal banking regulators) in exercising their jurisdiction over swaps, and may challenge each other's actions in court in the event of a dispute.

While the basic approach is comprehensive and quite straightforward, the definitional provisions are complex in detail. Care must be taken in evaluating the status of individual derivatives products. For example, the swap definition excludes certain transactions that are already regulated as securities, including options on securities and foreign exchange options traded on registered securities exchanges. Other exclusions remove from the scope of the Act commodity and security futures, leverage contracts, and forward transactions for non-financial commodities intended for physical settlement, as well as deposit and savings accounts, certificates of deposit and other 'identified banking products'. Swaps based on government securities (other than municipal securities) are excluded from the security-based swap definition and thus are subject to regulation by the CFTC.

Foreign exchange swaps and forwards, which were the subject of considerable debate during the legislative process, will be considered swaps. The Treasury Secretary may, however, make a reasoned determination based on specified criteria that such transactions, to the extent they are not cleared or traded through regulated facilities, should be exempt. Even if that determination is made, reporting requirements and certain business conduct standards apply.

Clearing and Trade Execution

The effort to require central clearing and exchange trading for many derivatives transactions is at the heart of two basic purposes of the Act – reducing systemic risk and increasing market transparency. At the same time, the mandatory clearing and exchange-trading provisions have been controversial, in particular due to the increased margin requirements (and hence increased costs) likely to be associated with central clearing.

The Act contemplates that the CFTC and SEC will, on an ongoing basis, review swaps and categories or classes of swaps with a view to determining whether clearing should be **mandatory**. Factors to be considered include the existence of significant outstanding exposures, trading liquidity and the availability of appropriate operational expertise and resources. Where the CFTC or SEC determine that a particular type of swap should be cleared but no clearing organisation accepts the swap for clearing, the CFTC or SEC are directed to investigate and take appropriate action. Mandatory clearing will not be applied to existing swap positions, so long as the positions are reported to swap data repositories in a timely fashion under rules to be promulgated by the CFTC and SEC.

Clearing organisations will be required to offset swaps with the same terms and conditions on an economically equivalent basis within the clearing organisation, and to provide for non-discriminatory clearing of transactions executed bilaterally or on unaffiliated facilities. In a similar vein, the Act calls on the CFTC and SEC to adopt rules, including possible ownership and control limitations, to mitigate conflicts of interest that may arise with respect to ownership of regulated clearing and trading facilities by bank holding companies, certain non-bank financial institutions, swap dealers and major swap participants.

Joint Study

The Act called upon the CFTC and SEC to conduct a joint study of the regulation of swaps and clearing agencies in the US, Asia and Europe and report to Congress. The key recommendations, released on 31 January 2012, to ensure compliance with the Dodd-Frank Act are:

- CFTC and SEC staff should continue to monitor developments at the national level across jurisdictions and should communicate with fellow regulators involved in efforts to regulate OTC derivatives.
- CFTC and SEC staff should continue to participate in international fora and actively contribute to initiatives that are designed to develop and establish global standards for OTC derivatives regulation.
- CFTC and SEC staff should continue to engage in bilateral dialogues with regulatory staff in the European Union, Japan, Hong Kong, Singapore, and Canada and should consider dialogues with additional jurisdictions, as appropriate.

The report goes on to state that regulation of the OTC derivatives is still in its 'beginning stage'. That further co-operation among regulators will ensure a well functioning market that in turn will ensure global financial stability.

3.   Reporting Requirements

Learning Objective

10.3.1   Understand the requirements to report derivative positions under the following circumstances and be aware of the impact and risk implications that fair value accounting may have on the derivative activities of banks and corporates: IAS 32 and IAS 39; merger and acquisition activities

IAS 39 'Financial Instruments: Recognition and Measurement' became part of the mandatory International Financial Reporting Standards (IFRS) in 2005 and was adopted on a global basis. It requires that an entity must report all financial assets and liabilities on its balance sheet. **IAS 32 'Financial Instruments: Presentation'** was established to complement IAS 39. Its objective is to establish principles for presenting/reporting financial instruments as liabilities, equities and for offsetting financial liabilities and assets. The classifications defined by IAS 32 are from the perspective of an issuer.

IAS 32 and 39 define a derivative as a financial instrument:

- whose value changes in response to the change in an underlying asset, such as interest rates, currencies, commodities, individual shares or an index (it later amended this to include weather- and climate-related factors)
- that requires no initial investment, or one that is smaller than would be required for a **cash market** contract, which had similar gains/losses to market/price movements – in other words, a **geared** instrument
- that is settled on a future date.

IAS 39 also includes embedded derivatives in this definition and treatment, if they produce a cash flow that is similar to a stand-alone derivative. Embedded derivatives require the same type of treatment as any other derivative.

The key requirement of IAS 39 as it pertains to derivatives is that it requires that all derivatives held by an institution, except those that are designated as a hedge, must be stated in all accounting statements at their **fair value**. Fair value is defined as the value for which an asset or contract could be exchanged, or a liability settled, between knowledgeable and willing parties in an arm's length transaction.

In other words, all derivatives must be **marked-to-market** and stated at their current market value in all financial reports.

The main exception to IAS 39's fair value derivatives rule, which the EU originally **opted out** of, was the requirement for fair value accounting of derivatives and certain aspects of hedge accounting on financial statements. These two 'carve outs' were intended to be temporary.

In light of this, the IASB published an amended version of IAS 39, which received support from the ECB. The amended version of IAS 39: Recognition and Measurement – the Fair Value Option (FVO) includes a restricted fair value option for all derivatives whose application is subject to principles and combined with extensive disclosure requirements, as well as the provision that any derivative that is stated to be a hedge does not have to be shown at its fair value, since they are expected to be held until maturity or the early settlement of the related transaction.

International accounting rules also clearly state that all derivatives positions and possible cross-share holdings must be disclosed and reported in the valuation of all takeover bids or merger transactions.

10

End of Chapter Questions

1. What is the main purpose and aims of regulation, in all markets globally?
   Answer reference: Section 1

2. How is MiFID expected to be affected by the UK's vote to leave the EU?
   Answer reference: Section 1.2

3. What are MiFID's main passportable services?
   Answer reference: Section 1.2

4. The Financial Services Act 2012 requires the FCA to consider eight principles when carrying out its work. What are they?
   Answer reference: Section 1.4

5. The FCA's Conduct of Business Sourcebook includes 11 key Principles for Businesses which authorised firms must observe. List them.
   Answer reference: Section 1.4.1

6. How does COBS define a professional client?
   Answer reference: Section 1.4.5

7. What are COBS best execution factors?
   Answer reference: Section 1.4.6

8. What is BaFin?
   Answer reference: Section 1.5.3

9. Define the two broad categories, in the new regulatory framework, into which the Dodd-Frank act divides previously unregulated derivatives.
   Answer reference: Section 2.7.4

10. What is the key requirement of IAS 39 as it pertains to derivatives?
    Answer reference: Section 3

Glossary and Abbreviations

Abandon

The decision of the holder of an option not to exercise his rights, due to the fact that the option is either out-of-the-money (OTM) or the transaction costs are greater than its intrinsic value.

Accrued Interest

The calculation of entitlement to interest on a bond, usually done on a daily basis. This needs to be reflected in the Invoice Amount in a bond future.

Against Actuals (AA)

See *Exchange For Physicals.*

Allocation

Assigning a completed derivatives trade to its originator, including registration into the correct account.

American Depositary Receipts (ADRs)

Represent ownership in the shares of a foreign company trading on US financial markets. ADRs are priced in US dollars, they pay dividends in US dollars and they can be traded like the shares of US-based companies. Their price is close to the price of the foreign share in its home market, adjusted for the ratio of ADRs to foreign company shares.

American-Style

An exercise style of an option. An option that can be exercised on any business day up to expiry on the last trading day.

Arbitrage

Trading simultaneously in one asset in two different markets to profit from short-term price differentials.

Asian Option

An option whose strike price is set at its expiration date. Its strike price is based on the average price of the underlying asset (the calculation is based on a pre-agreed fixing over the period).

Assign

Refers to options – following exercise by the option holder, the exercise is matched with a short position. Assignment is initiated when the exchange clearing house notifies the writer by an 'assignment notice'.

At-the-Money (ATM)

An option with an exercise price that is the same as, or very near to, the current underlying asset price.

Backwardation

When cash prices are higher than futures prices. Unusual for equity futures because of positive cost of carry. Normal for bond futures because bond yields are normally higher than money market yields (there is a negative cost of carry).

Barrier Option

An option that is activated or deactivated once the underlying asset's price reaches a set level. There are two main types, 'knock-in' and 'knock-out' barrier style options.

Basis

The difference between the present cash price and the nearby futures price of an asset. Calculation is cash minus futures. Basis will be negative in a contango market, and positive in a backwardation market.

Bear

An investor who believes the market in general, or a particular investment, will fall.

Bear Spread

A moderately bearish strategy. Uses call or put options for the same month but at different strikes (ie, vertical spreads), eg, buy 350 June calls, sell 300 June calls.

Bermudan Option

An exercise style of an option, which lies between a European and an American, in that it can be exercised on any various specified dates between the purchase date and the option's expiry.

Bond

A security issued by an organisation such as a government or corporation. Bonds pay regular interest and repay their principal or face value at maturity. One of the most common underlying assets for derivative contracts.

Bull

An investor who believes the market in general, or a particular investment, will rise in value.

Bull Spread

An options trade for the moderately bullish investor. Uses call or put options for the same month but at different strikes (ie, vertical spreads), eg, buy a 300 June call, sell a 350 June call. Can also be done with put options.

Bund

German government bond.

Buy-Write

An investment strategy involving buying a security and, simultaneously, selling calls against it.

CAC 40

The benchmark index of the French stock market. The index represents a capitalisation-weighted measure of the 40 most significant values among the 100 largest companies listed on the Paris Bourse.

Call

A type of option that gives the buyer the right, but not the obligation, to buy the underlying asset at an agreed price within a specific time for a set premium. Call sellers may be obliged to sell a specific asset at the set price if the call's holder chooses to exercise.

Cap

An option, which puts a ceiling to the interest rate at which a client borrows. A common term would be quarterly over three years. If the reference rate (eg, LIBOR) is above the cap the writer pays compensation. It allows the borrower to manage interest rate risk. Also used in foreign exchange.

Cash Settlement

Method of settlement where the underlying asset is not exchanged, just the cash difference between the contracted price and the official settlement price. Often known as a Contract for Difference. STIRs and Equity Indices futures are settled by cash payment rather than Physical Delivery.

Central Counterparty (CCP)

The entities that are used to clear OTC derivative trades, to reduce counterparty risk. Being established by new regulations.

Collar

The purchase of a cap, financed by the sale of a floor.

Combination

Strategy involving a variety of individual positions, such as puts and calls (eg, straddle, strangle).

Contango

A market where futures prices are higher than the cash price because of a positive cost of carry. Opposite of backwardation.

Contingent Liability

A potential liability for loss, over and above the amount invested, the amount of which cannot be established at the outset of a derivatives contract. For example, the seller of a future does not know how high the price could move against him – he is in a contingent liability situation.

Contract for Difference (CFD)

A contract involving the exchange of difference between the pre-agreed price and the closing price of the underlying instrument (such as an index or a share price). A contract involving cash settlement.

Convertible Bond

A bond that is convertible into another instrument, sometimes another type of bond, but more commonly into a company's shares at the set price which usually is above the current share price at the time of its issue.

Cost of Carry

The cost of holding an asset over time. Comprises borrowing costs and, for physical commodities, storage/insurance costs. For equities, the cost of carry will be reduced by dividends earned from the shares.

Covered Call

A short call option position that is covered because the writer also owns the underlying asset.

Counterparty Risk

Is the risk that one party of a contract will not live up to its contractual obligations. Counterparty risk is a risk to both parties and should be considered when evaluating a contract. In most financial contracts, counterparty risk is also known as credit or default risk.

Credit Risk

The exposure to loss associated with the payment default or failure on a payment due from a transaction/trade by a counterparty. It is also known as counterparty risk.

DAX

Deutsche Aktien Index – an index of 30 German equities. The principal German equity index.

Delivery

The settlement of a contract (such as a future) by delivery of the asset by the seller to the exchange clearing house. The long position holder takes delivery from the clearing house against payment.

Delta (Δ)

The measure of change in an option's premium or futures price given a change in the underlying asset. In options, delta can be thought of as the probability that the option will be in-the-money at expiry. The delta of futures will generally be about 1 or 100%. A £3 change in the cash price should cause the future to move by about £3 ($3/3 = 1$).

Derivative

Instruments whose price is derived from another asset. Examples include futures, options, FX forwards and swaps.

Dow Jones Industrial Average (DJIA)

The index of the share prices of the largest 30 companies listed on the New York stock market.

Electronic Communication Networks (ECNs)

Term used in financial circles for a type of computer system that facilitates trading of financial products on OTC markets. The main products that are traded on ECNs are equities and foreign exchange.

Equity Indices

Indices of blue-chip (ie, large) companies in various national or regional markets. Examples include S&P 500, FTSE 100, Eurostoxx. Major indices are used as the basis for derivatives contracts.

European Banking Authority (EBA)

EU's banking regulatory agency, whose main responsibility is to ensure that the EU banking sector functions efficiently and in an orderly manner, which in turn ensures financial stability.

European Insurance and Occupational Pensions Authority (EIOPA)

The EU regulatory authority whose responsibility is to ensure stability and and transparency in the insurance and pensions markets/system across the EU.

European Securities and Markets Authority (ESMA)

The independent EU authority whose goal is the safeguarding of the EU's financial system. One of its main goals is to establish a single rulebook across the EU's financial markets. The purpose of this is to create a level playing field for all investors and security issuers across the EU.

European-Style

An exercise style of an option. An option, which can only be exercised by the holder at expiry.

Exchange Delivery Settlement Price (EDSP)

The price at which maturing futures are settled (a Liffe term).

Exchange for Physicals (EFP)

The exchange of a future's position for a physical position. Also known as 'Against Actuals'.

Exercise

The decision by a holder of an option to take up their rights. In a call option, exercise involves buying the asset; in a put option exercise involves selling the asset.

Exercise (or Strike) Price

Refers to options – the price at which assets can be bought (call) or sold (put). In exchange-traded options, the exchange determines the intervals between strike prices.

Expiration

The date when a derivative contract, such as a future or option, ceased to exist.

Extrinsic Value

Another term for an option's Time Value. Basically the difference between its market price and its Intrinsic Value (the value that is equal to how much the option is In-the-Money).

Fair Value

The theoretical price of a future, ie, cash price plus cost of carry.

Financial Conduct Authority (FCA)

The new UK financial regulator that has assumed most of the authority of the FSA.

Flex Option

Exchange-traded options, where the investor can specify within certain limits, the terms of the options, such as exercise price, expiration date, exercise type, and settlement calculation.

Floor

An OTC option which guarantees a minimum return. If the reference rate (eg, LIBOR) falls below the floor level, the buyer of the floor receives compensation. See also collar.

Foreign Exchange (FX)

The name given to the general aspects of currency trading.

Forward

An OTC derivative on, for example, foreign exchange. Forward prices are based on the spot price and the interest rate differential of the two currencies, in the same way as exchange-traded FX futures.

Forward Rate Agreement (FRA)

An agreement where the client can fix the rate of interest that will be applied to a notional loan or deposit, drawn or placed for an agreed period in the future. Traded over-the-counter.

FTSE Indices

A range of indices that cover a wide range of asset classes and markets. The most well-known are those that measure the value of London-based shares, such as the FTSE 100 and the FTSE All Share indices.

Future

An exchange-traded contract that is a firm agreement to make/take delivery of a standard quantity of a specified asset on a fixed future date at a price agreed today.

Gamma

Measures the speed of change of Delta on a derivative for a given change in price of the underlying asset. Gamma is at its maximum for at-the-money options.

Gearing

An important feature of derivatives. Because only a small percentage of an asset's value is required when a contract is entered into (initial margin or premium) a small change in the underlying asset's value can lead to large percentage gains or losses relative to the initial investment. Also known as leverage.

Global Depositary Receipts (GDRs)

The non-US version of ADRs that are traded on non-US exchanges such as the London Stock Exchange.

Hedge

A strategy to protect or minimise a potential loss to an existing position or known commitment resulting from adverse price movements. For example, those owning assets can hedge by buying put options, protecting against a fall in value of that asset.

ICE Euro Interbank Offered Rate (EURIBOR)

The rates offered to prime banks on euro interbank term deposits. The ICE EURIBOR is set by the ICE Benchmark Administration. Loan maturities vary from a week to a year and their rates are considered among the most important in the European money market.

ICE London Interbank Offered Rate (LIBOR)

The average rate at which banks will lend currency including sterling, dollars, euros and yen to each other for periods such as one or three months. The ICE Benchmark Administration fixes these short term rates for five currencies. It also sets the ICE London Interbank Bid Rate (LIBID) to be calculated, which is how much banks would pay for deposits.

Initial Margin

A good faith deposit (in the form of collateral or cash) lodged with the broker or clearing house against potential liabilities on an open position. It is returned when the position is closed out.

In-the-Money (ITM)

An option with intrinsic value, eg, a call whose strike is below the underlying asset price.

Intrinsic Value (IV)

Indicates how much an option is in-the-money (ITM). One of the two components that make up an option's value. The intrinsic value represents the absolute minimum premium for an option. For example, a £1 call option would be worth at least 25p if the underlying asset's price was £1.25. Options which are in-the-money have intrinsic value. Intrinsically, a £2 put would be worth at least 50p if the underlying asset was trading at £1.50.

Invoice Amount

The amount a futures buyer pays to the exchange clearing house at delivery, for the underlying physical asset.

Last Notice Day

The last day for issuing of notices of intent to deliver against a futures contract.

Last Trading Day

The last day for trading futures with the current delivery month. All contracts outstanding/open at the end of the last trading day must be settled by delivery or by cash settlement.

Leverage

See *Gearing*.

Long

The buyer of an asset is 'long' the asset. Futures buyers are 'long' the futures. Options buyers or holders are 'long' the options.

Maturity

The final payment date of a financial instrument, such as a bond's principal or when a loan is repaid.

Margin

Collateral paid to the clearing house by the counterparties to a derivatives transaction to guarantee their positions against loss. Initial Margin is a security deposit that must be handed to the exchange clearing house by a broker (and to the broker by their client) for futures or short options. See also variation margin.

Mark-to-Market

The process of adjusting the value of investments to reflect their current market price. See also variation margin.

Naked Short

The practice of short-selling an asset without first borrowing the security or ensuring that the security can be borrowed, as is conventionally done in a short sale.

Netting

A system or agreement whereby all outstanding contracts of the same specification maturing, on the same date, between two counterparties can be settled on a net basis. This is an efficient way of reducing both settlement risk and counterparty risk.

Novation

The legal process where the exchange's clearing house becomes the counterparty to both the buyer and seller of futures contracts, substituting the original contract.

Operations Management Group (OMG)

An industry organisation of OTC market participants, that sets criteria of operational procedures and risk management of OTC contracts.

Open Interest

The number of contracts that have not been closed-out by being offset.

Open Outcry

Trading system where participants meet face-to-face and cry out their prices and sizes to the others on the floor. Used in many US exchanges.

Option

A contract that gives the buyer the right, but not the obligation, to sell or buy a particular asset at a particular price, on or before a specified date. Options are set at an agreed price (exercise price or strike price) and the exercise style would normally be American-Style or European-Style. The class of option either gives holders the right to buy (call) or the right to sell (put).

Out-of-the-Money (OTM)

A term used to describe an option whose strike price is less advantageous/profitable than the asset's current market price. For example a £1 call if the asset is trading at 85p. An OTM option has no intrinsic value, but a Premium may well be payable, but it would comprise only time value.

Over-the-Counter (OTC)

Transactions between banks and their counterparties not on a recognised exchange.

Physical Delivery

Where the settlement of a futures contract is by delivery of the physical underlying asset. Certain futures (eg, gilt futures, copper etc) will run through to physical delivery for final settlement. Other futures (eg, stock index futures and Short-Term Interest Rates) are cash settled.

Premium

The money paid by option buyers to option sellers. The price paid for the option.

Prudential Regulation Authority (PRA)

The part of the UK financial regulator that is now part of the Bank of England.

Put

A type of option that gives its buyer the right, but not the obligation, to sell the underlying asset at an agreed price within a specific time for a set premium. Put sellers may be obliged to buy the specified asset at the strike price if the put's holder chooses to exercise.

Put/Call Parity

The theoretical relationship between put premiums and call premiums for the same strike and expiry. The relationship (for European options) is:

Call premium – put premium = underlying asset's price - strike price (discounted to the present value).

Scan Risk

The basic evaluation of risk reflecting how these positions gain or lose value under particular combinations of price and volatility movement.

Screen Trading

Trading system where participants trade with each other by submitting prices and sizes onto a computer system from remote terminals.

Settlement Risk

The risk that an expected payment of an asset/security or cash will not be made on time or at all. This type of risk can be significantly reduced by establishing a netting system.

Series

Options of the same class (ie, calls or puts) with the same strike, date and underlying (eg, calls – 950, June, HSBC).

Short

1. To need an asset.
2. Another term for selling futures or selling/writing puts.
3. To hold a net sold position.

Short-Term Interest Rate (STIR) Derivatives

Common contracts for difference (CFD) derivative contracts, based on the interest on a notional sum of money for three months. For example, Euronext Liffe's June short sterling contracts are based on the interest on a notional cash deposit of £500,000 for the three months from June (ie, July, August and September). Priced as 100 minus the predicted rate, thereby replicating the inverse pricing behaviour of bonds and bond futures.

Single Stock Futures (SSF)

Futures contracts whose underlying assets are individual stocks/shares. Traded on several exchanges, such as OneChicago, where the contract size is 100 shares in an individual company.

Sovereign Wealth Fund

A state-owned and state-funded investment company that invests in a wide variety of domestic and international assets.

Spot

A term used to describe the current price of an asset. Also known as 'underlying' or 'cash'. Also used in foreign exchange where spot rates are the exchange rates for deals, which settle right away (usually T+1).

Spread

1. In futures – buying and selling different months of the same asset (intra-market spread) with a view about changes in basis.
2. In futures – buying and selling futures in different assets (inter-market spread). For example, a fund manager could increase his effective weighting of US stocks by buying S&P 500 futures and simultaneously selling FTSE 100 futures.
3. In options – see vertical spreads.
4. The difference between the bid and offer price.

Standard Portfolio Analysis of Risk (SPAN)

SPAN is a scenario-based risk programme, designed by the Chicago Mercantile Exchange, used for calculating daily initial margins across a portfolio. Essentially, it looks at the impact on a position if the price and volatility of the underlying change by set amounts.

Stop Loss

An order placed by an investor to buy or sell a security when it reaches a certain price. A stop loss order is designed to limit an investor's loss on an existing position.

Straddle

A combination of a put and a call option at the same strike. Buyers profit from volatility in the underlying asset.

Strangle

A combination of a put and a call option at different strikes. Buyers profit from volatility in the underlying asset.

Strike Price

The price at which a specific derivative contract can be exercised. For call options, the strike price is the price that the buyer of the call can buy the underlying security (up to or at its expiration date), while for put options the strike price is the price at which the buyer of the put is able to sell the underlying asset.

Swap

A contract to exchange a series of payments with a counterparty, eg, fixed for floating interest rates, currency A for currency B, income from asset C for income from asset D etc.

Swaption

An option to enter into a swap.

Synthetic

Manufactured position, eg, a synthetic future can be created by buying a call and selling a put option on the future.

Theoretical Intermarket Margining System (TIMS)

TIMS is a method used by the Options Clearing Corporation (OCC) and other clearing houses to determine the margin requirements for mixed portfolios of derivatives, particularly options.

Theta

The measure of the decline in an option's value based on the passage of time, as it approaches its expiration.

Tick

The smallest permitted variation between prices quoted to buy and sell on derivatives exchanges. For example, the tick for gold is 10 cents so prices of $390.00, $390.10, $390.20 can be quoted, but not $390.13.

Tick Value

The profit or loss that arises when prices move by one tick.

Time Value

An option's value that represents its time to expiry and the volatility of the underlying asset's cash price. It is the option's premium, less any intrinsic value. Time value will be higher the longer the option has to maturity. Sometimes known as extrinsic value.

Underlying

Is the term used to refer to the asset/instrument in derivatives trading, such as futures and options, who is the subject of and whose price is used to determine that of the derivative's contract.

Variation Margin

Margin is transferred from the account of the loser to the winner as prices move on a daily basis and positions are marked-to-market. The total accumulated variation margin equates to the profit or loss when a position is closed out.

Vega

The measure of how a 1% change in volatility affects an option's price/value.

Vertical Spreads

Calls (or puts) for the same month but at different strikes. For example, buy a 300 June call, sell a 350 June call. See also bull spread and bear spread.

Volatility

The measure of the probability of an asset's price moving. Usually calculated as annualised standard deviation. Volatility has an important impact on the pricing of options.

Warrant

1. A securitised option. An example is a security, which can be converted into shares in a company.
2. A document of title to goods; for example, warrants are used to satisfy the physical delivery of metals on the LME.

Yield Spread

The yield spread or 'credit spread' is the difference between the quoted rates of return on two different bonds which have the same or very similar maturities. It reflects the market's view and is based on the market's/investor's perception of the of difference in credit quality between the two borrowers.

Δ

Delta

ADR

American Depositary Receipt

AFM

Netherlands Authority for the Financial Markets

AMF

Autorité des Marchés Financiers

ATM

At-the-Money

BaFin

Federal Financial Supervisory Authority

BBA

British Bankers' Association

CBOE

Chicago Board Options Exchange

CBOT

Chicago Board of Trade (now part of the CME Group)

CBSL

Central Bank of Sri Lanka

CD

Certificate of Deposit

CDS

Credit Default Swap

CFD

Contracts for Difference

CFTC

Commodity Futures Trading Commission (US derivatives regulator)

CME
Chicago Mercantile Exchange (now part of the CME Group)

CMS
Constant Maturity Swap

CNMV
Comisión Nacional del Mercado de Valores

COB
Conduct Of Business

COMEX
A division of the New York Mercantile Exchange

CP
Committed Principal

CPI
Consumer Prices Index

CRD
Capital Requirements Directive

CSRC
China Securities Regulatory Commission

CTD
Cheapest to Deliver

CySEC
Cyprus Securities and Exchange Commission

DAX
Deutsche Aktien Index (German equity market index)

DCO
Designated Clearing Organisation (US)

DME
Dubai Mercantile Exchange

DMO
Debt Management Office (UK)

DTCC
Depository Trust & Clearing Company

EBA
European Banking Authority

ECB
European Central Bank

ECN
Electronic Communications Network

EDSP
Exchange Delivery Settlement Price (Euronext.liffe)

EFP
Exchange for Physical

EMIR
European Market Infrastructure Regulation

EONIA
Euro Overnight Index Average

EPS
Exchange for Swaps

ESMA
European Securities and Markets Authority

ETD
Exchange-Traded Derivative

EU
European Union

FCA
Financial Conduct Authority

FCM
Futures Commission Merchant

FIFO
First-In, First-Out

FLEX
FLexible EXchange

FOK
Fill or Kill

FpML
Financial Products Markup Language

FRA
Forward Rate Agreement

FRN
Floating-Rate Note

FSA
Financial Services Authority (former UK regulator)

FX
Foreign Exchange

GCM
General Clearing Member

GDP
Gross Domestic Product

GDR
Global Depositary Receipt

GFD
Good for the Day

GIS
Good in Session

GRY
Gross Redemption Yield

GTC
Good 'til Cancelled

HKEx
Hong Kong Exchanges and Clearing Ltd

HKMA
Hong Kong Monetary Authority

ICE
Intercontinental Exchange

ICE EURIBOR
Euro Interbank Offered Rate

ICE LIBID
London Interbank Bid Rate

ICE LIBOR
London Interbank Offered Rate

ICM
Individual Clearing Member

IFRS
International Financial Reporting Standards

IPE
International Petroleum Exchange of London Limited (now renamed ICE Futures)

IPO
Initial Public Offering

IRP
Interest Rate Parity

IRS
Interest Rate Swap

ISD
Investment Services Directive

ISDA
International Swaps and Derivatives Association Inc.

ISE
International Securities Exchange

ITM
In-the-Money

IV
Intrinsic Value

JADE
Joint Asian Derivatives Exchange

JGB
Japanese Government Bond

LIFO
Last-In, First-Out

LME
London Metal Exchange

LSE
London Stock Exchange

MAS
Monetary Authority of Singapore

MCX
Multi Commodity Exchange (Mumbai)

MDS
Market Data System

MiFID
Markets in Financial Instruments Directive

MIT
Market if Touched

MOC
Market on Close

MOO
Market on Open

MTM
Mark-to-Market Swap

NCDEX
National Commodity & Derivatives Exchange Ltd. (India)

NFA
National Futures Association (US)

NLV
Net Liquidation Value

NYBOT
New York Board of Trade

NYMEX
New York Mercantile Exchange

OCC
Options Clearing Corporation

OIS
Overnight Index Swap

OPEC
Organisation of Petroleum Exporting Countries

OPL
Open Position Limit

OTC
Over-the-Counter

OTM
Out-of-the-Money

PHLX
Philadelphia Stock Exchange

PM
Premium

POM
Public Order Member

PPP
Purchasing Power Parity

PPS

Protected Payments System

PRA

Prudential Regulation Authority (part of the Bank of England)

PSBR

Public Sector Borrowing Requirement (UK)

PSNCR

Public Sector Net Cash Requirement (UK)

RCH

Recognised Clearing House (UK)

RIE

Recognised Investment Exchange (UK)

RPI

Retail Prices Index

SCM

SwapClear Clearing Member

SDRT

Stamp Duty Reserve Tax (UK)

SEAQ

Stock Exchange Automated Quotation System (UK)

SEBI

Securities and Exchange Board of India

SEC

Securities and Exchange Commission (both separate Philippines and USA securities regulators)

SETS

London Stock Exchange Electronic Trading Service

SFC

Securities and Futures Commission (China)

SGX

Singapore Exchange Ltd

SHFE

Shanghai Futures Exchange

SPAN

Standard Portfolio Analysis of Risk

SSF

Single Stock Futures

STIR

Short-Term Interest Rate

STP

Straight-Through Processing

SWF

Sovereign Wealth Fund

SwML

Sign-Writing Markup Language

TAPO

Traded Average Price Option (LME)

TD

Transparency Directive

TIMS

Theoretical Intermarket Margining System (OCC)

TOIS

Tom/Next Indexed Swap

TRS

Trade Registration System (ICE)

TRS

Total Return Swap

TSE

Tokyo Stock Exchange

TSX

Toronto Stock Exchange

TV

Time Value

UAE

United Arab Emirates

UCITS

Undertakings for Collective Investments in Transferable Securities

UCP

Universal Clearing Platform

USF

Universal Stock Futures (ICE)

UTP

Universal Trading Platform

Multiple Choice Questions

The following questions have been compiled to reflect as closely as possible the standard that you will experience in your examination. Please note, however, they are not actual exam questions.

1. One of the differences between a CFD and spread betting is:

    A. A spread betting contract does not have a specific maturity
    B. A CFD has a single price differential, while a spread bet has at least four
    C. A CFD is legally conditioned as gambling
    D. A CFD does not have a specific maturity

2. Which of the following is TRUE when comparing an ETD's price with an OTC derivative?

    A. The OTC price will always have a tighter bid/offer spread
    B. Both are usually the same, since both are reported to the market
    C. The ETD price spread is wider, since it includes the initial margin
    D. The ETD price is more transparent, since it is quoted via the market

3. A speculator is anticipating an increase in lead prices and purchased 30 CFDs in three months' time at US$3,500 per tonne. The contract size is 25 tonnes. At expiry the position is closed out when the price has risen to US$3,525 per tonne. What is the profit?

    A. US$6,250
    B. US$7,500
    C. US$12,500
    D. US$18,750

4. If tick size is half a point for a future on the FTSE 100 index and is valued at £5, what is the profit for an investor who went long with the index at 4260 and then settled at expiry with the index at 4300?

    A. £20
    B. £200
    C. £400
    D. £4,260

5. What is the purpose of marking-to-market?

    A. To calculate the value of collateral
    B. To calculate any variation margin due
    C. To establish the daily settlement price
    D. To establish the spread margin requirement

6. The cash price for wheat is £166.90 per tonne. The finance cost is 4.5% pa, and storage and insurance costs are 1.5% pa. Calculate the fair value of a wheat futures contract for ten tonnes in six months' time.

    A. £17,691.14

    B. £17,190.70

    C. £16,940.36

    D. £17,065.53

7. A dealer buys £10,000,000 nominal of gilts, and sells gilt futures to the same value off-exchange, using Liffe's universal clearing platform to report the futures trade. What type of trade has he just executed?

    A. A FLEX trade

    B. A block trade

    C. An EFP

    D. A basis trade

8. A member firm executes, confirms and matches a trade, which it pre-registers to allocate the trade to another member firm. What is the term for this action?

    A. Assign to

    B. Call-up

    C. Give-in

    D. Give-up

9. If you buy an option, what is the effect, if any, of gearing for a given price change in the underlying asset?

    A. A similar proportionate change in the option value

    B. A greater proportionate change in the option value

    C. A smaller proportionate change in the option value

    D. None

10. How is the automatic exercise by ICE Clear Europe of ICE Futures options prevented?

    A. By filing an assignment notice

    B. By filing a give-up notice

    C. By filing a registration notice

    D. By filing a suppression notice

11. What method is used by SPAN to assess volatility in options' positions?

    A. Basis

    B. Deltas

    C. Gammas

    D. NLVs

12. A fund manager has positions worth €100,000,000 in bonds issued by 25 highly rated corporates located in a smaller European country. She is concerned that, because of uncertainty about that government's debt position, its corporates may have their credit ratings downgraded. The portfolio is currently producing a yield of 5%; while German bunds are yielding 2.75%. What action would you recommend to this fund manager?

    A. Purchase a credit default swap based on a significant fall credit event for the specified basket of securities

    B. Convert the portfolio into a collateralised bond obligation.

    C. Purchase a spread option on the portfolio versus German government debt

    D. Purchase a credit default swap based on a rating downgrade credit event for the specified basket of securities

13. How is standard deviation calculated?

    A. By calculating the arithmetic mean and the set of deviations from the mean, squaring each deviation and dividing the sum of the squared deviations by the number of observations to obtain the population variance and then calculating its square root

    B. By calculating the arithmetic mean and the set of deviations from the mean, dividing the sum of the deviations by the number of observations to obtain the population variance and then calculating its square root

    C. By calculating the arithmetic mean and the set of deviations from the mean, squaring each deviation and dividing the sum of the squared deviations by the arithmetic mean to obtain the population variance and then calculating its square root

    D. By calculating the arithmetic mean and the set of deviations from the mean, squaring each deviation and dividing the sum of the squared deviations by the square root of the number of observations

14. The type of option that combines the benefits of customisation of an OTC product with the advantages of being listed on an exchange is known as:

    A. An average rate option

    B. A Bermudan option

    C. A FLEX option

    D. A lookback option

15. An investor bought one June 100 call for 22 and sold one June 120 call for six. What market expectation did he have?

    A. Neutral

    B. Volatile

    C. Moderately bullish

    D. Bearish

16. Which of the following kinds of risk can be reduced by diversification within a portfolio?

    A. Counterparty risk

    B. Systematic risk

    C. Interest rate risk

    D. Equity risk

17. The benefit of a mark-to-market swap is:

    A. Its regular payments reduce any market risk from the underlying asset

    B. After each settlement date, any credit risk that has built up is removed

    C. It allows the value of the underlying principal to fluctuate after every settlement date

    D. The regular principal repayments fit its use as a hedge for bonds

18. A trader buys 500 March FTSE 100 futures and simultaneously sells 500 June FTSE 100 futures. Why might she have done this?

    A. Because the basis between the two contracts is expected to weaken

    B. Because the basis between the two contracts is expected to strengthen

    C. Because the basis is normally negative for contango markets

    D. Because the basis is normally positive for contango markets

19. How are members' contributions to the member default fund determined?

    A. According to the volume of clearing activity

    B. As an annual flat fee

    C. As a percentage of the firm's fees

    D. According to the status of the firm

20. If a borrower wants to hedge the risk that the floating rate on its loan will rise above a certain level, s/he will buy a:

    A. Floor

    B. Collar

    C. Swaption

    D. Cap

21. If you were to buy a 100 call for a premium of 13, what would be your maximum potential profit?

    A. 13

    B. 87

    C. 100

    D. Unlimited

22. FLEX options are hybrid products in what way?

    A. OTC-traded, but with standardised contract specifications

    B. Exchange-traded, but with choice of two exercise styles

    C. Exchange-traded, but with freely negotiable terms

    D. Options that can freely trade either on- or off-exchange

23. Which of the following is TRUE about EFP trades?

    A. Counterparty credit risk increases when an EFP replaces an existing OTC trade

    B. EFP transactions can be negotiated and registered round-the-clock

    C. OTC and futures positions can be swapped even if they differ substantially in value

    D. Margin and credit limits can be reduced by netting out OTC and futures positions

24. A client wishes to use the swaps market to convert floating receivables into fixed receivables, but is concerned about the credit risk associated with a counterparty who might, at the end of the period, be faced with a substantial unrealised loss on the transaction. Which of the following options would you suggest to the client?

    A. Don't use swaps if you have this concern. Investigate whether you can achieve the same result using futures because they are settled by a clearing house

    B. Use mark-to-market swaps

    C. Use FX resettable swaps

    D. Use FRAs because they can be novated by a clearing house

25. A fund makes an annualised return of 5.7% in a three-month period and its Sharpe ratio for that period is 45.65%. During the next period the fund continues to make an annualised return of 5.7% but its Sharpe ratio is now 56.52%. Which of the following conclusions can you draw from these statistics?

    A. The rate of risk-free return has increased

    B. The rate of risk-free return has declined

    C. The portfolio CAPM beta has declined

    D. The portfolio CAPM beta has increased

26. Which of the following might be a likely scenario for a futures hedge?

    A. An investor notices grain futures are cheaper in London than in Chicago

    B. A company dealing in a commodity wishes to capitalise on the rising price of that commodity

    C. A company requiring a commodity wishes to protect against possible price rises

    D. An investor anticipates a rise in bond yields following an interest rate change

27. How would you create a synthetic long future?

    A. Buy a call and buy a put

    B. Buy a call and sell a put

    C. Sell a call and sell a put

    D. Sell a call and buy a call

28. A sugar refiner bought 15 white sugar futures contracts on ICE at $275 per tonne. The contract size is 50 tonnes. The position was later closed out when the price was $270 per tonne. What was the loss?

    A. $750

    B. $1,875

    C. $3,750

    D. $4,125

29. An option's vega is useful, because it is a measure of:

    A. The relationship between an option's time decay and market sentiment

    B. An option's sensitivity to both market sentiment and current market conditions

    C. An option's hedge ratio and how it changes relative to price movements

    D. An option's sensitivity to market interest rates

30. Which order type on ICE is to be executed at the best price immediately available?

    A. Basis orders

    B. Stop orders

    C. Market orders

    D. Normal limit orders

31. An investor sells a July 100 call and buys a July 90 call on the same underlying. What strategy is this?

    A. Vertical spread

    B. Horizontal spread

    C. Diagonal spread

    D. Simple spread

32. Which of these four options will best hedge a short underlying position?

    A. A short future

    B. A long, deep-in-the-money put

    C. Two long at-the-money puts

    D. Two long at-the-money calls

33. Which of the following option positions is MOST likely to be exercised before its expiry date?

    A. Long-dated, deep-in-the-money, European-style

    B. Long-dated, out-of-the-money, American-style

    C. Short-dated, deep-in-the-money, American-style

    D. Short-dated, out-of-the-money European-style

34. Which COBS rule contains guidance on churning and switching?

    A. Suitability

    B. Client agreements

    C. Appropriateness

    D. Labelling of non-independent research

35. An investor has sold short CTD gilts with a nominal value of £22 million and a market value of £22.8 million. The price factor is 1.073. He wishes to hedge the position using long gilt futures. How many contracts are required?

    A. 236

    B. 294

    C. 502

    D. 245

36. An investor has bought 25 Brent Crude oil futures contracts on ICE Futures at US$63.25 per barrel and later closes out when the price is US$64.30 per barrel. The contract size is 1,000 barrels. What is the profit?

    A. US$6,250

    B. US$10,050

    C. US$16,075

    D. US$26,250

37. Which of the following types of client is LEAST well suited to an investment strategy containing a large number of derivatives?

    A. An investor looking for growth
    B. An investor looking for regular income
    C. An investor with no requirement for a high level of liquidity
    D. An investor with a long time horizon

38. CDs are issued:

    A. At deep discount to their face value
    B. With maturities typically between six and 12 months
    C. At a slightly lower rate of interest compared with T-bills
    D. With the possibility of withdrawal prior to maturity, but usually at a cost

39. How does ICE Clear Europe collect margin due on positions from members?

    A. By assigning collateral lodged by members
    B. By payments through a Bank of England account
    C. By requesting cash or collateral for each transaction
    D. By debiting members' accounts via the Protected Payments System

40. A long put option is normally considered to have the potential for:

    A. Unlimited profit and unlimited loss
    B. Limited profit and limited loss
    C. Unlimited profit and limited loss
    D. Limited profit and unlimited loss

41. Which of these correlation coefficients indicates the weakest relationship between two assets?

    A. +1
    B. +0.2
    C. −0.5
    D. −1

42. You are advising a package tour operator who has highly variable floating rate borrowing requirements throughout the year and wishes to lock in fixed- rate borrowing costs. What type of transaction is the most suitable for this company?

    A. An amortising swap
    B. A rollercoaster swap
    C. An arrears swap
    D. A forward start swap

43. According to the two most widely used option pricing models, an option's value will fall:

    A. When the underlying asset's volatility rises faster than market volatility.

    B. As the underlying asset's price moves below the call's strike price.

    C. As the underlying asset's price moves below the put's strike price

    D. As the underlying asset's price move above the call's strike price

44. An option that can be exercised by its holder at any time to up its expiration date is known as?

    A. American

    B. Asian

    C. Bermudan

    D. European

45. If a futures contract is trading significantly below its fair value, what strategy will an arbitrageur use?

    A. Spread

    B. Cash and carry arbitrage

    C. Reverse cash and carry arbitrage

    D. Reversal

46. How many bond futures will be traded to hedge an anticipated holding of €50 million nominal of the CTD bond assuming the contract size is €250,000, the price factor of the CTD is 1.112233 and the notional coupon is 6%?

    A. 180

    B. 200

    C. 222

    D. 247

47. Which of the following types of margin is exclusively paid by a client to the member?

    A. Intra-day margin

    B. Maintenance margin

    C. Spread margin

    D. Variation margin

48. A covered call is closest to which of these?

    A. Synthetic short put position

    B. Synthetic short call position

    C. Synthetic long call position

    D. Synthetic long put position

49. When obtaining a secured loan, which of the following is one of the benefits that the borrower can expect to receive?

    A. Lower up-front fees due to a higher interest rate

    B. A lower interest rate, since the lender can claim specific assets

    C. More favourable terms, since the debt can be switched into shares

    D. An upgrade of its credit rating, since secured debt is always investment-grade

50. The only credit risk associated with OTC options trading exists for:

    A. A bank that has sold an in-the-money put to a client

    B. A customer who has sold an at-the-money call to its broker

    C. A bank who has sold an in-the-money call to another bank

    D. A broker has a bought an out-of-the-money call from a client

51. Who pays the premium on an option?

    A. The holder of a put

    B. The writer of a put

    C. The writer of a call

    D. The seller of a put

52. Which of the following is typically the most conservative users of derivative products?

    A. Hedge funds

    B. Pension funds

    C. Corporate treasurers

    D. High net worth individuals

53. Which of the following highlights one of the key differences between an equity warrant and an equity options?

    A. A warrant is traded on an exchange, while most equity options are OTC-traded

    B. A warrant's exercise price is determined by its issuer, while it is the options buyer that chooses its strike price

    C. Since warrants are usually attached to a corporate bond, they are always European-style, while options have several exercise styles

    D. Warrants usually command a higher premium, since they are always issued with in-the-money exercise prices

54. Which of the following describes how CASS works?

    A. It is a special system to ensure daily internal reconciliations

    B. It requires firms to hold only retail client's funds in a separate account

    C. Its aim is to protect all clients' funds, such as the broking firm fail

    D. It sets the minimum balance that a firm must maintain as collateral

55. One of the reasons a bank may apply a haircut to the collateral that a client has deposited with them is:

    A. Because of regulatory requirements that apply to certain types of derivative contracts

    B. Because of exchange-based regulations that apply to all clearing members

    C. To secure protection from movements in the market

    D. To enable the client to exercise any options

56. Which of the following is TRUE about settlement?

    A. The net cash settlement amount is equivalent to the last day's variation margin

    B. The contract size for a particular commodity is standardised across exchanges

    C. For physical delivery, the buyer always initiates the settlement process

    D. Long government bond futures contracts have a single underlying deliverable asset

57. Which of the following is accepted by LCH.Clearnet as collateral?

    A. Australian dollars in cash

    B. Equities that are traded on AIM

    C. Japanese bonds

    D. US$ CDs

58. Which of the following would form is part of a passive rather than an active portfolio management strategy?

    A. Short selling securities that are overvalued

    B. Hedging an existing holding by using an OTC forward to take advantage of price movements outside of normal trading hours

    C. Selling options when their prices are inflated by high volatility

    D. Buying and selling index-based equity futures

59. The strike price of a put option is £2.00 and the current price is £2.20. The premium when this option was purchased was 15p and it is now 12p. What is the time value of this option today?

    A. 3p

    B. 12p

    C. 20p

    D. 32p

60. A portfolio has produced a return over a period of 5.7%. During that period the risk-free return was 4.9%, standard deviation of the portfolio was 2.3%, CAPM beta was −0.73 and the CAPM predicted return was 5.8%. What is the portfolio's Sharpe return?

    A. 13.79%

    B. 34.78%

    C. −1.10%

    D. −0.10%

61. Which of the following is normally part of the data used in the fundamental analysis method of evaluating a security?

    A. The company's historic prices

    B. Government policy

    C. The price volatility of the company's shares relative to its sector benchmark

    D. Evaluation of the company's shares' oscillators

62. Which of the following is an example of backwardation?

    A. Futures price at fair value, slightly higher than the cash value of the underlying

    B. Futures price below fair value, but above cash value

    C. Futures price below cash value

    D. Futures price has risen out of the arbitrage channel

63. When is a change in basis profitable for the short hedger (short the future, long the underlying)?

    A. Cash prices go down while futures remain steady

    B. Cash prices move from a premium over to a discount under futures

    C. Futures and cash move in unison

    D. Future price goes down while the cash price remains unchanged

64. If you sell a 240 put option for 17, what is your maximum profit?

    A. 17

    B. 233

    C. 240

    D. Unlimited

65. If an investor buys a call with a higher strike and a put with a lower strike on an oil future, what is this strategy called?

   A. Short straddle

   B. Long strangle

   C. Bear spread

   D. Bull spread

66. An increase in which of the following factors will cause all option premiums to increase?

   A. Time to maturity

   B. Risk-free interest rate

   C. A lower strike price

   D. Price of the underlying

67. Which of the following is the usual procedure when a futures contract is being physically delivered?

   A. The buyer nominates the time and place of delivery

   B. The clearing house gives instructions on delivery

   C. The exchange stipulates the delivery time

   D. The seller gives notice of intention to deliver

68. What did the Commodity Futures Modernization Act 2000 permit?

   A. FLEX options

   B. Single stock futures

   C. Swap futures

   D. Synthetic futures

69. A company needs to borrow $20 million for a period of six months in one month's time at LIBOR +1/16% and is concerned that interest rates may rise before then. LIBOR is currently 3.5%. It therefore buys a six-month (182 days) FRA at 3.4%. One month late LIBOR is fixed at 3.625%. What is the net settlement value of the FRA at the end of the period?

   A. $28,537.45

   B. $16,139.87

   C. $22,340.58

   D. $9,935.31

70. An investor buys 10,000 shares in Megacorp PLC at £5.25 per share and sells a call option at £5.50 for a premium of 15 pence per share. The Megacorp share price rises to £5.60. What is the profit to the investor?

    A. £5,000
    B. £2,500
    C. £3,500
    D. £4,000

71. An option has an exercise price of 600 and a premium of 65. What is the time value of both put and call options respectively if the market price of the underlying is trading at 543?

    A. 8 and 65
    B. 65 and 8
    C. 57 and 0
    D. 0 and 57

72. How is the member default fund funded?

    A. By bank guarantees
    B. By cash contributions
    C. By margin deposits
    D. By collateral deposits

73. An investor buys a January £5 call option at 25p. At the expiry, the stock is at £4.75. How much will the investor lose per share?

    A. 25p
    B. 50p
    C. £4.75
    D. £5.00

74. Which of the following removes the impact of cash flows in and out of a portfolio when measuring performance?

    A. Total return
    B. TWRR
    C. Holding period return
    D. MWRR

75. A call option has a strike price of £4. If the share is currently trading at £3.85, what is the intrinsic value of this option today?

    A. −15p

    B. Nil

    C. 5p

    D. 20p

76. An investment portfolio was valued at £1,500 on January 1 and grew in value to £1,800 at the end of the month. On 1 February it received an inflow of £1,000 and on 28 February it was valued at £3,000. What is its TWRR?

    A. 28.52%

    B. 100.04%

    C. 20.02%

    D. 42.86%

77. How is a bear spread constructed?

    A. Selling a put and buying a call with a higher strike price

    B. Buying a call and selling a call with a higher strike price

    C. Selling a put and buying a put with a higher strike price

    D. Buying a put and selling a put with a higher strike price

78. What is the normal contract size quoted for wheat futures in the commodity derivatives market?

    A. 100 tonnes

    B. 2,500 bushels

    C. 5,000 tonnes

    D. 5,000 bushels

79. What is the term used when a trader closes out a position for a nominal amount to crystallise a loss?

    A. Abandonment

    B. Assignment

    C. Cabinet trade

    D. Basis trade

80. Which of the following is involved in a long hedge?

    A. A stop order

    B. Selling short

    C. Buying futures

    D. Intra-market spread

81. What is the value of a 760 index put when the value at expiry of the underlying index is 772?

    A. –12

    B. 0

    C. 12

    D. 760

82. What are TIMS and SPAN used to calculate?

    A. Daily settlement prices

    B. Initial margins

    C. Maintenance margin

    D. Value of collateral

83. Which formula is generally used to calculate the invoice amount on a physically delivered contract?

    A. EDSP x scale factor x number of contracts

    B. (EDSP/scale factor) x number of contracts

    C. (Settlement price/scale factor) x number of contracts

    D. Traded price x scale factor x number of contract

84. A shipping company is concerned that rising fuel prices will push up its costs and reduce profits. What should the company consider doing?

    A. Sell put options on oil

    B. Sell oil futures

    C. Go long oil futures

    D. Go short oil futures

85. What is the main purpose of the CRD introduced as part of MiFID?

    A. To ensure orderly markets and improve client protection

    B. To make it easier for firms wishing to take advantage of passporting opportunities

    C. To improve client protection through the introduction of tougher sanctions against firms

    D. To improve trading liquidity across the EU

86. Which of the following events is the LEAST likely to trigger the need for rebalancing of the asset allocation within a portfolio?

    A. An increase in price volatility in a specific asset class

    B. A change to the rate of inheritance tax

    C. A change to the tax treatment of options and swaps

    D. The credit downgrading of a debt issue or news of a company takeover

87. How can a speculator avoid taking delivery of an underlying asset in their long futures position?

    A. By selling an option on the underlying

    B. By extending the terms of the future

    C. By selling an equivalent future

    D. By renegotiating the contract

88. The interest rate parity theorem states that:

    A. In FX forward rates, the higher interest rate currency commands a premium in the FX forward market

    B. In FX swaptions, the lower interest rate currency commands a lower premium payment

    C. In FX forward rates, the lower interest rate currency commands a premium in the FX forward market

    D. FRA rates are determined by the relative swap rates of the two currencies involved in an FX FRA

89. If you buy a 100 put for a premium of 13, what is your maximum potential profit?

    A. 13

    B. 87

    C. 100

    D. Unlimited

90. Where permitted, what does a credit line cover?

    A. Margin requirements of members' clients

    B. Tax liabilities when in default

    C. Purchase of the underlying asset on exercise

    D. Settlement payments of members

91. The current exchange rate is $1.65 = £1 and the interest rates in the US and UK for the next year are 3% and 4% respectively. What is the one-year forward rate of exchange using interest rate parity?

    A. $1.6341 = £1

    B. $1.6540 = £1

    C. $1.6995 = £1

    D. $1.7165 = £1

92. A European put option has a strike price of 350p, the current price of the underlying instrument is 275p and the premium is 65p. What is the best course of action for an investor?

    A. Buy the option and sell the underlying

    B. Sell the option and buy the underlying

    C. Buy the option and buy the underlying

    D. Sell the option and sell the underlying

93. What action will an investor take if they expect volatility to rise?

    A. Sell a call and buy a call on the same underlying

    B. Sell a put and buy a put on the same underlying

    C. Sell a call and sell a put on the same underlying

    D. Buy a call and buy a put on the same underlying

94. What is a block trade?

    A. A large transaction between an exchange member and a wholesale client, negotiated away from the central order book and reported after completion

    B. A large transaction between an exchange member and a wholesale client, according to the terms of the central order book and reported after completion

    C. An off-market transaction that involves the swapping of an OTC position with a futures position

    D. An off-market transaction that involves the swapping of an OTC position with a series of futures contracts

95. Which of the following types of margin covers the risk of default during the delivery process?

    A. Intra-day margin

    B. Maintenance margin

    C. Spot month margin

    D. Variation margin

96. Which of the following is normally used to settle a CFD?

    A. Exchange of documents

    B. Exchange of financial futures

    C. Exchange of the underlying

    D. Cash

97. Which organisation regulates options on stock indices in the US?

    A. CBOE

    B. CFTC

    C. NFA

    D. SEC

98. If an investor wants to change the interest rate and/or the currency exposure of a specific investment, the most effective way of doing this is to enter into:

    A. An asset swap

    B. A currency swaption

    C. A collar

    D. An interest rate swap

99. Which of the following is an example of an intra-market spread?

    A. Buying 250 June calls, selling 250 September calls.

    B. Selling 200 June puts, selling 220 September calls.

    C. Buying 240 June calls, buying 260 September calls.

    D. Buying September futures, buying November futures.

100. Which of the following statements is TRUE of price-takers?

    A. They are buyers of financial securities only

    B. Many market participants are both price-takers and price-makers

    C. Price-takers determine and deal on their own price

    D. Market makers are never price-takers

101. A fund manager has a portfolio of top UK equities, currently valued at £20,000,000. He hedges the portfolio by selling 400 FTSE index futures at 5250. The FTSE 100 currently stands at 5223. A day later the FTSE 100 has fallen by 13 index points and the future has fallen by 16 points. What are the hedged and unhedged portfolio values on day two?

    A. £19,950,220 and £19,956,620

    B. £19,950,220 and £20,014,220

    C. £19,950,476 and £20,014,476

    D. £19,938,733 and £19,990,733

102. If a UK exporter wants the hedge to risk associated with the euro-denominated receipts for its products, which of the following will provide an effective hedge?

 A. Euro FRA

 B. GBP swaption

 C. EUR/GBP forward contract

 D. EUR/GBP swap

103. A company treasurer buys a FRA on £17 million to start in one month's time to run for a period of six months, at a rate of 5%. LIBOR is subsequently fixed at 5.2%. If there are 182 days in the six-month period concerned, what is the net settlement amount at the end of the period?

 A. £16,524.95 payable to the company

 B. £16,748.59 payable to the company

 C. £20,676.29 payable by the company

 D. £20,956.38 payable by the company

104. Which of the following distinguishes LCH.Clearnet as operating a mutual guarantee system?

 A. A collective default fund

 B. Financial Services Compensation Scheme eligibility

 C. Insurance cover.

 D. Balance sheet reserves

105. When might the price of emissions contracts be expected to rise?

 A. When heavy polluters buy more contracts in order to hedge their exposure to pollutants

 B. If emissions in a specific pollutant increase

 C. As regulation tightens and pollution targets are reduced

 D. As pollution targets are reached

106. If a dealer wants to open a position by buying at the best available price, once a limit has been reached, what kind of order should be given?

 A. Stop limit order

 B. Limit order

 C. MIT order

 D. Spread order

107. Which of the following is the LEAST preferable collateral for a broker to take against a written GlaxoSmithKline put option?

    A. GlaxoSmithKline shares

    B. Cash

    C. CD

    D. T-bill

108. If you sell a straddle, what are you seeking to profit from?

    A. Time value

    B. Decreasing volatility

    C. Increasing volatility

    D. A rise in the price of the underlying

109. Which of the following describes a situation in which the futures price is lower than the cash price of the underlying?

    A. Positive basis

    B. Carrying

    C. Negative basis

    D. In contango

110. Which of the following is a type of wholesale trade recognised by ICE's universal trading platform?

    A. Basis trade

    B. Market order trade

    C. Cross trade

    D. Limit trade

111. Which of the following services does SWIFTNet FpML provide?

    A. A payments netting system across a range of OTC contracts

    B. A real-time matching system for a range of OTC confirmations

    C. A straight-through payment system for FX and swap transactions

    D. A real-time position and credit limit monitoring system

112. Which of these statements is true in relation to intrinsic value and for time value?

    A. Time value is based on the length of an option's risk period

    B. Time is measured by gamma

    C. Intrinsic value is negative for puts and positive for calls

    D. Only time value can fall to zero as expirations get closer

113. What action will an investor take if he is anticipating a change in the difference between a futures price and the cash price of its underlying asset?

    A. Naked purchase

    B. Basis trade

    C. Inter-market spread

    D. Naked sale

114. A Japanese investor expects to receive USD income from his portfolio of US government bond investments in three months' time. When and how might he hedge currency risk relating to this income?

    A. Buy yen spot value

    B. Sell a yen call/USD put option with a three-month expiration

    C. Buy yen versus the USD forward, with a three-month maturity

    D. Sell the US Treasury bonds

115. Assume that S&P 500 Index futures are priced at 1600 and the contract size is $250. How many index futures contracts are required to hedge a $15million portfolio of US equities with a beta of 1.12?

    A. 15

    B. 19

    C. 38

    D. 42

116. How is a yield curve described when short-term rates are the same as long-term rates?

    A. Concave

    B. Flat

    C. Inverted

    D. Normal

117. An investor is bearish on Megacorp PLC shares. They are currently trading at 115p. The investor decides to sell a CFD on 10,000 shares at that price. The investor's broker requires a 20% margin. Later, shares fall to 107p and the investor decides to close the CFD. What is the return on the cash that was invested?

    A. 6.95%

    B. 34.78%

    C. 7.40%

    D. 32.60%

118. Which of the following applies to broker margins?

    A. They can be greater than that of the corresponding clearing house

    B. They are 15% of the underlying contract value

    C. They are based on SPAN

    D. They must be equal to the margin determined by the clearing house

119. What price is used to mark to market all positions?

    A. Opening traded price

    B. Daily settlement price

    C. Mid-market traded price

    D. Weighted average traded price

120. Which of the following is an indication of a successful active fund manager AND a well-diversified portfolio?

    A. High Treynor ratio

    B. High standard deviation

    C. High Sharpe ratio

    D. Low information ratio

121. ICE Clear Europe calculates the amount of initial margin required to cover all contracts for each member by using:

    A. The difference between the settlement price and variation margin

    B. The gross value of all positions

    C. The marked-to-market value of net positions

    D. The net liquidation values

CISI
CHARTERED INSTITUTE FOR
SECURITIES & INVESTMENT

122. The type of swap that allows an investor to exchange the returns on an equity-based investment for the return on another equity-based investment is known as:

    A. Mark-to-market swap

    B. Equity swaption

    C. Commodity/equity swap

    D. Volatility swap

123. To liquidate a long position when the price falls below the prevailing market price requires which of the following orders?

    A. Sell stop

    B. Buy stop

    C. Sell limit

    D. Buy limit

124. If an investor goes long a call on three S&P 500 index futures where the premium is $1,500, what additional margin needs to be paid (if any)?

    A. $1,500

    B. $3,500

    C. $4,500

    D. Nothing

Answers to Multiple Choice Questions

1. **D** **Chapter 4, Section 2.3**

CFDs do not have a fixed maturity.

2. **D** **Chapter 1, Section 6**

Prices of all exchange-traded contracts are highly transparent, since they are listed by the exchange and have full public dissemination. All exchange members have access to all prices quotes at any given time.

3. **D** **Chapter 2, Section 6.2**

The speculator has made a profit of $25 per tonne after buying at $3,500 and selling at $3,525. The total profit = $25 x 25 tonnes x 30 contracts = $18,750.

4. **C** **Chapter 3, Section 4.2**

The profit is the tick value (£5) times the number of ticks moved. Because the tick size is half a point, the number of ticks moved is twice the number of points moved (40). So the equation is £5 x 40 x 2 = £400.

5. **B** **Chapter 5, Section 2.2.2**

At the close of each trading day all positions are marked-to-market based on the daily settlement price. The profit/loss on the day is measured and must be paid/received from the clearing house as variation margin.

6. **B** **Chapter 3, Section 5.3.1**

The cash price for ten tonnes is £16,690.00. Finance costs are £375.53 and insurance costs are £125.17. Add the three elements together to find the fair value. Incorrect answer A was calculated by using a whole year's financing and storage costs. C subtracted storage and D ignored it.

7. **D** **Chapter 3, Section 2**

A basis trade is the simultaneous exchange of a financial asset or instrument (eg, a government bond or a basket of shares), together with an appropriate offsetting number of futures contracts, in a privately negotiated transaction between two parties. Similar to block trades, the exchange allows the futures part of the basis trade to be executed outside the central order book.

8. **D** **Chapter 3, Section 8.2**

Give-ups are the sending of a trade to another member of the exchange. The member to whom the trade is given-up is said to be performing a give-in.

9. **B** **Chapter 1, Section 4**

The option value, or premium, is much smaller than the price of the underlying so a change in the value of the underlying will tend to produce a much greater proportionate change in the value of the option.

10.   **D**   **Chapter 6, Section 2.5**

If an ICE Futures option is not to be automatically exercised by ICE Clear Europe, a suppression notice must be filed.

11.   **B**   **Chapter 5, Section 2.4.1**

Options positions are affected by volatility, and London SPAN uses deltas to calculate the equivalent number of futures to quantify any potential offset.

12.   **C**   **Chapter 4, Section 7.2**

The fund manager can lock in the 2.25% spread by buying the credit spread option. It is a European-style option. In three months' time, if the spread has widened beyond 2.25%, the fund will receive the equivalent payment that will effectively lock-in that spread. Options A and D are not suitable because the maximum number of securities in a basket is 20.

13.   **A**   **Chapter 7, Section 4.2**

SD is calculated by finding the arithmetic mean and the set of deviations from the mean, squaring each deviation and dividing the sum of the squared deviations by the number of observations to obtain the population variance and then calculating its square root.

14.   **C**   **Chapter 4, Section 8.2**

FLEX options are exchange-traded options that allow buyers to customise contract terms.

15.   **C**   **Chapter 8, Section 5.1**

The investor has bought the call with the lower strike price, and sold the call with the higher strike price, creating a bull spread.

16.   **A**   **Chapter 7, Section 3.1**

Counterparty risk (credit risk) is the risk that your counterparty in a transaction cannot honour its obligation to you. All the others are risks that affect the financial system or market as a whole, and so cannot be diversified away.

17.   **B**   **Chapter 4, Section 6.8**

The payment of any changes in market value removes any credit risk between the two swap counterparties on a regular basis.

18.   **B**   **Chapter 3, Section 5.6.2**

Whenever the basis is expected to strengthen (irrespective of whether the market is in contango or backwardation), a trader should buy the spread. This involves buying the near-dated instrument and simultaneously selling the far-dated instrument, eg, buy March future and sell June future.

19.   **A**   **Chapter 5, Section 1.3**

Every clearing member contributes in cash to the member default fund according to the volume of its clearing activities.

20.   **D**   **Chapter 4, Section 5**

Caps are a type of option that allow the buyer to set a maximum rate on an underlying borrowing/loan.

21.   **D**   **Chapter 1, Section 3.3 & 3.4**

Loss is limited to the premium paid; for the buyer profit is potentially unlimited.

22.   **C**   **Chapter 1, Section 3.6**

FLEX options are exchange-traded, but key parameters such as exercise price, expiry date and exercise style are customised. Compared with OTC options, they have lower credit risk due to the use of a central clearing house.

23.   **D**   **Chapter 3, Section 2**

Margin and credit limits can be reduced by netting out OTC and futures positions; similarly, counterparty credit risk decreases as a result of an EFP trade. They can be negotiated on a 24-hour basis but must be registered during explicit times set down by the exchange. OTC and futures positions can be swapped only if they are substantially similar in value and/or quantity.

24.   **B**   **Chapter 4, Section 6.8**

A mark-to-market swap is one where settlements are calculated by revaluing the swap (ie, marking it to market) regularly and paying or receiving the mark-to-market loss or gain since the previous settlement. The benefit of this is that it removes, at each settlement date, any credit risk that has built up. FX resettable swaps are a form of mark-to-market swap, but they are only suitable for cross-currency swaps, and the question did not state that the cashflows were in two currencies.

25.   **B**   **Chapter 7, Section 4.3**

Sharpe ratio: (portfolio return – risk-free return)/standard deviation

Return on portfolio	5.70%	Sharpe ratio	45.65217391	first period
Risk-free return	4.65%	Treynor ratio	–1.438356164	first period
Standard deviation	2.30%	Jensen measure	–0.10%	first period
Portfolio CAPM beta	–0.73			first period
Return predicted by CAPM	5.80%			first period
Return on portfolio	5.70%	Sharpe ratio	56.52173913	second period
Risk-free return	4.40%	Treynor ratio	–1.780821918	second period
Standard deviation	2.30%	Jensen measure	–0.10%	second period
Portfolio CAPM beta	–0.73			second period
Return predicted by CAPM	5.80%			second period

26.   **C**   **Chapter 8, Section 3**

This is the typical reason for a hedge. If the company goes long a future in the commodity it wishes to purchase, then even if the price goes up, the value of the future will go up too, offsetting the extra expenditure the company will have to make on the commodity in the spot market. This is a long hedge.

27.   **B**   **Chapter 8, Section 7**

A synthetic long future results where matching short put and long call options positions are taken on a future. An investor will buy a call and sell a put with the same strike price and expiry.

28.   **C**   **Chapter 2, Section 6.1**

There is a loss of $5 per tonne after buying at $275 and selling at $270. Each contract represents 50 tonnes. Therefore $5 x 50 tonnes x 15 contracts = $3,750.

29.   **B**   **Chapter 3, Section 6.4.2**

Vega is the measure of how a 1% change in volatility affects an option's value. It is measure of how an option's value changes relative to changes in both expected or implied volatility and current market conditions.

30.   **C**   **Chapter 3, Section 2**

Market orders are to be executed at the best price immediately available. Normal limit orders are to be executed at the stated price or better.

31.   **A**   **Chapter 8, Section 5.1**

Vertical spreads, or price spreads, take place when an investor buys and sells options that have varying strike prices, but have the same expiry date. This investor has created a vertical, bull spread.

32.   **D**   **Chapter 8, Section 4**

A short underlying position has a delta of –1, so can be hedged by two long ATM calls (+0.5 x 2 = +1).

33.   **C**   **Chapter 6, Section 2.6**

American-style options can be exercised before their expiry date. It is feasible to exercise early when the following three criteria are met: i) American-style; ii) deep-in-the-money – having intrinsic value; and iii) close to expiry or short-dated, with very little time value left.

34.   **A**   **Chapter 10, Section 1.4.7**

The FCA's guidance on churning and switching is contained in the COBS rules on suitability.

35.   **A**   **Chapter 8, Section 3**

Number of contracts required =

$$\text{Price factor} \times \frac{\text{Nominal value of CTD portfolio}}{\text{Nominal value of the contract}}$$

Number of contracts needed to hedge =

$$1.073 \times \frac{£22,000,000}{£100,000}$$

= 236.06

= 236 contracts approx.

36.   **D**   **Chapter 2, Section 6.3**

The investor has made a profit of $1.05 per barrel after buying at $63.25 and selling at $64.30 and each contract represents 1,000 barrels. $1.05 x 1,000 barrels x 25 contracts – $26,250.

37.   **B**   **Chapter 9, Section 2.1**

As a rule, clients looking for income are usually not candidates for strategies that involve a high number of derivatives, unless they are investing a significant amount or their required income is in the middle or long future.

38.   D   Chapter 2, Section 2.4

CDs are issued at face value at maturities usually between three and six months, and pay a slightly higher rate of interest over government-issued T-bills to compensate for the extra risk. Because CDs are a form of time deposit, withdrawals are subject to a penalty.

39.   D   Chapter 5, Section 1.2

ICE Clear Europe calls on members for margin payments as necessary and these are paid through the Protected Payments System, an automatic debit from members' bank accounts.

40.   B   Chapter 1, Sections 3.3 & 3.4

Loss is limited to the premium paid. Profit is limited to the exercise price, less the premium (as the underlying price cannot fall below zero).

41.   B   Chapter 7, Section 3.2.2

High correlation between two assets gives a coefficient of +1.0 (perfect positive correlation) or –1.0 (perfect negative correlation). Assets with a high level of correlation (close to +1) tend to move in the same direction at the same time. Assets with strong negative correlations (close to –1) tend to move in opposite directions but are still strongly related to one another. Assets with a low correlation (close to 0) tend to move independently of each other and have the weakest relationships.

42.   B   Chapter 4, Section 6.2

A swap whose notional principal is allowed to increase and decrease during its life is known as a rollercoaster swap.

43.   B   Chapter 4, Section 8.1

According to any option pricing model, a call's price will fall as the price of its underlying asset falls below its strike price, making it further 'out-of-the-money'.

44.   A   Chapter 4, Section 8.1

There are three popular exercise styles for options. American style allows its owner to exercise it at any time, up to its expiration date.

45.   C   Chapter 3, Section 5.7

He will buy the future as it is relatively cheap and sell the cash asset – a reverse cash and carry arbitrage.

46.   C   Chapter 8, Section 3

To calculate the number of contracts needed the price factor is multiplied by the nominal value of the CTD portfolio divided by the nominal value of the contract. Therefore = 1.112233 x (€50m / €250,000) = 222.

47.   **B**   **Chapter 5, Section 2.2.3**

Maintenance margin is an arrangement between the member firm and its client. A firm will usually require a client to deposit more than the initial margin and allows for the payment of some variation margin to avoid referring back to the client every day. Once the credit breaches a preset limit, the member will issue a margin call expecting the client to replenish the account.

48.   **A**   **Chapter 8, Sections 5.1 & 7**

A long underlying and a short call together create the profit and loss profile of a short put. A synthetic short put is where an investor sells a call and buys a future – effectively a covered short call position.

49.   **B**   **Chapter 2, Section 3.2.1**

Secured debt usually gives the borrower more favourable terms, since the debt is tied to a specific asset, which the lender can claim, if the borrower cannot meet the payments.

50.   **D**   **Chapter 4, Section 8.1**

Since an option buyer usually buys the premium up-front, the only credit risk lies with any option buyer, no matter what type of option has been purchased.

51.   **A**   **Chapter 1, Section 3.2**

The buyer of any kind of option must pay the premium to the writer (seller) of the option.

52.   **C**   **Chapter 8, Section 10**

Hedge funds and high net worth individuals tend to have a greater appetite for risk than pension funds, which may also be constrained in their investment activities either through legislation or the client mandate. Corporate treasurers are the most risk-averse and will typically use derivatives to hedge price or currency risk associated with normal business activities.

53.   **B**   **Chapter 2, Section 5.3**

In the case of warrants, it is always the issuer that sets its exercise or strike price.

54.   **C**   **Chapter 10, Section 2.2**

Within CASS, the requirement to segregate client money from a firm's own money is aimed at ensuring that, if the firm fails, that money will not be used to repay its creditors. Usually this is done by ensuring that it is placed promptly in a separately designated client money account with a bank and ensuring that the bank treats it as separate from the firm's own.

55.   **C**   **Chapter 4, Section 11**

A haircut is applied to any type of collateral, to ensure that the broker/bank is fully covered as the value of the collateral changes, therefore the more volatile the collateral, the larger the haircut.

56.   **A**   **Chapter 3, Section 4**

The net cash settlement amount is equivalent to the last day's variation margin because it is the difference between the final closing price and that of the previous day. Contract sizes for commodities differ between exchanges and it is important to check the exact exchange contract specifications. For physical delivery, the seller initiates the settlement process. Delivery on long government bond futures contracts can be made from a list of eligible bonds as determined by the exchange.

57.   **D**   **Chapter 5, Section 2.5**

CDs denominated in sterling or US dollars are acceptable. Cash must be in one of eight approved currencies. Details of assets acceptable and not acceptable as collateral are set out in Section 2.5.

58.   **D**   **Chapter 7, Section 3.3**

Passive management requires the construction of an equity portfolio to track, or mimic, the performance of a recognised equity index. For portfolio managers employing this strategy, using index-based derivatives matches this specific portfolio management strategy, since the contract's underlying asset is the same, but also allows them to both reduce their trading-related expenses and increase their trading efficiency, since it is easier to buy/sell a index future or option than to trade the individual shares that are index components.

59.   **B**   **Chapter 3, Section 6.1**

The premium is calculated as intrinsic value plus the time value. Because we know the premium is 12p and the intrinsic value is nothing (because the option is out-of-the-money), we know that the time value must be 12p.

60.   **B**   **Chapter 7, Section 4.3**

Sharpe ratio: (portfolio return – risk-free return)/standard deviation

Return on portfolio	5.70%	Correct answer B	34.7826087	Sharpe ratio
		Distractor A	13.79310345	Sharpe calculated using incorrect divisor (CAPM return)
Risk-free return	4.90%	Distractor C	−1.095890411	Treynor ratio: (portfolio return – risk-free return)/beta
Standard deviation	2.30%	Distractor D	−0.10%	Jensen measure: portfolio return – CAPM return
Portfolio CAPM beta	−0.73			
Return predicted by CAPM	5.80%			

61. **B** **Chapter 7, Section 2.2**

Fundamental analysts attempt to study everything that can affect a security's value, including macro-economic factors, such as the overall economic and industry conditions, and company-specific factors, such as its financial condition, competitiveness and management. The method of evaluating securities by analysing the statistics generated by market activity, such as past price movements, volume and volatility, is called technical analysis.

62. **C** **Chapter 3, Section 5.4**

The market is said to be in backwardation when the futures prices are lower than the cash prices. If the futures prices are higher than cash prices the market is said to be in contango.

63. **D** **Chapter 8, Section 3.1**

Basis is the difference between the cash and futures prices. The short hedger has sold the future and holds the physical asset. Therefore he will benefit if he can close out his position by buying back the future at a lower price while still getting the same cash price for the underlying physical asset.

64. **A** **Chapter 1, Section 3.4**

The maximum profit for the writer of a put option is the premium.

65. **B** **Chapter 8, Section 6.3**

Strangles are constructed using calls and puts with different exercise prices. Here, the options are bought, so it is a long strangle.

66. **A** **Chapter 3, Section 6.1.4**

An increase in interest rates and the price of the underlying will cause call premiums to rise, and put premiums to fall.

67. **D** **Chapter 6, Section 1.3**

Futures sellers give notice declaring their intention to deliver the asset to the clearing house. The clearing house assigns the assets to the futures buyers and, if there is any flexibility in the contract, the seller can nominate what, where and when to deliver.

68. **B** **Chapter 10, Section 2.7.3**

In the USA, single stock futures were permitted under the Commodity Futures Modernization Act 2000.

69. **A** **Chapter 4, Section 2.2**

Principal	LIBOR + 1/16% rate	FRA rate	Days mult.	Days divisor	Top line of equation	Bottom line of equation	Answer
20,000,000	0.036875	0.034	182	360	29069.444444	1.018642	28537.45
	(3.625 + 1/16)/100				20,000,000 x (0.036875 – 0.034) x 183/360	1 + (0.036875 x 182/360)	29069.444444 /1.018642

Incorrect answer B: uses LIBOR of 3.5%							
20,000,000	0.035625	0.034	182	360	16430.555556	1.018010	16139.87

Incorrect answer C: forgets to add the margin of 1/16% to the LIBOR rate							
20,000,000	0.036250	0.034	182	360	22750.000000	1.018326	22340.58

Incorrect answer D: forgets to add the margin of 1/16% to the LIBOR rate, and used the wrong LIBOR rate of 3.5%							
20,000,000	0.035000	0.034	182	360	10111.111111	1.017694	9935.31

70. **D** **Chapter 8, Section 3**

If the price rises to £5.60 the option will be exercised. Thus the profit is:

10,000 x (selling price – strike price) +10,000 x option premium.

10,000 x (£5.50 – £5.25) +10,000 x £0.15= £4,000.00.

Distractor A used £5.60 as selling price, B ignored the option premium, and C used £5.60 as the selling price and also ignored the option premium.

71. **A** **Chapter 3, Section 6.1.2**

B transposed the results for put and call; C calculated intrinsic value instead of time value; D is as C but with the results for put and call transposed.

Exercise price	600				
Premium	65				
If share price =	543	Intrinsic value of put	57 (600 – 543)	Time value	8 (65 – 57)
		Intrinsic value of call	0	Time value	65 (65 – 0)

72.   **B**   **Chapter 5, Section 1.3**

Every clearing member contributes in cash to the member default fund according to the volume of their clearing activities.

73.   **A**   **Chapter 1, Section 3.3**

Rather than exercise the option, the investor abandons it and loses his premium – 25 pence.

74.   **B**   **Chapter 7, Section 4.1**

The holding period yield or return simply measures how much the portfolio's value has increased over a period of time and expresses it as a percentage. It suffers from the limitation of not taking into account the timing of cash flows into and out of the fund.

The MWRR is used to measure the performance of a portfolio that has had deposits and withdrawals during the period being measured. One of the main drawbacks of this method is that to calculate the return is an iterative process and so is time-consuming.

The TWRR actually removes the impact of cash flows on the rate of return calculation. This method is established by breaking the investment period into a series of sub-periods. A sub-period is created whenever there is a movement of capital into or out of the fund. Immediately prior to this point, a portfolio valuation must be obtained to ensure that the rate of return is not distorted by the size and timing of the cash flow.

75.   **B**   **Chapter 3, Section 6.1**

The intrinsic value is the difference between the current share price and the strike price, but only if that is a positive figure. The intrinsic value is zero.

76. **A** **Chapter 7, Section 4.1**

The formula: TWRR = [(1 + RSP1)(1 + RSP2)........(1 + RSPn)] – 1

	Workbook example	Correct answer A	Distractor B	Distractor C	Distractor D
Opening valuation	1,000	1,500	1,500	2,500	1,500
Opening valuation date	1 Jan	1 Jan	1 Jan	1 Jan	1 Jan
Second valuation	1,200	1,800	1,800	1,800	2,500
Second valuation date	15 Jan	31 Jan	31 Jan	31 Jan	31 Jan
Inflow	250	1,000	0	0	1,000
Date of inflow	16 Jan	1 Feb	1 Feb	1 Feb	1 Feb
Closing valuation	1,500	3,000	3,000	3,000	3,000
Closing valuation date	31 Jan	28 Feb	28 Feb	28 Feb	28 Feb
Step 1	0.200	0.200	0.200	–0.280	0.667
Step 2	0.034	0.071	0.667	0.667	–0.143
TWRR	24.08	28.52	100.04	20.024	42.8619

77. **C** **Chapter 8, Section 5.1**

For a bear spread you buy the high strike and sell the low strike.

78. **A** **Chapter 2, Section 6.1**

The contract size for wheat futures is 100 tonnes.

79. **C** **Chapter 6, Section 2.4**

A trader may need to crystallise a loss for tax or accounting purposes and instead of abandoning the option will close-out the position for a nominal amount. This is known as a cabinet trade.

80.   **C**   **Chapter 8, Section 3**

'Long' means 'buy' in derivatives jargon. Hedgers will offset risk by taking an opposite position in the futures market.

81.   **B**   **Chapter 3, Section 4.2**

At expiry, the put has no value to the holder as strike price is below the underlying price.

82.   **B**   **Chapter 5, Section 2.4**

They are both scenario-based risk programs used for calculating initial margins.

83.   **A**   **Chapter 6, Section 1.3.1**

For physically delivered contracts the futures buyers will receive an invoice for the asset and have to pay the amount stated in the invoice. This is calculated using the formula EDSP x scale factor x number of contracts. For bond futures the calculation differs to include the price factor and accrued interest.

84.   **C**   **Chapter 2, Section 6.3**

This is a hedge: rising oil prices mean rising fuel prices. The company should therefore go long oil futures, locking into the cheaper oil price.

85.   **A**   **Chapter 10, Section 1.3.3**

The main purpose of the Capital Requirements Directive is to set out regulatory requirements for capital that a firm must hold. This ensures orderly markets and improves client protection.

86.   **B**   **Chapter 9, Section 3**

A, C and D are all likely to have a significant effect on a portfolio, and effective regular monitoring is necessary in order to ensure that the asset allocation is rebalanced accordingly.

87.   **C**   **Chapter 1, Section 2.1**

A trader can remove any delivery obligations by taking an equal and opposite position before the expiry. This will crystallise any gains or losses.

88.   **C**   **Chapter 4, Section 3.1**

The interest rate parity theorem is the basis for the FX forward market, to ensure that arbitrage opportunities do not exist.

89.   **B**   **Chapter 1, Section 3.4**

The maximum gain on a long put = strike price – premium (100 – 13 = 87).

90.   **A**   **Chapter 5, Section 2.6**

Some exchanges allow their members to extend credit to their clients to cover margin requirements. These credit lines are subject to regulatory rules.

91.   **A**   **Chapter 2, Section 4.2**

The forward rate in one year's time will be based on the spot rate adjusted by the relative interest rates. So $1.65 x 1.03 will be equivalent to £1 x 1.04. The one year forward rate is based on $1.6995 = £1.04. Dividing both sides by 1.04 = $1.6995/1.04 = £1.04/1.04. The one-year forward rate = $1.6341 = £1.

92.   **C**   **Chapter 3, Section 6**

Exercise price (350p) – underlying price (275p) = intrinsic value (75p). The premium is 10p under its intrinsic value. The investor takes advantage of the low premium to buy both the option and the underlying so as to be able to deliver the underlying for a risk-free profit of 10p.

93.   **D**   **Chapter 8, Sections 6.1 & 6.3**

Calls and puts are bought in combination if volatility is expected to rise, creating a long straddle or long strangle.

94.   **A**   **Chapter 3, Section 2**

Block trades offer the opportunity to negotiate terms privately, providing that the order is reported into the exchange once completed. C and D relate to EFP and EFS transactions.

95.   **C**   **Chapter 5, Section 2.2.1**

A clearing house will try to minimise the speculative and delivery pressures by increasing the initial margin for those contracts where final settlement is by physical delivery. This is known as a spot month margin. This ensures that those position-holders contemplating taking the contract to delivery have either the underlying asset to deliver or have allocated sufficient funds to effect settlement.

96.   **D**   **Chapter 6, Section 1.3.2**

A CFD can only be settled in cash.

97.   **D**   **Chapter 10, Section 2.7.1**

The SEC regulates most US option products and option exchanges but does not regulate futures products or exchanges. The CFTC regulates options not covered by the SEC.

98.   **A**   **Chapter 4, Section 6.1**

An asset swap is the most effective way to change the total exposure of an asset.

99.   **A**   **Chapter 8, Section 2.1**

Spreads require buy and sell transactions on the same underlying asset. Intra-market spreads are trades based on the simultaneous buying and selling of futures with different expiry dates on the same underlying asset.

100.   **B**   **Chapter 1, Section 7**

A price-taker is a market participant who either requests the price, or deals through an intermediary on another participant's price. Thus, they do not set the price themselves. Many market participants including market makers may find themselves as price-takers in some circumstances, and price-givers in others.

101.   **B**   **Chapter 8, Section 3.1**

Correct answer B				
unhedged	20,000,000	5223	13	19,950,220
hedged:				
futures profit	400	5250	5234	64,000
hedged				20,014,220
Distractor A: failed to multiply futures calculation by £10 per lot				
unhedged	20,000,000	5223	13	19,950,220
hedged:				
futures profit	400	5250	5234	6,400
hedged				19,956,620
Distractor C: transposed FTSE index value and futures price for day 1				
unhedged	20,000,000	5250	13	19,950,476
hedged:				
futures profit	400	5223	5207	64,000
hedged				20,014,476
Distractor D: transposed price falls for the two instruments				
unhedged	20,000,000	5223	16	19,938,733
hedged:				
futures profit	400	5250	5237	52,000
hedged				19,990,733

102.   **C**   **Chapter 4, Section 3**

Forward FX contracts are a good means of hedging currency risk.

103.   **A**   **Chapter 4, Section 2.2**

The formula is:

Principal x ((LIBOR rate – FRA rate) x days in period/365)/1+(LIBOR rate x days in period/365) = settlement amount

ie, 17,000,000 x ((0.052 – 0.05) x 182/365)/1 + (0.052 x 182/365) = £16,524.95

Because the FRA is denominated in sterling, the days divisor is 365 not 360. Answer B used 360 days, C transposed the two interest rates in the formula, and D both transposed the rates and used 360 as the days divisor.

104.   **A**   **Chapter 5, Section 1.3**

All members of LCH.Clearnet contribute to a member default fund, which is available to cover the liabilities of a defaulting member. This system is known as a mutual guarantee system.

105.   **C**   **Chapter 2, Section 7**

Emissions contracts are initially bought by companies in order to offset levels of emissions that exceed set targets such as those established in the Kyoto Accord. The contracts will become more valuable when these pollution targets are reduced.

106.   **C**   **Chapter 3, Section 7.2**

An MIT order is an order to open a position that becomes a market order once the limit has been reached.

107.   **A**   **Chapter 5, Section 2.5**

The writer of a GSK put option has an obligation to take delivery of the shares and therefore needs cash to pay for those shares. If the put is exercised, it will be because the value of GSK shares is falling.

108.   **B**   **Chapter 8, Section 6.2**

Straddles are volatility trades, and an investor selling a straddle will profit if the underlying price is stable.

109.   **A**   **Chapter 3, Sections 5.4 & 5.6**

Positive basis describes a situation in which the futures price is in backwardation – below the cash price. Basis is calculated by subtracting the futures price from the cash price, resulting in a negative basis if the market is carrying/in contango.

110.   **A**   **Chapter 3, Section 2**

A basis trade is one of two types of wholesale trade recognised by ICE CONNECT™. It is the simultaneous exchange of a financial asset or instrument together with an appropriate offsetting number of futures contacts in a privately negotiated transaction between two parties.

111. **D** **Chapter 4, Section 12.4**

SWIFTNet FpML is a real-time confirmation and exception monitoring system for FX, money market and OTC derivative confirmations, whose main goal is to increase the efficiency of users' STP of OTC derivative confirmations.

112. **A** **Chapter 3, Section 6.1**

The intrinsic value is the difference between the strike value and the market price. Since the buyer is not obliged to exercise, the intrinsic value cannot be negative. Time value increases in proportion to the length of time the writer is at risk from the buyer exercising.

113. **B** **Chapter 8, Section 3.1**

Basis traders profit from the fluctuating difference between a futures price and the cash price of its underlying asset – that is, the basis. They take the form of intra-market, not inter-market, spreads.

114. **C** **Chapter 2, Section 3**

If USD weakens against JPY over the three months, the amount of yen that the investor will receive will fall. Therefore it makes sense to fix the exchange rate as soon as possible, to hedge any exchange rate risk. This is best done using a three-month forward contract.

115. **D** **Chapter 8, Section 3**

The correct formula is (portfolio value / (futures price x contract size)) x portfolio beta. Therefore the correct answer is ($15m / (1600 x $250)) x 1.12 = 42 contracts.

116. **B** **Chapter 2, Section 3.1.3**

If short-term interest rates are the same as long-term rates, the yield curve is flat.

117. **B** **Chapter 4, Section 2.3**

The profit is £800: (10,000 x £1.15) – (10,000 x £1.07). The investment is the margin of 20% (0.2 x (10,000 x £1.15) = £2,300), and the return on the investment is 800/2,300 = 34.78%. The distractors: A used the value of the shares at the start of the CFD, C used the value of the shares at the end of the CFD, and D is a random distractor.

118. **A** **Chapter 5, Section 2.1**

Broker margin must be at least equal to the margin required by the clearing house. As long as they meet this requirement, all other aspects are determined by the broker.

119. **B** **Chapter 5, Section 2.2.2**

At the close of each trading day, all positions are marked-to-market based on the daily settlement price. The daily settlement price can be referred to as the closing price as it is established at the end of the trading day. Other markets have different methods for calculating the daily settlement price.

120. **A** **Chapter 7, Section 4.3**

The Sharpe ratio measures return over and above the risk-free interest rate from an undiversified portfolio for each unit of risk assumed by the portfolio. The higher the Sharpe ratio, the better the risk-adjusted performance of the portfolio and the greater the implied level of active management skill. The Sharpe ratio therefore provides an objective measure of the relative performance of two undiversified portfolios.

The Treynor ratio takes a similar approach to the Sharpe ratio but is calculated for a well-diversified portfolio. Once again, the higher the ratio, the greater the implied level of active management skill.

The information ratio compares the excess return achieved by a fund over a benchmark portfolio to the fund's tracking error, calculated as the standard deviation of excess returns from the benchmark. A fund's performance may deviate from the benchmark owing to the investment manager's decisions concerning asset-weighting. If the fund outperforms, the ratio will be positive, and if it underperforms it will be negative. A low information ratio is therefore a sign of an unsuccessful fund manager.

Standard deviation is merely part of the calculation process for all the above and on its own is not a measure of success.

121. **D** **Chapter 5, Section 2.4.3**

Because initial margin requirements are based on the net positions held by the member firm and there may be a variety of positions held, the calculation of the amount due is based on the NLVs of the constituent parts of the portfolio.

122. **D** **Chapter 4, Section 6.10**

Volatility or equity swaps are the most popular method of switching the returns on equity or equity index-based investments.

123. **A** **Chapter 3, Section 7.2**

The stop will not necessarily be executed at the stop level – it will become a market order when the price falls to the stop level. A sell limit order could sit on the order book and remain unsatisfied.

124. **D** **Chapter 3, Section 6.5**

There is no initial margin payment on the purchase of an option because the counterparty's risk is covered by the premium.

Syllabus Learning Map

Syllabus Unit/ Element		Chapter/ Section
Element 1	**Introduction to Derivatives**	**Chapter 1**
	On completion, the candidate should be able to:	
1.1	**General**	
1.1.1	understand core concepts and key characteristics of forwards, futures and options contracts: • forward and futures contracts • contracts for differences • puts and calls • options on cash equities and futures • American, European and Bermudan • common path dependent and average pricing options	2, 3
1.1.2	understand the significance of gearing to exchange-traded derivatives: • how margin facilitates gearing • effect on derivative positions • reward versus outlay • reward versus risk	4
1.1.3	understand the purpose, risks and rewards associated with derivatives: • uses of derivatives: hedging, speculation and arbitrage • counterparty, market and liquidity risk • specific risks to buyers, writers and sellers	2.4
1.1.4	understand the differences between the two major measures of exchange-traded liquidity (open interest and volume)	5
1.1.5	understand the main features and differences of OTC-traded products in contrast to exchange-traded products: • how an OTC traded product is traded • standard size, versus bespoke OTC contracts • set maturity or expiry dates versus bespoke OTC contracts • margin requirements versus collateral • central clearing versus counterparty risk • liquidity from standard versus bespoke OTC contracts • risk profile of actively managed exchange-traded versus OTC hedging • market transparency versus confidential transactions	6
1.1.6	understand options diagrams and the characteristics and implications of long and short positions	3.3

Syllabus Unit/ Element		Chapter/ Section
1.1.7	understand the main markets, and roles of key participants: • FX, Money Markets, Equity, Fixed Income, Commodity • Regulators in major markets • Quote driven versus order driven • Floor versus voice versus electronic • Price Givers - Central banks, banks, major market corporates • Price Takers – Central banks, banks, corporates, asset managers, insurance companies, hedge funds, pension funds, private clients • Brokers/intermediaries including Futures Commission Merchants (FCMs) • Buy-side • Sell-side	7

Element 2	Underlying Assets	Chapter 2
	On completion, the candidate should be able to:	
2.1	**Money Market Instruments**	
2.1.1	analyse the main investment characteristics and risks of Treasury Bills: • purpose and method of issue • minimum denomination • term • redemption • zero coupons	2.3
2.1.2	analyse the main investment characteristics and risks of interbank deposits: • purpose and method of issue • minimum denomination • term • redemption • determination of interbank offer rates LIBOR, LIBID, EURIBOR, EONIA, SONIA	2.1
2.1.3	analyse the main investment characteristics and risks of Certificates of Deposit: • purpose and method of issue • minimum denomination • term • redemption	2.4
2.1.4	assess the risk implications of trading in money market contracts: • as a depositor • as a source of funding	2.2

Syllabus Unit/ Element		Chapter/ Section
2.2	**Fixed Income Securities**	
2.2.1	analyse the main issuers of government debt, and the key investment characteristics and risks of sovereign and government fixed income securities: • supranationals • sovereign governments • public authorities: local government/municipalities • index-linked • short, medium, long, undated and dual-dated • floating rate • zero coupon	3.1
2.2.2	analyse the main issuers of corporate debt, and the key investment characteristics and risks of secured and unsecured corporate fixed income securities: • corporates • financial institutions and special purpose vehicles • unsecured and secured debt • fixed and floating charges • asset-backed securities • mortgage-backed securities • convertibles	3.2
2.2.3	analyse the relationship between interest rates and bond pricing: • accrued interest, clean and dirty prices • interest rates, government bond prices and the risk-free rate • inflation, nominal and real interest rates • flat, normal and inverted yield curves • government and corporate bond yields • yield spread: government benchmark versus LIBOR-based spread • investment grade and non-investment grade bonds	3.3
2.2.4	analyse the main determinants of bond prices and bond valuation: • yield to maturity • role of rating agencies • credit rating and impact of changes • economic outlook, interest rates, inflation and impact of changes • trading volume and liquidity of domestic and international securities markets	3.3

Syllabus Unit/ Element		Chapter/ Section
2.3	**Foreign Exchange Instruments**	
2.3.1	understand the role, structure and main characteristics of the foreign exchange market: • market structure • quotes, spreads and exchange rate information • market participants and access to markets • margin and transaction costs • volume, volatility and liquidity • settlement dates and systems • risk mitigation: rollovers and stop losses	4
2.3.2	understand the determinants of spot foreign exchange prices: • currency demand – transactional and speculative • economic variables • cross-border trading of financial assets • interest rates • free and pegged rates	4.1
2.3.3	calculate forward foreign exchange rates: • relationship between spot and forward market • forward points, premiums and discounts • interest rate parity (IRP) and interest rate differential (IRD) • factors determining forward rates • quotation	4.2
2.3.4	understand the nature, characteristics, markets and uses of currency forward contracts including: • non-deliverable forwards • commercial and speculative uses • hedging uses in portfolio management • effect of time on open positions	4.3
2.4	**Equities**	
2.4.1	analyse the key investment characteristics and risks of the main types and classes of equity: • ordinary, bearer, preference and registered shares • voting rights, voting and non-voting shares • cumulative, participating, redeemable and convertible preference shares • ranking for dividends • ranking in liquidation • tax treatment of capital gains and dividend income	5

Syllabus Unit/ Element		Chapter/ Section
2.4.2	analyse how the following factors influence equity markets and equity valuation: • trading volume and liquidity of domestic and international securities markets • relationship between cash and derivatives markets, and the effect of timed events • market consensus and analyst opinion • changes to key pricing determinants such as credit ratings, economic outlook and significant events	5.4
2.4.3	analyse the key investment characteristics and differences between equity warrants and equity options: • purpose and issuers • benefits to an investor or speculator • time to expiry • where traded • strike prices • effect of exercise • settlement • gearing against the underlying • effect of corporate actions on equity warrants	5.3
2.5	**Softs and Agriculturals**	
2.5.1	understand the main softs and agriculturals and the influences on supply: • coffee, cocoa, white sugar, soya bean, wheat, rapeseed oil, grains, livestock • change in demand • change in production • holding cost	6.1
2.6	**Base and Precious Metals**	
2.6.1	understand the main base and precious metals and the influences on supply: • copper, nickel, aluminium, zinc, tin, lead, gold and silver • change in demand • change in production • marginal costs of mining • changes in industry • political or strategic • holding cost	6.2

Syllabus Unit/ Element		Chapter/ Section
2.7	**Energy Products**	
2.7.1	understand the main energy products and the influences on price: • crude oil, natural gas and emissions • change in demand • change in production • marginal costs of production • delivery costs • political or strategic • OPEC	6.3
2.8	**Other Products**	
2.8.1	understand the purpose and investment characteristics of futures contracts on weather, emissions, hybrids and property	7

Element 3	**Exchange-Traded Futures and Options**	Chapter 3
	On completion, the candidate should be able to:	
3.1	**Exchanges**	
3.1.1	understand the structure, physical and electronic trading processes, clearing mechanisms and main products of the major derivatives exchanges: • CME Group including CME, CBOT and NYMEX • Intercontinental Exchange (ICE) including ICE Futures Europe, US and Canada • NYSE Euronext, ICE Futures Europe and Liffe US • LSE Derivatives • NASDAQ Options Market and NASDAQ OMX Group • London Metal Exchange • EUREX • Tokyo Stock Exchange (TSE) • Shanghai Stock Exchange (SSE) • China Financial Futures Exchange (CFFEX) • Singapore Exchange (SGX) • National Stock Exchange of India (NSE) • Dubai Gold and Commodities Exchange (DGCX)	1.1

Syllabus Unit/ Element		Chapter/ Section
3.1.2	understand the membership structures (brokers, dealers and broker/ dealers, general clearing, individual clearing and non-clearing) and their principal rights: • executing trades for third parties • executing trades for their own account • executing trades for other members • capacity as broker • capacity as dealer • capacities of clearing members	1.2
3.2	**Trading Platforms**	
3.2.1	understand the essential details of the trading mechanisms • open outcry, telephone and electronic platforms • quote- versus order-driven • order matching • order types accepted by the markets • recognised trading strategies • record-keeping	2
3.2.2	understand the significance, implications and uses of wholesale trading facilities	2
3.3	**Exchange-Traded Derivative Contracts**	
3.3.1	analyse the range, key features and investment characteristics of the main types of exchange traded derivatives on: • equities • indices • interest rates • credit rates • foreign exchange • commodities • contracts for differences • exchange-traded funds	3
3.3.2	understand the trading mechanisms used for: • block trades • exchange for physicals (EFPs) and Exchange for Swaps (EFSs) • flex products	2

Syllabus Unit/ Element		Chapter/ Section
3.4	**Clearing Mechanisms**	
3.4.1	understand the matching and clearing process: • trade capture and order matching processes • delivery and settlement • physical versus cash settlement • establishment of settlement price • options into futures • initiation of delivery • purpose of mutual offset and where it exists	4
3.4.2	understand how the physical delivery methods for commodities operate and where they differ from other derivatives: • warehouses, warrants and good delivery • large position reporting • price discovery – official and closing price	4
3.4.3	calculate the profit/loss on delivery/expiry of futures and options	4.2
3.5	**Futures Pricing**	
3.5.1	understand the mechanisms for futures pricing and the relationship with the underlying cash prices, together with the significance of contributing factors: • contango and backwardation • price convergence at maturity • the concept of fair value according to IAS	5
3.5.2	understand the purpose, features and implications of the cost of carry including: • interest rates and asset yields • storage costs, insurance and interest costs	5.2
3.5.3	calculate the fair value of a future from relevant cash market prices, yields and interest rates	5.3
3.5.4	analyse the effect of basis: • behaviour at expiry • causes of basis strengthening or weakening • response to strengthening of basis • response to basis risk	5.6
3.5.5	apply appropriate strategies for cash/futures arbitrage trades: • identifying opportunities and risks of arbitrage • arbitrage calculations • arbitrage channel and effect of transaction costs • cash and carry • reverse cash and carry • hedging basis risk	5.7

Syllabus Unit/ Element		Chapter/ Section
3.6	**Options Pricing**	
3.6.1	calculate the intrinsic and time value of an option and understand the factors determining option premiums and pricing including: • influences on intrinsic value and time value • volatility • time to expiry • strike or exercise price • underlying asset price • interest rates • dividends/coupons	6
3.6.2	calculate a theoretical option premium using put/call parity to identify arbitrage opportunities: • application of the put/call parity theorem • adjustment for cost of carry • limitations in accuracy • identification of arbitrage opportunities • reversal and conversion arbitrage trading strategies	6.2
3.6.3	understand how delta is used in hedging a cumulative position	6.3
3.6.4	calculate the sensitivity of the option premium to changes in price by applying delta values to cumulative positions	6.3
3.6.5	analyse derivatives positions and hedging strategies by using the following 'greeks': • delta • gamma • theta • vega • rho	6.4
3.7	**Order/Instruction Flow and Order Type**	
3.7.1	understand how exchange-traded orders are processed: • acting as principal, agent or in dual capacity • how clients, brokers and exchange members are linked • principles of order flow on electronic and open outcry markets • opening, closing and cross trades • liquidity measures: volume and open interest • audit trail	7.1

Syllabus Unit/ Element		Chapter/ Section
3.7.2	understand the typical range of orders placed in derivatives markets and the reasons for using them: • market order • limit order • spread order • scale order • market if touched order • opening and closing orders • good til cancelled • immediate or cancel/fill or kill order • stop, stop limit and guaranteed stop orders • day order	7.2
3.8	**Trade Registration** On completion, the candidate should:	
3.8.1	understand the processes involved in trade registration, input, matching and allocation including: • differing requirements of electronic and open outcry markets • assignment to house, segregated or non-segregated accounts • reasons for allocating a trade to an account • use of give-up agreements • risk implications	8
3.9	**Market Transparency, Trade Reporting and Monitoring**	
3.9.1	understand the purpose, process and responsibilities of trade reporting including: • dissemination of information from exchanges to quote vendors • constituents of exchange price feeds and display screens • advantages of transparency to investors • monitoring volume and open interest	9

Syllabus Unit/ Element		Chapter/ Section
Element 4	**OTC Derivatives**	**Chapter 4**
	On completion, the candidate should be able to:	
4.1	**Forwards, FRAs and Contracts for Difference**	
4.1.1	understand the differences between the range of underlying assets, key characteristics, investment implications and applications of: • forward contracts • forward rate agreements (FRAs) • contracts for difference • spread betting	2
4.1.2	analyse the mechanisms for OTC derivative pricing and the relationship with the underlying cash prices together with the significance of contributing factors: • spot and forward rates • cash flow analysis and the zero curve • the role of interest rates and yields • other factors affecting pricing	2
4.1.3	calculate the price and net settlement amount of a forward rate agreement	2.2
4.2	**Foreign Exchange Forwards and Swaps**	
4.2.1	analyse the purpose, risks, benefits and costs of foreign exchange forwards and swaps	3
4.3	**Interest Rate Swaps and Swaptions**	
4.3.1	analyse the purpose, key characteristics and valuation of interest rate swaps and swaptions • types of swap agreements: vanilla, basis, coupon, index and currency • interest calculations (compared to bond markets)	4
4.4	**Caps, Floors and Collars**	
4.4.1	calculate the likely outcome of implementing caps, floors and collars: • purpose and construction • risks, benefits and costs	5

Syllabus Unit/ Element		Chapter/ Section
4.5	**Other Types of Swaps**	
4.5.1	analyse the key features and risk/reward trade-offs of other types of swap instruments including investment applications and relationships to other markets: • asset and total return swaps • amortising, accreting and rollercoaster • inflation • dividend • constant maturity • arrears • forward start • overnight index (OIS) • mark-to-market (MTM)	6
4.5.2	analyse the key features, risk/reward trade-offs and investment applications of commodity forwards and swaps	6.9
4.5.3	analyse the key features, risk/reward trade-offs and investment applications of equity forwards, swaps and swaptions: • volatility • bullet • variance	6.10
4.5.4	analyse the key features, risk/reward trade-offs and investment applications of environmental and property swaps	6.11
4.6	**Credit Derivatives**	
4.6.1	analyse the key features, risk/reward trade-offs and investment applications of credit default swaps: • credit events • credit default swaps: basic, index and basket • credit linked notes • agreements including compensation or settlement • option adjusted spreads	7.1
4.6.2	analyse the key features, risk/ reward trade-offs and investment applications of credit spreads: • credit default options • credit default obligations • synthetics	7.2

Syllabus Unit/ Element		Chapter/ Section
4.7	**OTC Options**	
4.7.1	analyse the key features, risk/reward trade-offs and investment applications of OTC option products: • main types: European, American, Bermudan • key differences between exchange-traded and OTC instruments • exotics: Asian, lookbacks and variants; ratchets/cliquets • clearing, settlement and delta-based collateral	8.1
4.7.2	understand the purpose, requirements and process of premium payment including: • when paid • credit exposure • the collateral process	8.1
4.7.3	understand the purposes, key features and risk/reward trade-offs of flexible exchange (FLEX) options including how they differ from standard exchange-traded and OTC options	8.2
4.8	**Structured Products**	
4.8.1	understand the purpose of structured products and how they utilise embedded derivatives to achieve a specific risk/return profile: • callable and puttable bonds • convertible bonds • index-linked notes • capital protected products	9
4.9	**Master Agreements**	
4.9.1	understand the potential impact of credit exposures on OTC positions and the documentation designed to protect against counterparty risk: • purposes and protocols of ISDA documentation • master agreement including main areas of content • confirmation • credit support annex documentation	10
4.10	**Collateral Management**	
4.10.1	understand the purpose and application of collateral management: • quality of collateral: volatility, creditworthiness, liquidity • acceptable types of cash and non-cash collateral • credit lines • valuation and pricing • thresholds and haircuts • delivery, return and minimum transfer amount (MTA)	11

Syllabus Unit/ Element		Chapter/ Section
4.11	**Trade Processing**	
4.11.1	understand the key features of the main platforms and mechanisms used for trading and settling OTC derivatives: • Bclear • SwapClear • MarkitSERV • SwiftNet FpML • TriOptima • ICE LINK • AffirmXpress	12
4.11.2	understand the main control processes in trading and processing OTC instruments: • order placement, deal tickets and term sheets • trade validation and confirmation • reconciliation processes: internal and external • cash flow/ asset movement instructions and control processes • profit and loss reporting and position management • risks of weak controls • close out or maturity instructions	13
4.11.3	understand the benefits of processing on straightforward OTC markets	**13.3**

Element 5	Clearing	Chapter 5
	On completion, the candidate should be able to:	
5.1	**Definition and Purpose of Clearing**	
5.1.1	understand the process of clearing, the risks involved and how these can be reduced: • market, settlement, currency and counterparty risks • eligibility and credit standing of counterparties • implications of default • mutual offset system • principal to principal • guarantee	1.1
5.2	**Structure of the Clearing System**	
5.2.1	understand the role played by the clearing house in the clearing process and the relationship between the clearing house, clearing members and non-clearing members: • trade reporting, confirmation, matching, registration and novation • use of payments systems	1.2
5.2.2	understand the benefits of centralised OTC clearing and how this is achieved in the major OTC markets	1.5

Syllabus Unit/ Element		Chapter/ Section
5.3	**Guarantee**	
5.3.1	understand the backing arrangements in place in the event of a member default, and how they are utilised: • margin and collateral • default guarantee fund • mutual and independent guarantees	1.3
5.3.2	understand the services offered by prime brokers as they relate to: • trade execution, settlement, custody and asset servicing • client services: global custody, stock lending, reporting • value-added services: introductions advisory and consulting services	1.4
5.4	**Margin**	
5.4.1	understand the purpose of margin, its various types, and how margin payments are paid or collected: • reduction of counterparty credit risk • initial, variation, intra-day and maintenance margin • advantages and risks of house, client segregated and non-segregated accounts • clearing house and broker margin • flow of margin	2
5.4.2	understand how initial margin is calculated and the factors that exchanges take into account when calculating initial margin: • systems – SPAN/STANS • spreads: spot and offset margining • purpose, nature and use of offsets • effect of volatility • inter-month charge • inter-month spread • spot market spread • short option minimum charge	2.2.1
5.4.3	calculate variation margin based on marking to market	2.2.2
5.4.4	understand the purpose of settlement price limits and position limits including: • key features and differences • who imposes limits • the effects of their application: • action in the event of breach	2.3

Syllabus Unit/ Element		Chapter/ Section
5.4.5	understand methods of margining involving delta and SPAN and their implications: • application of delta • SPAN: scenario risk analysis • STANS: portfolio-based margining • effect of price change in the underlying asset • net liquidation value	2.4
5.4.6	understand methods of margining centrally cleared OTC products and their implications: • calculation of exposure • what margins are applied • payment of margin	2

Element 6	Delivery and Settlement	Chapter 6
	On completion, the candidate should be able to:	
6.1	**Futures**	6
6.1.1	understand the purpose of closing contracts compared with rollover or delivery, and the main methods for performing close-outs	1.2
6.1.2	understand the purpose, key features and differences between cash settlement and physically delivered contracts: • factors used in ascertaining the invoice amount • warrant delivery • differences between financial and commodity products	1.3
6.1.3	understand the importance and implications of the delivery of open contracts at expiry and the significance of the short position: • purpose of open contracts • financials versus commodities • avoidance of delivery – reasons and methods • seller's choice of delivery time and method • underlying asset delivery to the clearing house • relevance of first notice day, last notice day and delivery day or period:	1.3
6.1.4	understand the processes for physical delivery including: • exchange delivery settlement price (EDSP) and the factors affecting its value • auction process • calculation of the invoice amount on a physically settled contract	1.3, 1.4
6.1.5	understand the processes, merits and limitations of cash settlement of contracts for differences	1.3.2

Syllabus Unit/ Element		Chapter/ Section
6.2	**Options**	
6.2.1	understand the processes and implications of the exercise of options, the assignment of obligations, abandonment and expiry: • purpose of assignment of obligations • instigating an assignment notice • receiving an assignment notice • abandonment • which options are most likely to be exercised before expiry • exercise at expiry • European, American and Bermudan options • action upon exercise • reasons for assignments • effect of assignment • advantages to the investor • probability of assignment	2
6.2.2	understand the significance of automatic exercise: • purpose of automatic exercise • options that may be subject to automatic exercise • reasons for clearing houses to adopt automatic exercise • benefits to members and holders of long positions • prevention of automatic exercise	2.5

Element 7	Portfolio Research and Construction	Chapter 7
	On completion, the candidate should be able to:	
7.1	**Market Information and Research**	
7.1.1	understand how to access and use regulatory, economic and financial communications: • news services • government resources and statistics • broker research and distributor information • desk research • regulatory resources	2.1
7.1.2	understand the different types, uses and availability of research and reports: • fundamental analysis • technical analysis • volatility in underlying sector: benchmark and relative • sector-specific reports	2.2

Syllabus Unit/ Element		Chapter/ Section
7.1.3	assess key factors that influence derivatives markets and sectors: • responses to change and uncertainty • volume, liquidity, and nature of trading activity in domestic and overseas markets • volatility • risk-based regulations and restrictions	2.3
7.2	**Portfolio Construction**	
7.2.1	analyse the main types of portfolio risk and their implications for investors: • systemic risk • market or systematic risk – asset price volatility, currency, interest rates, commodity price volatility • investment horizon • liquidity, credit risk and default • counterparty risk	3.1
7.2.2	understand the core principles used to mitigate portfolio risk: • correlation • diversification • active and passive strategies • hedging and immunisation	3.2
7.2.3	understand the key approaches to investment allocation for bond, equity and balanced portfolios: • asset class • geographical area • currency • issuer • sector • maturity	3.2
7.2.4	understand the main purposes and applications of derivatives in portfolio management strategies and styles: • indexing/ passive management • active/ market timing • passive-active combinations • growth versus income • immunisation • long, short and leveraged • contrarian • yield enhancement	3.3

Syllabus Unit/ Element		Chapter/ Section
7.2.5	assess portfolio risk and return using the following measures: • holding period return • total return and its components • standard deviation • volatility • covariance and correlation • risk-adjusted returns • benchmarking	4

Element 8	Trading, Hedging and Investment Strategies	Chapter 8
	On completion, the candidate should be able to:	
8.1	**Futures Spread Trading**	
8.1.1	analyse futures spreads and the scenarios in which they may be appropriate: • intramarket spreads • motivations and uses in differing market conditions • situations resulting in profitability/loss	2
8.2	**Hedging with Futures**	
8.2.1	calculate the number of contracts required to hedge a portfolio of Cheapest to Deliver bonds (CTDs): • price factors • highest implied repo rate • understand the basis of adjustment for non-CTD bonds	3
8.2.2	calculate the number of contracts required to hedge an exposure to a single equity holding or equity portfolio	3
8.2.3	calculate the change in value caused by movement in basis, know the implications of basis risk and understand how changes in basis can be used to advantage by an investor	3.1
8.3	**Hedging Using Options**	
8.3.1	analyse an investor's net long/short position using delta hedging	4
8.3.2	calculate the number of contracts required to hedge a long underlying position by: • buying a put option • selling a call option	4.1
8.3.3	calculate the number of contracts required to hedge a short underlying position by: • selling a put option • buying a call option	4.2

Syllabus Unit/ Element		Chapter/ Section
8.3.4	apply covered calls and covered puts as part of an investment strategy: • characteristics and risks • motivation for the writer of a covered short call • motivation for the buyer of a covered short put • calculation of the outcome on expiry • maximum upside and downside • uses in different market conditions	4.3
8.4	**Options Spreads**	
8.4.1	apply vertical spreads as part of an investment strategy: • characteristics and risks • bull call and bear call spreads • bull put and bear put spreads • calculation of the outcome on expiry • maximum upside and downside • uses in differing market conditions	5.1
8.4.2	apply horizontal and diagonal spreads as part of an investment strategy: • characteristics and risks • horizontal spreads • diagonal spreads • calculation of the outcome on expiry • maximum upside and downside • uses in differing market conditions	5.2
8.5	**Options Combinations**	
8.5.1	apply long and short straddles and strangles as part of an investment strategy: • characteristics and risks • long straddle • short straddle • long strangle • short strangle • calculation of the outcome on expiry • maximum upside and downside • uses in differing market conditions	6
8.6	**Synthetics**	
8.6.1	understand the use of synthetic positions by combining futures and options: • characteristics and risks • synthetic long and short futures • synthetic long and short calls • synthetic long and short puts • calculation of the outcome on expiry • maximum upside and downside • uses in differing market conditions	7

Syllabus Unit/ Element		Chapter/ Section
8.7	**Comparison of Exchange-Traded and OTC Hedges**	
8.7.1	analyse the advantages and disadvantages of using exchange-traded versus OTC products in hedging: • exposure flexibility versus contract specification • ease/cost of closing OTC transactions versus exchange-traded positions • margins versus collateral processes • counterparty exposure versus centralised clearing • price transparency • best execution • documentation • settlement mechanism	8
8.8	**Indirect Investments**	
8.8.1	analyse the main types, features, styles and applications of derivatives-based indirect investments: • accounts • pooled funds • speculative, guaranteed and synthetic funds • retail schemes • onshore and offshore funds • taxation, access and cost considerations	9
8.9	**Application of Derivative Strategies and Funds**	
8.9.1	analyse the relative attractiveness of derivative positions or investments to specific client circumstances: • private client investment portfolios • high net worth portfolios • institutional asset managers • corporate treasurers • hedge funds • structured funds • sovereign wealth funds	10

Syllabus Unit/ Element		Chapter/ Section
Element 9	**Investment Selection and Administration**	**Chapter 9**
	On completion, the candidate should be able to:	
9.1	**Advisory Process**	
9.1.1	apply a range of essential information and factors to form the basis of appropriate financial planning and advice for clients: • financial objectives • current and future status risk profile • level of knowledge about investments • existing debts and investments	2.1
9.1.2	analyse and select strategies suitable for the client's aims and objectives in terms of: • investment objectives • risk tolerance • liquidity, trading and ongoing management • mandatory or voluntary investment restrictions • tax and cost considerations	2.2
9.1.3	analyse and select derivatives suitable for a particular portfolio strategy: • direct holdings, indirect holdings and combinations • rationale • impact on client objectives and priorities • balance of investments	2.2
9.2	**Administration and Maintenance**	
9.2.1	apply key elements involved in managing a client portfolio: • systematic and compliant approach to client portfolio monitoring, review, reporting and management • selection of appropriate benchmarks to include market and specialist indices, total return and maximum drawdown • arrangements for client communication	3
9.2.2	apply measures to address changes that can affect a client portfolio: • client circumstances • financial environment • new products and services available • administrative changes or difficulties • investment-related changes (eg, credit rating, corporate actions) • portfolio rebalancing • benchmark review	3

Syllabus Unit/ Element		Chapter/ Section
Element 10	**Regulatory Requirements**	**Chapter 10**
	On completion, the candidate should be able to:	
10.1	**Scope of Regulation**	
10.1.1	understand in outline the scope of regulation of derivatives markets and related activities in the main developed and emerging economies: • UK, USA, Japan and Europe • India, China and South America • passporting and cross-border agreements • business versus investment activity	1
10.1.2	apply FCA principles and Conduct of Business Rules when advising on, trading in or managing derivative based investments and products for clients: • client classification • treating customers fairly • suitability and appropriateness of the transaction/product • best execution • justification and risk warnings	1.4
10.2	**Principal Differences Between EU and US Regulations**	
10.2.1	understand the role of European regulation on EU derivative markets including the UK: • MiFID and the Transparency Directive • clients' money • clients' accounts • margining practices • unregulated markets • access to overseas markets • access to overseas clients	2
10.2.2	understand the principles set out in the European Market Infrastructure Regulations (EMIR) and European Securities and Markets Authority (ESMA) regarding: • central clearing obligations • central reporting obligations	1.3
10.2.3	understand the role of the Securities and Exchange Commission (SEC) in the regulation of derivatives: • regulated investments • regulated exchanges	2.7

Syllabus Unit/ Element		Chapter/ Section
10.2.4	understand the role of the Commodity Futures Trading Commission (CFTC) and the National Futures Association (NFA): • NFA delegated functions including "screening and registration of all firms and individuals who want to conduct futures-related business with the public" • regulated investments • regulation of other entities • dispute resolution	2.7
10.2.5	understand the prohibitions of CFTC Part 30 (Foreign Futures and Segregation of Customer Funds)	2.7
10.2.6	understand the Commodity Futures Modernization Act 2000 and the principles governing trading of single stock futures in the US: • physical delivery or cash settlement • market regulators • restrictions	2.7.3
10.3	**Reporting Requirements**	
10.3.1	understand the requirements to report derivative positions under the following circumstances and be aware of the impact and risk implications that fair value accounting may have on the derivative activities of banks and corporates: • IAS 32 and IAS 39 • merger and acquisition activities	3

Examination Specification

Each examination paper is constructed from a specification that determines the weightings that will be given to each element. The specification is given below.

It is important to note that the numbers quoted may vary slightly from examination to examination as there is some flexibility to ensure that each examination has a consistent level of difficulty. However, the number of questions tested in each element should not change by more than plus or minus 2.

Examination specification		
80 multiple choice questions		
Element number	Element	Questions
1	Introduction to Derivatives	4
2	Underlying Assets	10
3	Exchange Traded Futures and Options	13
4	OTC Derivatives	13
5	Clearing	7
6	Delivery and Settlement	5
7	Portfolio Research and Construction	7
8	Trading, Hedging and Investment Strategies	12
9	Investment Selection and Administration	4
10	Special Regulatory Requirements	5
	Total	80

A two-hour examination of 80 multiple choice questions.

Candidates sitting the exam by computer based testing will have, in addition, up to 10% additional questions as trial questions that will not be separately identified and do not contribute to the result. Candidates will be given proportionately more time to complete the test.

CISI Chartered MCSI Membership can work for you...

Studying for a CISI qualification is hard work and we're sure you're putting in plenty of hours, but don't lose sight of your goal!

This is just the first step in your career; there is much more to achieve!

The securities and investments industry attracts ambitious and driven individuals. You're probably one yourself and that's great, but on the other hand you're almost certainly surrounded by lots of other people with similar ambitions.

So how can you stay one step ahead during these uncertain times?

Entry Criteria for Chartered MCSI Membership

As an ACSI and MCSI candidate, you can upgrade your membership status to Chartered MCSI. There are a number of ways of gaining the CISI Chartered MCSI membership.

A straightforward route requires candidates to have:
- a minimum of one year's ACSI or MCSI membership;
- passed a full Diploma; Certificate in Private Client Investment Advice & Management or Masters in Wealth Management award;
- passed the IntegrityMatters with an A grade; and
- successfully logged and certified 12 months' CPD under the CISI's CPD Scheme.

Alternatively, experienced-based candidates are required to have:
- a minimum of one year's ACSI membership;
- passed the IntegrityMatters with an A grade; and
- successfully logged and certified six years' CPD under the CISI's CPD Scheme.

Joining Fee:	Current Grade of Membership	Grade of Chartership	Upgrade Cost
	ACSI	Chartered MCSI	£75.00
	MCSI	Chartered MCSI	£30.00

By belonging to a Chartered professional body, members will benefit from enhanced status in the industry and the wider community. Members will be part of an organisation which holds the respect of government and industry, and can communicate with the public on a whole new level. There will be little doubt in consumers' minds that chartered members of the CISI are highly regarded and qualified professionals and as a consequence will be required to act as such.

The Chartered MCSI designation will provide you with full access to all member benefits, including Professional Refresher where there are currently over 60 modules available on subjects including Behavioural Finance, Cybercrime and Conduct Risk. CISI TV is also available to members, allowing you to catch up on the latest CISI events, whilst earning valuable CPD hours.

Professional Refresher

Self-testing elearning modules to refresh your knowledge, meet regulatory and firm requirements, and earn CPD hours.

Professional Refresher is a training solution to help you remain up-to-date with industry developments, maintain regulatory compliance and demonstrate continuing learning.

This popular online learning tool allows self-administered refresher testing on a variety of topics, including the latest regulatory changes.

There are currently over 70 modules available which address UK and international issues. Modules are reviewed by practitioners frequently and new topics are added to the suite on a regular basis.

Benefits to firms:
- Learning and tests can form part of business T&C programme
- Learning and tests kept up-to-date and accurate by the CISI
- Relevant and useful – devised by industry practitioners
- Access to individual results available as part of management overview facility, 'Super User'
- Records of staff training can be produced for internal use and external audits
- Cost-effective – no additional charge for CISI members
- Available to non-members

Benefits to individuals:
- Comprehensive selection of topics across industry sectors
- Modules are frequently reviewed and updated by industry experts
- New topics introduced regularly
- Free for members
- Successfully passed modules are recorded in your CPD log as Active Learning
- Counts as structured learning for RDR purposes
- On completion of a module, a certificate can be printed out for your own records

The full suite of Professional Refresher modules is free to CISI members or £250 for non-members. Modules are also available individually. To view a full list of Professional Refresher modules visit:

cisi.org/refresher

If you or your firm would like to find out more contact our Client Relationship Management team:

+ 44 20 7645 0670
crm@cisi.org

For more information on our elearning products, contact our Customer Support Centre on +44 20 7645 0777, or visit our website at cisi.org/study

Free to CISI members

Professional Refresher

Top 5

SCORM COMPLIANT

Integrity & Ethics
- High Level View
- Ethical Behaviour
- An Ethical Approach
- Compliance vs Ethics

Anti-Money Laundering
- Introduction to Money Laundering
- UK Legislation and Regulation
- Money Laundering Regulations 2007
- Proceeds of Crime Act 2002
- Terrorist Financing
- Suspicious Activity Reporting
- Money Laundering Reporting Officer
- Sanctions

Financial Crime
- What Is Financial Crime?
- Insider Dealing and Market Abuse Introduction, Legislation, Offences and Rules
- Money Laundering Legislation, Regulations, Financial Sanctions and Reporting Requirements
- Money Laundering and the Role of the MLRO

Information Security and Data Protection
- Information Security: The Key Issues
- Latest Cybercrime Developments
- The Lessons From High-Profile Cases
- Key Identity Issues: Know Your Customer
- Implementing the Data Protection Act 1998
- The Next Decade: Predictions For The Future

UK Bribery Act
- Background to the Act
- The Offences
- What the Offences Cover
- When Has an Offence Been Committed?
- The Defences Against Charges of Bribery
- The Penalties

Conduct Rules
- Application and Overview
- Individual Conduct Rules – FCA & PRA
- Senior Management Conduct Rules
- Obligations on Firms

Pensions Advice
- Advice or Guidance?
- Advice During Accumulation
- Defined Contribution Pension Freedoms
- Transfers and Decumulation
- Problems with Accessing New Freedoms

Retirement Planning
- Pensions and Provisions
- Money In
- Money Out

Financial Planning (An introduction)
- Related Activities
- The Financial Plan
- Cash Flow Planning and Modelling
- Behavioural Finance and Financial Planning
- Risk
- The Regulatory Framework
- The Future Landscape

Senior Managers and Certification Regime
- Definitions
- Obligations
- Certification
- Conduct Rules
- Scope of the Rules
- Conclusion and Future Developments

Operations

Best Execution
- What Is Best Execution?
- Achieving Best Execution
- Order Execution Policies
- Information to Clients & Client Consent
- Monitoring, the Rules, and Instructions
- Best Execution for Specific Types of Firms

Approved Persons Regime
- The Basis of the Regime
- Fitness and Propriety
- The Controlled Functions
- Principles for Approved Persons
- The Code of Practice for Approved Persons

Corporate Actions
- Corporate Structure and Finance
- Life Cycle of an Event
- Mandatory Events
- Voluntary Events

Wealth

Client Assets and Client Money
- Protecting Client Assets and Client Money
- Ring-Fencing Client Assets and Client Money
- Due Diligence of Custodians
- Reconciliations
- Records and Accounts
- CASS Oversight

Investment Principles and Risk
- Diversification
- Factfind and Risk Profiling
- Investment Management
- Modern Portfolio Theory and Investing Styles
- Direct and Indirect Investments
- Socially Responsible Investment
- Collective Investments
- Investment Trusts
- Dealing in Debt Securities and Equities

Banking Standards
- Introduction and Background
- Strengthening Individual Accountability
- Reforming Corporate Governance
- Securing Better Outcomes for Consumers
- Enhancing Financial Stability

Suitability of Client Investments
- Assessing Suitability
- Risk Profiling
- Establishing Risk Appetite
- Obtaining Customer Information
- Suitable Questions and Answers
- Making Suitable Investment Selections
- Guidance, Reports and Record Keeping

International

Foreign Account Tax Compliance Act (FATCA)
- Foreign Financial Institutions
- Due Diligence Requirements
- Reporting
- Compliance

MiFID II
- The Organisations Covered by MiFID
- The Products Subject to MiFID's Guidelines
- The Origins of MiFID II
- The Products Covered by MiFID II
- Levels 1, 2, and 3 Implementation

UCITS
- The Original UCITS Directive
- UCITS III
- UCITS IV
- Non-UCITS Funds
- Future Developments

cisi.org/refresher

Feedback to the CISI

Have you found this workbook to be a valuable aid to your studies? We would like your views, so please email us at learningresources@cisi.org with any thoughts, ideas or comments.

Accredited Training Partners

Support for examination students studying for the Chartered Institute for Securities & Investment (CISI) Qualifications is provided by several Accredited Training Partners (ATPs), including Fitch Learning and BPP. The CISI's ATPs offer a range of face-to-face training courses, distance learning programmes, their own learning resources and study packs which have been accredited by the CISI. The CISI works in close collaboration with its ATPs to ensure they are kept informed of changes to CISI examinations so they can build them into their own courses and study packs.

CISI Workbook Specialists Wanted

Workbook Authors

Experienced freelance authors with finance experience, and who have published work in their area of specialism, are sought. Responsibilities include:
*   Updating workbooks in line with new syllabuses and any industry developments
*   Ensuring that the syllabus is fully covered

Workbook Reviewers

Individuals with a high-level knowledge of the subject area are sought. Responsibilities include:
*   Highlighting any inconsistencies against the syllabus
*   Assessing the author's interpretation of the workbook

Workbook Technical Reviewers

Technical reviewers provide a detailed review of the workbook and bring the review comments to the panel. Responsibilities include:
*   Cross-checking the workbook against the syllabus
*   Ensuring sufficient coverage of each learning objective

Workbook Proofreaders

Proofreaders are needed to proof workbooks both grammatically and also in terms of the format and layout. Responsibilities include:
*   Checking for spelling and grammar mistakes
*   Checking for formatting inconsistencies

If you are interested in becoming a CISI external specialist call:
+44 20 7645 0609

or email:
externalspecialists@cisi.org

For bookings, orders, membership and general enquiries please contact our Customer Support Centre on +44 20 7645 0777, or visit our website at cisi.org